W9-ANP-520

NORTH AMERICAN INDIANS

AN INTRODUCTION TO THE CHICHIMECA

NORTH AMERICAN INDIANS

AN INTRODUCTION TO THE CHICHIMECA

George Pierre Castile
ASSOCIATE PROFESSOR OF ANTHROPOLOGY
WHITMAN COLLEGE

McGraw-Hill Book Company
NEW YORK ST. LOUIS SAN FRANCISCO AUCKLAND BOGOTÁ DÜSSELDORF
JOHANNESBURG LONDON MADRID MEXICO MONTREAL NEW DELHI
PANAMA PARIS SÃO PAULO SINGAPORE SYDNEY TOKYO TORONTO

This book was set in Palatino by Black Dot, Inc. (ECU).
The editors were Eric M. Munson and James B. Armstrong;
the designer was Joan E. O'Connor;
the production supervisor was Donna Piligra.
The drawings were done by J & R Services, Inc.
R. R. Donnelley & Sons Company was printer and binder.

See Notes and Acknowledgments on pages 294–302.

NORTH AMERICAN INDIANS: AN INTRODUCTION TO THE CHICHIMECA

1234567890DODO78321098

Library of Congress Cataloging in Publication Data

Castile, George Pierre.
North American Indians: an introduction to the
Chichimeca.

Includes bibliographical references and index.
1. Indians of North America. I. Title.
E77.C33 970'.004'97 78-8112
ISBN 0-07-010233-3

To the Bozos and
to Jeanne for entirely
different reasons

CONTENTS

PREFACE xi

CHICHIMECA: INTRODUCTION AND PERSPECTIVE 1

Chichimeca? Circle the Wagons or the "Noble Savage" versus the "Murdering Redskin" Will the "Real" Indian Please. . . ? Level of Approach Anthropology and the American Indian Anthropology? Some Key Concepts Forward into the Past!

PART I
INDEPENDENT DEVELOPMENT AND VARIATION

I. FIRST MAN 21

The Wrong Monkeys Bridges and Bullboats Early, Earlier, Earliest Blood and Bones Babel Artifacts and Eoliths Big Game Hunters?

II. WORLDS TO CONQUER 39

Living in, Efficiently: The Archaic The Desert Bands Making a Living The Boys in the Band Rabbits and Foreign Affairs It Works! From Sea to Shining Sea Traditions and the "Chichimecness" of the Chichimeca

III. CORN MOTHER 63

High and Dry Tacos to Go Beans and 'Baccy Fruit of the Loom Lady with a Hoe Of Pots and Pueblos People in Grass Houses

IV. LEFT-HANDED MEXICAN CLANSMAN 79

Social Bookkeeping Oedipus and Mother's Brother Who's in Charge Here? One Thing Leads to Another

V. THE GREAT SPIRITS 94

Prime Movers and Coyotes Things That Go Bump in the Night Peyote and Pain Take Two Chants "Emics" and "Emetics" Shamans and Sun Kings

VI. LORDS OF THE CHICHIMECA 114

Tombs and Temples Stinkards Beloved Men Conspicuous Consumers Noble, Nobler, Noblest "Always Giving Blankets Away while Walking"

INTERREGNUM: SOME ALTERNATIVE PERSPECTIVES 137

Messages from Home and "Elsewhen" Those Gods-forsaken Chariots "Elsewhen" Shalom, White Man Mysticism and Mu! Rah, Rah—Ra! Bodhisattvas and Berserkers Made in Japan On the Eve

PART II CONTACT, ACCULTURATION, AND ACCOMMODATION

VII. CIVILIZATION, SALVATION, AND LAND CLEARANCE 163

Iron Men and Wooden Ships First Blood Mr. and Mrs. John Smith Move Over, Brother

VIII. TREATIES AND TEARS 182

Sachems and Saviors   Forest Statesmen   The Utmost Good Faith   Removal and Revitalization   Gaiwiio: The Code of Handsome Lake   Staying out of the Melting Pot

IX. WARRIORS AND WAGONS 203

Way Down Yonder in the Indian Nation!   Close, but No Cigar!   Lakota, Nakota, Dakota—Sioux?   The Light Cavalry Finale   The Earth Surface People   The Last Roundup

X. THE HEADLESS HORSEMEN 226

Off with Their Heads   Trust Me   Off with Their Hair   The Unvanishing American   Beet Farmers?

XI. SECOND THOUGHTS 244

The "Indian Problem"   Collier and the I.R.A.   A Little Bit Pregnant!   Ready or Not   What Now, White Man?

XII. WHAT IS TO BE DONE 266

Been Down So Long   OPEC and the Chichimeca   Who Speaks for the People?   "With the Consent of the Secretary . . ."   Let My People Go?   Title 25 and Catch 22

NOTES AND ACKNOWLEDGMENTS 294

INDEX 303

PREFACE

After some years of trying to teach anthropology courses about the Native American peoples, I found that the approaches which came to seem most valuable for increasing student awareness of the realities of the Indian experience were nowhere expressed in a text. This book represents the results of my attempts to provide an overview and perspective that will allow those who may know the Indian only through movies and television to understand something of the 20,000 years of diversity and development that preceded the few fictionalized, colorful moments of violent conquest.

The arrangement of this book is basically chronological. The first half begins with the question of the arrival of the Indian in the Americas and ends with the first contacts between European and Indian. There is, however, also a developmental sequence tying together each chapter.

Each is keyed to a specific cultural topic, but the complexity of the cultures considered tends to increase. Ecological issues are addressed in the earliest chapters in terms of simple hunting and gathering peoples, religion and politics are examined in regard to more complex agriculturalists and Mississippian Mound Builders. I have not provided a complete "ethnography" of any one people nor have I strung together several such ethnographies, each drawn from a particular culture area, which is the basic arrangement of most available texts. Such an approach can indicate the range of diversity, but it cannot provide a coherent picture of the developmental unity that makes the Indian peoples what they are. In the language of the anthropologist, I have tried to be "holistic" and have selected illustrations and examples from many areas without "zonal" limitations.

There is a brief digression in the middle where I have taken time out to make some appraisal of the more bizarre theories about the Indian peoples. There are so many books of a "mystical" character that are very popular now that I felt it worthwhile to put in my anthropological 2 cents. It really isn't much of a scientific issue, but it is a thing that many people wonder about, and books ought to answer questions that are being asked.

The second half of the book is devoted to the impact of European contact on the Indian peoples. This treatment, too, is primarily chronological, beginning with first contacts and ending with the Indian situation in 1977. While following the historical events and indicating the complexity of the contact of different cultures, I have again sought to build a developmental sequence focused on the shifts in the nature of Indian-white relations. In particular I have tried to understand the motives and events that led to the reservation system. The final chapter explores the "Indian problem" as it currently exists.

Born in "Mound City" (an early name for St. Louis) and raised in tidewater Virginia (Hampton), I grew up aware of Indians only as peoples of the past, since both the Mound Builders and the Powhatans had long since vanished. When I did my anthropological training in Arizona and then came to live and teach in Washington State, I became exposed to the confusion that most people feel about the "special" status of the Indian. It doesn't hurt anyone very much if the peoples of the East or even most of the West think of the Indians as befeathered horsemen. The problem is that in some of our states (including Arizona and Washington) the Indians are real, not imaginary, and the curious notions held by the non-Indians have a great deal of impact on what happens to them. I have had many motives in writing this book, but among them was a desire to give the reader a key to a perspective that will allow the tangled issues being debated about Indian affairs to be more clearly understood.

In Washington State the weekend fisherman who argues that it is unfair for Indians to be allowed to fish when he cannot is thinking, as we all usually do, only of the present. In terms of today alone, the federal court decisions about Indian fishing rights seem to make no sense and only provoke outrage. But supposing, instead of arguing about how many fishermen there are or who is paying the fees that support the hatcheries, we were to consider how we all got here in the first place—fish, Indians, and whites? Why were the treaties on which the decisions were based written the way they were? Why were they signed in the first place? What were the reservations intended to accomplish? What were the Indians doing before the whites arrived? How did we come to get all the state and they end up with the reservations and the right to some fish? Perhaps this book can help with the understanding of such questions.

It seems sad that I have to point out that I have tried to be objective and evenhanded. Unfortunately so many books about the Indian take such strong emotional positions that the reader has come to expect a great deal of subjectivity in these areas. My biases probably creep in here and there, but I have avoided supporting the very popular "devil theories," which attribute the downfall of the noble and sensitive Indian to the machinations of rotten, land-grabbing settlers and the ineptitude of the Bureau of Indian Affairs. I have also avoided the earlier popular position (still held in many quarters where Indians threaten land, water, or fishing rights) that the murdering savages who massacred kindly missionaries have gotten exactly what was coming to them. If I have an axe that is being ground here, it has to do with the conviction that the Indian peoples have a right to continued existence *as Indians* and that they need some help in getting to wherever it is they want to go. Whether or not that is going to happen, and whether or not it is desirable that it happen, is something that perhaps the reader will think about after finishing the book; in coming to a conclusion, perhaps the reader will make some use of the past as well as the present. If so, the book will have been worth writing.

George Pierre Castile

NORTH AMERICAN INDIANS

AN INTRODUCTION TO THE CHICHIMECA

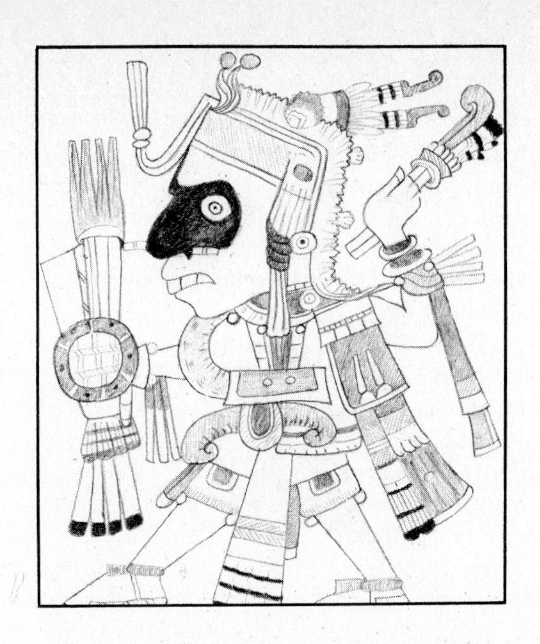

CHICHIMECA: INTRODUCTION AND PERSPECTIVE

Here I stand, I cannot do otherwise.
Martin Luther

Chichimeca?

This is not a familiar word, so let us begin the introduction to this book and to the peoples with which it deals by explaining the choice of title. An accurate phrase is "native peoples of North America," but that is a description and not a name easily used. The normal, indeed unavoidable, term for those peoples in question is "Indians," which is often modified to "American Indians" to distinguish them from the Indians of India or to "North American Indians" to indicate a separation from the native peoples south of the United States–Mexican border. These terms reliably conjure up thoughts of the appropriate area and groups, and their usage is so thoroughly established that it would be foolish to attempt to change it. I will indeed use the term "Indian" throughout the book, but for the title, and as something of a gesture, I want to propose another term that seems to me more appropriate.

"Indians," as surely every literate American knows, is a label derived from the mistaken notions of Columbus that he had arrived at the fringes of the realm of the Great Khan, "the Indies," when he landed on the islands of the Caribbean. It seems sad somehow that this foolishness should solidify into a permanent label for a people. Sadder still, it is not a native term at all but was imposed by outsiders who ultimately dispossessed those peoples of much of their newly labeled land—America.

Use of the term "Americans" in place of "Indians" does not have the drawback of being a geographical absurdity, but it is in no sense native in origin, deriving as it does from the map-making activity of an Italian geographer and explorer, Amerigo Vespucci. (God bless Vespucciland?[1]) The term has been preempted in any case by the European populations currently residing in the "Americas." To apply it to the pre-Columbian peoples (another legacy), it is necessary to add "native" to Americans. References to "Americans" are a source of some irritation to persons south of the United States–Mexican border, where there are some who think that all who live in the Americas (North and South) are Americans and not just "the Americans," who are after all only *Norteamericanos.*

Why not use some term employed by the peoples themselves from their own languages? As we shall see, the area is a veritable babel with regard to languages, but almost all of the peoples' terms for themselves mean something like "the people" or "the men," and their terms for others usually have some reference to "the enemy" or, in disdain, to objectionable creatures, as in "the snakes." In any case terms for themselves and others usually apply to specific small groups known to the peoples in question and are not general labels applicable to the whole "Indian" area.

There is one exception which, with a little generosity of interpretation, can do the job—"Chichimeca." This is a Nahuatl term used by the mighty Aztec to refer to the "barbarians of the north." It is not without honor, since the Aztec insisted that they themselves were Chichimeca from a mysterious northern locale called Aztlan, and it is with Chichimec invaders that much of the story of the rise of Mexico is involved. Chichimeca has the virtue of being a native American term used, at least roughly, to designate the native peoples of the area who are usually

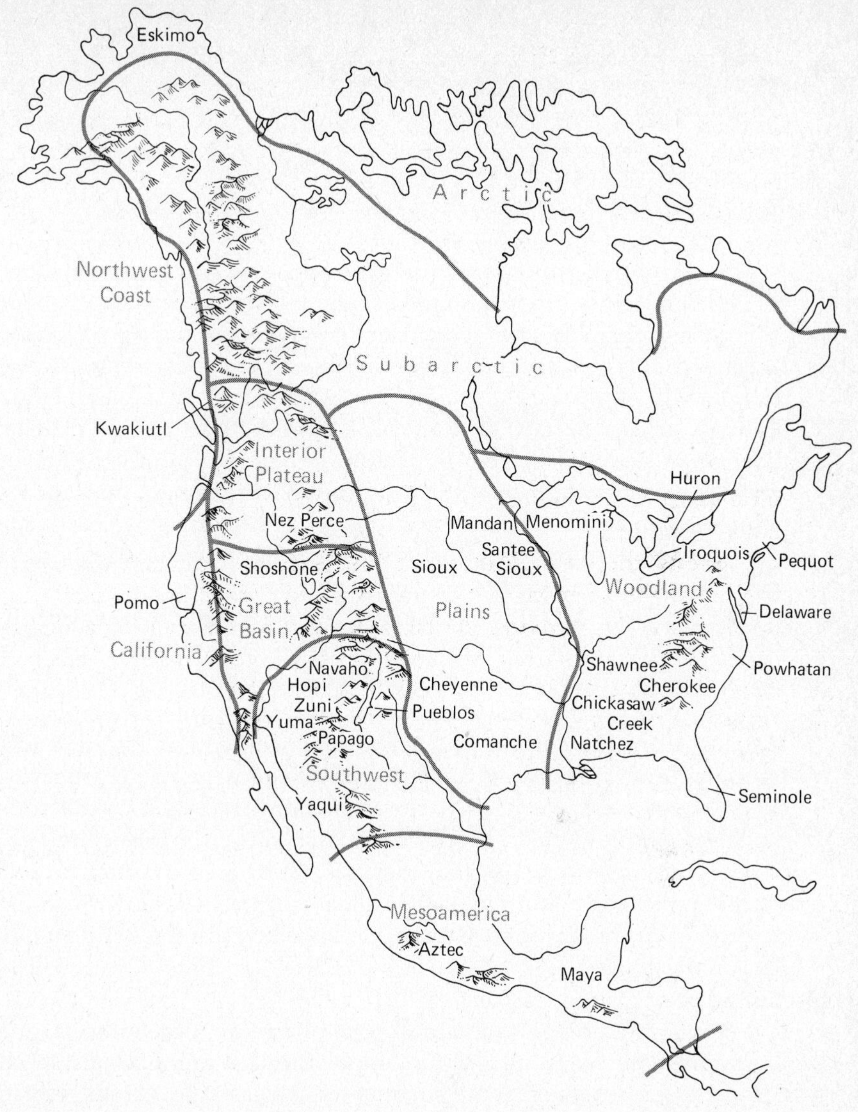

Culture areas of Native North America. Tribes shown are those mentioned significantly in the text. Areas and locations indicated are only approximate.

labeled "North American Indians." If there is no term current in the North American area itself for these peoples, it is better perhaps to use a label devised by the native culture of highest development in all of the American tradition.[2]

Indians? Chichimeca? Whatever the name applied, we are talking about the native peoples of that part of the New World now known as the United States, Canada, and the northernmost provinces of Mexico.

Explaining why this is a logical unit of study, representing something more real than arbitrary, will be one of our tasks in the following chapters.

Circle the Wagons, or the "Noble Savage" versus the "Murdering Redskin"

Anyone who has grown up in the United States and has been subjected to high school history texts, movies, and television, knows all about the American Indian. Indeed Americans have always known all about the Indian—that is to say, there has always been some prevailing view of this unavoidably noticeable people. The problem is that what everyone knows is seldom related to the real nature of the people and usually has more to do with our current difficulties in dealing with the Indians than with the Indians themselves. This is more unfortunate than it sounds, because from earliest times the Indians have been subjected to actions and policies based on these sometimes very curious misconceptions held by the invading and dominant European populations.

At one pole is the "noble savage," who very kindly gives gifts to the grateful Pilgrim fathers, and the romantic Pocahontas, who saves the life of the handsome (we presume) Englishman John Smith. (Some doubt ought to be thrown on the validity of these images when we recollect that virtually all of the coastal peoples who welcomed the Pilgrims and the Puritans have disappeared, some like the Pequots purposely exterminated by those same Puritans, who rejoiced in having sent the Indians' "heathen souls to hell.") There has also always been some body of opinion, as there is today, that idealizes the Indian as one who follows some simple and natural life-style that is more in tune with the inner harmonies of the universe than that followed by the crass and materialistic American. Indians today are looked on as some sort of "groovy" natural ecologists.

At the opposite pole, and in the position more frequently assigned to them in our history, are the Indians of the late-night television show. Almost any evening on some channel we can see kindly settlers forced to circle their wagons to defend themselves against a pack of howling, bloodthirsty savages, who fortunately are not able to hit the broad side of a Conestoga with their weapons and who are mowed down in droves by John Wayne. The murdering savage—torturing, scalping, burning, and generally carrying on in a manner justifying his extermination—has always been a great comfort to us when, as rarely happens, we have sought to wonder about our right to occupy the North American continent and confine its surviving original inhabitants to small parcels of undesirable land.

In both the "noble" and "murdering" aspects, the archetypal Indian has always been the befeathered horseman of the Plains with his tepee,

This bookplate, which illustrated an 1883 edition of Fenimore Cooper's The Wept of Wish-Ton-Wish, *reflects the view of the "savage" Indian that has been held during much of our history. (Whitman College Library)*

buffalo hunts, painted face, and colorful beaded costume. Most people are amazed to discover that the horse, having long been extinct here, was reintroduced to the New World by the Spaniards in the 1500s. It was only in the 1700s that the horse, having gradually spread across the continent, became the foundation for the spectacular buffalo-hunting cultures represented most often in the popular image by the Sioux. This pattern of life, which is "typical" in our minds of the Indian, in fact rose and fell (both events caused by European actions) in not much more than a hundred years, while, as we shall see, there have been peoples living in North America for at least 20,000 years.

Will the "Real" Indian Please . . .

At this point we can begin to explain the reason for writing and reading a book about the Indian as something other than a mere display of academic erudition. Obviously the intention is to say something about the "real" American Indian beyond the simplistic labeling just indicated. No part of the human experience can be understood through such stereotypes, and, at a minimum, the aim here is to provide a broader exposure to the full range of the Indian reality so that, whatever the reader's motivation for undertaking the study, there is some solid foundation in fact and perspective for understanding. Though the author holds no brief for the image of the Indian as a murdering savage, we are no closer to understanding the reality of the Indian through the wave of new popular writings that attempt to idealize the Indian as hapless victim of thoroughly rotten European settlers and in possession today of some superior and natural philosophy and wisdom. It is not intended here to present Indians as either heroes or villains, since they, like all other humans through all time, have been both (depending, of course, as always, on who is defining the nature of villainy and goodness). As we shall see, it is part of the anthropological perspective to avoid making such judgments, since what is good and proper in one society (polygamy) is an unnatural and illegal outrage in another (bigamy!).

This 1905 photograph by "Major" Moorhouse of Pendleton, Oregon, shows the overly romantic view of the Indian most often represented by Pocahontas. Inevitably, the Indian maiden is a "princess." (Whitman College Library)

In a positive way the intention is to provide a representative sample of the full range of diversity of Indian societies over time and space. There is no single "Indian" way of life, just as there is no single "Indian" language. The proud horsemen of the Plains *do* exist, but so do simple foot nomads of the desert, grubbing a precarious living from a harsh environment; and while no group of Chichimeca approach the complexity of central Mesoamericans in the possession of cities and empires, there are some, such as the Mississippian peoples, who construct huge temple-mound complexes and organize themselves into classes of nobles and commoners ruled by a divine "king." There are religions and ideologies that emphasize harmony with nature, but then again there are groups such as those of the Northwest Coast who approach, if not surpass, the conspicuous-consumption orientation of American society today. There are totally egalitarian societies and societies that hold slaves. The Chichimeca may not have shown in their 20,000-year existence every possible variation known in human societies, but their diversity is truly enormous.

Although the arrangement of this book is fundamentally historical, running from the arrival of these peoples to modern times, it represents an anthropological perspective, not a history, and its focus is not on reciting an isolated series of events but on understanding a process of development and adaptation. We want to explain and to understand the variety of the peoples and how such variety came to exist, with the higher purpose of understanding more about the nature of human societies. In this light the Chichimeca represent a long line of independent development from Old World peoples, and the events of their Old World experience compared with those of the New World can, in their similarities and differences, tell us much of social process.

Many people find the idea of using the Indian as a "laboratory study" rather distasteful and seemingly exploitative of the Indian for the benefit of the social scientist. The Navaho matrilocal family has been jokingly described as consisting of a woman, her husband, their married daughters, their daughters' children, unmarried sons, and an anthropologist. In their diversity the Indian groups *are* a laboratory for a comparative science, but then so is all mankind, and social scientists are to be found poking about everywhere in their attempts to understand and illuminate the human condition. Which of us has not found on the doorstep at some point or other a sociologist with a questionnaire in hand? Yet we do not define the American nuclear family as including a sociologist. Perhaps the unease is caused by the fact that the Indian is being studied by a non-Indian, but even though there are anthropologists today who are themselves Indian, it is ridiculous to operate on the assumption that "it takes one to know one." To divide up the species into noncommunicating, autonomous segments is unwise, since the proper study of man is man—*all* men.

Level of Approach

As the subtitle of the book suggests, the intention is to introduce the reader to an understanding of the Indian, and that has important implications. We are dealing with a general overview of a very broad subject indeed, and there is no pretension here to cover all possible details or viewpoints that have been advanced. There are thousands of writings on the subject that the serious student can explore (some of which are indicated at the end of each chapter), and our approach merely provides a framework, and not the only one possible, for entering this complex world.

This approach has dictated some characteristics of the book. Although I hope that what I am presenting will be regarded by my colleagues as an acceptable distillation of our findings, the book is not written for them. In every chapter I have provided important sources and suggestions for further readings, but to preserve interest I have not supported every specific statement with its original bibliographic reference. Consulting their bibliographies in "some readings" will get you started and into the maze of scholarship. This book is for students and teachers who want to begin, and no single book can pretend to do more than start this process.

Anthropology and the American Indian

While this is a book about the American Indian, it is also a book about anthropology since it is written by an anthropologist and makes use of the perspectives of that discipline. For beginning students it is perhaps necessary to add some statement about the nature of that discipline so that, at a minimum, they can be aware of the extent to which an anthropological approach differs from one that might reasonably be taken by a historian or other investigator.

Anthropology as an organized discipline with its own coherent body of theory and method is a very recent phenomenon, so recent that Franz Boas, who only died in 1942, is often referred to as the "father of American anthropology." Our solid beginnings date no earlier than the 1800s with such writers as Lewis Henry Morgan who, though primarily remembered as a proponent of the theory of cultural evolution, was deeply involved in the study of the Indian, particularly in matters of kinship patterns. Though hardly to be counted an anthropologist, Thomas Jefferson was among those sufficiently interested in the Indian to excavate their "mounds." It was such explorations of the archaeological past and the necessity of dealing with living Indians during the westward expansion of the United States that have had much to do with the growth of American anthropology.

It is a harsh and uncomfortable fact that just as British social anthropology developed out of the necessities of the imperial control of Africa and Asia, so American anthropology grew out of the conquest of the Indian. This is not to say that anthropologists have acted as the agents of domination and conquest, but that the "Indian problem" provided an impetus for study and that the fact that such a distinctive people should be in our own backyard (recently acquired) made it inevitable that many of our comparative social studies would develop there. There have been, of course, anthropologists who have exploited the Indian, or at least disregarded the Indians sensibilities in favor of their own interests, but in general, because of the very nonethnocentric character of the discipline, anthropologists have been in the forefront of attempts to improve the Indian's condition and protect his cultural integrity. The programs of the Bureau of Indian Affairs (BIA) under the administration in the 1930s of John Collier, an anthropologist, were perhaps until very recently the most effective and responsive approach to Indian problems we have undertaken. Though it has become fashionable to decry social scientists as exploiters of the populations they study, an examination of the record of the relationship between Indians and anthropologists probably shows that we have done more good than harm and that, at a very minimum, we have consistently tried to support the aspirations of the Indian people during periods when they have had few other supporters.

Anthropology?

For those students who are using this text in a course and have no background in anthropology, I have listed at the end of this chapter several excellent introductory books to the general field. For those students who have some background in anthropology, the definitions and concepts that are introduced here will be familiar, but given the diversity of anthropological theoretical positions, even for them the list of books will be useful in revealing the author's particular bias. Basically I want to give some warning of the general anthropological perspective and introduce some key concepts that organize much of our thinking.

There are almost as many definitions of anthropology as there are anthropologists, but virtually all circle around the "culture" concept, and I tend to prefer Leslie White's label of "the science of culture."[3] A. R. Radcliffe-Brown's "natural science of society" also carries the necessary implication that we are dealing with a science and not an art or one of the humanities.[4] Literally, the word anthropology means "man study," and quite often definitions such as the "holistic science of man" are offered to emphasize the fact that we study man in all his aspects. But, as Leslie White has pointed out, man is a constant in the cultural equation, unless one wishes to take a racist position and argue that cultures can be explained by the different physical characteristics of the individuals who make them up.

Culture is the phenomenon we wish to explain in our science, and the unit of study is a culture, not an aggregate of human beings. The Navaho, for example, constitute such a culture. An individual Navaho is born, *learns* the Navaho way, and dies; but the Navaho *culture* is there before the individual's birth and continues after his or her death, illustrating the fact that culture is a thing of itself and that it is a *superorganic* system based on organic man but with a temporal existence beyond that of the members. The Navaho way is a *system* with many interlocked parts, including means of making a living, beliefs about the nature of the universe, and all else necessary to allow it to continue to survive and *adapt* over time to the environment in which it exists. How such systems or lifeways come into existence, take the forms that they do, and change as they do are the problems that anthropologists seek to solve. The Navaho value sheep and horses above all else and try to maintain a harmonious balance with the universe as they conceive it. The Kwakiutl value rank and prestige, make their living through fishing, and are fiercely competitive. Both cultures work by the only really useful definition, which is that they continue to survive over much time, but still they are very different. Why? Anthropology is still in the process of trying to find out, and some of our understandings are presented in this book.

Anthropology is traditionally divided into four fields, representing four aspects of our method of approach to explanation. *Physical anthropology* is the attempt to understand the biological character of the human species in its development and in its modern variation. As we shall see, such studies of the American Indian shed important light on questions of the origins of the peoples and their relation to the races of the Old World. *Linguistics* is the attempt to deal with human language, and this too can tell us much about the relations of the peoples. Most important and basic, however, are *ethnography* and *archaeology.*

Ethnography is the field that, through participant observation, attempts to describe and analyze the workings of ongoing, living cultures. Ethnographers are at work today on Indian reservations, and others like them have been making investigations ever since the days of Lewis Henry Morgan. Many early studies pushed back the amount of cultural time covered by emphasizing "memory cultures" that relied on the recollections of old men such as the Sioux named "Black Elk," who remembered what lifeways had been like in the days before the disruptive arrival of the whites. Actual field ethnographic investigation has, of course, always been supplemented by the use of historical documents, such as the reams of reports from government Indian agents, though these most often tell us more about the problems experienced with the Indians than they do about the nature of Indian society itself.

Archaeology is the subfield of anthropology that allows us to fill in the vast time span that we wish to understand. Even if we were to assume that immediately on arrival the invading Europeans made accurate observations about every group they encountered, which is obviously far from the case, we are still only back to the 1500s, leaving us with most of our 20,000 years unexamined.

As everyone knows, archaeologists dig holes in the ground and recover all sorts of "neat" Indian relics, particularly arrowheads, just like that beautiful collection your Uncle Charlie has on the wall of his den. As a matter of fact, archaeologists are little interested in "neat," uniquely beautiful relics, since their object is the reconstruction of extinct, prehistoric cultures from the traces left behind, and the garbage dump and the lowly potsherd tell us far more than the beautiful weapon point. In the article "Archaeology as Anthropology," Lewis Binford illustrates how the trick is done in greater detail than I can provide here.[5]

Basically the *artifacts* of a culture—the material traces they leave behind them—are arranged in the *context* in which they are discovered by the nature of the system that used them. We can, if this context is carefully preserved and analyzed, go quite far in working backward toward the reconstruction of the kind of society that left these remains. Your Uncle Charlie is not helping us, since pot-hunting amateur diggers destroy this context, and once destroyed, it can never be useful in reconstruction. Through rather sophisticated mathematical analysis of potsherds we can, for example, tell you whether we are dealing with a matrilineal people—but not if your uncle has burrowed his way into our material.

Some Key Concepts

Obviously we cannot present all of the important theoretical and methodological constructs of the discipline, but I do want to point out a few major considerations that influence the way material is arranged in this work.

ADAPTIVE/EVOLUTIONARY MODEL

This is the basic conceptual framework for organizing understanding in anthropology. In examining the diversity of the Indian cultures and their range from simple to complex in organization and technology, we are looking at a process of adaptation to surrounding environmental circumstances, both physical and cultural. Though the comparison can easily be overworked, the general process is closely similar to that of evolution in biology. A particular culture at any given moment is, to the extent that it changes at all, simply trying to maintain itself in existence by responding to changes in its surrounding environment; at this level *(specific evolu-*

tion) change is nondirectional and certainly not to be thought of in the popular "onward and upward" sense that has distorted the basic Darwinian concept of evolution. But, over much time and much space, we do discover complexity emerging from simpler forms *(general evolution),* and usually we can order these forms in levels of complexity—as we shall do in this book, for example, in terms of the band, the tribe, the chiefdom, and the state.

CULTURE AREAS

Most books about Indians are arranged according to the culture-area concept, as when the peoples discussed are put into groups labeled the Northwest Coast, the Southwest, the Eastern Woodlands, and so on. Peoples so grouped are obviously thought of as having more in common with each other than with the members of the other groups. There is considerable validity to this concept for two reasons. All the people in a particular region are confronted with a similar environment, which in a general way presents them with a set of problems different from those found in some other zone. The other aspect is simple propinquity; that is, the people living in such zones have more contact with each other than they do with groups at some distance and in other zones. It is a handy construct as long as we remain aware that it is only roughly useful. The Southwest, a usual culture area, contains food-gathering foot nomads, horse nomadic raiders, pastoralists, irrigation agriculturalists, floodwater agriculturalists, and the city of Phoenix. Clearly these are not all the same, and something more is required to explain this cultural range.

DIFFUSION

A much abused but vital concept. Cultures differ from biological populations in that they may borrow characteristics from other cultures and incorporate them into their own structure. No matter how much a giraffe may admire a tiger's claws and fangs, there is no way it can acquire them. The Navaho, however, have cheerfully lifted everything from agriculture to weaving from other cultures and have made them their own. For complex reasons, not all cultural traits, even those that seem singularly useful, move from group to group. A classic example is the Navaho rejection of the Ghost Dance religion that spread to groups all around them, basically because the religion promised the return of the dead ancestors, and the Navaho view of the dead is such that this is exceedingly distasteful. Diffusion requires some contact but can take the form of *stimulus diffusion.* Here a classic example is that of the Cherokee, Sequoyah, who knew that the whites could write their own language. He knew that the thing could be done, although he didn't know *how* it was done, so under this stimulus he invented his own method, which in no way resembles our own alphabetical system.

STRUCTURE AND FUNCTION

No structure, no function. Cultures are systems which, in Anthony Wallace's "organismic analogy," seek to maintain themselves.[6] All cultures therefore must make provision for certain necessary structures to provide essential functions. All must have some means, for example, of enculturation, that is, reliably teaching new members the appropriate behaviors they must perform in the ongoing culture. If these behaviors fail for some reason, the culture must make appropriate structural adjustments or it will begin to collapse. One problem for reservation cultures, as we shall note later on, is that many of their essential functions are crosscut by structures controlled from the outside. In the case of enculturation, reservation schools, which are instruments of enculturation, are directed by white society for its purposes rather than the purposes of the Indian.

CULTURAL RELATIVISM

The reverse side of ethnocentricism. The general, and indeed virtually inevitable, human tendency is to assume that everything we do is right and proper (why else would we do it?) and, to the extent that they differ from our own, other people's ways are wrong, loathsome, or the like. Cultural relativism is an anthropological perspective which amounts to ethical neutrality in its insistence that what the many diverse peoples of the earth believe and do is right, proper, and appropriate for them. For those who practice polygamy, it is right, and for those who practice monogamy, that too is right. Values are a function of the culture to which they pertain, and attempts to erect universal standards of judgment are doomed to ludicrous failure. It may be difficult for you to accept something like ritual torture as "right," but once you begin to apply your own arbitrary standards to other people's customs it is hard to stop.

Cultural relativism must, of course, include sexual and racial relativism as well. At no point in this book are Indian cultural differences linked with biological/physical characteristics. Sexism, given the nature of the English language, is a little harder to avoid in writing, and I have chosen to use the word "man" in its generic sense and mean it to be read as including both male and female. Similarly, I have tried to avoid cumbersome language and have used the seemingly masculine pronoun "he" and words such as "tribesman" and "kinsman" in order to avoid constant repetition of the compound "he or she" and of grammatical atrocities such as "tribespersons." The occasional apparent overempha-

Red Cloud, a very real man who did as much as any person could and succeeded longer than most. Red Cloud's War was one of the few instances where Indian peoples won not only a battle but also a campaign to reclaim lost territory. (Edward Curtis)

sis on the masculine is intentional, since that was the nature of many of the Native American cultures in question, and it would be ethnocentric of me to insist that male-dominated societies be presented as having achieved sexual equality.

Forward into the Past!

One more thing to be noted is the arrangement of the book into two parts. Part I deals with independent development and evolution of the Indian societies prior to sustained white contact. In this part we will examine the variety of adjustments that the Indian peoples made in their populating of the New World. Part II deals with the period of white contact and conquest up to the present reservation situation. This range of response to contact, generally referred to as *acculturation* in anthropology, is our primary interest here and will lead us into a consideration of possible future directions for the Indian peoples.

Some Readings

General Introductions to the Field of Anthropology

Friedl, John, and John E. Pfeiffer: *Anthropology: The Study of People,* New York: Harper & Row, 1977.

Harris, Marvin: *Culture, Man and Nature,* New York: Thomas Y. Crowell, 1971.

Hoebel, E. Adamson, and Everett L. Frost: *Cultural and Social Anthropology,* New York: McGraw-Hill, 1976.

Kottak, Conrad Phillip: *Anthropology: The Exploration of Human Diversity,* New York: Random House, 1974.

General Works on the American Indian

Driver, Harold: *Indians of North America,* 2d ed., Chicago: University of Chicago Press, 1969. An encyclopedic collection of ethnographic facts about the Indian.

Farb, Peter: *Man's Rise to Civilization as Shown by the Indians of North America,* New York: Dutton, 1968. Title is actually longer. A readable, if somewhat overstated, treatment that leans heavily on the evolutionary stages of Elman Service.

Murdock, George Peter, and Timothy J. O'Leary: *Ethnographic Bibliography of North America,* New Haven: Human Relations Area files, 1975. For the truly serious student, a monumental collection of sources for research and further study (five volumes).

Newcomb, William W.: *North American Indians: An Anthropological Perspective,* Pacific Palisades: Goodyear Publishing Co., 1974. One of several general introductions organized around culture areas.

Oswalt, Wendell H.: *This Land Was Theirs,* 2d ed., New York: Wiley, 1973. Recently revised older survey organized around culture areas.

Underhill, Ruth: *Red Man's America,* Chicago: University of Chicago Press, 1953. Very readable but somewhat romanticized general survey.

PART I

INDEPENDENT DEVELOPMENT AND VARIATION 20,000 (±) B.C. TO A.D. 1492

CHRONOLOGICAL OUTLINE FOR PART I

	Pre-Projectile Point cultures?		
25,000 B.C.			Possible first arrivals from Asia
12,000 B.C.	Big Game cultures		First *certain* evidence of arrival: skeletal remains, fluted points, other tools
	Clovis		
	Folsom		
8000 B.C.	*Plano*	Desert	Extensive/collecting-oriented Desert tradition begins
			Gradual extinction of Pleistocene megafauna
6000 B.C.	*Archaic*		
			General shift toward extensive specialized subsistence techniques with increasing regionalization
1500 B.C.	Specialized regional cultures emerge—Arctic/California/Woodland/Plateau/Plains/Northwest/Southwestern/Subarctic		

Dates and events vary widely from the examples cited.

	Woodlands (Ohio-Mississippian)	Southwest	
1500 B.C.			Woodland pottery (possibly 2000 B.C.). Settled villages—presence of agriculture uncertain
800 B.C.	Adena		Adena/Hopewell—burial mounds and other monumental earthworks. Long-range trade in cult objects
300 B.C.	Hopewell		
100 B.C.		Mogollon Hohokam	Agriculture and settled village life in the Southwest (possibly 300 B.C.) Hohokam shows influence/contact with Mesoamerica: ball courts, temple mounds, art themes
A.D. 600	Mississippian		Mississippian temple mounds and tombs
A.D. 700		Anasazi	Agriculture in Mississippian area and strong Mesoamerican resemblances
A.D. 800			Hohokam massive irrigation works
A.D. 1000		(Athabascans?)	Great Pueblo period
			Athabascans enter Southwest somewhere in this time bracket
A.D. 1400			Pueblos decline in area
		(Athabascans?)	
	Natchez	Rio Grande pueblos	
A.D. 1540		*Coronado Expedition*	First contacts between European and Chichimeca
A.D. 1542	*DeSoto Expedition*		

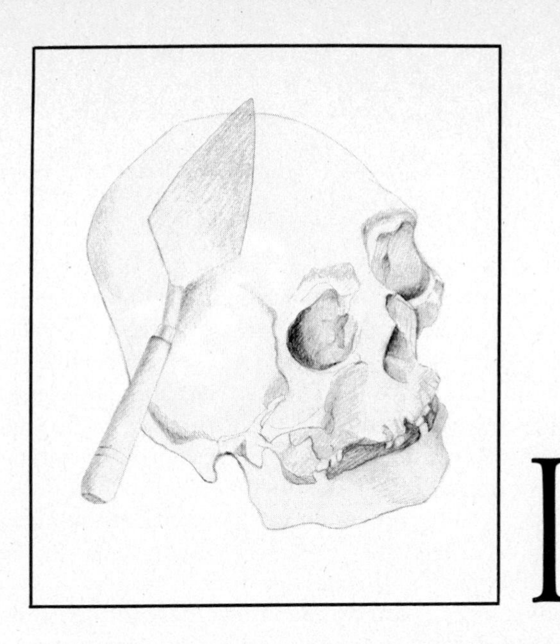

I
FIRST MAN

The White Bead Woman wished now to have her own people. She wished to have a people that she could call her grandchildren. They would carry on the lore that she would teach them. They would respect and hold holy the prayers and chants that she would give them.

She took a white bead stone and she ground it to powder. She put this powder on her breasts and between her shoulders, over her chest and on her back; and when this powder became moist she rubbed it off her body and rolled it between her fingers and on the palm of her hand. From time to time a little ball dropped to the ground. She wrapped these little balls in black clouds. They arose as people. She placed these people on the shore of a big body of water.

. . . Then the White Bead Woman asked the Twelve Holy Beings to lead her children far away from the Great Water. She said that the shells should be planted for corn and for different kinds of food plants. So the people made ready and they moved far inland from the sea.

Fragment of Navaho origin myth[1]

Virtually all groups have been fascinated with questions of their origins and have provided themselves with explanations, either in legendary form, such as this portion of the origin myth of the Navaho, or in some more or less factual recounting of migrations. The Navaho version is, as a matter of fact, a little of both, since the Diné are Athabascan-speaking peoples who appear to have moved into their current southwestern homeland in relatively recent times. They have northern linguistic relatives, some of whom are indeed coastal peoples, so their traditional account probably reflects some recollection of the reality of their migration.

Archaeology and physical anthropology today give us a strong foundation for satisfying *our* curiosity about these beginnings, though there yet remain great gaps and confusions in our understandings. As an introduction to what we think we know, let us examine an anthropological origin myth.

> First man entered the New World, although he did not know it, walking rapidly and steadily westward across a marshy and muddy land, annoyed by clouds of insects. His interest and attention were focused on a herd of large animals, moving some distance before him. These were mammoths, though there were many other varieties of huge herd animals available for the skillful hunter. First man and his people have been following this herd for some days, hoping to trap them in some bog or gully for they are too dangerous to approach without some special advantage, armed as he and his kinsmen are, only with spears tipped with delicately worked stone points.
>
> He is not *going* anywhere, except where the pursuit of the game on which his life depends leads him. He was probably born and will die within a hundred miles of where he now stands, for unlike later arrivals he has no desire to conquer and own the land but only to seek and enjoy the abundant game. Tonight, if there has been a kill, there will be singing and dancing as the men boast of their prowess—a fitting celebration as well for their arrival in the New World.

This reflects our conviction that the first inhabitants of the Americas were hunters of big game animals, drifting into the New World toward the end of the Ice Ages when Asia and Alaska were connected by a wide land bridge with a climate much like that of the modern Canadian tundra. Whatever the details, something like this must have occurred, for no person—not the Puritan Founding Fathers, nor the mighty Aztec, nor the humble seed gatherers—is a "native" American in the strict sense, since man's homeland lies elsewhere. The first great issue in our understanding of the peoples of America is when and in what condition did they first come here. It may be necessary to point out that, while all are immigrants, some have held squatters' rights for perhaps 20,000 years and would seem to have some proper prior claim to the title "native."

The Wrong Monkeys

Though much about man's origins is in dispute, one thing is certain and that is that man did not develop in the New World. Although, as shall be seen in a later chapter, there have been at various times those who have insisted that the American Indian came from Mu or Atlantis or represents one of the rather remarkably far-flung "lost tribes" of Israel, there is no one who suggests that the species was born here. Theories of migration and influence have been bizarre indeed, including most recently the theory of mysterious "gods from outer space" directing the high civilizations of the Americas, but at least all concede migration and not separate creation of New World man.

North and South America, like Australia and its famous marsupials, are zones of some zoological interest because they have undergone long periods of isolation, broken by occasional contacts and consequent movements of animals from Old to New World. In South America, for example, in the Oligocene period there flourished, in the absence of more efficient, competing mammalian carnivores, a huge, flightless meat-eating bird (*Phororhacos*) that looked something like an ostrich, only larger and with teeth. The monkeys of the New World would appear to have separated from their Old World relatives in the order *Primates* sometime in the Eocene (40 million to 60 million years ago) and developed entirely separately thereafter. Old World monkeys and New World monkeys look and behave enough alike that casual observation would not point up the differences that are so significant to the anthropologist.

In recent years man's evolution has been reliably traced back for at least 2 million years to the first upright biped who used tools—*Australopithecus*, or *Homo africanus*, of Africa. A great deal of evidence has been amassed that strongly indicates that man first became man at this time and place.

Physical anthropologists, considering both modern man and the fossil remains of our ancestors, have long been able to show that we stand in close relation to the relatively specialized Old World Primates adapted to brachiation (swinging through the trees), whose living representatives are the great apes. We share with these apes a basic skeletal orientation to the vertical, because bipedalism and brachiation both require verticality, and man's bipedalism is almost surely the result of the utility of the brachiators' skeletal preadaption to the upright posture.

No such creatures exist in the New World. Indeed the New World monkeys are sufficiently different to be placed in a separate suborder of Primates. The dental arrangements, blood serums, facial structures, prehensile tails, and myriad other differences totally disqualify the New World monkeys from playing a part in human development. There is no suitable ancestor here, and this statement is reinforced by the fact that nowhere in the New World are there found any fossils of any man or manlike creatures that differ significantly from modern man of our own species, *Homo sapiens.* In the Old World there are the remains of our two great predecessors—*Homo erectus* and *Homo africanus* (*Australopithecus*), but here there is nothing but ourselves. Man must have come to the new land as fully developed, biologically, as he is today.

If he was not born here, then from where did he come? How? When? What sort of man was he?

Bridges and Bullboats

From where and how are relatively easy questions to answer, since for the how at least there are only two possibilities. Our first man either walked across a land bridge, as the opening "myth" suggests, or somehow crossed the oceans that once made this "Fortress America." We will not deny the possibility, and even the likelihood, that at certain times there have been seaborne visitors from Europe, Africa, Oceania, or Asia, such as those suggested by the spectacular voyages of Thor Heyerdahl. It is, however, extremely unlikely that the *first* contact could have been made in this way, since other evidence suggests that the event occurred at such an early date that nowhere in the world were there peoples who possessed oceangoing craft. One archaeologist has suggested that contacts could have been made by people using very simple craft, like bullboats—wicker frameworks wrapped with hide—but considering the distances involved, this seems extremely unlikely, and certainly no evidence exists to support it.

There is really little doubt that man came here on some land bridge connecting New and Old World. A glance at a map immediately shows that there is only one real possibility for such crossing, and that is the area where Alaska and Asia are separated only by a narrow stretch of water. Presumably many are familiar with the "drifting continents" theories in geology that suggest that the continental arrangements were once very different; but those arrangements, while fascinating to contemplate, took place many millions of years before man's existence and so do not serve as an alternative solution to the contact problem.

Similarly a glance at the map would seem to suggest the Aleutian Island chain is the most likely site for land contact, but there is deep

A hide and wicker "bullboat" of the Mandan. Such craft were all that existed during the period of earliest arrival, and it seems unlikely that they would have been suitable for the crossing of the North Atlantic. (Edward Curtis)

water there, and while it is possible that island hopping might have occurred in later periods, that was not the location of the land bridge. The obvious point is the Bering Strait, narrowly separating the Asian and North American continents. It is fairly easy to cross even today in the simplest of boats. Again we emphasize that at various times there could easily have been movement across ice and water in much the same manner that modern Eskimos, the most recent immigrants, travel through the Arctic region.

More important is the land bridge that periodically has existed in this area. During the Pleistocene (Ice Age) much of the world's water was trapped in the great continental ice sheets, and areas now submerged were then dry land. The Bering Strait during this epoch was high and dry and formed a natural corridor for the movement of men and animals between the continents. The image that pops to mind is that of a narrow path, like a plank laid between housetops, but this land bridge was at times as much as 1300 miles wide, and primitive men could easily have crossed it without knowing that any dramatic event had occurred. We know for certain that there was considerable animal migration in both directions across the bridge—the most fascinating migrant being the horse, which, fossil evidence shows, once resided in the New World, although it later became extinct. When the Spanish reintroduced it to the New World, the horse was simply coming home and happily proliferated in its ancestral habitat, eventually becoming a vital part of the Plains Indians' culture.

Travel across ice is not impossible, but both men and animals probably moved into the new land through ice-free corridors such as the Mackenzie River Valley and radiated out into the rest of the continent. There is considerable debate as to how rapidly man expanded in numbers and how quickly he reached the South American area. This issue is tied up with the problem of when man first arrived and how many separate waves of migration occurred. Considerable evidence suggests the presence of man at the very tip of South America at 14,000 to 10,000 B.C. Unless man moved very, very rapidly indeed, this is disquieting to some who have tended to believe that man first arrived in the North American area at about that same time.

The issue remains unresolved, and the answer will continue to be obscured until dating methods become more refined. On the basis of our current reliable dates it looks as if the New World was populated very rapidly, and that is not inconsistent with what we know about the expansion of animal species that find themselves in a new environment which was previously unexploited and in which they have few or no natural competitors. The situation of the horse, which multiplied and spread very quickly, is a case in point.

One must not, however, slip into imagining a man jogging steadily southward mumbling "Tierra del Fuego or bust." When we say "rapid," we mean many, many generations. Human populations at this level tend to expand in accord with a sort of budding model. A hunting and gathering group, however rich the animal resources on which it depends, tends to reach an optimum carrying capacity—a balance between the available resources and the size of the population. The original group then splits into smaller groups, and some members move on into new hunting grounds. Each such move involves new adaptations to the circumstances of each new ecozone entered, and the split-off groups eventually produce split-off groups of their own, radiating out, as has been suggested, all over the North and South American continents.

Complicating the reconstruction of settlement in the New World is the certain fact that there have surely been several waves of migration. The Eskimos are the most recent immigrants, and the Athabascans also clearly intruded into areas already occupied by earlier peoples. The question is again how many such waves were there, and again we have no certain answer, though some have postulated on the basis of physical and linguistic evidence that there may have been as many as twelve separate waves. What we do know about the migrations and the truly crucial issue of timing can best be considered through examination of existing evidence and the positions taken in the interpretation of the evidence.

Early, Earlier, Earliest

The comparative youthfulness of anthropological science is apparent in the fact that not until 1926 did we produce evidence that could place the earliest Americans in the Pleistocene period. Reacting against wild-eyed speculation in the area of physical anthropology in the 1800s, such persons as Ales Hrdlička, who insisted on *hard* evidence, held to about 3000 B.C. as the earliest proven date.[2] Sloppy archaeological techniques, confused geological findings, and dubious dating techniques combined to make easy the rejection of earlier dates as unproven and unreliable. But in 1926, at Folsom, New Mexico, careful digging in clearly undisturbed geological deposits revealed the bones of extinct bison in clear-cut association with projectile points (Folsom points) of undeniable human manufacture. Man *had* to have been here at the close of the Pleistocene, and the gates were open at last to dates of 10,000 or more years ago for man's arrival in the New World.

Currently there are three fundamental positions on the arrival date, with decreasingly solid evidence the farther back one wishes to push it. For the period between 15,000 and 10,000 B.C., there is hard and essentially incontrovertible evidence of man's presence in the New World. For the period between 35,000 and 20,000 B.C., there is little evidence that is undeniable, but material is continually accumulating that makes this a possible and increasingly likely position. Beyond this it is essentially blue-sky speculation, with virtually no solid evidence to back it, which suggests that man may have come as early as 100,000 B.C. Even this interpretation, I hasten to point out, is not impossible, but in the absence of evidence, it is held only by a fanatical few.

Blood and Bones

Physical anthropologists address the issues of man's arrival in the New World in two ways. One is the examination of modern living Indian populations with regard to such characteristics as the distribution of blood types. The other is the study of skeletal and fossil remains of extinct populations. In both, the principal question is the degree of similarity or difference between the Indians and other human populations, with an eye to determining the degree and timing of the isolation of the Indian from these other populations.

Beginning with the bones, we have already cited one very significant conclusion, which is that of all of the fossil remains we have discovered none differs significantly from the various characteristics we find in living modern Indian populations. If man did arrive in the New World in 100,000 B.C. or earlier, then we would be on the edge of man's transition from *Homo erectus* to *Homo sapiens*, and we would expect some very fundamental differences in our fossils. To be fair, we should point out that there are only a very few currently known "early men," and it is entirely possible that others will be discovered. It is conceivable that we will find evidence for more primitive men, though no such evidence now exists.

There is a general argument as to the racial classification of the Indian that also bears on the issue of the timing of arrival and the analysis of the bones. Very early arrival is associated in the minds of some people with the idea of "proto-Mongoloids"—some hypothetical racial variety that in the Americas goes on to become the Indian and in Asia to become the true Mongoloid. While argument is possible in terms of the interpretation of differences between modern Indian and Asian populations, there is nothing in the bones that the majority of anthropologists accept as evidence for the proto-Mongoloid position. To the extent that skeletal features can reflect race, which is mostly a matter of cranial characteristics, the earliest finds show virtually no differences from modern populations.

Physical anthropologists have also extensively studied living populations of Indians and have discovered that they bear very close resemblance in most of their physical characteristics to the living peoples of east Asia. In most classifications of the large geographical or continental races Indians are included in the Mongoloid group. They differ sufficiently from these Asian peoples, however, so that many regard them as a separate, though ultimately related, group. This is, of course, strong reinforcement for the conclusion that the peoples of the New World migrated from Asia much as we have described.

The degree to which the Indians differ from the generalized Asian population suggests that they have existed in isolation in the New World long enough for these differences to become established. Unfortunately this sort of evidence doesn't do much more than verify our conclusion that the Indians have been here for some thousands of years, since there is no agreement on how long it would take for the observed variations to arise, whether through a process of adaptation to climatic/environmental conditions or through some other process such as genetic drift. It is significant that while there is certainly variation among American Indian populations, most observers think there is considerable uniformity among the groups as compared with the much wider range of variation seen in other continental races.

As generalized Mongoloids, the Indians have such characteristics as straight, dark—usually black—hair which rarely grays and rarely all falls out. Indians have very little body hair. High cheekbones and the relatively frequent occurrence of the epicanthic eye fold within a smooth, relatively flat face reinforce the Indian resemblance to the Mongoloid stock. Skin color, which seems so important in most people's concept of race, falls within the Mongoloid range, although Indians' skin is generally lighter than that of the Asian Mongoloids and has a greater tendency to tan. The true "redskins" are the Europeans, who sometimes have very florid complexions, while the Indians are actually "ivory-brownskins."

Genetic characteristics that distinguish the Indians from Mongoloids, as well as from all other races, are rather subtle. Physical anthropologists place great importance on traits, the occurrence of which they can trace and which they can use as markers and indicators of population isolation, whether or not these traits seem very important to the layperson. Thus we find that Indian groups tested have a high incidence of shovel-shaped incisor teeth and a very low incidence of hair on the middle segment of the fingers. These traits obviously have no great significance for the survival of the people, or indeed any particular utility at all, but they do indicate a degree of genetic isolation from other groups.

Blood types, which have the advantage of being easily tested, are very definite indications of the separate status of Indians as a distinctive genetic population and of their uniformity as a group. In the A-B-O system, Indian groups show an almost complete absence of A and B blood types and a very high incidence of O. On the blood factor M-N Indians show a very high frequency of N, and the Rh+ factor is far more common among them than the Rh− factor. Still another factor, Diego, is confined almost exclusively to American Indians and a few peoples of east Asia. In these and other elements there are, of course, variations and exceptions. The Blackfoot show one of the highest incidences of type A blood in the world, and the Hopi have a very high frequency of albinism. The more recent arrivals, the Athabascans and the Eskimos, naturally show more resemblance to Asian peoples and less to the earlier arrivals in the New World.

Babel

Do you speak Indian? While estimates vary, there were probably about 200 mutually unintelligible languages, not counting dialects, being spoken in the Chichimec area shortly before the arrival of the European. For North and South America combined, estimates run as high as 2000 separate languages. While some other aspects of language will be considered, the point here is in the relevance of this confusion of tongues to the problem of origins and arrival dating. As with the physical evidence, the important question concerns how long it would take to develop such diversity of languages, since we can scarcely entertain the idea that there were hundreds of separate migrations.

Linguistic analysis groups these languages into basic stocks on elaborate criteria of similarity, and within limits it is generally assumed that these related languages all evolved from some basic protolanguage. Thus there is a *Na-Déné* language group that includes Athabascan speakers of the subarctic and Pacific Coast regions and the Navaho and Apache speakers of the Southwest.

Obviously it would take time for such diversity to develop, and in a general way we are again simply affirming our conviction that it was a long time indeed. How long? There is a method, the absolute accuracy of which is in doubt and much debated, but which suggests at least some approximate times or the eventual possibility of deriving them. The method, known as "glottochronology," works on the same basis as the method for grouping languages in the first place; it is fundamentally a statistical analysis of the number of cognates in supposedly related languages. The English *father* and the German *vater* are such cognates, which, along with a great many others, lead us to group English and German as related languages.

Glottochronology is based on the assumption that two groups speaking the same language will, when isolated from each other, gradually modify their language and come to differ from each other at a predictable rate. This is measured in terms of a core of cognates, which are nouns for common objects such as *the sun* or verbs such as *to eat* that we assume occur in some form in all languages. It is assumed that this core is conservative and changes only slowly and predictably. Using a list of some 100 to 200 core words, the rate of change seems to indicate that two languages will retain 66 percent of the same cognates after 1000 years. In some cases archaeological evidence has borne out this method of dating, as with Eskimo and Aleut languages, but unfortunately a number of other investigations do not show such regularity in rate of change. Glottochronology remains a promising tool, but for the moment it can really only indicate "a long time," as do our other dating methods.

Artifacts and Eoliths

In one area, archaeology, we stand on very solid ground; indeed, it is here that we can give definite and reliable dates for our earliest Americans. Archaeologists can provide us with both *absolute* and *relative* dates for the remains man has left behind in the New World. Absolute dates place the object being dated at some definite point on the calendar—say, 1000 B.C.—while relative dates give its age relative to something else—Clovis points are older than Folsom points—a fact that can be determined stratigraphically, even when an absolute date is unavailable for either item.

This use of stratigraphy is an example of how important context is in archaeology. If a site is peeled down layer by layer, then the material discovered can be described in terms of "strata," or layers; material found farther down in the layering is obviously older than that found in the upper levels, because time is required for deposits to build up. It is in the nature of geological process that the younger layers overlie the older. For this reason, as well as others, it is necessary to record carefully the context of the material as the site is dug. An archaeologist under whom I studied compared the digging of a site to the reading of a book, but as each "page" of a site is read, it is destroyed forever, so *everything* must be recorded.

Archaeologists today have developed or borrowed from other disciplines a wide variety of dating techniques, the most notable of which is the carbon 14, or radioactive carbon, method. The various and ingenious dating techniques include paleomagnetism, which depends on the mapping of the movements of the magnetic poles; palynology, which through pollen analysis determines vegetation types and thus climate and, in turn, rough dates for various climates; patination and hydration, which both depend on the rate at which stone, once chipped, builds up chemical layers—measurement of the layers can yield the date of original chipping.

Carbon 14 dating, the most common and useful technique, is based on analysis of the proportion of carbon 12 to carbon 14 in a sample of wood, bone, shell, or similar organic material. The proportions of these forms of carbon present in the atmosphere are presumed to be constant, and when an organism dies, it ceases to take in both forms. The unstable, radioactive carbon 14 then begins to break down at a fixed and predictable rate, which is expressed as a "half-life" of 5730 years. That is, in 5730 years there will be only half as much carbon 14 as there was at the beginning. There are technical problems that create some uncertainty, and all dates are expressed as ± to indicate a range of variation. A good discussion of this and other technical archaeological problems can be found in *An Introduction to Prehistoric Archaeology* by Hole and Heizer, cited at the end of this chapter.

We can date objects precisely, or reasonably precisely, but what are we dating? Essentially we are looking for man himself, in skeletal materials, which are very rare indeed, or in indisputable evidence of his presence, his works. More actual human physical remains of early age are being unearthed, as at the Marmes site in Washington, but it is man's artifacts on which we must principally rely. There is some confusion as to why human fossils are so rare, but the basic assumption is that man himself was not a numerous species in the early period and was spread very thinly over the land (as wolves are less numerous than the herd animals they kill). More speculatively, we can also assume that intelligent individuals were far less likely to end up in bogs or tar pits than were less bright game animals, and fossil preservation occurs best under such circumstances, where the remains are sealed against the effects of the elements.

In the absence of human fossil remains, we need evidence of man's passage, and that poses a problem in distinguishing between artifacts and eoliths. An *artifact* is most simply defined as any aspect of the environment altered by the hand of man—a stone tool, a posthole, a fireplace, or a Frisbee. An *eolith*, unfortunately, is an object that is formed by natural processes, not by human hands, but which *looks* like an artifact. Stone can be chipped by many actions other than the hunter's shaping, and if a tool is simple enough it is difficult to distinguish between it and a chipped stone.

There are two overlapping cultural traditions which are usually lumped together as the "Big Game Hunters." Their tools give us unmistakable evidence of the presence of man in the New World around 10,000 B.C. These are the traditions called Folsom and Clovis, both originally verified in the Southwest and called after towns near the type sites—Folsom and Clovis, New Mexico. Each is characterized by projectile points, which are presumably lance points rather than arrowheads as is sometimes popularly assumed. They are classified as lance points because of their large size and because of evidence that suggests the bow was not in use until thousands of years later. There is no confusion about these points as artifacts because a single glance will show there is no way they can be natural occurrences. Indeed, until very recently, the technique of making them was beyond the talents of archaeologists who sought to reproduce them.

The most noticeable characteristic of these points is a flute or long central channel in an already thin flaked point, which greatly reduces its thickness. The purpose of this channel is obscure, but it probably made the point easier to haft or eased its penetration into the animal when it was used as a thrusting weapon. The Clovis point is usually larger and not so finely made as the best of the Folsom points, nor is it fluted along its whole length. Some points have been found in good stratigraphic context and are well dated, but others are also widely distributed in the Chichimec area as undatable surface finds.

The points are, of course, only the most readily identifiable artifacts of the peoples who made them. Their tool kit was made up of a variety of other less distinctive implements, including less elaborate points. There are such stone tools as hammerstones, scrapers, blades, and gravers. Since most sites of this period are kill sites rather than camp or habitation sites, it is unlikely that we have the full range of the tools and artifacts of these peoples. We will return to these peoples later to consider what their life was like, but for the moment the point being made is that on the basis of these materials there is no dispute over the fact that man was present on this continent around 10,000 B.C.

The materials of the Big Game Hunters were rather sophisticated and must have developed somewhere at some earlier time from simpler forms and techniques, as we know has occurred with every other tradition. There must be sites in Asia, if these theories of origin are correct, where there are materials that resemble the American finds. Work in Asia is not yet well developed, but there is evidence accumulating in Siberia and at other east Asian sites to support these assumptions. As yet, none of it can be regarded as clearly conclusive, and very little can be of use in dating man's entry into the New World. There is the same lack of developed evidence from the far north of America, in areas such as Alaska, where we would also logically expect to find very early evidence of preceding stages of development. In both cases the problem is, to some extent, the result of the difficulty of digging in remote areas, and until recently archaeologists have concentrated on other more accessible and more productive regions. Archaeologists are human after all, and it is more fun to dig a rich Mayan temple than to grub in the frozen tundra for a few stone chips. Some evidence of migration may, of course, never be recovered if any part of the path of movement was down the coastal plain, because that plain, which was exposed at times during the Pleistocene, is now under deep water.

In the central Chichimec area, however, there are a number of sites that have been dug in recent years that show dates in the neighborhood of 30,000 to 25,000 B.C. (or so some contend) and that could be the hoped-for evidence of a pre-Projectile Point horizon. None of these sites has any artifact so clearly and indisputably of human manufacture as the Clovis and Folsom points, and this very lack is argued to be evidence of their antiquity. Although a great deal of the material advanced to support this position appeared as surface finds and therefore is automatically of limited utility for dating, some material has been found through digging at sites such as Friesenhahn Cave in Texas and Santa Rosa Island off the coast of California.

The unfortunate fact is that the support for this position is primarily a matter of believing that there *ought* to be evidence at this time level. None of the current sites is accepted widely as demonstrating beyond question the presence of man. There is evidence of fire, but it could be the result of natural burning. There are extinct animal remains, but nothing to make certain they were killed by man rather than by other carnivores. There are some toollike objects that may simply be natural occurrences, and there are other toollike objects that are probably artifacts, which are not clearly associated stratigraphically with the time period. The dating of any of this evidence is confused, sometimes because of poor associations and often simply because we are at the outer limits of our most reliable dating technique—carbon 14.

There are, as indicated, some who contend that man's arrival might have been very early indeed. L. S. B. Leakey, the famed popularizer of the *Australopithecus* finds in Africa and a man who did much work to determine the antiquity of the extremely crude tools of that man of 2 million years ago, has been among those who have endorsed such sites as Calico in California, which dates back at least 50,000 years on geological criteria. The problem with this "very old" position is that the largest number of the finds are surface finds, and the largest number of purported artifacts, lacking good contextual association, have been dismissed as eoliths. While the 25,000- to 30,000-year position has some substantial acceptance by reputable archaeologists, at least to the point that there is debate over the validity of the finds, only a dedicated few support the earliest finds in the face of the general judgment that none of their evidence is even debatable. Just as with the crude "Olduwan" tools that finally were associated with *Australopithecus* remains through contextual analysis, the simple stones of America may possibly turn out to be tools; but in the absence of context that rules out natural forces, one could stroll along a stream and fill the bed of a pickup truck with "tools" every bit as persuasive as those currently being used as evidence.

In summary, then, we can be sure that man came here from Asia and that he was flourishing as a Big Game Hunter by the end of the Pleistocene period. Most of us are convinced not on the basis of any very good evidence but by the logic of man's condition and the level of his cultural development that we *will* find evidence of an earlier arrival date than any we can now prove. Why are we so concerned? As noted at the beginning, we are trying through our study of the American peoples to make some statements about the nature of cultural phenomena in general. When we can pin down how much time elapsed between man's arrival in the New World and the time of Columbus, and thus how long it took for the cultural diversity that was observed at that time to develop, and if we can verify that the culture of the peoples at the time of arrival was relatively uniform and simple, then we can make more accurate observations about the nature and rapidity of cultural evolutionary/adaptive processes.

Big Game Hunters?

It has been mentioned that the cultures whose existence is undeniable were "Big Game Hunters," but in that simple statement there is a wealth of information about the nature and complexity of the culture of these earliest Americans. In the next chapter the simplest levels of cultural development characteristic of Indian beginnings will be described, but we can note here a few of the things we have learned about these peoples through archaeological evidence and inference.

They were surely hunters, since no evidence of domesticated plants or any equipment necessary to deal with such plants appeared until thousands of years later. Because most of the sites were not camp or habitation sites we have little evidence of the technology associated with plant gathering and processing. However, except in special environments (among the Eskimos in the Arctic, for example), we know of no human societies that do not rely heavily, and indeed primarily, on the plant-collecting activities of women, supplementing those food supplies with the more sporadic kills by the men. There is, as we shall see later, evidence (8000 B.C.) in the southwestern United States of a cultural pattern that very nearly overlaps the pattern of the Big Game Hunters. This other pattern, usually called the "Desert Tradition," was very heavily oriented toward plant-processing technology. It may well be that we have simply failed to find enough to fill out this side of the same picture, but for the moment the image of the Big Game Hunters is one of a highly specialized hunting way of life.

Just as we think of the Plains Indians of historic times as having a virtually symbiotic relation with the bison, so these people seem to have oriented their lives around the pursuit of particular species of big game common in the Pleistocene. Where evidence of association is obtainable, Clovis points are to be found with mammoths, as at the Blackwater Draw site near Clovis, New Mexico, or at the Naco site in southeastern Arizona. Folsom points are usually found with the extinct and larger-than-modern *Bison antiquus*, as at the Lindenmeier site in Colorado or at the Folsom, New Mexico, type site. This pattern of dependence on a single species is similar to that of the Upper Pleistocene peoples of Northern Europe at around the same time, and some enthusiasts, on the basis of such similarities, have postulated the very unlikely possibility of contact or common origin. It is to be noted that there are animal remains other than the primary species present, but they are nowhere nearly as abundant or frequent.

The kill sites show considerable evidence of sophistication in hunting techniques, since large animals like mammoths were not easy to kill with stone-tipped spears. The kills were usually in some spot of special advantage to the hunter, such as bogs, ponds, and streambeds where the animal could become mired and helpless, either by accident or, as is more likely, by being driven there by the hunters. The purposeful driving of the game is also evident at sites where the animals have been driven over high drops or into box canyons. Although there is no doubt on other grounds, such cooperation in a drive makes clear the existence of language and suggests the necessity for some degree of organization among the hunters to facilitate coordination.

How sophisticated were these peoples? Their tools are finely made, at least in the case of the points, indeed so finely made as to suggest definite aesthetic traditions and high standards of workmanship. In addition to the difficult art of fluting, they made use in some cases of prepared core techniques for blade making, a procedure that in the

European sequence is often offered as evidence of abstract and *sapiens*-level thought that earlier men were not capable of achieving. Still, the range of tool types was not great, and the overall assemblage simple and utilitarian.

There is nothing in the New World culture to correspond with the "art" of the European Upper Paleolithic, at least nothing that has been preserved, nor is there any evidence of such abstract ideological considerations as would be implied by the discovery of purposeful burials. They may have buried their dead in some fashion that militates against preservation (platform burials, for example), but whatever the case we lack evidence.

The little we know of camp sites is consistent with the requirements of nomadic hunters who must follow the game. The sites do not appear to have been occupied continuously for any long period of time, and there is no evidence of permanent structures to serve as housing. The size of the sites argues, as does other evidence, for small groups, probably no larger than thirty to fifty persons in a single band. Studies of the location of the camps seem to indicate proximity to a water source and normally to a ridge or other elevated spot overlooking a hunting area, a not unnatural pattern for hunters. The sites are generally open, and protection from the elements must have been provided by the fire that the hunters controlled and by some sort of perishable shelters that have left no clear traces. Perhaps the men wore skin clothing, a part of the Asian tradition, although there is no New World evidence for it at this point, unless one assumes that the stone scrapers found here were used, as they were in historically known cultures, for the purpose of hide preparation.

Of the less tangible aspects of their life, we know little and will probably never know much more. Religion? They leave us no carvings of spirits or offerings in graves to indicate a belief in an afterlife. We may assume, if we like, that they brought with them from Asia some aspects of belief, and many suggest that the common elements in historically known belief systems, such as shamanism or more particularly the use of drugs as an aid to contact with the supernatural, may trace back to these beginnings. These beliefs have left no recognizable clues, though they are plausible assumptions. Social organization? As we shall see in the next chapter, we can assume much on the basis of the small size of the groups as to the simplicity of the social organization required, but its exact nature is not known. In regard to later groups we have been able to infer with some confidence the nature of kinship structures on the basis of pottery distributions, but here there is nothing so usefully informative.

Politics? Mythology? Language? We are discovering much about their diet and average life span, and perhaps even one day we will develop some notions of their relations among groups (interband cooperation=politics?), but in general the leap from the technological realm, the artifacts, to the sociological and the ideological is too much for us on

An Assinboin hunter using dogs as pack animals, probably in much the same way that the earliest immigrant hunters, who lacked the horse, used them. (Edward Curtis)

the basis of such slender evidence. What they said to each other and in what language we will never know because there are no fossil phonemes, and this was a preliterate period that left no inscriptions. Their songs, their fears—all are lost, and perhaps beyond recovery.

Whoever they were, these first men, they were the conquerors of two continents of a totally new world. They endured and established a cultural tradition that goes on for thousands of years to give rise to the many lifeways that we know today as those of the American Indian. Pioneers in a strange land, they made it their own and planted the seeds of the traditions that led to the great Aztec as well as to the humble Shoshone, even though their own special adaptation of Big Game hunting was to perish at the close of the Pleistocene, swept aside (along with the big game animals on which it was founded) by the Great Death.

Some Readings

General Survey of Prehistoric Archaeology

Hole, Frank, and Robert F. Heizer: *An Introduction to Prehistoric Archaeology,* 3d ed., New York: Holt, 1973. The best introduction to the basic nature of archaeology and its methods.

General Surveys of Chichimec Archaeology

Jennings, Jesse D.: *Prehistory of North America,* 2d ed., New York: McGraw-Hill, 1974.

Willey, Gordon: *An Introduction to American Archaeology,* vol. 1, *North and Middle America,* Englewood Cliffs, N.J.: Prentice-Hall, 1966.

Early Man in the Americas

Claiborne, Robert, et al.: *The First Americans,* New York: Time-Life Books, 1973. Beautifully illustrated and readable treatment of the "early man problem." An unfortunate tendency to consistently favor the more spectacular and radical interpretations.

Jennings, Jesse D., and Edward Norbeck (eds.), *Prehistoric Man in the New World,* Chicago: University of Chicago Press, 1964. A collection containing a number of useful articles, including one pertinent to this chapter by Alex D. Krieger, "Early Man in the New World."

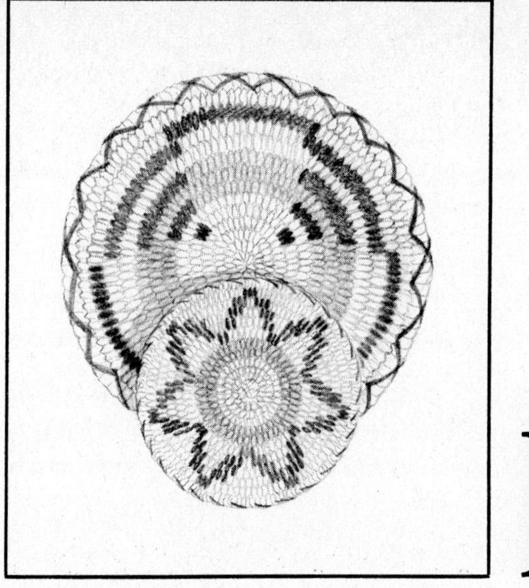

II

WORLDS TO CONQUER

Be fruitful and multiply, and replenish the earth, and subdue it.
Genesis 2:28

Great Death? We left off in the last chapter with a mention of this somewhat ominous-sounding phenomenon which requires some explaining. In this chapter we shall be generally concerned with some aspects of the development of diversity in the Indian tradition which can be closely linked to man's intimate relation with his environment. The study of such relationships is generally referred to as "ecology," and when one seeks to explain the nature of human social forms in terms of the influences and limitations of the natural environment, the perspective employed is usually labeled "ecological." Beginning with the Great Death, the period we are about to examine, essentially that labeled "Archaic" by most archaeologists, is one where these sorts of influences are most important and most visible. As the cultures become more complex, the direct influence of the environment becomes less critical, and the nature of the patterns of change is not entirely explained by environmental considerations.

The relationship between man and nature can be no more direct than that of the hunter who depends almost exclusively on the pursuit of a single species, as was apparently the case both in North America and Northern Europe in the last stages of the Pleistocene. If that species disappears, the culture based on it must disappear as well, as the hunters are forced to find new resources to sustain themselves and to develop new life-styles around new patterns. In a period from about 12,000 to 8000 B.C., this is precisely what happened when the mammoth and the giant *Bison antiquus* on which the Folsom and Clovis traditions depended became extinct.

The Great Death remains a controversial and vaguely mysterious problem in archaeology, with explanations ranging from increases in cosmic radiation to devastating plagues. What is most curious is that the pattern of extinction is largely confined to megafauna (large animals), and mostly those who browse and graze in large herds. Mammoth, bison, and the horse are the most significant, but the group would include the dire wolf and the camel, as well as the giant sloth. The conventional wisdom has long been that the close of the Pleistocene brought with it dramatic climatic changes as the ice sheets withdrew from large areas of northern America and that this directly caused the extinctions. While it is certainly true that some of the more northern areas were subject to gross fluctuations, they were by no means abrupt and did allow species to migrate gradually as conditions changed. More confusing is the fact that large areas populated by the megafauna changed only slightly and very gradually. In much of North America the change was one of increased warmth and decreased moisture, with a slow enough transition to enable most animal species to adjust themselves to the changes. Why were the megafauna affected so drastically, while others survived unscathed?

There are those today who have suggested persuasively that man was the culprit in the extinction of the mammoth and some other species at this time, as his modern descendants have been responsible for the virtual elimination of once-numerous species such as the bison and passenger pigeon. In general, predators such as wolves are beneficial in a balanced relationship with the animals they hunt, serving the ultimate interests of both species by controlling overpopulation and maintaining the fitness of the hunted species by eliminating primarily the weak and unfit. It is possible, however, that man simply became too efficient in his hunting, as witness such techniques as the "jump kill," which could be wasteful and indiscriminate. Man, radiating through the habitat of the large browsing animals at a time when they were under other pressures to adjust to climatic change—while increasing his own numbers and applying his efficient predatory techniques—may have been enough to tip the balance against the survival of these species. Man was the straw that broke the camel's, and the mammoth's, back.

Living in, Efficiently: The Archaic

Although we cannot as yet be certain that it was man who pulled the ecological rug out from under himself, there is no doubt that the megafauna disappeared and man necessarily turned to adaptation to sustain himself. As long as man could depend on a reliable supply of food, such as that represented by an ambulatory mound of calories like the mammoth, there was no need to look further. He could, and apparently did, ignore the possibilities of lesser food sources that existed all around him, an interesting illustration of the intervention of culture in the supposed "natural" relation with the environment. Nowhere on earth at any time do men exploit *all* the potentially exploitable resources of their surroundings; always, for a complex variety of cultural reasons, they make choices. A modern four-wheeler enthusiast with a busted axle and without a cooler full of salami sandwiches and beer would rapidly starve in the southwestern desert that once comfortably supported many groups of Indians. One man's desert is another man's supermarket.

For the American Indians there was a general tradition, commonly called the Archaic, which became well established by 6000 B.C., though beginning earlier and overlapping the Big Game adaptation in some areas. A problem in describing the Archaic lies in the fact that, by its very nature, it was a collection of regional traditions and did not possess the uniformity on a wide scale that was characteristic of the Big Game Hunters. The essence of the Archaic was the extensive and intensive exploration and exploitation of the resources of a particular ecozone, and as these zones varied so did the manifestations of the Archaic. It is illustrative again of the variability in the relationship between man and his environment that hunters and gatherers at this level, like those of the Big Game stage, had important aspects of their culture closely defined by the nature of their physical surroundings. Large, complex societies such as our own are little influenced in any direct way in their fundamental patterns by such physical factors. The desert city of Phoenix and the relatively frigid city of Minneapolis do not reflect nearly as much difference in the daily lives of their inhabitants as that which existed between earlier hunters and gatherers occupying equally dissimilar zones. Houses, offices, TV, food—all these are so much the same and are sufficiently free from environmental influence that a man traveling from airport to airport and chain motel to chain motel could find himself without a clue as to where he was. The man who gathered nuts and berries and hunted rabbit in the desert would likely not have found such familiarity were he to have been magically transported to a village of Northwest Coast whalers and salmon fishers. As we shall see in later chapters, the more complex the society, the less the influence of environment in any but gross ways until the limits of growth are reached.

The Archaic has been described as a process of "living in" the environment, and this has important consequences both for the nature of the Archaic and as a kind of prelude to the introduction of agriculture. "Living in" means that man had to become familiar with the nature of his surroundings, developing appropriate techniques for the use of available resources instead of relying on a single resource, as in the Big Game period. Only in a few special zones, like the Northwest Coast with its fantastically abundant and reliable salmon runs, was this a simple process. Elsewhere it required a complex and carefully timed and balanced use of a multiplicity of individually inadequate resources. Each zone or region offered different resources in varying quantity and with varying timing, so the adaptation was nowhere exactly the same. In some areas, such as the Desert Southwest, the extreme aridity and sparse resource base prevented the possibility of something other than a precarious life-style, while in the richer forests of the Northeast, the contrasting abundance allowed a comfortable adjustment that the introduction of agriculture did little more than supplement.

In describing these cultures, one anthropologist, Joseph Caldwell, contributed a very useful concept of "efficiencies," as in "forest efficiency," to describe the complex of techniques that developed in this period in each ecozone.[1] It is in reference to the balanced exploitation of these efficiencies that some of the popular notions of Indians as "natural" ecologists has some real validity, although there is nothing inherent in the Chichimec genes or psychic character to cause this "naturally." It is a cultural pattern that has existed in other parts of the world at various times and consists of a very stable and successful life-style that depends on the preservation of a careful balance between man and the world around him, with the avoidance of disrupting any part of that world. Much evidence has been accumulated to indicate that hunters and gatherers in such situations are not engaged in a desperate struggle for survival but maintain their own numbers at a level below the "carrying capacity" of their resource base. They do not multiply indiscriminately but have cultural means to stay at a level that maintains both themselves and the plants and animals upon which they depend.

The life-style of the Archaic was, indeed, so successful in propitious environments that it endured in some of the eastern forest zones well

"The Bowman," a fisherman in a rich environment. (Edward Curtis)

into historical times. To illustrate in a gradual, developmental way the essence of the Archaic at this point, we should to turn to an examination of the southwestern tradition usually known as the Desert culture. This is chosen for a number of reasons. It is the oldest of the Archaic traditions, overlapping the Big Game period at around 8000 B.C., and is probably the most well-explored because the whole southwestern area has long been the site of very active archaeological investigation. It is also uniquely documented in terms of objects that are usually perishable but which endure there because of the continuously dry desert air. This not only produces natural mummification of burials but preserves seed plants and such things as basketry and sandals of plant fibers that simply do not last in other areas. Finally, the Desert culture is among the simplest of these Archaic traditions both materially and socially, largely as we shall see because of environmental limitations, but this makes it more comprehensible as an illustration of basic aspects of the developing Indian cultures. The range of complexity is great and our illustrations focus purposely on the simplest of all as a beginning point for understanding.

The Desert Bands

In order to give a properly comprehensive picture of this level of cultural adaptation, it is necessary to combine archaeological findings with a certain amount of ethnographic analogy to flesh out the material remains. From the dry caves dating to 8000 B.C. we have found tools and food remains which are so similar to those of the historically and immediately prehistorically known cultures of this same area that we feel safe in assuming at least broad similarities between the life-styles represented. The environment confronted by later Shoshonean-speaking peoples and the techniques they employed were much the same as the ancient ones, and so we assume not a detailed identity with earlier peoples in language and belief but similar solutions to similar problems.

The generalized Desert culture is, archaeologically, defined in terms of an apparent similarity of adaptation to the conditions of aridity existing in a wide area. Within this broad zone there are many localized variations around the theme. The artifact assemblages of the Great Basin, the California coast, and southern Arizona are by no means identical, but in each area they seemingly focused on the efficient exploitation of sparse vegetation and scarce game resources. In contrast to the preceding Big Game tradition, it was a rich and inventive material culture, as new means were contrived to cope with the challenge of the harsh environment. Within the zone some areas are richer than others and offer varying resources. Some Desert peoples leave us evidence of fishhooks and decoys to show that they had contrived to exploit fish and waterfowl in the none-too-frequent lakes and rivers of this generally arid region, while others leave only evidence of plant gathering and small game hunting.

Making a Living

Although we have available to us the usual nonperishable evidence, such as stone tools, the apparent preference for many of the Desert peoples to camp in caves or use them for storage caches with pits dug for the purpose has provided us, in combination with the aridity already noted, an excellent range of normally unrecoverable organic materials preserved over thousands of years. Projectile points associated with this period are generally considerably smaller than those of the preceding Big Game era, and this might lead some to speculate that the bow and arrow were already in use—were it not for the fact that sufficient wooden pieces have been preserved to show us that these things were actually used as dart points in combination with a clever throwing aid—the atlatl.

The atlatl is found in many parts of the world, and Australian Bushmen have used it in recent times. An atlatl is simply a short wooden shaft into which the butt of a spear or dart is fitted for throwing, which increases the force of the throw by lengthening the lever arm. Although it appears clumsy to the amateur, there is no apparent loss of accuracy, and the increase in force allows for greater distance in the cast and/or greater impact in the short throw. The points used are frequently notched or stemmed, indicating a variety of means of hafting, and they come in an assortment of shapes and sizes in contrast to the relative uniformity of the Big Game points. This same atlatl was still in use at the time of the Spanish conquest as a military weapon by the Aztec.

The variety of points is probably to be seen as additional evidence of the wide range of game taken. Archaeology and ethnography both show that the most important game animals were the antelope and the rabbit, but virtually all animals that could be hunted were taken, including a wide variety of birds, mountain sheep, fox, rats, weasel, and skunk. It is probably safe to say from evidence of historically known Shoshonean-speaking peoples that the men of the desert hunted and ate everything that moved and that smaller animals such as snakes, gophers, or insects were in combination quantitatively more important than the larger game animals.

Plant resources as well show a pattern of wide-ranging exploitation. Modern groups are known to have collected as many as a hundred different wild plants, and evidence analyzed from the dry caves indicates the use of forty to sixty varieties. Many of these plants were those with hard-shelled seeds, easy to collect, and more readily preservable and transportable than the roots and leafy vegetables which were utilized when available. In areas where they were abundant and reliable, the piñon (pine nut) and the acorn were staples. In parts of California the acorn made possible a stable, predictable subsistence for such peoples as the Pomo of the Russian River area, and in Nevada the piñon allowed many Shoshone groups to remain settled throughout the winter months, eating the nuts preserved in storage pits.

Some kinds of stone tools are indicative of this adaptation even without the evidence of the actual plant materials. Stone slabs are found on which the hard seeds were obviously ground with milling stones like the modern Mexican mano and metate. The dried corn and the wild seeds collected at this time had to be specially prepared to be easily edible, and the Desert peoples made a mush or gruel of these ground wild seeds, as Mexicans today do with corn. To facilitate the grinding, the seeds were parched or toasted using flat baskets on which the seeds and hot coals were shaken. Cooking was done by a variety of means but included stone boiling, which is a technique where the mush is heated in a basket in which hot stones have been placed. Ample evidence exists of the use of fire and of the wooden fire drills used to make the fires. These techniques for processing wild plants were, as suggested, adaptations that turned out to be useful when domesticated plants were introduced into the area.

Pottery, the archaeologist's delight, was the invention of a later period and, in its fragility, not useful for peoples who were very frequently on the move. Basketry, however, developed in this period and served most of the uses of pottery. Baskets of locally available, suitable fibers—yucca, willow, and the like—were first made by a twining technique and later by coiling in a wide variety of patterns. Baskets were used for cooking, carrying, storage, and even as water containers. Sandals, sometimes made of hide, were also woven of plant fibers, as were belts, aprons, and cordage for carrying and strapping. In later periods in the Southwest, and especially in what is now California, basketry was brought to artistic heights nowhere surpassed. Rabbit fur was twisted into strips and woven into a kind of cloth out of which robes for winter were made, and the evidence of bone awls and stone scrapers suggests a wide use of animal hide for a variety of purposes, supplementing the basketry.

Although this is the simplest of the Archaic cultures and, in comparison to later societies, a bare-minimum adaptation, the cultural inventory is rich in relation to the preceding period. It includes spoons, knives (wooden-hafted), crude choppers, scrapers, awls, rattles, gaming sticks, effigies, pegs, wrenches, sickles, tubular pipes, bird-bone whistles, and ornaments and articles of less certain function. We even frequently find *Olivella* shells among the ornaments of these inland sites, indicating some degree of trade and contact with the California coast. It was a simple technological tradition but a highly efficient one, and what little they had was cleverly adapted to the needs of the environment.

The technology was limited not by the lack of inventiveness of the people but by a sort of environmental/technological interrelationship. The Desert peoples were nomadic wanderers, and in the absence of draft animals such as the then-extinct horse, nomads were limited in their material possessions to what could easily be carried on their backs. Contrast if you will the things you "need" to live comfortably in your house or apartment with what you would take on a backpacking trip. Some things such as stone milling slabs can be left in a place of storage to be used if a particular campsite is to be frequently visited, but these and other substantial material goods could not then always be available. The

This Havasupai home suggests something of the simplicity of the arid-land peoples, including these dwellers in the Grand Canyon. (Edward Curtis)

phenomenon was essentially one of an inability to accumulate more property of any kind than could be carried, and this necessarily limited technology.

It is something of a chicken/egg proposition. The people are nomadic because they lack the means to sustain themselves in one location, and the nomadism contributes to their inability to develop those means. The Desert people were not, however, truly nomadic in the sense of absolutely free wandering but tended to range over a predictable and well-known, limited area, with the size of the range and density of the population per square mile varying with the food resources. In the Archaic cultures of the East, the resource base was sufficiently rich and was distributed both seasonally and spatially, which allowed more or less permanent villages.

With the Desert peoples there was no aimless wandering in the hope of finding something to eat, but instead a regular and purposeful pattern of planned foraging. Both plants and game were thin on the ground, and infrequent rainfall could make an area that was relatively productive one year unsuitable for men or their game in the next two. As part of this plan of "living in," the people moved frequently, but in such a way that they timed their travels to be in the best area for hunting and collecting as the seasons changed and in accordance with their experience as to which places had had rain or had not been hunted over too recently. An antelope drive or rabbit hunt in a particular valley meant that it would be a matter of years before that place would likely be worth hunting again. The piñon nuts could only be profitably harvested at the beginning of winter, and not necessarily in the same place each year. Some zones were richer than others, and so the distance wandered or the amount of time spent at any particular spot varied. The acorn-collecting groups of California were able to maintain a sedentary existence much like that of the eastern Archaic culture.

One of the adaptations of the hunting and gathering life-style, and a consequence of the sparseness of the resource base, was the small size of the typical Desert band. Just as the groups could not remain permanently in one area without depleting the game, no group could be too large without increasing the difficulties of food getting. In most of the areas group size was forty or fifty, with an outside limit of approximately a hundred persons—the largest population that could conveniently forage together without straining the resource base and jeopardizing the life chances of its members. These limited numbers were not maintained as the popular Malthusian concepts would indicate, with starvation, disease, warfare, and other disasters forcing an ever-expanding population back to lower levels. Disease, at least in its devastating epidemic forms, was less of a problem for widely scattered hunters than it was for the city dwellers of later eras who were susceptible to infection by their neighbors. Warfare was almost entirely absent, and intergroup violence was minimal, as was murder and other forms of intragroup violence. Infant mortality appears to have been very high, presumably due to the rigors of the constant mobility, but the compensating high birthrate usually postulated for primitive groups does not seem to have constantly driven up the numbers. Most recent investigations have begun to suggest that hunters such as these limited their own numbers through cultural means, not necessarily because of an awareness of the problems of overpopulation but for a variety of other purposes. We know that modern Shoshone practiced occasional female infanticide, for example. There are many other techniques available to reduce the birthrate, such as spacing births through prolonged nursing or establishing periods of sexual taboo after birth. Why a particular group takes such action usually will have to do with personal convenience or belief, but the groups that act will have increased the efficiency of their adaptation and will be more likely, in an evolutionary sense, to perpetuate their customs. Whatever the details, it appears that such a stability was maintained and, contrary to popular thought, the life of these peoples, hard though it was, was not a matter of desperation, with people scrabbling at the edge of starvation. The balance was delicate and perhaps occasionally disastrous for a particular group, but the life-style endured virtually unchanged for 10,000 years—scarcely possible under conditions of misery unless we assume a masochistic people.

The Boys in the Band

With such small groups it is obvious that we would expect the web of human relationships to be as simple as the material aspects of the culture. Twenty-five people do not require elaborate structures to govern their dealings with each other, and if their relations with other groups are infrequent and constantly shifting, then external affairs, too, will not need to be highly structured. Members of a hierarchical and highly diverse society such as ours placed in a small-group situation tend to immediately elect a president or otherwise replicate the structures of the larger society. Aboriginal desert groups had no such models to replicate and no need to develop such structures. It is only in our society that we have developed the saying "Too many chiefs and not enough Indians"; the fact is these early peoples had no chiefs at all.

Julian Steward, in describing the social organization of the historical Shoshone, refers to it as essentially "familistic," and we presume the same model appropriate for the early peoples.[2] The functional group in which most of the essential activities of daily life took place for most of the year was composed of an "extended" family, which was basically a collection of related nuclear families. The nuclear family was simply a man and a woman and their unmarried offspring. It became extended "vertically" if the sons married and remained, along with their children, with the sons' parents. It became extended "horizontally" if a group of brothers remained together along with their own offspring. I say "sons" because at this level the general pattern of postmarital residence seems clearly to have been patrilocal, the men remaining and the women marrying out. Exogamy, the insistence that you may not marry within your own band, inevitably raises the issue of postmarital residence, and hunting bands worldwide seem to tend to patrilocality. We presume that this indicates the importance of male cooperation and familiarity with territory as aspects of the hunt. Matrilocality, not impossible at this level, only becomes the preferred pattern at a later stage and apparently is associated with the development of simple garden-plot agriculture where the use and ownership of land by women is critical.

Within the band the relationships between persons were structured in terms of kinship and little else. The horse nomads of the Plains, who will be discussed later, also lived in small, wandering groups, but they were participants in more elaborate structures of clans and voluntary associations such as warrior societies that did not exist here. The only significant personal distinctions that existed formally were those of age and sex. All the men had much the same role to play, but there was a difference between adult and child and between elder and younger man. Women gathered while men hunted, and there were other obviously biologically based differences between the social identity of the sexes, centered on child bearing and rearing. Conspicuously absent, from a modern Anglo point of view, were distinctions of rank and privilege based on wealth or position. These were equalitarian societies, where no man had more than any other in material goods or in social privilege, and represent the sort of thing the Marxists have in mind when they speak of "primitive communism."

Every man made his own tools and hunted his own game and established his own relationship with the supernatural, learning these things from his father and transmitting them to his son. Everyone was directly involved in wrenching a living from the environment, and no man—priest or chief or skilled craftsman—was supported by the productivity of another. Some men were obviously better at some things than others, and a man could become a shaman because everyone recognized that he was especially efficient at dealing with the supernatural realm. He was, however, primarily a hunter and not a full-time practitioner of his specialty, because the delicacy of the economic balance did not allow such an adjustment, and social mechanisms did not exist to support it.

Leadership existed but only in terms of ephemeral evaluation of personal qualities. A man recognized as a skilled hunter would have been listened to more seriously than others when hunting decisions were to be made, but no one need follow his directions as if he were a chief who commanded. What was lacking here in our terms was the concept of "office"—we give obedience to an individual because of position, the office, and not because of the individual's personal characteristics. At the band level there was no "office," hereditary or elected, such as chief or priest, but only a very personal appraisal of individual capabilities subject to constant reappraisal. For a more detailed discussion on this topic, see Chapter 6.

Obviously this sort of loose structure could only function in such a small group where all the members were in constant face-to-face interaction. They had all grown up together and, like the members of a family, had long since developed a pattern of predictable behaviors that needed no more formalization than the interaction that exists in a contemporary family. Deviance, failure to play by the rules of the group, was not controlled by laws and courts but by more subtle "familistic" means. In some sense the solidarity of the group was the solidarity of "identity," since in the absence of a maze of different social roles, all persons were in agreement because they were the same persons socially.

In such small groups techniques such as gossip and ridicule served sufficiently to warn of and control deviant behavior, and at the ultimate extreme a member could be ostracized. Withdrawal of group support was tantamount to a death sentence, since no man could survive on his own, and all were aware of this. Such confrontations that would lead to ostracization were carefully avoided by a procedure that even more sophisticated levels of Indian society utilize in present-day reservation societies. It resembled what Lyndon Johnson referred to as "consensus politics": Decisions are endlessly discussed until everyone gradually comes to a unanimous understanding of what all will accept, and no "majority" view will be enforced against the will of a minority. As we shall see, such procedures at the "political" level are cumbersome and have caused the Indians much trouble in their dealings with the more rapidly decisive white society.

The exchange of goods between persons—an act that we naturally group under general economic considerations such as those discussed in the section on "making a living"—was characteristically thought of by these peoples in terms of social relations rather than economic relations. Karl Polanyi, an economist who considered, as economists rarely do, the nature of "primitive" economics, coined the word "reciprocity" to describe an exchange system that is literally describable as "gift exchange."[3] Americans are market-oriented people, and in all our transactions we seek to maximize our gain, even in our gift exchange. The college student who sends home a twenty-five-cent Christmas card may not be acting from unadulterated generosity, but hopes by this display of filial devotion to remind his father of his obligation to provide a ten-speed bicycle. The system of generalized reciprocity of the band is of a different order.

"Bread cast upon the waters" best describes generalized reciprocity, because the giver does not in fact know precisely where the return of the gift will come from nor in what quantity. In a hunting society, particularly one like the Desert peoples who lived in an environment of scarcity, an individual hunter could not reliably count on getting sufficient game every day that it was needed. When he did not, however, it was likely that some member of his band had and that that member would share with him. In our own society we would, of course, expect the only man who has killed an antelope to immediately raise the price of antelope and make a big profit, but this is not the shrewd approach in an economy of scarcity that it is in one of abundance. The hunter who fails to share with his kinsmen will himself not receive when the others have killed, and such a total failure of group obligation would withdraw all forms of cooperation necessary to survive. The sharing through distribution of gifts evens out the life chances of all members of the group and can be thought of as a form of social insurance. As Pogo and Albert stated in the comic strip in reference to the Soviet Union, "All is equal! . . . All is starvin! . . . Yes, but all is *equal* starvin!"[4]

Rabbits and Foreign Affairs

For most of the year each individual band of the Desert peoples existed as an autonomous society performing within its own familistic structure all of the functions that a society needs to maintain itself, but there were regular and necessary relationships with other similar groups. MacNeish, in his archaeological investigations in the Tehuacan Valley of Mexico, discovered evidence to support the notion that the earliest Desert peoples behaved as modern ones did in terms of shifting micro- and macro-bands.[5] His digging showed small campsites, briefly occupied, coexisting with large camps occupied for longer periods of time, which reflected variable patterns of group affiliation, probably largely seasonal in their occurrence.

In the American Southwest and Great Basin there is ample evidence to suggest a similar pattern, presumably extending far back in time to the beginnings of the Desert tradition. The Great Basin Shoshone wandered through their foraging rounds as single bands, but during the winter, when the piñon groves were fruitful, several such bands would come together and settle down to harvest the nuts. This was not a cooperative activity but one in which each group, in spite of acting independently, respected the right of the others to whatever segment of the harvest they could gather. In different areas there would be occasions when the bounty would be great enough to support several groups, at least for a time, and then there would be a mingling involving visiting, exchange of information and gossip, and simple social activities such as dancing and singing. As in the Tehuacan Valley, these occasions must largely have been determined by the seasons; good rains might produce so rich a hunting and gathering opportunity that several bands would gather to exploit in a valley where only one would normally forage.

The Great Basin Shoshone engaged in a kind of periodic pattern of group cooperative hunt that illustrates something of the kind of intergroup relations we are postulating for the whole sequence. The game characteristically available was small enough and widely scattered enough to make the normal pattern of individual and small group hunting an efficacious procedure. Bands, however, encountering other familiar groups and exchanging information with them, would gradually become aware that some particular spot was bountifully supplied with rabbit or antelope, and several groups would move by common and informal agreement to take advantage of the situation. The nature of a hunt of this kind illustrates a number of important aspects of band society, but before considering its significance, let us consider the scenario of such a hunt.

Jackrabbit populations apparently are given to unpredictable fluctuations, so that periodically a specific area will be overrun with the beasts. Several groups whose regular wanderings tended to overlap would come together at one such place for a rabbit drive under the leadership of one or more "rabbit bosses," the closest thing to formal offices that these peoples possessed. The rabbit boss was most frequently the man who owned the net necessary for the drive, but also an older man whose skill and wisdom in such matters were usually recognized. The net or nets were something like tennis nets, one or two feet high and as long as possible. The nets would be strung across a valley under the supervision of the boss, and some of the cooperating band members would station themselves in concealment around the net. The rest of the group would go far up the valley and, whooping and hollering, beat down the valley, terrorizing the rabbits and driving them toward the nets. At the nets the rabbits would turn back or become entangled (with a great many obviously escaping), and the beaters and those lying in wait would kill them with clubs. The meat could not be preserved for long, so there was a feasting on rabbit shared equally among the cooperative groups, and, perhaps more important, the hide with fur was twisted into strips for making the fur cloth for winter robes.

Similar cooperation occurred in periodic antelope hunts. Here, however, there is strong historical documentation of a technique of "charming" the antelope into enclosures or into proximity to concealed hunters by an antelope shaman. The shaman drew the antelope into this trap supposedly through the power of his songs and ceremonial understandings. There are presumably many possible naturalistic explanations of this, the most likely being that the antelope is a fatally curious animal.

In the roles of the antelope shaman and the rabbit boss there were obviously the seeds of more formal organizations, but for the Shoshone the role of leader was activated only very rarely and not always in relation to the same groups. These occasional macro-bands formed for the hunt or at the piñon gathering—groups did not form the basis for some more permanent, larger grouping because the same bands did not necessarily gather on each occasion. The only formal connection between the groups was a system of regular exchange of women, forming a network of marriage alliance. Since they were exogamous, the periodic gatherings and encounters provided the opportunity for marriages to be arranged between the bands; and the more regular such exchange—we marry your women and you marry ours—the greater the basis for cooperation between two groups. Eventually, as we shall see in the consideration of tribes, the web of kinship implicit in this became more formally recognized, but at this familistic level of things it was very informal, and people saw themselves as related to other bands only very loosely.

Territoriality, a thing many people have been brought to believe is some sort of innate characteristic of humankind, is highly variable in the Desert tradition and reflects the precariousness of the environment. Any group committing itself to a particular piece of territory and ferociously defending it against outsiders condemns others to starvation if that spot is the only productive one—and condemns themselves to starvation if it should fail. A rich resource base such as the Washo concentration around Lake Tahoe in Nevada may have reflected such a pattern, as might have the sedentary acorn cultures of California, but for most of the Desert region the resource base was too unpredictable, and groups maintained peaceful, equal access to the shifting productive zones as in the piñon harvests. There was a kind of recognition of property rights conferred by use. Whoever harvested a particular grove had the right to do so, but the next year some other band could arrive first and claim that area. As we shall see, it was only with the rise of agriculture that careful sorting out of actual ownership of the land became an important feature of Indian societies, and that led to forms of social bookkeeping that ensured orderly inheritance of such "property."

Even to the extent that rights to a particular area did exist, they were not personal, individual property rights. The use of the land was an attribute of the group and not of the individual. That pattern, which persisted to higher levels, will be examined later as a profound difficulty in the "treaty" period when nonexistent Indian chiefs signed away nonexistent rights to very real land. An individual "owned" only those things intimately associated with his person, the sorts of items that might be buried with him, or the sorts of things that our law would not strip from a man in a bankruptcy proceeding—watch, loincloth, and so on. From the Marxist point of view this becomes "communism" because there is no private ownership of the "means of production" or, in Morton Fried's definition of the stratified society, "the basic resources that sustain life."[6]

At the considerable risk of making the life of the Desert bands sound too idyllic and too much like Rousseau's "noble savage," it should be pointed out that the evidence—historical and archaeological—seems to indicate an absence of anything we would recognize as war. The reasons for this are not nobility of spirit but a lack of ability and motivation. A delicately balanced small group cannot sustain prolonged concentration on war and, equally, cannot bear losses of material and personnel that would be associated with it. Besides, what's the point? In the absence of territoriality, and with apparently stable populations in sparse surroundings, "conquering" anything is senseless. Bringing other peoples under one's rule is equally pointless for an undifferentiated hunting society which has nothing in particular it would like the captives to do. Violence surely existed, since a carnivorous primate like man seems to have to have some outlet for his aggressiveness. The level of violence was, however, that of feud focused on an attempt to maintain, in this as in all else, a balance between the groups. One didn't seek to wipe out the offending group but only to redress the wrong done by means of an equivalent vengeance. This will be discussed further, as it has signifi-

"The Burden Bearer," a Pima woman in the rugged environment of the Southwest, which in spite of its harshness gave rise to complex and sophisticated traditions—Hohokam, Mogollon, and Anazazi. (Edward Curtis)

cance in the conflict with the Anglo conceptions of the supremacy of law over personal vengeance.

It Works!

The culture of the Desert peoples, modern and ancient, suggested here was remarkably simple in both material and social terms, but each band had the capability of performing within its simple structures all of the necessary functions for the maintenance of a society so long as it maintained minimal stable relations with other similar groups. In this familistic context, goods necessary for life, from food to sandals, were reliably produced and distributed to those who required them. New members were reproduced and instructed in the knowledge and behaviors essential to make them fully functioning members of the group and placed in relationship to others so that the pattern of activity and transmission smoothly proceeded. All members of the group were motivated to reliably carry out all necessary activities in cooperation with other members so as to maintain the total system. So long as the numbers of the group were held below the carrying capacity of the environment and all neighboring groups maintained a similar balance, a perfectly satisfactory life resulted, albeit one that involved hard work and perhaps only a minimum of what we would regard as comforts and pleasures.

A problem that shall be pursued throughout this book is why, when all that is "necessary" has been achieved, do human societies go on to pursue levels of what seems "unnecessary." The reason for increasingly complex cultural patterns does not appear to lie in an adaptation to a relatively unchanging environment but in a sort of feedback phenomenon involving the interaction of one group with others. The Desert peoples in modern historical times encountered pressures from other societies more complex and in some sense more efficient than themselves. When the horse was introduced into the area, many of the former Desert groups adopted it and, with it, many of the culture traits of the buffalo-hunting complex of the Great Plains. In the Southwest the Desert culture gave way much earlier to an agricultural tradition that culminated in the modern Pueblo peoples. Only in the most marginal zones in the most desolate areas, seemingly not usable by more complex peoples, did the old tradition survive into the recent past to be finally swept away by the conditions of the reservation system.

From Sea to Shining Sea

During the Big Game period the Indian established his presence in the New World and trickled out over all of its surface. During the Archaic this human stream soaked into virtually every nook and cranny that would support human life. We do not know what the population of the Chichimec area might have been at this point, although that is one of the issues that is currently being addressed, but we are certain that it was far larger than that of the preceding period. We have described briefly the peoples of the Desert zone, but during this same period cultural traditions were established on the East and West Coasts, on the plains and inland plateaus, in the high mountains and along the great rivers, in the forests and even in the frozen Arctic. It is inappropriate in this general introduction to attempt to provide details of description, but a few words to indicate the range would be useful to avoid the impression that the Desert peoples are some sort of archetype.

In almost every other part of the continent, the resources are richer and more varied than they are in the Desert zone, and the Archaic populations consequently larger. In much of the East there are archaeological sites that seem to indicate relatively permanent settlements, usually associated with a great many traces of temporary campsites, reinforcing the impression of a shifting seasonal exploitation, but one that ranged from a fixed point. There seem to have been two distinct focuses of general adaptation. There was a coastal version with an emphasis on fishing and shellfish-collecting, as evidenced by the remains of a wide range of tools including fish weirs and traps and shell middens. The interior or forest adaptation had a greater emphasis on plant-collecting and hunting technology. Ground stone rather than chipped stone was abundantly used, including implements with an obvious forest focus—axes, adzes, and the like.

Everywhere the inventory is variable in accord with our conception of specialized adaptive efficiencies. In the region of the Great Lakes we find a remarkably early tradition called the Old Copper culture which made use of raw natural copper for a wide range of implements. Metallurgy never developed to levels equivalent to those found in the Old World, and the tools found here were simply hammered from native copper and not smelted or cast. There are in many places examples of fine and elaborate stone working including peculiar objects which have long been in pot-hunters' collections as "bird stones" and "banner stones." These were in all likelihood simply stone weights to be fixed on the atlatl to improve its throwing characteristics. Organic preservation is not everywhere comparable with that of the desert area, but we find burnt and carbonized remains of an incredible profusion of plant and animal material to indicate a complex pattern of exploitation and a wide range of tool materials other than stone—bone, antler, shell, horn, wood—which were all widely used.

We know very little of the less tangible aspects of the cultures represented in the Archaic, although it is possible to do as we have done with the Desert and project into this prehistoric past our understandings of what these people had become by historical times. Burials with grave goods and curious nonutilitarian objects give some evidence of ideological complexity that comes to be clearly evident in the complexes of burial mounds of later derivative cultures such as Adena and Hopewell. These will be examined later, but the social and religious elaborateness that these represent must have had their origins in this early period. If the groups were larger and more densely packed than in the Desert, there were presumably earlier manifestations of more complex social mechanisms and the development of societies more nearly like those described later as tribes and chiefdoms. We are certain these things must have had

A Hupa fish weir indicates (although this photograph is actually historically late) the theme of special technological adaptations to special environments during the Archaic period. (Edward Curtis)

origins in this period, but evidential demonstration is still in the stage of speculation.

Traditions and the "Chichimecness" of the Chichimeca

Much that we characteristically think of as "Indian" in a material and technological sense became well established in the Archaic. Cradleboards, pipes, baskets, beads of stone and shell, and rattles and effigies of animals are all things that we think of as "Indian," although individually many occur elsewhere in the world. An issue should be raised here, not in terms of such simplistic material traits, but focused on the overall characteristics of a tradition which make it distinctive. Edward H. Spicer has spoken of the "Yaquiness of the Yaqui," a northwestern Mexican group whose name is widely familiar in the image of Carlos Castaneda's Don Juan.[7] Spicer was talking of what is left after filtering out all the aspects of a culture which have some universally describable quality. A people practice agriculture and they use a digging stick as their principal implement. They practice polygyny and reckon kinship matrilineally. They wear sandals instead of shoes or moccasins. All well and good, and many other peoples do the same, but why does this particular group do it in just that particular combination, and in just that particular way? What is so "Yaqui" about the Yaqui, or in the present instance, what is so "Chichimec" about the Chichimeca? The social sciences have not gone far enough toward isolating the general causality that governs cultural things, but in our rush to fill that gap there remains a need to consider questions about what appears to be uniqueness, as a kind of causal issue in itself and one that is not easily explained by reference to environments and technologies.

If you examine any of the general treatments of North American archaeology that have been cited, you will see that all make use of some version of "cultural areas" as an organizing principle. In each area, out of the generalized early traditions, which seem everywhere much alike, there begins to appear, from the Archaic on, regional "traditions" which are clearly distinguishable. In what is now the southwestern United States we find developing out of a generalized Desert level three separate and archaeologically definable traditions: Mogollon, Anazazi, and Hohokam. Separate as they were, they were more alike than were those of another regional sequence, such as the Upper Mississippi culture, where the Archaic Old Copper tradition yielded to effigy/burial mound traditions like the Hopewell. Both of these in their later phases were sedentary agricultural traditions; was it only the variation in the natural surroundings of the Southwest and the Upper Mississippi that produced the differences?

Complicating the issue, one of the Southwestern traditions, the Hohokam, showed remarkable affinities to the Mesoamerican model, including as did the later Mississippian cultures, the use of large earthen temple mounds. Even at this level of things, although both presumably the result of some degree of contact and diffusion with the Mesoamerican heartland, the Hohokam and Mississippian versions were not the same. Are we forced at this point of developing regional diversity to abandon the idea of the whole Chichimec zone as a common tradition until the intrusion of Anglo society and the reservation systems begin again to create commonality of experience for all Indians?

Yes and no. We will in general be content with a sort of ecological perspective which suggests that different areas require different adaptive strategies and that through diffusion those living in proximity to each other will develop similar solutions to similar problems. A set of ideas is more readily acceptable if the peoples concerned are confronted with the same situation to which it can be applied. A gradual accretion of these solutions constitutes an area co-tradition which can be distinguished from others, and we can step up from there in terms of broader and broader zones to distinguish Mississippian from Hohokam and both from central Mesoamerican. The separate Indian regional traditions are not alike, but they are more alike than Indian and Asian or Indian and European. Everywhere in the world certain cultural developments promote similarities—as with the technical requirements of agriculture or its promotion through irrigation. In the evolutionary long run such similarities may be more significant than the differences, but a Chinese social system of water control is not the same as a Pueblo system, and that remains significant if blocks of time less than thousands of years are considered.

Less ecologically, however, we are also concerned with a question of persistent cultural systems, the basic core of which seems in some way to survive a great deal of technological and even environmental change. The Navaho are a relatively recent case in point whose pattern of "incorporative" change will be examined in some detail later. For the moment let us simply point out that the Navaho are only slightly earlier arrivals in the Southwest than the Anglos; starting as foot nomadic hunters and gatherers they have, through contact with Pueblo, Mexican, and American societies, become horse nomads, farmers, pastoralists, and finally wage workers. They have incorporated weaving from the Pueblos, silversmithing from the Mexicans, and pickup trucks from the Anglos, but they remain Navaho. They have altered everything in this torrent of change and have made it their own and have done so without any apparent sense of having ceased to be Navaho.

In their latest theoretical efforts, archaeologists have endorsed a view of cultural things which serves to some extent to illuminate this cultural persistence or identity persistence. The suggestion is that all aspects of a society are a reflection of a cultural "code" which exists in the minds of the members of the society. In this view human cultural behavior is to be considered as language in the sense that the behaviors are a response to a set of instructions contained in cultural rules which the members have incorporated. Linguistically the difference between a rat and a cat is in the difference between the sounds represented by *r* and *c*. The difference between a mother and father terminologically is sex, and one behaves differently toward them on the basis of this distinction. A complex of such instructions is what culture *is* according to this view. Archaeologists are, of course, suspiciously fond of this view to which many objections can be made, because it allows them to relate the material to the nonmaterial.

Claude Levi-Strauss, the French anthropologist and humanist, is the principal proponent of an idea derived from these linguistic analogies that suggests that all human behavior in a group is governed by some single set of rules in the same way that languages are generative in their grammars. The way that people organize their kinship and marriage behavior is in terms of particular codes or rules which reflect a certain basic way of looking at things and organizing them that is reflected in all aspects of a society. This is beguiling to archaeologists, for it suggests that if they discover principles of organization in pottery they will also have discovered some principle that can be applied throughout the society, and to those ephemeral areas that can never be recovered archaeologically.

I raise this perhaps alarming example of the metaphysical wrangles of anthropological theory only to point out that it is in some such model that there is a hope of explaining the cultural persistence mentioned. The Navaho remain the Navaho because the basic organizing principle, the code of "Navahoness," remains the same regardless of the particular material it has to work with—in the same way that the rules of grammatical expression remain the same regardless of what is being talked about. If it were possible to discover some universal codes or rules in the overall Chichimec experience, we might be able to more realistically address the issue of the "Chichimecness" of the Chichimeca. This issue of the "Indianness" of Indians will recur in later chapters in regard to problems of the modern reservation. It is mentioned here simply as an area of inquiry that may one day be of use in filling in the limitations of the evolutionary approach of explaining the unique.

For all practical purposes, after the Archaic there was no single culture but a myriad of (admittedly related) local variations. The unity which exists in the following chapters and permits generalization is an adaptive evolutionary unity focused on the notion of "levels" already enunciated. A tribe, wherever it may be, is demonstrably another sort of beast than a band or state, and groups of horse nomads have by the nature of their adaptation certain things in common not to be found among horticulturists or foot nomads. It is around this developmental unity that the first part of this book is organized, while it is around the commonality of coping with Anglo society that the second part is organized.

Some Readings

For this and the chapters throughout the first half of the book, the appropriate sections in the general surveys of Chichimec archaeology cited in Chapter 1 will be useful.

Caldwell, Joseph R.: "The New Archaeology," *Science*, **129**:303–307, 1959. The concept of "efficiencies" discussed in the context of the Archaic.

Haynes, C. Vance: "Elephant-Hunting in North America," *Scientific American*, **214**:104–12, 1966.

Martin, Paul S.: "The Discovery of America," *Science*, **179**:969–74, 1973. An excellent brief discussion of the peopling of the new world.

Mason, Ronald J.: "The Paleo-Indian Tradition in Eastern North America," *Current Anthropology*, **3**:227–278, 1962.

Steward, Julian H.: *Theory of Culture Change*, Urbana, Ill.: University of Illinois Press, 1955. A short description of Desert Basin bands and a landmark treatment of cultural ecology.

III CORN MOTHER

Now it is planned, in the East is the Corn.
Now it is planned, in the South is the Bean.
Now it is planned, in the West is the Pumpkin.
Now it is planned, in the North is the Tobacco.
Navaho Mountain Chant[1]

A popular vision exists, for those with some limited historical knowledge, of the difficulties in persuading the Indians to settle down to farming during the reservation period. There is a very popular quotation from Smohalla, the prophet of the Dreamer religion during the time of the Nez Percé wars: "You ask me to plough the ground. Shall I take a knife and tear my mother's bosom? You ask me to dig for stone. Shall I dig under her skin for her bones? You ask me to cut the grass and make hay and sell it and be rich like white men. But dare I cut off my mother's hair?"[2] There is no doubt of the sincerity of these sentiments, but it must be recalled that they are the sentiments of the horse nomads of the Plains who form much of the stereotype of the Indian people. In this as in much else they are anomalous, for agriculture was the backbone of the majority of Indian cultures and, far from a desecration, the growing of crops was regarded as a sacred and holy activity surrounded with elaborate ceremony, as in the Navaho chant quoted above. It is in a consideration of the cultivation of corn that we make the transition from the hunters of the Archaic to the more complex Indian cultures.

As wheat is the "staff of life" in the biblical tradition and in Europe, corn is the fundamental food plant of all America. It is in many traditions a miraculous gift from the gods, associated with Our Mother Corn or some other female bringer-of-life, like the Navaho White Bead Woman. It required ritual to ensure the harvest, bring the rain that must fall when needed, and thank the gods whose gift it was. Farming may have been distasteful to the nomads, but it was vital to many others. The nomads, too, depended on it, obtaining corn by raiding or trading with the settled farmers with whom they maintained a symbiotic relationship.

Corn—maize as it was known to the Mexicans who first domesticated it and scientifically called *Zea mays*—is entirely a New World plant. Some confusion may exist in the mind of the reader who has seen references in histories to Roman concern for the control of African corn or mention in English translations of the Bible of the existence of corn. Used in this sense, "corn" is a general term for grain. Maize was first called "Indian corn," and it has only recently preempted the term "corn" exclusively for itself. There was no corn in the Old World before Columbus.

High and Dry

Corn is the most important of the New World domesticates, and its history is the most thoroughly investigated, so an examination of its beginnings will illuminate the problems associated with the rise of domestication and its implications. Curiously, in both the Old World and the New World, the major domesticates are plants whose wild habitats are relatively arid highland zones. As wild grasses wheat and barley are known to have originated in the "hilly flanks" of Iraqui-Kudistan rather than in the fertile valleys of the Tigris and Euphrates Rivers, where they later become the source of the first civilizations. Similarly, in the New World corn seems to have been a native of the high and arid mountainous plateaus of central Mesoamerica rather than of the rainy gulf coast where the first high civilizations based on its cultivation appear.

There is a certain logic in this since the high zones in question are marginal for effective hunting and gathering, and the cultures existing there were of the Desert tradition type examined above. The suggestion has been made that the precariousness of the life of the food gatherers gave motivation to the encouragement of plant growth through some form of cultivation that was not as likely to occur in a richer zone where wild plants and animals produced a sufficiency without human aid. Whether or not this was the critical factor, it is certainly true that the domesticates first appeared in such zones and not in the richer areas.

No wild corn exists today. It is everywhere a true domesticate in that it is incapable of self-propagation, or even of surviving without human aid. Some suspect it might have originated elsewhere than in the New World, but the presence of distinctive pollen in drilling cores from the Valley of Mexico indicates the existence of wild corn 80,000 years ago. Two plants which do occur without cultivation, *Tripsacum* and teosinte, are relatives of corn; but botanists have concluded that they are not its direct ancestor and that modern corn is the product of repeated hybridization with these plants and its putative original form.

Tacos to Go

The earliest evidence of domestication in the Chichimec area lies in what is now southwestern United States, at Bat Cave in New Mexico. Here, in a dry cave representative of the Desert culture, are found the remains of primitive corn virtually undeveloped from a wild form and similar to the earliest types found in Mexico. This is a high, arid area similar to those in Mexico that grew corn, and the suggestion is currently made that corn, not yet having adapted to alternative climates, diffused northward along the mountain chains that provided a suitable environment. The Mogollon Mountains of New Mexico were the seat of the earliest of the settled agricultural village traditions, developed around 100 B.C. to A.D. 400, and it seems clear that the diffusion of agriculture lay along the lines of these arid highlands at these early dates. Although Bat Cave shows some indication of plant domestication at 2000 B.C., similarly primitive traces existed in Mexico around 5000 B.C., and settled villages based on agriculture were flourishing there by 2000 B.C., making inescapable the primacy of Mexico in the development of domestication.

Domestication probably developed in a number of places more or less simultaneously once the basic idea had occurred, since there is considerable evidence of rapid hybridization in the earliest sites. In the Mexican state of Puebla is the high valley of Tehuacan, and it is there that we have a sequence of evidence for an early transition from hunting

Women of Hopi pueblo grinding corn (maize), the New World staff of life. (Edward Curtis)

and gathering to settled village agriculture that is unique in the world. No one will ever be able to say exactly where or when the first American Indian said to himself "Aha!" and began to understand that plants could be helped along. The seasonal cycle of plant growth would have been long since known to a foraging people, as would have the conditions under which plants grew most abundantly; so the "invention" of agriculture required only the decision to take a hand in this well-known process. It might have occurred first at Tehuacan, but the only thing we know for certain is that the effects were felt there earlier than anywhere else we have excavated.

Mesoamerica is only our concern to the extent that developments there were important to the Chichimeca, but Tehaucan is worth describing in that context. The earliest material of interest in this valley dates from 7000 to 5000 B.C., a period called "El Riego" by Tehaucan's excavator, R. S. MacNeish.[3] At this point we find the remains of a typical Desert adaptation with abundant evidence of a wide variety of gathered wild plants and animals associated with scattered, small, temporary campsites. In the "Abejas" phase, dating from 3400 to 2300 B.C., there were permanent pit-house villages; and while gathering still supplied important amounts of subsistence, there was a reliance on domestication, as evidenced by the presence of hybridized maize, beans, squash, and even cotton. The material in the valley shows a shift from plant collecting at 5000 B.C., when primitive and possibly domesticated maize first appeared, to fully settled village agriculture at 2000 B.C. This is reflected clearly in the ever increasing proportion of cultivated plants to wild plants in the refuse deposits and in the shifting form of the plants themselves as they were altered by the process of cultivation. First seen as a wild grass no more important than others, corn became the basis of subsistence and shifted from a tiny, self-sufficient seed plant to the dependent, husk-confined ear of modern maize. Such a record in one place, and so complete as this, rarely occurs in archaeology, and nowhere do we have such clear-cut evidence in the Chichimec zone of any such transition, which reinforces our conviction of Mesoamerican origins.

Once it had begun in the heartland, the basic plant, corn, spread gradually (as eventually did a number of others), changing and adapting as it went on to become the foundation of all the more complex traditions except those of the Northwest Coast. As noted, the Mogollon tradition of New Mexico had its beginnings around 100 B.C., almost certainly through direct Mesoamerican influence. The Hohokam tradition, centered on the Gila and Salt Rivers near modern Phoenix in Arizona, appeared at approximately the same time. There is clear-cut evidence of actual Mesoamerican derivation and the Hohokam tradition may, indeed, have been the result of migration, including as it did, ceremonial ball courts and extensive irrigation works.

The wastes of Texas may have been a barrier to diffusion, and there is considerable suggestion that influences from further to the east may have arrived separately across the Gulf of Mexico or along the Gulf Coast. The Mississippian centers of the great river valley are the first ones with clear remains of corn cultivation, at around A.D. 500, and these also reflected considerable evidence of Mesoamerican influence in their arts and in the temple mound complexes characteristic of this culture. Mound builders earlier than the Mississippian are the Adena-Hopewell of the Ohio-Kentucky area, manifest from 800 B.C. to A.D. 600, but these do not appear at this time to have been demonstrably agricultural; they were apparently based in a highly efficient Archaic hunting and gathering complex. Considerable argument rages over this point, with many convinced that agriculture was necessary at this earlier date, while others would have it introduced into the East by 1000 B.C., earlier than its introduction into the Southwest.

By A.D. 1000, agriculture had spread to all the areas where it would be found at the time of Columbus. The parts of the Southeast and Northeast that were under Mississippian influence by this time had well-established maize cultivation. The river valleys of the plains—the Republican, the Missouri, and so on—seem to have been the last to adopt cultivation, with evidence to suggest a movement into this area by some peoples from the East only around A.D. 1200 to 1300. Here again there is argument, with some finding resemblances with the Southwestern traditions and postulating the source of cultivation in that direction.

Hunting and the gathering of uncultivated plants never ceased to be important, even in the most populous and sophisticated of sedentary traditions. Many areas, even though exposed to the idea of cultivation by their neighbors, never adopted it. California, which is closely connected with the Southwest, never became an agricultural center, and the peoples of the Great Basin and the Plateau areas of the Northwest also failed to make this adaptation. The prosperous fishermen of the Northwest Coast maintained one of the most elaborate life-styles of all, without ever engaging in cultivation.

Beans and 'Baccy

Though corn was the most important basic food plant, the New World was also the home of a great many other domesticated plants, some of which may have preceded corn as a cultigen. Several varieties of bean, including the lima and kidney bean, were grown almost everywhere that corn was grown, often in the same field. Squash and pumpkin were equally ubiquitous, and the combination of corn, beans, and squash has been referred to as the trinity of American agriculture—and was known as the "Three Sisters" to the Iroquois. Sunflowers were widely grown on the edges of corn fields for their seeds and may have been cultivated earlier than corn. Amaranth (pigweed) appears to have been similarly cultivated at very early times, possibly preceding the introduction of maize. Bottle gourds were grown for their value as utensils. Perhaps it is worth pointing out that many plants not particularly important in the Chichimec area proper but now vital to our modern tastes had a New World origin. These include potatoes, manioc, tomatoes, chili peppers, cacao (chocolate), henequen, sisal, peanuts, avocado, sweet potatoes, rubber, and vanilla.

Tobacco is a uniquely New World plant, but its exact origins are still obscure, though it is assumed to be a tropical plant. Tobacco appears, or at least pipes apparently for its use, earlier than clear evidence of agriculture, but in general it would appear to have spread more or less simultaneously with maize. It was used vitually everywhere including areas that had no other agriculture. Plains buffalo hunters, after abandoning agricultural enterprises, continued to grow tobacco through sacred men's societies entrusted with this holy duty. Pipes of many forms were the most common means of using tobacco, but it was also rolled into cigars, while cigarettes were made with corn husks. In most cases the smoking of tobacco had definite ceremonial aspects and supernatural associations. First brought to Europe by the Spaniards, the custom was popularized, as every schoolchild knows, by Sir Walter Raleigh, and, in view of the recent Surgeon General's warnings, seems to have constituted a long-term joke by the Indian on the European.

Though the variety of plants is as great as, if not greater than, in the Old World pattern, the Chichimeca never seem to have made any important efforts at animal domestication. The horse had become extinct, and no other suitable domesticable draft animals existed, although the llama was important in Peru. The turkey was domesticated, although in some cases for the feathers as much as for the food. The only domesticated animal most Indian peoples knew was the dog, which seems to be not only man's best friend but also his oldest. There is no certainty as to when the dog was domesticated in the New World, and there is some reason to believe that man and the dog have been partners long enough for them to have come across together from Asia in earliest times. The Aztec, like the Chinese, raised a small breed of dog specifically for food, although many Chichimec cultures tended to view the eating of dog much in the light we do. The only really important domesticate to fundamentally affect Indian life was the horse after its reintroduction by the Spaniards, but the enthusiasm of the love affair between the Plains Indians and the horse makes clear that the lack of domesticated animals was nothing more than a reflection of the lack of suitable candidates.

Fruit of the Loom

Prior to the domestication of plants, Indians wove many materials into mats, baskets, and cloth, using wild plants like reeds, yucca, and willow. Even feathers and animal fur strips were in some places woven into fabric, and beaten bark was made into cloth, as in the famous "Chilkat" blankets of the Northwest Coast. At about the time that other domesticates were being introduced, cotton was becoming important as a reliable source of fiber for weaving.

New World and Old World cotton are undeniably relatives, and which originated where is a confused and as yet unanswered question. It may be that the same plant was domesticated independently in both areas, though many tend to see the common usage as proof of transoceanic contacts and influences. It is only in the Southwest that cotton and the techniques for its use were important to the Chichimeca, although it was widely traded from there to other areas. Spindle whorls for the making of thread and the loom, both horizontal and vertical, were in use.

In the Southeast bark cloth was so finely made that it was mistaken for cotton, and in the Northwest looms and spindles were likewise highly developed for the use of wild, rather than domesticated, plant materials.

To modern Americans, the most famous weavers of all are the Navahos with their famous blankets, but the Navahos learned weaving secondhand from the Pueblos, probably as late as the Spanish period when many Pueblo peoples fled to refuge with the Navahos. The Navahos learned to weave wool from the Spaniards, often, in the earliest days, unraveling Spanish cloth for the colored thread to decorate their own less bright materials. The modern blankets are almost entirely a recent phenomenon, brought about by the encouragement of traders after 1900. The Navaho themselves have long since produced these items strictly for sale, preferring the commercial "Indian" blankets for utilitarian purposes. Though, as with much else, the techniques and even the designs are not originally Navaho, the Navaho have added elements to their weaving that makes it unique.

Lady with a Hoe

The agriculture of the Indian was not quite what we are used to thinking of as agriculture. The plow was not used anywhere in the New World, and the small scale of cultivation of garden plots with hand implements is sometimes referred to as horticulture to distinguish it from European practice. For most cultures the primary implements were the hoe and the digging stick. The sharpened stick was punched into the ground, a few seeds were dropped in, and the hoe was employed occasionally to weed. Fields were cleared with stone axe or adz, and the cuttings were burned prior to planting. The fields were planted until yields diminished to the point that another field was needed. This pattern of rotation is often called "slash and burn" and is highly productive so long as population density does not require the fields to be reused too frequently.

Only in the dry areas of the Southwest was agriculture more complex than has been described. The Pueblo peoples necessarily made use of all available water, planting in scattered plots near springs or in sites that took advantage of runoff moisture. In suitable spots they built small dams and impounded water to irrigate small terrace plots called *trincheras*. Some of the Rio Grande Pueblos and the Hohokam built actual irrigation systems of canals and dikes to utilize river water more effectively. The Hohokam built canal systems that ran for miles through the desert, more impressive than any found in the so-called Mesoamerican heartland.

Gardening is not an unnatural outgrowth of plant collecting and processing, so it should not be surprising to learn that, with the exception of the Pueblos, it was primarily the job of women to tend the fields, and as will be discussed in regard to kinship, it was through

Corn was grown in many ways and in many places, even in these near-desert conditions by the Hopi mesas. (Edward Curtis)

women that fields were inherited and regulated. Men, of course, participated in the work, particularly in the clearing of the fields. The typical Chichimec pattern was not an exclusive dedication to agriculture but a balance between cultivation and gathering and hunting. In an age before the equalizing effects of powered machinery, men were inevitably better candidates for some tasks as a result of their greater size and strength. Women were not only less suited to certain work because of their limited strength but also because of the limitations of childbearing and rearing: they could not range freely as was required in hunting. The Iroquois, who will be examined in the historical period, exemplified this sexual division of labor so strongly that has been suggested that it was a society of nomadic men and sedentary women. Because of the importance of hunting, and later of trade and warfare, agriculture remained women's work, which in view of the importance of cultivation to the economy, does much to explain the relatively high position of women in most Indian cultures.

The processing of wild plant materials produced a technology of food preparation that was most adaptable to the cultivation of corn; there was simply more reliance on a single seed plant and a consequent concentration of methods. Stone grinding slabs and hand stones became somewhat more elaborate in the form of manos and metates, but the principle was the same. In the woodland areas, wooden mortars and pestles were more often used. In general, the only difference was that the range of equipment became larger and more elaborate as consequences of sedentariness and the freedom from being confined to the tools that could be carried on the back.

The cooking process was not radically different from what had gone before for plant gatherers. The hard, flinty kernels of corn, unless eaten green, required some form of cooking. Green corn was a seasonal delicacy (as corn on the cob), but a main advantage of the plant was the fact that when dried, it could be stored for long periods, which is how it was primarily used. To eat it required that it be popped (yes, Indians were the originators of popcorn) or ground into meal. Ground corn was used as a drink mixed with water, as a gruel, and was of course made into cakes and a number of kinds of bread often resembling the tortillas of Mesoamerica. Unprepared dried corn could be, and was, eaten as a kind of iron ration, but anyone who has chipped a tooth on the remains in the bottom of the popcorn box knows the limitations of this food.

Of Pots and Pueblos

The effects and implications of the process of domestication were profound but were more visible in some areas than others. Many of the Eastern woodlands tribes had already established a settled and stable economy and simply added cultivation as one more seasonal resource. It was in the Southwest that the shift was most dramatic, moving from the simple Desert gatherers discussed above to agricultural settlements like Pueblo Bonito, a giant D-shaped tiered apartment structure of some 800 rooms. In this area, which was extremely limited in its ability to support the hunter and was also the earliest to utilize domestication, the potential of cultivation stood out clearly.

Some aspects of ethnographically known agricultural tribes will be examined shortly, but the archaeological record of Pueblo development can be used to illustrate the beginnings. The first of the cultures to shift from the Desert hunting and gathering pattern to the settled agricultural life was the Mogollon. The Hohokam, perhaps equally early, were a special case, reflecting a unique degree of Mesoamerican influence and diffusion.

Somewhere in the vicinity of the Mogollon Mountains of New Mexico, a century or more before the time of Christ, a band of Desert gatherers became interested enough in the idea of growing corn to attempt it. Mesoamericans had already reached high levels of civilization, and some of them, perhaps traders or even missionaries, had to have introduced this idea to the Mogollon and had to have provided the seed itself. Perhaps the people of the Mogollon even stole the first seeds. Such details, however romantic, are unknowable.

What we do know is that at this time the wandering gatherers began to build permanent villages. Only with agriculture does life become predictable enough for peoples in this kind of environment to settle down in one place, secure in their control of the food supply. The villages were not large, since with primitive techniques agriculture was none too productive in this area, but for the first time the Indian was in control of some part of his environment. Agriculture can be expanded by increasing the area under cultivation or by improving techniques to accommodate shifts either in the availability of other food resources or in changes in the numbers of people. Wild plants and animals may not be effectively manipulated, but once the trick of cultivation is learned it can support a thousand people where only fifty could live before—or, as in our modern situation, 200 million, with enough left over to export. Compared with gathering, farming is predictable, controllable, and easily expansible, though our image of farmers rightly acknowledges their sensitivity to weather conditions that threaten their crops.

The first steps probably involved planting of seed and then leaving it to its own devices while the band continued to wander, returning only at the time of harvest. Once confidence in this resource was established, more or less permanent settlement during the growing season occurred, until eventually villages existed year-round. The first Mogollon settlements were not impressive, consisting of only a handful of semisubterranean pit houses usually in an elevated area such as a low ridge overlooking farmland. The houses, built of timber and roofed with matting and covered with earth, were primitive enough but were far more effective as shelters than were the windbreaks and lean-tos that were generally all that nomads were probably able to erect for their short and temporary stays in one spot. The remarkable skin tents that we normally associate with Indians (tepees) were, of course, only possible for horse nomads who had the means to transport such materials through the use of draft animals. A foot nomad was not going to lug a cluster of poles and a bundle of buffalo hides on his back just to provide a more secure shelter.

Many of the early villages had larger-than-usual pit houses associated with them which may have been community buildings of some kind. For historic Pueblos we have much information about the importance of underground ceremonial chambers called *kivas,* which remained after Pueblo architecture had shifted to aboveground structures. Although unclear, it is very likely that such ceremonial chambers date to these early periods. The Mogollon never appear to have developed much more elaborately than these beginnings would indicate, and the neighboring and probably related Anasazi must be examined for evidence of further complexity.

The Anasazi (Navaho for "ancient ones") were centered around that area known as the Four Corners, the place where present-day Arizona, New Mexico, Utah, and Colorado meet. Probably having learned agriculture from the Mogollon by A.D. 700 to 900, the Anasazi, from similar simple beginnings, were originators of the true Pueblo tradition. The most obvious and spectacular feature was the shift from the simple single-unit pit house to a pattern of linked aboveground rooms. Consisting at first of only a few rooms, often with an underground ceremonial chamber, the pueblos grew larger until they were the apartment house dwellings so familiar to tourists of the Southwest. The construction techniques were not particularly sophisticated. They were made essentially of rough stone loosely mortared with adobe and did not use arches or other complex techniques. Each room appears to have been the dwelling of a single family with some other rooms set aside for storage and other common purposes. The rooms, roofed with wooden beams and often entered from the roof by ladders, were sometimes windowless and probably used for sleeping and storage, with most work done on the roofs or in the courtyards.

The period from A.D. 1000 to about 1400 was when the largest and most impressive pueblos were constructed; there was a general abandonment of many of them at the end of this period. These "great pueblos" were usually located in a highly defensible spot, "cliff palaces" and the like, hard to reach except by ladders or steps cut in the stone. This must have been so inconvenient for daily life that it would have had to come about for good reason, and the logical assumption is some threatening enemy. There is considerable speculation about the "Great Pueblo fall," and it has been traditional to attribute it to the Athabascans (Navaho and Apache), who moved into the area at about this time. Sober reflection, however, makes it seem unlikely that a handful of foot nomads could be a serious threat to so numerous and well-organized a group as the Pueblos. The historical Pueblos were not the entirely peaceful people that some early writers have described them as being, and their participation in battles against the horse warriors in cooperation with the Spanish does much to invalidate the notion of their being helpless farmers. The period in question seems to have been one of general drought. It may well be that as the land became less able to support them, it was the Pueblos who threatened each other. Internecine warfare and dwindling crops forced the defensive architecture, then a retreat to richer farming country around the Rio Grande, where the majority of Pueblos are found today.

The Pueblo archaeological record indicates many things of importance to the understanding of agriculture. The size of human groups that the unchanged environment could support is seen dramatically in the shift from camps to castles. With groups that were so much larger, changes must necessarily have occurred in social complexity in order to cope with the larger number of persons in constant interaction. The Pueblos in general seem to have developed at an early date an elaboration of kinship into units called clans. The nature of these will be described in the next chapter, which deals with the Mandan and others who, like some Pueblos, had the matrilineal form of clan so common in the Chichimeca. In their later days, the Pueblos showed signs of still more complex structures of a political order, but that will be discussed in the chapter on chiefdoms and states in other better-known areas.

People in Grass Houses

There are two consequences of cultivation from which most of its impact follows—sedentism and surplus. Sedentism can be achieved in other ways, but in the long run agriculture is the only way to maintain permanent populations without shifting in response to environmental fluctuations. That stability is itself the result of surplus. As a contributor to sedentism, surplus simply means that farmers can grow and store more than they immediately need to consume and so provide themselves with a cushion against environmental vagaries. Sedentism and surplus go hand in hand in opening the door to cultural complexity.

Surplus, the production of more than is immediately needed to be consumed, becomes particularly significant when it is reinvested rather than simply used to provide a hedge against bad times. Reinvestment has a wide range of results and underlies the complexity of the social entities we generally think of as civilizations. The fact that one farmer can produce enough to support himself, with some left over, means that for the first time some persons can spend their full time at activities that are not directly productive of food. A shaman, who works with the supernatural only part-time because his primary task, like everyone else's, is getting enough to eat, can, with surpluses, now becomes a priest, a full-time religious practitioner, fed by the productivity of others who, in turn, benefit by his specialist skill at manipulating the beyond. The skilled organizer can now become a full-time administrator and decision maker, a chief, increasing the order and efficiency of his group and earning indirectly what he does not produce directly. The Pueblos did not expand this possibility very far, but the peoples considered in the next chapters illustrate clearly the development of what is still only a potential at this point. The full potential of cultivation was never reached, being shortcircuited by invasion and destruction from Europe.

Once sedentary, technological or material accumulation becomes possible. People in grass houses, as the joke has it, shouldn't stow thrones; indeed, the nomad cannot accumulate much of anything. Once you stay put, however, as with the houses themselves, the material conditions of existence can be improved. Tools can become larger, more elaborate, and more numerous, and the consequence of this is a technological snowball. Pottery is the simplest example but one of the most dramatic.

The Mogollon were the earliest people to use pottery in the Southwest, and it clearly diffused there along with the maize complex from Mesoamerica. It could only become established there after sedentism was achieved, for among its many characteristics, pottery is fragile and unsuitable for the hurly-burly of nomadic life. The earliest Southwestern pottery is usually described as a polished brownware and is undecorated and occurs in simple bowl and jar forms. In the East we have something of a puzzle: in the Northeast there was pottery occurring at 1000 B.C. of a type usually called Woodland, and still more remarkable, in the Southeast there was pottery being made at 2000 B.C., both much earlier than current evidence for the Southwest. The Woodland, a grit-tempered pottery, was usually roughened on the surface through the use of some tool, such as an incised paddle or cord-wrapped stick; and while it has some Mesoamerican resemblances, many feel that it may reflect a continuing influence from northern Asia. The fiber-tempered southeastern pottery may also ultimately have been of Mesoamerican derivation, but in view of its early occurrence, some have felt it to be possibly an entirely independent development. The fact that it occurred earlier in these areas than in the Southwest is perhaps explicable by the fact that we are confident that sedentism preceded agriculture in these richer zones, and settled villagers could have been introduced to and accepted pottery before the full range of other innovations, including maize itself, became acceptable.

Pottery, as elsewhere noted, is the archaeologist's delight because its characteristics are remarkably variable, but the variation is not dictated by the nature of the material or by the uses to which it is put. The shape, form, and decoration are matters of personal and, more importantly, cultural taste, and that taste seems to have been reasonably conservative. A pot can be flared at the lip, or have no lip at all. It can bow out toward the bottom or at the top or in the middle or not at all. It can be painted or incised or grooved or punctated or beaten with a cord-wrapped stick or simply smoothed with a stone. It can be tempered with grit or potsherds or fiber or feathers or even shell. A particular pot is made with some combination of these characteristics not because it *must* be but because that is the way somebody thought it *should* be.

People make pots in styles characteristic of their cultures and in styles that illustrate much about the nature of culture itself. A Pueblo pot in one period is in just such a shape with just such a handle and just such a lip and decorated with just such a pattern. So are most of the others to be found with it at that given time and place. Why? Why are you wearing a pair of trousers and shoes rather than a loincloth and sandals? Because that's the way it's done! Styles are simply matters of common agreement in areas where necessity does not dictate and, as such, are reliable guides to indexing cultures. We can reliably assign a pot of particular pattern, even if we have no actual association or date, to a particular culture on stylistic grounds alone.

The Pueblo peoples, having become sedentary and having found pottery useful and usable, can thereafter be kept track of by the shifts in their choices of shape and decoration. As Pueblo life became more elaborate, so did the pottery. It began as a few simple forms, largely undecorated, and at its height was represented by an incredible wealth of vessel shapes and highly stylized polychrome decorations, ranging from geometrical designs to realistic animal depictions. As did many other peoples, the Pueblos adopted the metal utilitarian cookware of the invading Europeans, and while pottery never ceased to be made, it was not for a long time representative of this great tradition. Here again commercial demand has resulted in a renaissance, this time with the potters of the Pueblos. In some cases archaeologists have contributed to the revival by providing the modern potters with the designs they have

Corn made possible the sedentary town life represented here by the multilevel architecture of a Hopi pueblo. (Edward Curtis)

discovered while excavating ancient places, and these designs have come to life once again.

As the architecture and the tools became more complex after sedentism became established, so did virtually all other aspects of Pueblo society. The historical Pueblos were, indeed, too complex socially and politically to be suitable as an illustration of the next level of social organization—the tribe. It would be best to move, therefore, in time and space to other groups of the tribal level of organization. The clans and secret societies of the Pueblos were of a tribal character but somewhere, lost in the archaeological sequence, they passed beyond the simplicity we require for explanation.

Agriculture did not everywhere lead to the same thing, but it did represent a new level of adaptive possibility. Some hunting and gathering societies were larger and more complex than some agricultural peoples. The Kwakiutl and other Northwest Coast peoples were fortunate in the richness of their wild resources, while the Pima of the Arizona desert, even with agriculture, had all they could handle in maintaining themselves. The practice of agriculture, even in a relatively rich environment, did not in itself guarantee great cultural complexity. The surplus productivity of domestication was only a potential that *could* be harnessed to make possible levels of culture higher than those that gatherers, in however rich an environment, could hope to reach. As in the discussion of environmental factors as limits rather than direct causal factors, agriculture raises us to a new *level* with new limits, but it does not in itself determine the variation within those limits. Natchez, Mandan, Zuni, Aztec, Chinese, and English are all agricultural peoples; obviously that alone is not a sufficient explanation for their cultural differences.

Some Readings

Dozier, Edward P.: *The Pueblo Indians of North America*, New York: Holt, 1970.

Dozier, Edward P.: "The American Southwest," in E. B. Leacock and N. O. Lurie (eds.), *North American Indians in Historical Perspective*, New York: Random House, 1971.

Flannery, Kent V.: "Archaeological Systems Theory and Early Mesoamerica," in Betty J. Meggers (ed.), *Anthropological Archeology in the Americas*, Washington: The Anthropological Society of Washington, 1968. Despite the forbidding title, a readable discussion of the issue of cultivation.

Mangelsdorf, Paul C., Richard S. MacNeish, and Walton C. Galinat: "Domestication of Corn," *Science*, **143**:538–545, 1964.

IV LEFT-HANDED MEXICAN CLANSMAN

His sisters and his cousins, whom he reckons up by dozens.
Gilbert and Sullivan, H. M. S. Pinafore

The kind of society most characteristic of the Chichimeca was not the simple band but a more complex (but still primarily kinship-based) organization usually called a tribe. As the peoples became settled in permanent communities and adopted reliable sources of livelihood, the number of persons who had to be dealt with on a regular basis gradually became too great for the simple familistic pattern of the nomadic band. Once settled, each village had to deal not only with its own members, who now could number in the hundreds rather than the dozens, but also with its settled neighbors. At the same time that the numbers in interaction grew, there was an increasing importance in regulating the use of resources like agricultural land; the growing of products and their distribution were both less simple than the collection of wild products, which clearly belonged to whoever picked or killed them.

The essence of the tribal level of organization was defined by Elman Service in his concept of the "pan-tribal sodality," which in simplest terms is a unit of social structure whose membership crosscuts all the groups that make up a tribe.[1] Two kinds of structure perform this function: One is based on a much-extended kinship, the clan; the other is the principle of "voluntary association" resulting in such self-selected entities as warrior or curing societies. A tribe can be thought of as a sort of "multiband" entity for the purpose of describing these structural arrangements, but in fact the critical operating segment of the tribal society is really a new and different sort of unit entirely—the corporate kin group. All of this takes some explaining, since much of it is entirely alien to our own organizational principles. As has already been noted, a failure to understand these differences underlies much of the tragedy of Indian history in relation to white society.

Social Bookkeeping

A band, though familistic, is, strictly speaking, a loosely aggregated group whose only true rule of membership is residence with the group. Though patrilocal postmarital residence and group exogamy create a situation where the continuity of males is preserved, it is only at the tribal level with the clan that these de facto groupings are given cohesiveness by *rules* for membership. The rule in defining the clan is one of kinship reckoned through a line of descent, real or mythical.

This becomes difficult for most of us to comprehend in that the line in question is a "unilineage," tracing descent *only* through males or *only* through females, producing either a matrilineage or a patrilineage as the basic element of the clan. Our system, as noted elsewhere, is bilateral in that we reckon ourselves equally related to our father and mother, and our mother's brother is as much an uncle as our father's brother. A clear picture of a patrilineal principle in action can, however, easily be gained by simply examining the way in which we inherit our last names. I am a Castile and any of my children will also be Castiles, but if my sister were to marry a Ferndock her children would become, of course, Ferndocks and not Castiles. The name descends through a *line* of males, and if you simply tote up all of those who bear the name (discounting female name changing upon marriage), you have described a patrilineage. The problem with this example is that we do not actually reckon kinship in this fashion but inherit *only* our names unilineally. I am, indeed, as related to my mother's kinfolk, the Smiths, as I am to the Castiles, even though I bear the Castile name. My rights and obligations to one group are neither more nor less than they are to the other.

Perhaps in attempting to mentally thread your way through the morass of persons to whom you can consider yourself related, you perceive the advantage of the unilineal principle. Bilateral descent becomes too diffuse too quickly for efficient social bookkeeping. It can be done, and corporate kin units will be examined which are bilateral (usually called cognatic clans), in relationship to the chiefdom where they are important, but the unilineage is far more common at the tribal level. The origin of the patrilineal emphasis can easily be seen in the situation of patrilocality combined with exogamy, but matrilineality is more difficult to explain.

In a patrilocal band the shift to patrilineality is simple. In *Theory of Culture Change* Julian Steward has shown convincingly that patrilocality, because of the advantages of preserving the continuity of males, can be formalized into patrilineages in situations where it is important to define group membership.[2] Matrilineality in a very general way is associated with circumstances where it is female economic activity that is basic to subsistence. In the case of early agriculture it was women who farmed, and it was women's rights to the use of land, including particularly the matter of land inheritance, that required the social bookkeeping. Matrilineality combined with matrilocality creates a number of social problems, as shall be seen, and seems to be possible only for groups who are closely settled, so that while the males live in their wives' villages they are not far from their own. The origins of these unilineages have been hotly debated since the beginnings of anthropology, and I will not pretend to resolve the matter here.

Marriage has frequently been functionally defined as "the legitimization of parentage," and the lineage-clan principle is made more understandable if it is realized that the important thing being accomplished is the definition of groups and the assignment of children to membership in one group or another. Our own lack of interest in kinship as an organizing principle is dramatically emphasized in the confusion that results after a divorce as to whom the children belong. The *unit* of importance in our society is the nuclear family and not any lineage or other larger kin entity, so when the nuclear family is broken by divorce the children are essentially up for grabs, because their *unit* of membership has ceased to exist. In the unilineal society the children are clearly members of either the father's group or the mother's group, and it simply does not matter what happens to the marriage that produced them. Our important social units are not kinship-based at all.

This makes it necessary to clarify the concept of the *corporate* kin unit. You could reckon genealogically your relationship to a multitude of supposed kinfolk, but this would be an imaginary unit since none of these persons has any real, important connection with you through some pattern of mutual obligation. A corporate unit is an actually functional social unit much like the corporation, conceived of in modern law as a legal person capable of holding property, suing, being sued, and the like. The corporate kin unit defined by the principle of unilineality is a *lineage*, and that lineage holds real property, like land, or rights to ceremonies, names, songs, or other less tangible property. The lineage acts as a unit and is not just an abstract reckoning of relatives. A matrilineage will own land, granting the right to the use of the land to individual women; however, they do not own it in the sense that they may freely dispose of it. This is the principle of usufruct as opposed to simple ownership, and acting on this principle is just one of the problems the Indians had in confronting Europeans. As will be seen, the Dawes Act of 1887, in attempting to create Indian freeholders in the European pattern, struck hard at this concept of limited communal ownership.

Before getting futher into the implications of these kinship concepts, the relationship of the lineage to the clan and other higher groupings should be emphasized. A lineage generally is localized in a single village where all of the members can actually reckon their genealogical relationships; everyone knows who is related to whom. Several such lineages will constitute the membership of a single village. Lewis Binford has suggested several persuasive propositions in a paper called "Post-Pleistocene Adaptations," among which is a kind of budding model where sedentary villagers regulate their number below carrying capacity by establishing new daughter villages as numbers become too great.[3] In some such process can be seen the origins of the extension of the lineage principle to form the clan.

If representatives of several lineages form a new community and eventually still another community is formed from that one, then at some time it becomes inevitable that a preliterate group will lose track of its actual detailed line of descent but retain the certainty that it is somehow related to the people of another village. In human affairs, the solution is inevitably some sort of mythological explanation which shows that the lineages in different villages are really the same because they are all descended from some common ancestry. The lineages so related all belong to a named group—the Wolf Clan—because they are all descended from the Wolf. In every village of a tribe will be representatives of each clan, all of whom believe themselves to be related, and act toward each other as if they were in fact relatives, including not marrying anyone within one's own clan. The ceremonial and mythological life of tribes, more complex than that of bands, centers around reinforcing these beliefs.

Clans themselves can be combined into still larger units. Several clans within a tribe may regard themselves as more closely related to each other than to the rest, again through some mythological connection. If clans are divided into two such exogamous groups, it is called a moiety (e.g., the Mandan), while if the groupings number more than two it is called a phratry (e.g., the Hopi). In all cases the point is to establish between still larger groupings a rationalization of kinlike relationship as a basis of orderly interaction. This, I hasten to point out, is not a conscious intention since the persons in each instance may have a wide variety of beliefs about the real nature of their behavior.

Clans as pantribal sodalities provide a basis for interaction among large numbers of persons. The Mandan of the Missouri River area, when visited by George Catlin, lived in six large villages and numbered perhaps 2000. The Iroquois represented an ultimate extension of kinship principles into a political level where clan membership was an important fact in tying together perhaps 20,000 persons. Contrast numbers of this kind with the handful characteristic of the band and the utility of the tribal system is apparent.

Voluntary association will be considered in detail in terms of religious societies in the next chapter and again in describing the horsemen of the Plains, among whom it was highly important and elaborate. The various warrior societies and ceremonial brotherhoods and sisterhoods added yet another element of social glue holding together the elements of a tribe. In any village a man could expect to find clansmen who would welcome him and treat him as kin whether or not they had ever seen him before in their lives. In the same way, members of a warrior society knew what to expect from fellow members in other villages, though this was most important when many branches of the tribe came together as in the great annual buffalo hunts of the Plains where the men's societies served as organizers and police for the great encampment.

Voluntary associations can be formed by many means and for many purposes, but they always have some fairly specific focus and are sometimes called special-interest groups. Always, however, they differ from clans and other kin units in that membership is by choice, not necessarily in that the individual chooses but that somebody chooses; it is not an automatic process. A man is a member of his clan willy-nilly, because he was born so. A man can become a member of a curing society by having the disease that the society is dedicated to cure, a Dog soldier through invitation because of his prowess in war, a Contrary (a society of the Plains whose members do everything backwards) through dedication and purchase, and a member of some Pueblo societies by "ritual trespass"—that is, by seeing a secret part of a ceremony, one is obligated to join. These are not, or ought not to be, difficult for Americans to understand since our society is overrun with similar special-interest brotherhoods, ranging from college fraternities and sororities to the Ku Klux Klan. The Indian versions also have exit and entrance rites, named offices, sacred paraphernalia, and the like. They differ as ours do from simple ephemeral friendship groups by possessing structure and a corporate character that allows them to exist beyond the lifetime of the particular collection of individuals that make them up at any given moment.

Oedipus and Mother's Brother

The intricacy of kin relations suggested in the tribal level is not the feeble thing it is in our own society. Virtually everything that is important in the life of the individual is tied up with the lineage of which he is a member. There are other larger groups to which he has ties, but the truly vital one for defining his behavior is his lineage. One way in which this importance is indicated is in the nomenclature used.

Nomenclature—in this instance, what you call your relatives—is presumed to reflect what is of interest to the people that use the system. Our own, which we naturally think of as the only right way, reflects our interest in the nuclear family above all else. As can be seen in the kinship diagram, we name all the members of that group separately but lump others of both the mother's and the father's side together, making no distinction between one sort of uncle and another or between cousins. Unilineal systems like that of the Iroquois make important distinctions not only between the two sides as to uncles and aunts but also between types of cousin; the fundamental principle is to which lineage the individual belongs rather than to what nuclear family.

There are many puzzling features to these systems from our point of view, too many for us to examine in this brief coverage, the purpose of which is only to indicate that the differences are profound. References to the sport of kinship analysis are provided at the end of the chapter. Still, you will note that in the Iroquois system, the speaker (ego) does not

American/Eskimo system of kin terms. A cousin is a cousin is a cousin. Compare this system, where great emphasis is placed on the nuclear family and where other kinfolk tend to be lumped together, with that of the Iroquois. Circles represent females, and triangles represent males; equal signs show affinal ties (marriage); and vertical lines indicate lines of descent.

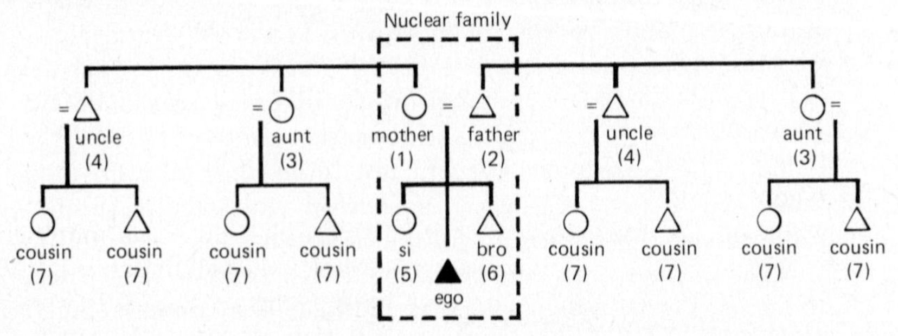

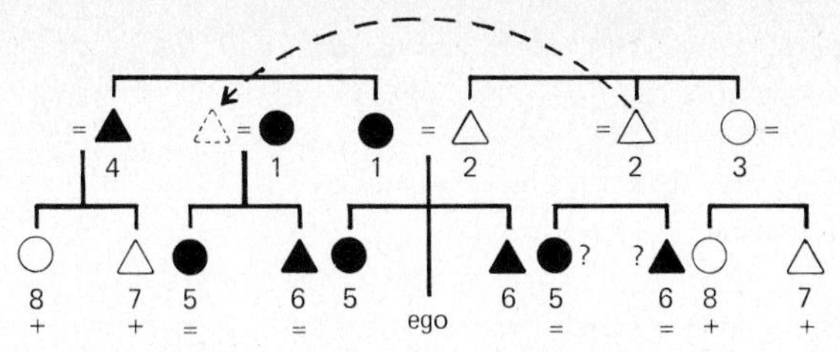

Iroquois system of kin terms. Much of the difference between the American/Eskimo system and the Iroquois system can be understood by noting the shaded figures, which represent members of ego's own matrilineage. Distinguishing between cross and parallel cousins is important, since some are "clan sisters," while others are preferred marriage partners in a system of unilineal reckoning.

seem to be able to tell the difference between his father and his father's brother or between his mother and his mother's sister. He seems to regard his brothers and sisters in the same light as some of his cousins but not in the same light as others of his cousins. Early Europeans encountering such systems tended to conclude that they reflected some pernicious pattern of group marriage, total promiscuity, or other licentiousness that made it impossible to know who one's parents were!

Let us first note that the impression that you cannot tell your uncles apart is obviously false; it just takes you a phrase rather than a single term: "mother's brother" as opposed to "father's brother" or "uncle on my mother's side" as opposed to "uncle on my father's side." So, too, the unilineal peoples can distinguish father from father's brother, but they do not customarily do so any more often than we customarily distinguish uncles. The key, as can quickly be seen on the kinship diagram, is that the term we gloss, or translate, as "father" really means "elder male member of my lineage" (assuming the system is patrilineal). The terms for the cousins are somewhat more complex but follow the same principle of emphasizing lineage membership.

The "cousin" terms point out the importance of marriage alliance as between lineages. If the system is patrilineal, the children of my father's brother will, of course, be members of my lineage and hence socially equivalent to my brothers and sisters. The term being used generally glosses more accurately as lineage or clan sister/brother and will be extended to all those of one's own generation in that patriline. Those cousins who can be traced through the same sex line—brother of my father or sister of my mother—are called "parallel cousins," while those where a sex line is crossed are called "cross cousins." The cross cousins are not only not members of ego's own lineage but in many cases of preferred cross-cousin marriage represent those of other lineages that he is most likely to marry. In a patrilineal system it is easy to see that the children of one's father's brother will be clan brothers, but the other parallel cousins, the children of one's mother's sister, are harder to explain. The answer is fairly simple if we assume a pattern of balanced marriage relationships (symmetrical connubium) such that ego's father and ego's father's brother will both marry women of the same lineage or clan or moiety. In fact, the expectation is that those represented on the diagram as the children of ego's mother's sister could be the children of ego's father's brother. Indeed, since sororal polygyny is not uncommon, they could be actual brothers and sisters if ego's father had married not only his wife but her sister as well!

The terms only very dimly reflect the fact of actual kinship behaviors. A man whom you call by the same term as your brother is entitled to the same kind of treatment that you would afford your own brother. We define incest, for example, only in terms of the nuclear family, but groups of this kind extend incest prohibitions to a much wider group. The Navaho recognize an ailment called "butterfly sickness" where the victim is drawn to cast himself into a fire like a moth to the flame. This is the result of incestuous thought or behavior and can be caused not only by lusting after one's sister but also by such thoughts about any clan relative in the class one is forbidden to marry. In a great many other ways important aspects of human relations are determined by considerations of lineage membership.

Matrilineality is no more complicated than patrilineality but is harder to deal with because of its unfamiliarity and also because it does have certain built-in problems. Although membership in the clan and even place of residence are determined through tracing a line of females, these societies are not in any sense matriarchal. There are nowhere on earth human societies that *consistently* vest authority in females, although obviously females may *occasionally* hold great power, as witness Queen Victoria. I will not argue with the feminists that this should be so, but it *is* the case. Given this fact, there are problems.

In a particular matrilineage or clan it is the male members of the lineage who exercise authority. If one looks back at the Iroquois diagram and interprets it as a matrilineage, it is immediately obvious that a child's father is *not* a member of his matrilineage. The elder male who stands closest to the child who is a member of the lineage is the mother's brother, and it is to this person that the child must look for those things which we in our society think of as inextricably connected with the role of father. This is the man who controls the use and inheritance of lineage property, who knows the ceremonies of the lineage, who in virtually all things stands in a position of authority over the child. The actual biological father has something of the position of uncle in our own society because while omnipresent and well beloved he is not the one who decides much that is important.

Ego's father does, indeed, as a male, have important duties to perform—but not in the household in which he resides. With the children of his sister he is the one who has the patriarchal role, and it is in his own lineage of origin that his voice is important. Obviously there are built-in tensions in such a system, and it should be noted that in such societies marriages are very fragile. House, land, and children belong to the mother, or rather to her group, and, as with the Zuni, a husband can return to find his loincloth and other possessions on the doorstep and the marriage dissolved. With the Iroquois, the women and their children form the core of social continuity, with the wandering males drifting in and out, frequently returning from year-long hunting and trading trips to find themselves divorced. The men with stable relations to the group are not the husbands but the sons.

One obvious deduction from this, as Bronislav Malinowski pointed out long ago, is that the Freudian concept of the Oedipus complex can hardly be universal.[4] In matrilineal societies it is not the father who plays the role of awesome, dominating male figure but the mother's brother.

This Mandan earth lodge was the property of a particular matrilineage, and several nuclear families would reside there, all related through female descent, with the males taking up residence in the lodges of their wives. (Edward Curtis)

Harder than this to understand, in view of all the Indian "lovers' leaps" to be found in the United States, is that marriage is an important transaction between corporate kin groups and not the result of romantic love. It is only in societies like ours, where the nuclear family is the critical unit, that individual preferences override all else. Elsewhere marriage is an important arrangement between groups—not to be decided by selfish personal taste because, among other things, it is the means by which the group perpetuates itself. If Pocahontas went at all willingly, it was as a representative of her people and not as an adolescent romantic.

The modern Navaho have as one of their most frequent complaints about the children who have gone off for many years to school the fact that they "don't know who their relatives are." By this they mean the children do not understand the intricate web of mutual obligation and respect that are due kinsmen, and for a tribal people it is this web that defines much of what it is to be a Navaho. Kinship is of the essence at this level of social organization, and little that the Indian peoples did in reaction to the Europeans is understandable without taking this factor into account. No single man owns or disposes as an individual but only acts with the advice and consent of his kinsmen. Europeans found the principles of collective identity and collective responsibility important here only vaguely comprehensible—only European noble and royal families had a similarly corporate character. The dilemma of the King of England who abdicated to marry the "woman I love" would have been easily recognized by most Indian peoples as a denial of important kinship obligations.

Who's in Charge Here?

The tribe, while more cohesive than the band, is by no means as tightly ordered as the centralized bureaucratic states typical of the Europeans. Each of the kin units that make up the group is in large part an autonomous social entity whose relations with the rest of the tribe are loosely structured and difficult to reliably coordinate. Elman Service, in his theoretical consideration of these matters, has suggested that it is only the pressure of surrounding peoples that maintains the unity of the tribe which otherwise has centrifugal tendencies.[5] In Indian–white dealings, many of these characteristics had important and often disastrous manifestations.

The most evident weakness of the system lies in the lack of any clear-cut concept of offices, like that of chief, wherein some individual has the power to make decisions for the group as a whole which are binding on the group as a whole. There is instead a continued reliance on very informal leadership based on recognition of the personal qualities of some particular charismatic individual. A great many Indian groups recognized a distinction between "war chiefs" and "peace chiefs," which is a reflection of this shifting approach. Generally, elder men of wide experience and proven wisdom will be influential in most group decision making, while younger men of known daring and bravery, and possessed of good luck, will lead in matters of warfare. In both cases the pattern of leadership is one of example and persuasion, not command, and the position of chief is subject to constant reappraisal.

The Roman centurion in the Bible who illustrated his authority with the words, "I say to this man go and he goeth; and to another, Come and he cometh" (Matt. 8:9), stands in contrast to the Indian leader at the tribal level who could never be certain who would goeth and who would cometh. Organizing a war party among most peoples was not a matter of issuing orders but an act of salesmanship. A particular leader and those who actively supported him would propose such an event and rally around them others who were persuaded of its wisdom. Each would make his own decision based on his appraisal of the leader's plan and of the leader himself. Those who did not agree would simply not participate, and if at any time during the expedition it appeared that the adventure was ill-fated or that the leader's relationship with the supernatural necessary to such undertakings was weak, the followers would simply fade away. As shall be seen, in any individual military action, Indian tactics might win the day, but the informality of organization time and again robbed them of the ability to sustain a campaign long enough to capitalize on a victory or coordinate a strategy involving more than one battle at a time.

Typically, warfare among tribes was a matter of small-scale raid and ambuscade with neither side mounting sustained campaigns, because as was the case at the band level there was little point to wars of conquest. There was, indeed, far more military activity here probably because of the increased importance for sedentary peoples to define and protect their territorial resources. In general, these small-scale raids were primarily intended to harass the enemy and maintain a balance of terror and protect the status quo. In fighting the Europeans, such tactics were only temporarily effective and usually only in situations where the Europeans were isolated and overextended, as was the case with Red Cloud's successful war to close the Bozeman Trail.

Among the tribes themselves a contributing factor to the centrifugal tendency was the custom of feud. Each clan or lineage, if it found itself injured by a member of another clan, even within the tribe, or from still another group, took action as a clan to redress the balance. Feuds between groups were undertaken constantly to equalize the damage done, but as with the Hatfields and the McCoys of American legend, the thing could go on for many years. The problem for the European invaders was the fact that any clan could act independently in these matters, and while most of a tribe would make peace, some segment could continue to make war until satisfied that vengeance had been properly exacted. The start of Chief Joseph's War was at least in part due to this principle when some of Chief Joseph's band killed whites to revenge the death of a kinsman. The seriousness of the problem can be seen in the fact that when the Cherokees began their attempts to organize themselves to resist white encroachment, one of their first acts was to outlaw clan vengeance. They were at that time essentially shifting to a state form of organization, one of whose most important defining characteristics is the "monopoly of organized sanctions." In the state, only the state itself has the right to adjudicate grievances and mete out punishments. Individual action, taking the law into one's own hands, is the rule for the tribe and contributes to its lack of coordinating ability.

The pattern of feud and vengeance had another unfortunate characteristic for Indian-white relations in its group character. From the Indian point of view, the death of an individual is primarily an offense to his kin group by another kin group, and vengeance need not necessarily focus on the specific culprit. If you have killed one of ours, we will kill one of yours, and it doesn't really much matter which one. Thus if a lawless prospector or trapper were to kill an Indian, his kinsmen would seek vengeance and, knowing little of white intricacies of organization, might very well kill some utterly innocent and well-meaning settler. From the Indians' point of view, justice was accomplished, while to the Europeans a senseless atrocity had been committed. The whites, too, were prone to strike out at the nearest band of Indians, innocent or not, as in the famous Sand Creek massacre of Black Kettle's band of Cheyennes led by Colonel Chivington, in which the Europeans were proceeding in violation of their own custom and on a wholesale basis of slaughter. Eventually, of course, both sides in the conflict tended to take the view of the other that the only good one is a dead one.

In peace as in war, organization is loosely structured and leadership highly personal. The Cherokee had a class of leaders called "beloved men" and this phrase reflects important custom. A leader held his position on the basis of the respect that he could command. Elder males and, as with the Cherokees, sometimes older women, would speak out on their views as to what ought to be done in any particular dispute. Oratory was an important consideration, and debates would customarily be lengthy. The principle in operation was a kind of "consensus politics," where the purpose of discussion is to feel out the range and mood of feeling rather than to force the issue. Decisions were necessarily carefully tailored to be acceptable to all since no power existed to coerce compliance. If it became obvious that some action would be unacceptable to a large number of persons, then no decision at all would be made. The system was, of course, rather conservative and unwieldy if rapid and radical action had to be taken. Even today, debates at Navaho chapter meetings tend to have this quality of seeking consensus and avoiding any action that cannot be made palatable to all, resulting in a rather ponderous decision-making process from the point of view of the Bureau of Indian Affairs.

One Thing Leads to Another

The characteristics of the tribal peoples in many ways resemble those of the smaller and simpler bands. Most of the differences are reflections of increased size and agriculturally based sedentism, although tribalism is not confined to agriculturally based groups. The tribes also contain within them the seeds of greater complexity, and examining any particular group will show not a "pure" ideal type but a wide range of

Antelopes and Snakes, members of Hopi voluntary associations, dancing in a public ritual at Oraibi Pueblo. (Edward Curtis)

variation around a theme. It is particularly difficult to sort out the nature of the aboriginal tribal organizations because contact with Europeans tended to produce change before good observations were made. It is then difficult to say what is the result of contact and what an aboriginal pattern. As will be seen, the European insistence on dealing with "chiefs" is something of a self-fulfilling prophecy in that European action created the chiefs by recognizing and strengthening their authority.

More highly structured than the bands in terms of extended kinship and voluntary associations, the tribes resemble the bands in the lack of centralized authority. Although generally agricultural, in most cases the surplus productivity of agriculture remains only a potential that is not yet harnessed and exploited, notably in the continued absence of full-time specialists. With tribes as with bands, the society is essentially homogenous, and if one man is not equal to another, it is a matter of personal achievement and not a feature of the social structure. Each man or woman does much the same sort of thing as any other and the families of "chiefs" grind their own corn. Though individual private ownership is weak, the tribe does recognize ownership of real property for the kin groups that compose it and asserts territorial claims as a whole against other tribes. Groups like the Mandan seem to have been immediately involved in trade and other market activities but, in general, economic exchange still moved through a pattern of reciprocity. At this level, however, the gift exchange is more structured and less balanced, beginning to shift in the direction of redistribution, a system of economics characteristic of the chiefdoms to be discussed in Chapter 6. In general, no man has more than another and the exchange of goods is still more important to reinforcing social ties than as a means of maximizing gain and concentrating economic power.

In areas of ideology the tribal peoples have become more complex than the bands because the intricacy of their social relations calls for more elaborate justification and explanation. The religious mechanisms of ceremonial life not only tie together the tribesmen in matters of common identity but are also among the elements that lead to higher forms of organization. These will be examined in the next chapter.

Just as the bands gave rise to the more complex tribes, so, too, the tribes in some places give way to still more complexity represented by chiefdoms and, ultimately, states. In the same way that bands continued to exist into the historical period, various tribes remained even though other groupings which had gone beyond them in sophistication, had formed. Although it was in fact the Europeans who destroyed the pattern of tribal life, the end was already under way as larger and larger societies with more centralized organizations were beginning to assert themselves. The Aztec empire of Mexico was only the last of several great civilizations that brought much of that area under its sway and which molded the simpler peoples in its own complex image. The Chichimeca had already begun to generate similar great organizing civilizations at the time of intrusion that would inevitably have had the same result in reducing tribal diversity.

Some Readings

On the Concept of the Tribe

Basehart, Harry W.: "Mescalero Band Organization," *Southwestern Journal of Anthropology*, **26**:87–106, 1970. Excellent illustration of many of the complexities of understanding leadership and authority in non-state societies.

Sahlins, Marshall: *The Tribesmen*, Englewood Cliffs, N.J.: Prentice-Hall, 1968.

Service, Elman R.: *Primitive Social Organization: An Evolutionary Perspective*, New York: Random House, 1964.

On Kinship

Fox, Robin: *Kinship and Marriage: An Anthropological Perspective*, Baltimore: Penguin, 1967. A comprehensive survey of key concepts in understanding kinship.

Schneider, David, and Kathleen Gough (eds.): *Matrilineal Kinship*, Berkeley: University of California Press, 1961. Illustrates with some American Indian examples the nature of matrilineal systems.

THE GREAT SPIRITS

I am like the Most High Power Whose Ways Are Beautiful.
Before me it is beautiful,
Behind me it is beautiful,
Under me it is beautiful,
Above me it is beautiful,
All around me it is beautiful.

Navaho—White Corn Boy chant[1]

Until now the concern has largely been with the technological and the sociological systems of society without any direct focus on the ideological. It is impossible to talk sensibly about any one of these aspects of a society without considering them all, so closely are they interrelated, but the realm of ideas and beliefs has not so far been emphasized. As the cultures developed increasing social and technological complexity, there was a comparable development in the area of ideological systems. In our own tradition, at least in its modern manifestations, there is sharp separation between and compartmentalization of those things we would label "religious" and the "real" or "practical" world. For most American Indian societies there is no such clear-cut dichotomy, and the worlds of the natural and the supernatural cannot so easily be separated. Hunting and planting and the curing of disease are all as much religious as practical acts, and belief and practice grow up together.

The placing of these matters in a separate chapter, as has been done here, would probably have made little sense to most American Indians to whom magic, science, and religion are really conceptually much the same. Ralph Linton, in an effort to deal with "nativistic" religious movements, attempted to separate the "rational" from the "magical," but this and all other such categorizations represent the notions of the outsider and not of the native practitioner.[2] A man casts corn pollen to the four winds not because he is a superstitious fool but because he believes, indeed he *knows*, that if this is not done his enterprise will fail. People believe in what we call magic in the same way we believe in science. Every flight on a Boeing 747 is, after all, an act of faith, since most of us have no real notion as to why the 747 flies, and just looking at it would certainly suggest a magical process. We take airplanes for granted in the same way that most Indian people took the active interaction of the supernatural and natural for granted. Virtually all human societies insist on controlling and explaining the world around them, and if no naturalistic solution is at hand, then something else must be found in the realm of the supernatural.

Prime Movers and Coyotes

The "Great Spirit," in whose name so many treaties were sworn, was almost entirely the product of the white man's powers of self-deception, combined with the fact that it was the whites who wrote down what the Indians said. The famous Stevens treaties negotiated in 1855 with the tribes of the Washington Territory were explicated to the Indians in the "Chinook jargon," a trade language of a few hundred simple terms. One of these treaties begins with the words, "The aforesaid confederated tribes and bands of Indians hereby cede, relinquish and convey to the United States all their right, title and interest in and to the lands. . . ."[3] The language of the treaty is Anglo and could never have been conveyed to the Indians in this form through the jargon. In the same way, the innumerable instances of calling on the "Great Spirit" are simply attempts by white men to put into their own terms complex Indian concepts. Words like the Sioux *wakan* or the Algonkian *manitou,* which tend to describe a condition of holiness or powerful spirituality, were apparently consistently personalized and translated into references to a Judeo-Christian single god. No Chichimec group was monotheistic in the strict Western sense; although some did postulate "prime mover" creator gods who, while not alone like the jealous Christian God, were more important than others.

Popular theological concepts of the West were and are inadequate to describe the range of Indian belief and, for that matter, can be easily misinterpreted in this discussion. The Spanish had a great deal of difficulty coping with the resemblances between their own Catholicism and the complex faith of the Mesoamericans, which included baptism, virgin births, reincarnated savior gods, confession, communion, and celibate orders of monks and nuns. This could only be the work of the devil mocking the true faith. The English did not really care and tended to dismiss Indian faith as idolatry, devil worship, or the like. At treaty time it was convenient to assume that everyone believed in the same god for purposes of getting on with the transfer of land, and this contributed more than anything else to the "Great Spirit" approach.

The range of Indian religious belief is very great, but by comparison to European belief, certain general observations can be made, though they do not apply to each and every society. As noted, the belief systems are polytheistic rather than monotheistic, but even that is something of a distortion since the "gods" do not have the character, attributes, or degree of worshipful respect accorded to the Judeo-Christian one god. If a particular supernatural entity is but one among many, without the omnipotent and omniscient qualities of the "almighty," attitudes and behaviors toward it are likely to be less clearly worshipful and obedient. Like the Greek Olympians, these gods can be powerful beings, but one is also likely to find them sitting down to share a feast with the people or whispering advice in one's ear on the eve of battle. Through dreams and visions, the supernaturals of the Chichimec cosmos are in frequent, intimate, even sometimes trivial, contact with the "Earth Surface people."

"Animism" is a term frequently used to suggest a characteristic of Indian belief which is the tendency to endow much of the universe with a spirit or "soul" like that of man—in essence, to animate the inanimate, or make conscious the unconscious. The lines of separation between organic, inorganic, and superorganic are blurred or are at least very differently drawn from European practice. A coyote was somehow connected with "Coyote," the spirit or god. There could be a coyote clan, all of whose members had some special relation with both these supernaturals, while at the same time some individual had a personal relationship with Coyote granted through a vision. A masked dancer could actually become Coyote temporarily or at least could serve as the

Komugi—a ritual mask of a legendary sea monster used in Kwakiutl ceremonial. The sophistication of the Northwest Coast artistic tradition is evident. (Edward Curtis)

vehicle through which he spoke. A grove or a table rock or other place sacred to the Coyote had a spiritual vitality conferred on it beyond the usual. What was sacred and what was mundane is not easily defined.

The animistic complexities can be more easily understood if we add the concept of spiritual "power," or what the peoples of the South Seas call *mana*. Many things can be considered to have force or power of this kind, with the supernatural beings having or controlling more of it than men, and some men having greater access to the power than others. We are familiar, because of John Wayne movies, with the notion of "strong medicine" or our own concept of a charmed life or a lucky man, which approximate the nature of power. Some are perhaps familiar with the ancient "caloric" theory of heat which had heat as a fluid that flows from body to body. *Mana*/power can be considered as such a fluid but one whose transfer is a dangerous and delicate matter. A person who has undergone a Navaho curing ceremony is overloaded with spiritual power and is dangerous to contact for some time after the ritual. Just as we deal with radiation or electrical energies with confidence but caution, these spiritual energies can be handled by those who understand them, but are dangerous to the ignorant. Religious life is to a great extent the manipulation of these forces in a beneficial way.

The power of some of the spirits is great, and when they are angry it might be necessary to approach them with fear and trembling, or at least to seem to be fearful and tremulous. In general, however, the flavor of the Indian approach to their supernaturals is not abject self-abasement, as might be appropriate with the all-powerful creator gods, but a more familiar and workaday manipulation of beings who might be more powerful than men in some ways but who can, nonetheless, be outwitted or outmaneuvered. Much shamanistic magical activity or community public observance has an inevitable quality. If the songs are sung properly, the dances danced appropriately, and the paraphernalia handled well, then the supernaturals *must* yield the proper results. If the proper results are not forthcoming, the cause is not that the gods refuse—for, indeed, they cannot refuse—but that some mistake was made in the ritual. Not all of the supernaturals can always be controlled in such an inevitable way, but this theme of orderly contractual transactions is far more prevalent than purely hopeful worship. The gods, of course, can be utterly capricious and some even consistently malevolent; but most can be pleased, cajoled, tricked, bought off, flattered, or otherwise brought into some understandable and beneficial relation with man.

The Navaho roughly divide the spiritual universe between the "Holy people" and the "Earth Surface people." The Earth Surface people are essentially the Navaho themselves, while the Holy people include all of the non-Navaho entities, most of which cannot be considered gods but simply beings of greater or at least different spiritual substance from the Navaho. Some, like Changing Woman (also called White Bead Woman), and her sons the Hero Twins, have such great importance as creators and teachers of the Navaho that they would fit our common conception of "gods." Many of the Holy people are not necessarily friendly to man, including a range of monsters, most of whom were destroyed by the Hero Twins, but some of which survive to plague man. There are also animal spirits like Coyote, who is a mischievous trickster, and Spider Man and Woman, who taught the Navaho how to weave. All of these can be dealt with by careful observation of the rules of proper behavior and manipulated through elaborate rituals called "sings," which restore disturbed harmonies.

The range of the Chichimec spirits is obviously very great, varying enormously from region to region and tribe to tribe. The Huron have a female-creator goddess Astaentsic, like the Navaho Changing Woman, but where Changing Woman is consistently friendly to the Navaho, Astaentsic seems to have regretted her act of creation and made much trouble for the Huron. Her son, Iouskeha, is the one who taught the Huron useful arts and watched after their interests against his mother's malevolence. Coyote, however, is not only widespread but appears relatively uniformly in the role of trickster, something like Shakespeare's Puck. The Kwakiutl, fascinated with property and rank, are deeply concerned about guardian spirits associated with family lines or inheritance, while Pueblo peoples of the Desert spend much spiritual energy on spirits connected with the rains, like the Zuni "Shalako." The spirits vary as much as do the peoples and their interests.

The supernatural realm of most Indian groups is complex, at least in terms of the numbers of types of supernaturals, but ultimately does not emerge as theologically sophisticated. By this I mean that the cosmology of most peoples seems strewn with contradictions and inconsistencies. A good deal of this is doubtless due to the distortion of time, as fewer and fewer persons remembered the myths and stories of their people as their societies were disrupted by white intrusion. Since most groups did not have full-time priests, religion was something more of an amateur undertaking with less concern for the intricate niceties of mythological exegesis characteristic of professional religious practitioners. Perhaps in the long run our failure to fully understand the internal consistency of some of the beliefs is simply a function of the religions having been transmitted through oral traditions and none of them frozen for our scrutiny in written bibles.

Things That Go Bump in the Night

If the scale of the spirits is more manageable than that of the European, there are nonetheless many "things" out there that mean man no good and are to be feared and avoided. The Navaho night is populated with enough of these to make it inadvisable to walk alone, and while the Navaho fear of the night and the dead is extreme, they are not alone in postulating things "that go bump in the night." The Kwakiutl myths involve, for example, a great cannibal bird, while people of the Cochiti Pueblo were convinced that many animals might actually be malevolent witches. An area where there is great variation in belief is in attitudes toward the dead and their ghosts, if any.

To the Navaho, the dead, however beloved and friendly they may have been in life, are greatly to be feared after death. Contact of any form with the dead is dangerous and requires ritual purification. Efforts to avoid contact lead to extreme measures such as abandonment of a house in which a death has occurred. The Ghost Dance, a religious movement which swept over many reservation tribes in the nineteenth century, promised the return of the dead ancestors as part of its message. The Navaho never participated in this movement, in large part because from their point of view trafficking in the dead is horrifying in the extreme. The Comanche of the Plains seem to have treated ghosts lightly in early days, but a recent study seems to indicate a very Navaho-like orientation for modern Comanches. The Iroquois, who had elaborate "mourning" rituals to console the grief of those who had lost a loved one, were close to the opposite extreme in their attention to the remains of the dead and care for their resting places. However, they also regarded them as potentially dangerous, although they were more concerned with witches.

Witches and the fear of witchcraft are important factors in a great many Indian societies. Clyde Kluckhohn, in his classic work, *Navaho Witchcraft*, suggested that a more correct title than "witch" would define a class of persons who are engaged in "influencing of events by supernatural techniques that are socially disapproved."[4] Witches in a general sense are persons who tap the potential of supernatural forces (in itself an acceptable act) for evil, selfish, and harmful purposes, or by methods which are disgusting, horrible, or otherwise such that no normal person could use them. Navaho witches work at night, commit incest, and work their magical evil through the use of means like "corpse poison" (dried human remains), and can assume the form of wolves.

It is difficult to discuss the actual practice of witchcraft because with some few exceptions there really weren't any practitioners. Some shaman might hint that he had such powers to achieve some end, or a psychotic might claim them, but in most Indian societies, some injunction must have been at work similar to the biblical one, "Thou shalt not suffer a witch to live (Exod. 22:18)," and anyone suspected of witchcraft was at least potentially marked for death. What is truly significant here is the belief in witchcraft and the social stress that accusations of witchcraft reflect. Magic there surely was, but persons who consciously thought of themselves as evil and malevolent traffickers in the foul and the obscene were few and far between.

At a time when the League of the Iroquois had fallen into ruin and the peoples of the League were despairing, the prophet Handsome Lake, who rose to preach a message of salvation, concerned himself deeply with the threat of witches. The fear of witchcraft and the witch hunt are usually symptomatic, as in this case, of a society in trouble. Witchcraft accusations seem to multiply under the same conditions and at the same times as suicide rates, alcoholism, violent crime, and other reflections of social disintegration. As observed by Kluckhohn, the majority of those accused by the Navaho were prosperous and well-to-do. Fear of being accused as a witch out of envy would serve to reinforce customs of generosity and guarantee a kind of equality of distribution; in general, it would tend to enforce good relations with one's neighbors and relatives. In a sense, the accusation of witchcraft is only the ultimate expression of social disapproval for actions that have failed to be controlled by lesser sanctions such as gossip.

Peyote and Pain

One very characteristic aspect of the supernatural practice of the American Indian is the altering in some way of a "normal" human mental or physical condition to promote interaction with the supernatural realm. Many European peoples have regarded some forms of "madness" as holy. Epilepsy was widely regarded in this light. The Indians of the Americas are not unique in their interest in such matters, but the degree of emphasis in some cultures and the wide range of techniques employed to induce some abnormal but "holy" condition is distinctive. The "vision quest" of the Plains Indians has received most attention but is only a dramatic part of a broader picture.

If madmen are closer to the gods by some associative process that links the not-normal with the super-normal, then it is not a long step to purposeful alteration of the conditions of "normality" to achieve a closeness to the gods. The rituals of purification, sacrifice, and the vision quest have some quality of making the individual "worthy" or otherwise receptive to supernatural contact. The Cherokee and other of the civilized tribes of the Southeast made use of the "black drink," an emetic, as a necessary cleansing and purification on important occasions, with the same consistency that the Plains peoples sought supernatural assistance through self-mortification and mutilations.

Fasting, sexual abstinence, and sweat baths were all mild forms of physical means of altering the spiritual condition and were very widespread among the Indian peoples. The horse nomads of the Plains went further than most in the means employed. Young men seeking to establish a personal spirit relation went beyond fasting to such methods as courting physical exhaustion by endless running or sunstroke by exposing the body without water or shelter. The famous "Sun Dance" and the lesser-known but related "Okipa" ceremony of the Mandan both emphasized dancing to exhaustion and self-mutilation by ripping free skewers pierced through the skin. All induced shock and fainting as a desirable condition in which the mind was open to spiritual contact through vision and dream.

An amazing variety of drugs were in use to alter the mental condition in a similar way. Given the mystique of drug use, it is perhaps

Hamatsa—an initiate of the Kwakiutl Cannibal Society emerging from the wood. He is possessed by the spirit that the dancers attempt to portray in a simulated cannibalistic frenzy. (Edward Curtis)

necessary to note that, with a few exceptions such as tobacco, the exploitation of drugs by American Indians was not recreational but religious in character. The taking of peyote buttons by the modern Native American Church as a sacrament most frequently involves vomiting and illness, and it is often said that the peyote road is hard. Extremely mild in its narcotic effect and rigidly directed through ritual in a spiritual path, the peyote ceremony can scarcely be thought of as "getting it on," as many of its opponents have suggested. Most Indian drug use involved specific religious purpose and frequently pain and danger.

Weston La Barre, a leading student of peyotism, has noted the remarkable fact that the New World peoples "knew some forty local species of hallucinogens; whereas all the inhabitants of the rest of the world had scarcely half a dozen."[5] Alcoholic beverages were relatively rare and largely limited to the Southwest, a reflection of connections with Mesoamerica, but drugs like peyote included *Datura stramonium* (jimsonweed), mescal, *teonanacatl, Amanita,* and many others about which La Barre observes, "In all instances, the principle was the same; the mind-moving effect of the plant was proof enough to them that it contained supernatural 'mana' or power."[6] While the writings of Carlos Casteneda have little or nothing to do with the lifeways and religion of the ethnographically and historically known Yaqui of Sonora, the themes of "power" may in some sense be considered useful reflections and generalizations on less specifically tribally designated shamanistic practices in the Chichimec area as a whole.[7]

In general, the taking of drugs and the mortification of the body are involved with the attempt by an individual to establish a personal relation with a spirit, though there are exceptions such as the group character of the modern peyote cult. There are instances, such as the pattern of the Ghost Dance, of dancing and chanting monotonously and endlessly as a group until many of the persons fall into trances and share the same structured vision. Both the Ghost Dance and the Peyote cult, while undoubtedly rooted in pre-Columbian tradition, are modern and show many signs of Anglo influence. They arose in circumstances of great stress, so it may not be possible to view them as reflecting a common pattern.

Take Two Chants

The world of magical/religious practice is far too wide and varied to completely treat of any aspect of it in this short introduction. Just as the spirits are many and various, the focus or purpose of the supernatural life of the individual peoples is highly variable. Agricultural peoples seek to influence the rains and the fertility of their crops. Hunters seek to increase the abundance of their game and improve their hunting luck. Priests in sophisticated traditions labor to maintain the existence of the sun and the universe itself against the threat of darkness.

One theme that can be discussed to sample the variety is that of curing, or medical magic, because it is a virtually universal interest in the simplest and the most complex cultures. If magic and religion seem most often to concern themselves with the control of the uncontrollable or the explanation of the inexplicable, it is not surprising to find human illness so common a focus. There are peoples in the world who refuse to accept any death as "natural," and the American Indian interpreted illness very often as the result of offense to the supernaturals or in other "unnatural" terms. The Indian might not understand the "true" cause of illness (bacteria, vitamin deficiency, and so on), but by attributing it to the influence of the supernatural, he created at least the illustion of being able to cope with it rather than accepting it as inevitable and inescapable. For those too quick to scoff, it is well to remember that the great plague in Europe was widely regarded as a punishment for sin, and that the placebo is still a powerful tool in modern materia medica. The belief that one is going to be cured is a long step toward an actual cure regardless of the ailment, and the Indian curer combined the ability to create this feeling with a wide range of practical medical knowledge of a nonmystical character. None set out to splint a broken bone magically.

Obviously when an ailment whose cause has none of the evident quality of the broken bone strikes, the first problem is diagnosis, particularly when cure is closely linked to cause. Some, like the Navaho, had specialized skilled diagnosticians, such as the "hand trembler," who, because of his special gift, could move his shaking hand over the patient's body and locate the source of ailment and indicate its probable cause. In other cultures some other method might be used, such as an actual physical examination to determine whether some foreign material was lodged in the patient's body, placed there by witchcraft perhaps and surely the cause of the illness, while others, such as the Iroquois, might find a diagnosis in a dream.

The cause of the illness most frequently was thought to lie in some violation of the necessary rules of life, just as our modern physicians constantly assure us that any nonspecific malady lies in being overweight, in smoking, eating, working, or the like. Ghost sickness is very common and is any illness brought on by contact with the dead or through angering the ghosts. Navaho warriors could be contaminated by the ghosts of slain enemies and required a specific ritual to rid them of this risk; otherwise, they could become very ill. Also among the Navaho, inquiry would reveal that at some point the person who was sick had had incestuous thoughts about his sisters or clan sisters, and thus brought "butterfly" sickness upon himself. Perhaps he had been careless in disposing of his bodily wastes or hair trimmings, and some witch whom he had offended was using these to create the illness. Cherokees as well as Navaho and others felt that a hunter could, through improper action, offend the spirits of the animals he pursued and so fall victim to "bear sickness' or other diseases specific to the animals concerned. Food taboos or contact with menstruating women or a thousand other violations of the imperatives of an orderly existence could lie behind disease.

A Navaho masked dancer, an important participant in Navaho curative "sings," where the "Holy People" were represented. (Edward Curtis)

Once the cause was known, some hope of cure existed if the supernatural forces could be coerced or manipulated into compliance. A witch's curse could be turned against the witch if its identity could be discovered. The spirit of the bear could be placated by prayer and sacrifice. Ghost sickness could be removed by a "sing." Foreign substances lodged in the body could be sucked out by the skill of the shaman. Iroquois who had dreamt of an appropriate image could be cured by the performance of the dancers of the "False Face" society. Ritual performances and shamanistic healing sessions would, of course, be supplemented where necessary with dietary restrictions, herbal medicines, sweat baths, and other continuing therapy. It should not really be so surprising that the patients had a great deal of faith in these curing practices, which to us are obviously without value. The magical medical practitioners had a relatively good rate of cure, and where the rituals and medicines failed there were acceptable explanations. Most common diseases are ultimately self-curing; they run their course and if the patient does not die they disappear of their own accord. So long as what the shaman does is not actually harmful, he will seem to have been responsible for these "cures." If the patient *does* die, inquiry into the situation can usually establish that it was not the fault of the curer since the patient will be found to have failed to observe the dietary restrictions, or some close relative was guilty of incestuous thoughts during the ceremonies, or there was some other violation of necessary conditions for which the curer could hardly be blamed.

"Emics" and "Emetics"[8]

A distinction important in much anthropological work should be noted here between the purpose a social action seems to serve from the analytical point of view of the outside observer ("etic") and the purpose and meaning it has for the actual participant in the culture ("emic"). Curing practice as ceremonial activity illustrates part of this phenomenon of perspective.

Navaho ceremonials ("sings") almost invariably have a specific "patient," the curing of whose ailments the sing is meant to achieve. Sings are, however, very elaborate affairs taking anywhere from one or two nights to five nights, and the process may ideally be repeated four times. Many of the patient's kinsmen are involved, not only by attending the event but also by helping to pay for such obviously expensive treatment. Particularly for those sings that have a public aspect, a *yeibichai* dance or the like, many nonrelatives will also attend. The chanting and the dry paintings (sand paintings) of the ceremonies, dedicated as they are to the curing of a specific patient, are also a recitation and reaffirmation of the myths, of origin and otherwise, of the Navaho people. In all of this there is a confusingly wide range of motivation and intention beyond the medicinal.

If one were to have asked a Navaho about the meaning and purpose of a specific sing, the first answer would likely have stressed the illness of the particular person for whom the ceremony was being given. Further inquiry might elicit the fact that while given for individuals, it is also true that ceremonies must be given with some frequency to maintain the harmonious balance necessary between the Navaho and the world. The more ceremonies that are given, the better the balance of things between people and their universe, though it would not likely be phrased in such terms. All of these are "emic" perceptions of those actually involved.

The outsider—for example, Clyde or Dorothea Kluckhohn, the famous anthropological students of the Navaho—might also observe that men of wealth find themselves under pressure to sponsor ceremonies (lest they be accused of being "stingy") regardless of any actual illness in their families. Such an outsider would observe that such a procedure, given the costly nature of the event, serves to level differences in wealth and ensure equal distribution of resources. A sophisticated and thoughtful Navaho and the hypothetical outsider might both come to observe that the ceremonies provide an opportunity for the young to understand something of the origins of their heritage through the mythology represented in the chants, and so serve the purpose of enculturation. Widely scattered kinsmen come together on these occasions and youth of marriageable age can meet potential partners outside their own exogamous clans in the "squaw dances" or at the edges of the firelit gatherings.

The Mandan annually hold the Okipa ceremonies specifically as a kind of "rite of passage" to adulthood for young men, but even older men may vow to undergo the torments of the rite. The ceremony is a reenactment of the origins of the Mandan and contains a supernatural explanation of the identity of the Mandan as a people and a justification of the rules that govern life. This myth and the myths of other groups, along with the public ceremonials which recite them, serve in the "etic" perspective to increase the solidarity of the people by reinforcing the belief systems which make customary behavior meaningful. Men need to be occasionally reminded that "proper" behavior has the sanction of the gods.

The Iroquois place a great deal of emphasis on dreams for avowedly religious/magical reasons. Great effort is lavished on fulfilling the implications of a dream once its meaning has been properly interpreted. Anthony Wallace, who has studied the matter, points out that in fact the Iroquois approach is essentially psychoanalytical, although couched in language such as "wishes of the soul."[9] The Iroquois believed, as do the Freudians, that failure to fulfill these wishes of the soul expressed in dreams would lead to calamity. There are other peoples who have similar views, but in some sense all of the myths and ceremonies have some such element of fulfilling individual psychological needs at the same time that they fill social needs. The widespread Ghost Dance offered each individual dancer a chance to escape at least momentarily into a vision of heaven at the same time that it held out the promise of making that vision a reality for the society as a whole.

Shamans and Sun Kings

We do not ordinarily think of ideological systems as "evolving" in the simple-to-complex progression we associate with technology. We have long since abandoned the simplistic unilineal evolutionary scheme posited by the earliest students of the Indian, which tended to accept any form of monotheism (for obvious ethnocentric reasons) as proof of sophistication and advancement. Still, it is true that the ideological needs and supporting structures of simpler societies are not the same as those of more complex cultures, and the loosely organized shamanistic practices of the band peoples are very different from the priestly hierarchies necessary to properly worship a divine king. If ideological patterns are to be considered, as some suggest, as the social oil that smooths the functioning of social systems, then different kinds of societies have differing requirements for lubrication.

The Shoshone, who previously have been examined, have as little structured complexity in their ideological dealings as in anything else. As there are no chiefs, there are no priests; and as there are no clans, there are no medicine societies. Each man seeks to establish his own special and personal relations with the supernatural. Some who have special gifts are sought out as curers of disease just as some who may be possessed of special ability to charm the antelope will be sought to conduct the antelope drives as shaman. No one holds such a position full time, and it carries with it no special social rewards or power beyond the fact that a shaman may be feared for the possession of witch powers. There is neither a need for complex systems nor the means to support them.

Tribesmen like the Navaho or the Mandan require more sophisticated arrangements to coordinate their ideological affairs. Although still with a strongly individualistic bias, as in the vision quest, the size of the group and its multiunit structure necessitate a more reliable and enduring organization of belief. Not all members of the tribe are related to one another in a simple family system, and the casual learning of belief and behavior that serves in that context is inadequate at this level of things. More complex purposes must be served by ideology as in the need to reinforce the solidarity and common identity of persons who have no clearly visible family bonds to tie them to one another. Men have to be motivated to cooperate with persons they may never have seen before and to undertake activities which may have no immediate, directly perceivable benefit to themselves.

Tribesmen have no full-time religious specialists (priests) any more than they have full-time administrators (chiefs), but the complexity of religious practice may have already begun to create men of special training and learning—shaman, generally—but there are other possibilities, such as the Navaho singers. An excellent picture of the tribal shaman in the form of a modern Comanche "medicine woman" is provided by a short and readable book by David Jones, *Sanapia.*[10] Sanapia, an "eagle doctor" who cures through the ability to tap the supernatural power of the eagle, can do so only by virtue of her careful training and observance of ritual taboos and procedures. In such part-time specialization of magical practitioners lie the seeds of true priesthood.

The Navaho singer is more nearly a full-time religious specialist, at least in modern times, than is typical of our picture of tribal peoples. Most Navaho men had some degree of ceremonial knowledge, at least to the point of being able to assist in the preparations, and the Kluckhohns have estimated that perhaps 20 percent of the older adult men could perform simple chants. They point out, however, that "The singer who knows one nine-night chant must learn at least as much as a man who sets out to memorize the whole of a Wagnerian opera: orchestral score, every vocal part, all the details of the settings, stage business, and each requirement of costume."[11] All the details of the ceremonies must be learned precisely and correctly without variation from the wording of the chants to the exact figures to be laid out in the sand paintings. This can only be done by apprenticing for a lengthy period to an older singer who is served and who is paid for his teaching. Some men know several of the longer ceremonies, and since, to be efficacious, the ceremony involves a fee paid to the singer, a popular singer can make most or all of his livelihood in this role.

In general the specialist in religious affairs at the tribal level is a healer of some sort rather than the official representative of a god. He is more of a doctor with special supernatural backing than a minister of a faith, and his influence is limited to a clientele of individual patients. More complex and community-focused ceremonial affairs are likely to be in the hands of some "medicine society" or other form of voluntary association, and the officers of these organizations may begin to resemble priests in their permanency.

The Pueblo peoples of the Southwest have perhaps the most dazzling array of ceremonial societies, particularly those of the western Pueblos which focus on the "Katchina" cults. The Iroquois "False Faces" are similarly organized as a curing society on the principle of voluntary association, and even the rank-conscious chiefdoms of the Northwest Coast have ceremonial societies, although the principle of social position and kinship intrudes in these organizations.

Although tribal peoples in general make use of secret societies, the Pueblos have so intertwined them with their religious, social, political, and economic life that even today their role is crucial. There are great problems in dealing more deeply than has been done here with matters of Pueblo religion which date from the time of Spanish attempts to stamp out "pagan" practices and which were reinforced by misguided attempts by the Bureau of Indian Affairs in early days to similarly suppress non-Christian activity. The Pueblos generally became participants in Spanish-Mexican Catholicism and oriented their political structure in accord with Spanish expectations. At the same time they continued their ceremonial life in secret, in the underground kivas, for example, and guarded it from intrusion by the severe penalties imposed on their own members. Even in very recent times this secrecy has prevented all but a very few studies being done, as the Pueblos continue to protect the integrity of their institutions from at least the memory of past persecutions.

The governing bodies of the Pueblos, superficially of Spanish character, with judges and chiefs and war captains, are indicative of the curious "compartmentalized" system worked out by the Pueblos, with the heads of the traditional secret societies generally responsible also for filling the offices in the "non-Pueblo" sector, although this dual leadership is itself covert. In the past no part of Pueblo life was entirely free of the influence of the societies.

The Pueblo of Sia, one of the Keresan-speaking peoples, according to Leslie White, had ten major societies with two more of only semiautonomous character.[12] The Zuni had six such basic societies, while the number varies rather widely among the other Pueblos. In many tribal societies virtually everyone belongs to some form of sodality, but for most Pueblo groups the active membership in any particular society always seems to have been small. The actual members of the society act essentially as organizers for ceremonial activities in which most or all of the members of a village participate to greater or lesser degree and in this light resemble priests to some extent. Most of the societies have some curing function in addition to their special purposes, which may be hunting, warfare, weather control, or the like. For all of these purposes the members have charge of a body of special knowledge, including dances, myths, songs, and a set of varied paraphernalia such as that for the Katchina societies, which includes the masks with which the supernatural Katchinas are impersonated.

The societies function not for the benefit of a particular family or lineage but for the good of the community as a whole. The members of the group imitate the Katchinas or dance the snake dances to bring rain or health for all of the people—in contrast to the client-centered practices of the shaman—though individuals can be treated and cured by the members of some societies. Membership is acquired in a number of ways, most usually by means of a vow, as in the Mexican Catholic notion of a *manda*. If an illness threatens or if in some other way the assistance of the supernaturals is required, an individual will promise to join and serve in a particular society if the desired end is granted. Similarly, parents may "pledge" a child's membership for the same reasons. Since much of the Pueblo ceremonialism is strictly secret, persons trespassing

A Plains platform burial, one of many American Indian ritual means of dealing with the dead. (Edward Curtis)

within defined bounds around the areas where the society is engaged in its ritual are forced to join the group if caught. For some of the medicine societies, anyone cured of a disease by the society must join that society.

For the Mandan and some other peoples, there may be a linkage between communitywide ceremonialism and clan organization that to some extent resembles the operation of the voluntary associations. For the Mandan, each important ceremonial has associated with it a "medicine bundle," which contains a variety of objects of sacred significance and without which the ceremony cannot be given. The great Okipa ceremony mentioned above has an associated bundle, and this, like all the others, "belongs" to a particular matrigroup, even though the ceremony is performed for pantribal benefits. Both in this instance and in the "ownership" by particular Pueblo societies of ceremonies, one can see a social mechanism that serves to guarantee the preservation and transmission of complex ritual through formal structure, replacing a diffuse and casual passing-on of knowledge.

Both Mandan and some Pueblos, including Sia, not only mix clan and sodality mechanisms in the organization of religious affairs but add the element of dual or moiety structure. In the case of the Mandan, the group is divided into halves, each of which has certain ceremonial and political privilege and responsibility on the basis of clan membership. At Sia there are two "kiva groups," the Wren and the Turquoise, membership in which is determined by geographical location in the pueblo, and which can be altered if one moves from one sector of the pueblo to another. A Mandan obviously cannot change his moiety membership since it depends on clan membership.

When, as in the Pueblo sodalities, there are offices within the group which have attached to them authority and privilege, a long step has been taken away from the totally equalitarian pattern most typical of band and tribal society. When these sorts of offices begin to involve full-time specialization, which is necessarily supported by the labor of others, a new era of "organized" religion has been entered. Like the "state" level of social organization with which such formality of belief is associated, these "religions" are rare in the Chichimeca.

The discussion of this level of ideological complexity of organization leads into the next chapter where the very few manifestations in the Chichimeca of truly complex social systems at the chiefdom and state levels will be considered. The Natchez of the Mississippi Valley were ruled by a divine "king," the Great Sun, a descendant of the sun itself, and its representative here on earth. Eternal flames were tended by this king and his priestly hierarchy atop great earthen temple mounds, following a tradition many centuries old in the Mississippi Valley. In life, the word of the Great Sun is law, and on his death many of his followers are strangled and follow him into the beyond. Such a centralized cult is a reflection of the character of the state in which it exists and whose purposes it serves. The Natchez, as will be seen, are the last of a long line of "Mound Builder" traditions, which represent the highest level of sophistication achieved by Chichimec peoples.

Some Readings

Kluckhohn, Clyde: *Navaho Witchcraft*, Boston: Beacon Press, 1944. An excellent classic study.

La Barre, Weston: *The Peyote Cult*, New York: Schocken Books, 1969. Classic study which in this edition includes a very useful preface and reprints of recent review articles by La Barre.

La Barre, Weston: "Materials for a History of Studies of Crisis Cults: A Bibliographic Essay," *Human Organization* **12**:3–44, 1971. A comprehensive review of sources pertinent to the rise of social movements, a subject touched on more fully as an acculturation phenomenon in Chapter 10, but many of the Indian movements pertain to the themes of this chapter.

Lessa, William A., and Evon Z. Vogt (eds.): *Reader in Comparative Religion: An Anthropological Approach*, New York: Harper and Rowe, 1965. Wide ranging collection with numerous articles dealing with Indian religion including treatments of the vision quest, shamanism, and totemism.

Underhill, Ruth: *Red Man's Religion*, Chicago: University of Chicago Press, 1965. Like Underhill's more general work, a very readable if somewhat romantic overall survey.

VI

LORDS OF THE CHICHIMECA

Oh you do not come twice on to the earth,
Chichimec Lords!
Let us be happy. Does one take flowers along to the
Land of the dead?

Aztec poem[1]

The great potential of agriculture as the source of economic surplus which could be harnessed to support more complex social orders was briefly considered earlier. In Mesoamerica the culture we call the Olmec appeared on the Gulf coast around 1000 B.C. out of the simple, equalitarian villages of the formative agricultural period. The Olmec, at their great site of La Venta (in the state of Tabasco), built huge pyramids, erected great stone colonnades and altars, hauled huge blocks of stone many kilometers, and carved them into portrait heads of their gods or perhaps their rulers. Something had occurred so that some men were in position to dispose of the surplus productivity and direct the labor of others, putting it to uses of no immediate direct benefit to any individual but only for the glory of the gods. A social order had arisen that gave some persons great power over others, reflected in the glorious costumes the stone carvings show us on some personages and in the great tombs that house a few noble dead—while most were buried simply. Other peoples all over Mesoamerica were influenced to greater or lesser extent by the Olmec styles and rich art. Many have suggested that the Olmec probably represented a "cult" or great religion unifying diverse peoples in its service and spreading the good news widely and beginning similar traditions everywhere.

In this chapter the extent to which similar phenomena have occurred in the Chichimec area to produce sophisticated and far-flung traditions and other forms of complex social organization beyond that of the equalitarian tribes and bands will be considered. Basically our interest is in chiefdoms and states, what Morton Fried in his *Evolution of Political Society* called "rank societies" and "stratified societies."[2] Such levels of organization are by no means "typical" of the Chichimeca, but the extent to which they existed gives us some shadowy idea of what a purely Chichimec advanced society might have come to be. Like the Aztec whose level of sophistication surpassed all others, the "lords" of the Chichimeca were swept aside by the white man's conquest, before their promise could be fulfilled.

A few brief definitions would be useful at this point, though the issues will be illustrated more thoroughly as the examination of complex Chichimec cultures proceeds. Specifically, a clarification should be made of the ways in which the words "power," "rank," "stratification," and "state" are used. I shall largely follow Fried. Power can be best defined by distinguishing it from authority, as Fried does when he says, "Authority is taken here to refer to the ability to channel the behavior of others in the absence of the threat or use of sanctions. Power is the ability to channel the behavior of others through the threat or use of sanctions."[3] In the simple, equalitarian societies of tribe and band, a leader may possess authority in the sense that his suggestions are likely to be followed, but he does not possess power in that there is nothing he can do if his suggestions are not followed. He may lead but he does not command. In the nonequalitarian societies someone to greater or lesser degree possesses the ability to command and to enforce adherence to the commands. How this power is obtained and distributed will be considered in appropriate context.

"A rank society is one in which positions of valued status are

A Kwakiutl house and "totem" pole, both of which portray the wealth and importance of a "chief." (Edward Curtis)

somehow limited so that not all those of sufficient talent to occupy such statuses actually achieve them."[4] Anyone can be a hunter who has the skill, but not everyone who is capable of handling the job can be the chief or lord of the revels. There may be a hundred candidates for a single office. In this society, some are now more equal than others, but both Fried and Elman Service insist that differences in rank are not necessarily equated with differences in wealth in the sense of actual economic imbalance. This point is emphasized in Fried's definition of a stratified society as "one in which members of the same sex and equivalent age status do not have equal access to the basic resources that sustain life"[5]—in other words, a class society with unequal control, in the Marxian sense, of the means of production. This may necessarily imply the existence of the territorial state to maintain the order of stratification. The nature of state and chiefdom will be made clearer, but one thing should be obvious: whatever the nature of these organizational forms, they are not equalitarian, and human productivity is being channeled for ends other than simple survival.

Tombs and Temples

In terms of the massiveness of construction and the level of labor lavished on monumental architecture, some of the early archaeologically known cultures seem to have reached heights not maintained by their historically known descendants. Scattered widely through many of the eastern states and along the great Ohio River and Mississippi River drainages are the works of the Mound Builders. Elaborate burial mounds are typical, but they include in the Mississippian area huge, flat-topped, pyramidal "temple mounds." At Cahokia, Illinois, across the river from St. Louis, in the rich river-bottom lands, is a complex of over eighty mounds which includes the largest of all—Monks Mound—which is over 30 meters high and approximately 200 by 300 meters around the base. This immense structure involved incredible labor since it was built of countless "basket-loads" of earth hand dug and transported to the temple construction site. Whatever else such colossuses may represent, they reflect some form of centralized social organization that could mobilize, feed, and control large numbers of peoples scattered over large areas, and maintain this control over long periods of time. These are not bands.

Adena and Hopewell are very early traditions (approximately 800 B.C. to A.D. 600) which appear to indicate the existence of some such complex organization, if the evidence of monumental architecture alone is conclusive. The most remarkable feature of these cultures is that they may well have reached heights of sophistication of this order without agriculture to support them, but instead with a highly efficient hunting and gathering economy as described for the Woodlands Archaic, the cultural period with which these peoples of the Ohio-Kentucky area are associated.

As with the other peoples who are known only through archaeological remains, we must paint with a broad brush, but some things are clear even on this scale. Studies done of the remarkable stone heads of Easter Island and the process of their manufacture have demonstrated that relatively small groups of people can erect monumental structures if they are willing to devote disproportionate amounts of effort over long periods of time to the task. Sweat is required, but the number doing the sweating is variable. In general, in the Adena-Hopewell period, we find that the effort is spread among great numbers and, therefore, reflects large centralized social organizations. The size of the burial mounds persuades us of such large social units.

The fact that they are indeed mortuary structures (tombs) is revealing, regardless of estimates of the labor required for their construction. They are generally conical mounds of earth, though sometimes they are arranged as animal "effigies" in some related cultures. The structures cover in some cases the log tomb of only a single individual, while in others they have been used as a final resting place for many. We are dealing here with what archaeologists refer to as status burials. The effort devoted to the interment of some personages is immensely greater than that awarded to the common man. Here and in Egypt (pyramidal tombs), Scandinavia (ship burials) and other places, the fact that some are more equal than others is dramatized by their graves.

We actually know very little of the nature of these peoples except what we have recovered from the burials. To the extent that they have been investigated at all, the village sites reveal small, scattered hamlets whose remains have told us little and do not seem impressive. The "grave goods," however, reflect a complex and sophisticated artistic tradition. Individuals buried in Adena and Hopewell mounds were accompanied by artistic treasures on a lavish scale, reflecting the importance of a "death cult" in the lives of these peoples. Finely worked stone pipes, incised and painted pottery, pottery figurines, ornaments of sheet copper and mica, even fragments of textiles have been recovered from Hopewell sites. Materials used were imported (presumably through trade) from as far away as Florida and the Black Hills.

Hopewell, which overlaps Adena but is more widespread, includes in its pattern more elaborate "earthworks" as well as more elaborate offerings associated with the tombs. Adena sites frequently have circular ramparts or enclosures, but the Hopewell sites have elaborate embankments, palisades, and other earthern structures. Some have suggested that these were defensive works, but it seems more likely that they were ceremonial in nature. The "moats" (where earth was taken to build the walls) are inside the structures not outside, scarcely defensive logic. The elaborate complexes of Hopewell sites probably represent, as did their counterparts in Mesoamerica, "vacant towns" uninhabited except during important ceremonial occasions when many would gather from the surrounding countryside to bury their important dead, honor the sacred beings, and build or enlarge their great mounds.

The spread of these elaborate practices so widely by the Adena-Hopewell may have many explanations. Some have postulated influences or actual migrations of peoples into the area from Mesoamerica. Some

A serpent "effigy" mound in southern Ohio. Such earthworks are obvious indicators of massive investments of time and labor. (Courtesy Ohio Historical Society)

have seen the cultures as a wave of conquering invaders. There is no clear answer, but the explanation most often heard is the rise and spread of a cult, a religious movement, as is generally accepted to be the case with the Mesoamerican Olmec. Whatever the impetus, the Hopewell in all its richness soon flickered out and the mounds ceased to be erected. In the Mississippi Valley a cultural tradition had already begun to rise which continued into the historic period to confound the eye of French explorers.

Stinkards

Concentrated in the Mississippi River Valley itself, the "Mississippian" culture is manifest throughout what is now the southeastern United States. Its influences and sites run from Louisiana to Wisconsin and from Texas to Florida. The time range is from approximately A.D. 600, for earliest evidences, to the historic Natchez who represented a much diminished form of the Mississippian culture in 1700. There is little doubt that these cultures represent some degree of Mesoamerican influence, but the extent is much debated. The Olmec of Mesoamerica had long since been superseded by more sophisticated civilizations, and the Mississippian period began at approximately the end of the Classic, when the mighty empire of Teotihuacan fell, to be followed by a series of militarist cultures culminating in the rise of the Aztec empire in the 1400s.

The Hohokam culture of southern Arizona shows signs of Mesoamerican contact as early as 100 B.C. and, perhaps not entirely coincidentally, from A.D. 500 to 900, a period generally called the Colonial, these influences were very strong. In addition to domesticates and resemblances in artistic themes, the Hohokam constructed flat-topped pyramid mounds and even (at a site called Snaketown) a ceremonial ball court which was undeniably Mesoamerican in conception. Some students of these times, such as Charles Di Peso, have produced persuasive evidence for the existence of what amounts to trading outposts of Mesoamerican cultures in adjacent, northernmost Mexico which are doubtless responsible for such influences.[6]

For the Mississippian peoples we have less clear evidence for contact of such intensity. The area of southern Texas and northeast Mexico seems never to have supported pre-Columbian agricultural manifestations of any sophistication and represents a gap between the Mississippians and the northernmost outposts of the Mesoamericans, which appear to have extended no further than the Huasteca of southern Tamulipas. There is no doubt that contacts did occur, by land or by sea, possibly at some points along the Gulf itself. The difficulty of the intervening terrain probably made these sporadic and limited. While some have thought that it is possible that actual Mesoamerican populations migrated into the Hohokam area, there are few who believe that the Mississippians represent any such intrusive migrants.

The maize-cultivation complex is, of course, conclusive evidence of contact; but the Mississippian peoples show an entirely new range of ceramic styles in contrast to the preceding Woodland styles of the area (though the two blend in places), with many artistic themes and techniques that are strongly Mesoamerican. Most dramatic and obvious is the huge, earthen, flat-topped temple mound, undeniably Mesoamerican, which becomes a central defining feature of the Mississippian peoples. The arrangement of these and other structures around a central plaza is still another evidence of influence. Whether they were missionaries of some cult, traders, or simply wanderers and explorers, some persons from Mesoamerica had some degree of contact sufficient to produce these transformations. It is perhaps useful to think again of the concept of stimulus diffusion, that is, the concept that an idea can be transmitted sometimes with only very minimal actual movements of persons from one area to another. The "cult" argument is strong because of the widespread, uniform, and distinctive artistic themes associated

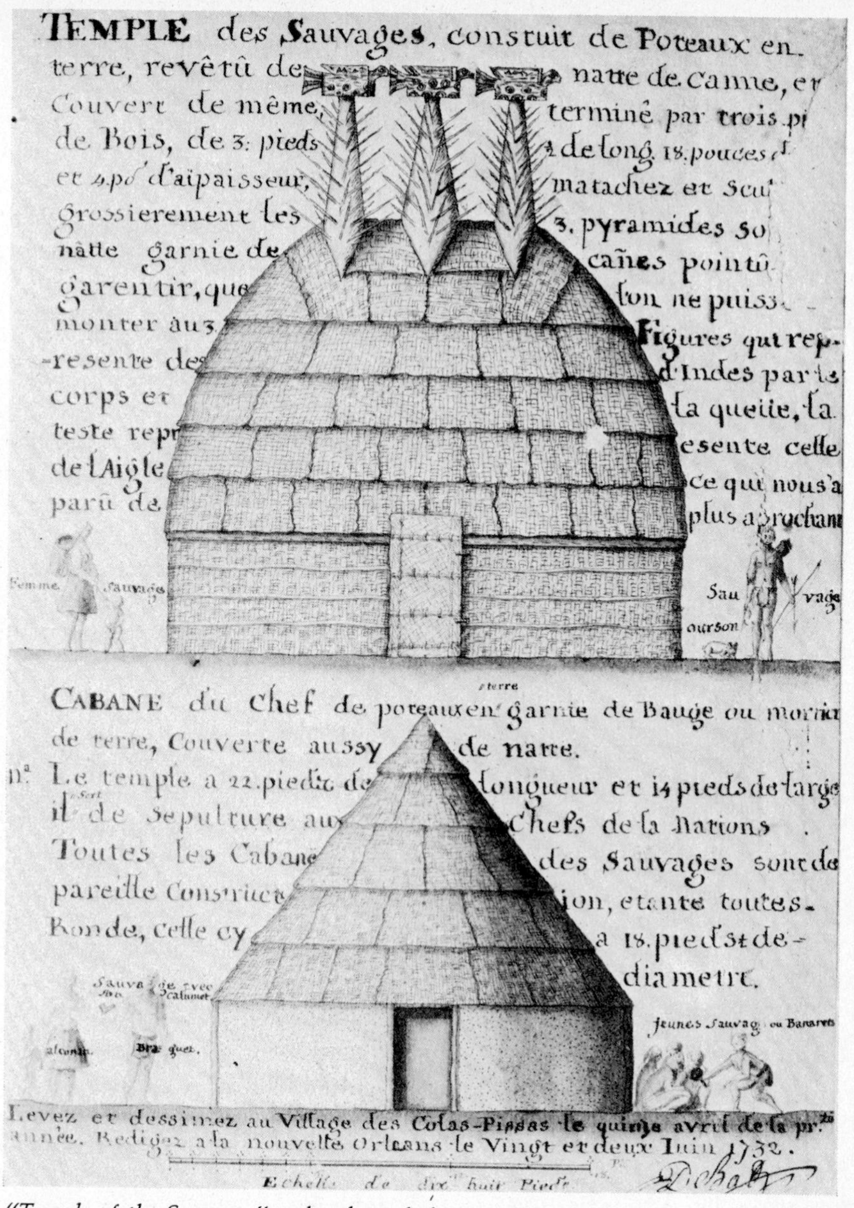

"Temple of the Savages," a sketch made by an obscure Frenchman, A. DeBatz, in 1732 of a Mississippian temple structure. (Courtesy National Anthropological Archives, Smithsonian Institution)

with what has often been called the "southern cult," which is representative of much of the work of the Mississippian peoples.

There is some evidence to suggest that the great ceremonial mound groups, such as that at Cahokia, may still have been in active use when first European contacts were made. The only peoples, however, for which we have any documentary evidence to help our imaginings are the Natchez, who were contacted and ultimately destroyed by the French. The Natchez, who when first clearly seen numbered something like 3500 persons in nine villages, appear to have been a remnant of far larger and more powerful organizations. The area where earlier village remains can be found at Cahokia stretches for all of six miles. The Natchez ceased to exist, except as dispersed refugees among their Cherokee and Creek neighbors, by 1731; and while no good evidence currently exists, it is possible that other Mississippian peoples fell earlier, not as the Natchez, in the face of European arms, but from the effects of disease that spread far ahead of the advance of European settlement.

An aspect of the situation that persuades us that the Mississippians might once have been more numerous and sophisticated than their historical remnants is the "unnecessary" complexity of their social order. The Natchez had a "class" society with a divine hereditary ruler, the "Great Sun," his relatives themselves forming a noble class of "Suns," and then, in descending order of rank, "Nobles," "Honoreds," and the common people who were referred to by the noble as "Stinkards." The Natchez were a matrilineal people, so the "Great Sun" inherited his rank through his mother, who was called "White Woman." The rules of class membership are clouded at this distance with confusing features requiring a decline of rank each generation for men such that sons of Suns become Nobles, sons of Nobles become Honoreds, and so on. The implications have been much debated, since there are apparent impossibilities in the systems as variously reported. Whatever the case, the Great Sun and others of his Nobles of high office clearly possessed the power of command up to the point of ordering the immediate execution of those who displeased them. The other ranked "classes" had associated with them rights and privileges, which, while generally only sumptuary (rights to dress and decoration), appear also to have involved some degree of real political and economic power. Even in attenuated form, these are characteristics of a state.

The sacred fires burning atop the temple mounds, while ultimately the responsibility of the divine Great Sun himself, were served by a hereditary order of priests who governed all ceremonial matters. The "Great War Chief," along with lesser secular Nobles, had responsibility for practical matters, including war and the hunt. The problem that emerges when examining the elaborate rituals and organization of officials within the already complex class system is why there was so much organization for so few people. This is, indeed, a case of too many chiefs and too few Indians, if we are to accept at face value the French reports. It must be remembered that the Natchez, from the moment of French contact, were in decline, so the picture is confused and in many cases contradictory. A level of social complexity of this kind would be appropriate and necessary for a society of many thousands of persons spread over wide territories, and the archaeological record gives us some reason to believe that at their height the Mississippians were such a people. The Natchez "Great Sun" may have borne the same relation to previous "Great Suns" as the medieval Byzantine "Emperors of the Romans" (who controlled only their own city of Constantinople) did to their predecessors, who had borne the same title but who had reigned over the known world.[7]

Beloved Men

The Natchez and their Mississippian ancestors are only dimly seen, but in the East (east of the Mississippi River) there were peoples who survived into the historical period long enough to be clearly described and whose complexity was of a high order. These include the cultures that will later be referred to as the civilized tribes: Creek, Cherokee, Choctaw, of the Southeast, and also the Iroquois of the Northeast. The Iroquois and Cherokee, who figure importantly in the historical chapters, will be treated at greater length there. Here there will be a more general description of southeastern sophisticated traditions. This sequence is followed because the town-dwelling farmers of the Southeast appear to be the direct heirs of the monument-building peoples, although in historical times their energies were not directed toward such constructions. Most are of the language group called Muskogean, though the Cherokee speak a language classified with that of the Iroquois.

The Cherokee and the Iroquois, because of their confrontations with the Europeans, created undeniable state forms of social organization. Aboriginally, however, the organization of most of the civilized tribes seems to have been a curious amalgam of tribal characteristics and the beginnings of a territorial state expressed in very loose and shifting confederacies. Even with historical documents to guide us, much eludes us because the observers simply did not understand what they saw or recorded only what was of interest to themselves. For example, while there is no doubt that the Creek were a group possessing matrilineal clans, there seem to be contradictions as to whether a mico (a hereditary office) was inherited by the nephews, as would occur if the position were hereditary in a matriclan, or by the sons, which is not possible matrilineally since a son obviously is not a member of the same matriclan as his father. Either mistakes were made in observation or the positions were not consistently hereditary in a single matriline. All we can do in this, as in other cases of confusion, is to weigh what is likely to have prevailed on the basis of the preponderance of evidence. Most evidence indicates that some positions were, indeed, hereditary in particular clans, and they passed through the line of females and not from father to son. Certainly this will be seen to be the case with the Iroquois. Not infrequently a position was hereditary in a particular matriline, but the specific office-holder was selected by the group as a whole, which again was also found among the Iroquois.

The Creek basic unit of social life was the *talwa* or township. In historical times there were between fifty and sixty towns making up the Creek confederacy. These were divided usually into "Upper" and "Lower" Creek towns. Pushing the dual division principle still further, the towns were divided into either "Red" or "White" towns, also called respectively "Peace" and "War" towns. Estimates vary, but all of the tribes which made up the confederacy and were called Creeks by the Europeans numbered in the vicinity of 20,000. While this unit could never actually act together, it possessed some degree of structure which forced Europeans to make it a factor in their plans and calculations.

The *talwa* was a scattering of individual house compounds concentrated around a central plaza bordered by public council buildings—a Mesoamerican and Mississippian pattern. Households usually comprised several "cabins" around a courtyard and were the property of the matrilineage of the women who lived in them. The central plaza was the heart of public life, and councils, ceremonies, and "chunkey" games (games where poles were cast at a rolling stone disk by two players while onlookers wagered) were held there. The *talwa* was the largest social body that consistently acted together as a cohesive unit, and its adherence to the actions of the other towns with which it was associated was never guaranteed. Actually, even within the *talwa* unit, clan loyalties could override community loyalties, as when members of an injured clan continued to seek vengeance after the community as a whole had made peace with another group. The Cherokee, when they began to organize their state, made it one of their first concerns to outlaw clan vengeance as disruptive to the interests of the group as a whole. In essence, they sought to guarantee a monopoly of power to the state itself to minimize centrifugal tendencies.

The kinship organization, essentially of a tribal nature, is not the reason for introducing the Creek here. In addition to kinship elements, the Creek had a kind of political organization that mixed hereditary positions with elective positions and positions of charismatic achievement. It was a similar kind of organization that the Cherokee and Iroquois were able to extend into a true state, while the Creek floundered under white pressure before adjustments could be made to make the unwieldy system more responsive and reliable.

The individual town had a "governing" council whose membership was linked with a larger council of the confederacy as a whole. The dual division or moiety principle was again important as clans within the town were associated with Red/White or War/Peace. Although the same clans occurred in many towns, they were not always necessarily of the same moiety in each town. From a particular clan in each town came the mico, who the Europeans tended to view as a king of some sort. James Edward Oglethorpe, the founder of the Georgia colony, however, perceived the limited nature of the power of these "kings" with a clarity worthy of a trained ethnographer, saying:

> Their Kings can do no more than persuade. All the power they have is no more than to call their old men and captains and to propound to them the measures they think proper. After they have done speaking, all the others have liberty to give their opinions also; and they reason together with great temper and modesty, till they have brought each other into some unanimous resolution, then they call in the young men and recommend the putting in execution of the resolution with their strongest and most lively eloquence.[8]

Clearly, from our state-oriented point of view, the mico is more of a master of ceremonies or a chairman of a board where other members of the board have equal voting rights. The "old men and captains" referred to are the other "officers" that make up the governing council. Some of these are of a class called "beloved men," who seem simply to have been older men who had somehow distinguished themselves in war or council and whose advice would be sought and heeded. Others held more formal, even sometimes hereditary, offices, though the mico was the only figure that stood out (large towns sometimes had more than one mico). There was often a war leader, said in some cases to be chosen from a particular clan, but more often the office was apparently held by a man on the basis of his personal achievements and reputation in a formal extension of tribal practice. This "great warrior" had a group of similar men of prowess associated with him who were also part of the class of "captains" referred to by Oglethorpe. Other men, called *henini,* were responsible for ceremonial affairs, including the "black drink," and apparently inherited this duty through membership in particular clans. In all but the looseness of the organization and the limitation on the power of leaders, the Mississippian pattern was evoked.

At the town level, as Oglethorpe suggests, none "commands"; but obviously the organization is more formal and ultimately more centralized than is characteristic of tribes, though less than true states. The mico, and through him the other officers, were spared some of the burdens of life so as to facilitate their service as specialists. The council received a portion of the productivity of the fields and the hunt for the support of "public works." Fines could be levied against those who failed in cooperating in community work, although ultimately any serious offenses were matters to be settled between the clans of the persons offended. Though cumbersome in decision-making, the *talwa* was a cohesive political mechanism aboriginally.

The confederacy of the Creek was represented by periodic councils of micos and other representatives from the various towns whose decisions could not command but whose influence was great. Such councils were more frequently held in the "capitals" within the groupings of Lower or Upper Creek towns, but gatherings were held for common discussion among all Creek towns on an annual basis or more often in times of particular crisis, usually as a result of pressure for treaties by the whites.

These great councils of the Creek were essentially enlarged versions of the procedures followed at the township level. The larger scale of the general council tended to guarantee that arriving at a consensus would be an arduous and frequently impossible process. Each town or group of towns had divergent interests and followed the decisions of the council only to the degree they found convenient. The Creek are often cited as having pursued a "policy of neutrality" in seeking to avoid involvement in the machinations of the French, English, and Spanish colonists pressed against the Creek borders. Though they pursued this goal more successfully than other less-cohesive tribal groups could have done, they nonetheless consistently failed as one town or the other fell away from the overall consensus to seek its own salvation. To pirate Benjamin Franklin's phrase, failing to hang together, they all hung separately as the tide of white settlement swept them away.

Conspicuous Consumers

Completely separated from these Eastern developments with their Mesoamerican flavor were the peoples of the Northwest Coast (Kwakiutl, Tlingit, Haida, and so on), concentrated in the rich coastal rain forests of the modern state of Washington and of the province of British Columbia. Making no use of agriculture and influenced more profoundly by Asia than by Mesoamerica, the coastal chiefdoms, although they are virtually always discussed at length in any treatment of the Indian, are typical of nothing but themselves. They do, however, reflect in a clear, even exaggerated way, the essential features of that kind of society called the "chiefdom," which most scholars presume to be transitional from the equalitarian tribe to the stratified state. The chiefdoms in the other Chichimec cultures differed profoundly from those of the Northwest Coast, but these dramatic peoples help us to understand this order of things through exaggeration, in the same way that the desert Shoshone in their simplicity illustrate band society. The Creek are not clearly tribe, chiefdom, or state, but there are no doubts about the Indians of the Northwest Coast.

The best known of the groups, thanks largely to early ethnographic attention, including the work of Franz Boas, are the Kwakiutl.[9] These people lived on what is now Vancouver Island and on the adjacent strip of mainland coast and numbered in the vicinity of 8000 (by some estimates) prior to white contact. This group, when first officially counted by whites, numbered something less than 3000, a dramatic decline, but one that can be closely associated with recorded outbreaks of introduced diseases after permanent white settlement at Fort Rupert. The population density was as great as that of most of the Southeast, even greater when it is considered that the northwestern villages were confined to narrow land strips hemmed in by the coastal mountain ranges. The communities were in most cases located directly on the beaches, not arranged around plazas as in the Mesoamerican mode, but in a line along a common street or the beach front. Unlike the Creek, this "unit" of 8000 possessed no common structure above the single village, though interrelations were complex.

The coastal peoples were unique in their art, which is spectacular and distinctive, and in their fascination with rank and privilege which, particularly among the Kwakiutl, is central to much else in their lives. The potlatch, a dramatic ceremonial means of distributing property, was an unusual characteristic of the Kwakiutl, as was the fact that the cultural complexity rested on an ecologically balanced maritime adaptation found almost nowhere else. The narrow strip inhabited by these nonagricultural folk yielded a variety of resources with great regularity and remarkable abundance. The great salmon runs are at the heart of this richness, along with those of the oulachon (candlefish).

The climate of this coastal zone is essentially a rain forest with a year-round temperate but very wet climate produced by the warming effects of the Japanese current. The coast is broken into islands and fjords, making travel almost exclusively a matter of boats: the peoples of this area built large, seaworthy craft, dugouts with "sewn-plank" superstructures. The subsistence base was a complex pattern of seasonal exploitation of marine resources and land resources. In most areas there were several runs annually of salmon and oulachon, which were smoked or preserved in oil to provide the stable, year-round resource equivalent in abundance and reliability to agriculture. The full range of resources exploited included shellfish, sea mammals, and for some, such as the Nootka, an occasional whale. The land strip provided additional plant resources and game animals, while long-established trade inland further enriched the mix of the economy. These northwestern peoples had no real worries in regard to subsistence and, indeed, there was an almost embarrassing abundance of food.

Wood and the technology for its use are the most notable and distinctive aspect of coastal art and practical crafts. Techniques for decoration and manufacture were nowhere equalled. In addition to the sewn-plank method, and perhaps equally enthralling, were the "bent wood boxes" so cleverly made and so well made that they were used for water storage or as containers for oulachon oil. Masks, totem poles, house fronts, spoons, boxes—virtually everything—was elaborately carved and painted in an intricate style. I will attempt no real description, referring the student instead to the bibliography at the end of the chapter for photographs and descriptions of this fabulous art.

The focus of the art was the "crest," a symbol owned and displayed by a particular individual who had inherited the right to display it and would pass it on to other kinsmen. Some analogy can be made with our own system of ownership of trademarks, whose use is closely and jealously guarded. A closer comparison, in view of the nature of the social structure, is to the escutcheon or coat of arms of feudal Europe which identifies not a product but a man, his family, and the importance of that family. A coat of arms is recorded for "Castile" which, could I show connection, would allow me to display two banana trees, a tower, and a mortar on my shield—if I had a shield. The totem pole, the most well-known manifestation of Northwest Coast art, is also among the most misunderstood. The poles, which could be erected for a number of purposes, are primarily a sort of personal advertisement listing the various ranks, privileges, and honors held by a particular man, as represented by the "crests"—animal and mythological figures—carved upon it. It is not, as is commonly shown in the funny papers, an "idol" or other object of worship, except inasmuch as the peoples of this culture area can be said to have worshiped rank. It was also confined to this area and was not a universal feature of Indian peoples, as one might think from those same funny papers, which frequently depict a thirty-foot cedar pole standing outside the tepee of what are clearly meant to be horse nomads of the Plains. Perhaps it breaks down into sections for transport?

Noble, Nobler, Noblest

The social organization of the Northwest Coast is varied, including northern peoples who are primarily matrilineal and southern groups who are largely patrilineal. All, however, make some important use of the principle of rank in addition to simple kinship-based lineage groupings. The Kwakiutl have a form of kin group that Boas called the "numayn," which is at first glance a patrilineage but which has, on closer examination, a confusing and apparently inconsistent bilateral tendency. Organizations of this kind have been called "ambilineal" when both matri- and patrilineal principles are used in apparent alternation. Like much else about the Indian, the concept is only difficult because of its unfamiliarity.

The numayn is basically a single household, although it may in fact include the residents of more than one dwelling in a village. Kwakiutl houses are plank-constructed "long houses," which may have from ten to twenty nuclear families residing within, all related to the house chief, who is the highest ranking man in the lineage that owns the house. The house is an example of property or privilege that passes more or less strictly through a unilineal process of descent, and most of the persons resident in the typical numayn are related to the chief patrilineally. The ambilineality comes in when we discover that some of the persons within the household are not sons of the male line but daughters with husbands. Although it is more common with the matrilineal northern peoples, we may even find avunculocality, as when a couple that upon marriage goes to live with the group of the groom's mother's brother (maternal uncle). Still more distant relations are sometimes found residing in this supposedly patrilineal group.

It becomes very simple when we remember the Kwakiutl fascination with rank. The persons associated with a numayn are engaged in a process of choice in their kinship attachment in which they seek to reside with or be in close contact with that kinsman or set of kinsmen which will maximize their chances of gaining rank. Parents can exercise some degree of choice on their children's behalf in regard to residence. In essence, they can choose as they see fit to pursue their matrilineal connections or their patrilineal ones. Later the child can make the same choice or revert to another of his options. It can even occur that a father can exercise a rank privilege that is inherited through his wife on behalf of his sons until their majority.

What? Again the feudal European model may be of some help in this matter, or even the example of my grandmother (maternal). Anyone who could show relationship to a king, however distant, conferred upon himself some degree of nobility if others would recognize the connection. As in any instance of hereditary nobility, the closer the relation the greater the possibility of inheriting something, even if one is not in the direct line of descent. With any luck, all of your wife's brothers and uncles will be wiped out and you will receive some part of their inheritance. There is an old British movie, *Kind Hearts and Coronets,* where such a distant relative sets out to murder everyone between himself and the title. My grandmother could trace my relation to the founding families of the city of St. Louis by a long, intricate process of switching back and forth from female line of descent to male line. The object is to trace descent through any means to a person of importance (a rank!) and studiously ignore the horse thieves. The Kwakiutl simply used this principle as the basis for the formation of corporate residential groups much in the same way a European king would find his court heavily populated with relatives. The greater his importance, the more relatives he would have.

A Kwakiutl village was composed of several affiliated numayn, and this unit, sometimes called a tribe, is the largest reliably cooperating corporate group that existed, although the numayn individually were far more important for most purposes. Within the village/tribe the numayn were ranked in relation to each other, and some wider organization existed in that villages tended also to be ranked in relation to other villages. This allowed on some occasions for the combining of more than one village into a "confederacy." Except for cooperation in the occasional raiding "war" party, there was no real coordination of intervillage activities, although relative ranks were well understood.

Rank, it must be understood, including that of the "chiefs," was generally not a matter of command or power, either economic or political, but of relative prestige. It has been suggested that in such societies each individual forms a "class" all his own, although in a general sense one could describe two categories of persons—the noble and the not-so-noble. Virtually everyone except an orphan would hold *some* rank or privilege, but some persons had so few, and those so unimportant, that they constituted a class of de facto commoners. Those who had many ranks and privileges were, in this same quantitative definition, the noble. The chiefs were simply the most noble, not the only noble, of the nobility, and the youngest son of a chief might inherit so few privileges as to rank as a commoner.

There is another "class" of persons which has not been mentioned because its members were not really part of the social order but apparently only a category of property. The Northwest Coast peoples had as one of the purposes of their raiding warfare the taking of captives as slaves. The position of slave was seemingly without rights; however, the slave would generally live in the household and might even marry, although the children would themselves be slaves.The kinsmen of the captive slave would make every effort to ransom him and then give potlatchs to clear away the disgrace that would fall on all the members of the enslaved person's lineage. As property, the slave was valuable, but not so valuable (compared to a "copper," for example) that he might not be sacrificed at any time as part of a display of contempt for wealth. In a manner reminiscent of Polynesian custom, a slave might be put in the hole during the erection of a totem pole. The word "sacrifice" is inappropriate because it appears that the act had no more significance than any other instance of property destruction.

"Always Giving Blankets Away While Walking"

The title of this subsection is a hereditary, ranked name recorded for one of the Kwakiutl numayn. Its emphasis on the honorableness of "giving away" will serve to lead into a discussion of the potlatch, a coastal ceremonial activity that makes plain many of the essential elements of the chiefdom and rank-oriented societies. Giveaways—the distribution of presents on important ceremonial occasions—are widely known among Chichimec societies and elsewhere in the world, but in the Northwest they were more flamboyant and dramatic than elsewhere. The exaggerated "rivalry" potlatch is probably, according to best modern thought, the result of increased wealth combined with declining population, both brought about after and as a result of white contact; but the potlatch in some form seems always to have been important in this area.

In a rank-oriented society such as the Kwakiutl, the potlatch had particularly great significance because no name could be inherited, no privilege exercised, without validation of the right of the individual to the honor involved. That validation could only be achieved through the giving of a potlatch, and failure to do this meant that the honor was undeserved and that the privileges could not be exercised. In an "etic" perspective (the analytical outsider) the potlatch serves an economic purpose equivalent to the principle of "redistribution" described by Karl Polyani as one of the alternatives to the marketplace of our economy.[10] A society which produces surplus, like that of the coastal peoples, can evolve mechanisms whereby the surplus is concentrated at some point (in the hands of the chief) and then disbursed (redistribution) to those who are in need or employed for some important public purpose—the earthworks of the Mound Builders, for example. Though undertaken for other purposes (the "emic" point of view), such as guaranteeing rights to prestige, the final effect of the potlatch can be considered, despite its dramatic quality, as functionally equivalent to taxation in our own society. Goods are taken from all who have them to spare, concentrated, and then reallocated to those who have need, or they are utilized for the common good. At a minimum, the process guarantees a constant circulation of goods, assuring the life chances of all, as did the reciprocity system described for simpler groups. Because surplus productivity is involved, the scale is much larger here; and the possibility of support for nonproductive specialists—chiefs, priests, artisans—exists along with the means to undertake public works, ceremonial and otherwise.

Preparation for a potlatch generally began well in advance of the chosen date so that property might be accumulated. The chief, or anyone who had need of a potlatch to verify a title, would begin a series of credit transactions among his kinsmen, lending them property to be paid back at usurious interest rates at the time of the potlatch, usually 100 percent in six months. The system should be familiar to our own credit-based society, although not in the kinship structuring of the transactions. At any given time there were far more "blankets" (a Chilkat blanket or, later, Hudson's Bay blankets) in theoretical circulation as a kind of currency than actually existed, just as there was always more paper money than actual gold to back it in the United States even before we went off the gold standard. Both systems depend on a degree of faith to prevent runs on the bank in the form of everyone calling in all his debts at once. An important factor in holding the system stable was the "copper," a shieldlike item of beaten native copper, usually heroically named, which accumulated value each time it changed hands until it could be reckoned to be worth many thousands of blankets. Like a check in our system, it could have any value the parties concerned could agree upon. The concept of ever-increasing value is familiar enough in our society in the sale of art objects, stamps, and the like. At some point the copper would be ceremonially destroyed in a potlatch, taking the burden of several thousand nonexistent blankets with it.

When sufficient property had been accumulated, the invited group (often the lineage of the potlatch giver's wife) would arrive for the festivities. The activities of the potlatch point up not only the fascination with rank but also much of the system of priorities and privileges so highly valued that were purely ceremonial and activated only at the potlatch itself. The right to sit in the presence of the king granted to some English nobility is a more familiar example of a purely ceremonial but highly valued hereditary privilege. This honor was no doubt lowered in prestige when a tall prince, later George IV, granted all officers of the British navy the right to toast the royal name sitting down after he himself had banged his head on the low beams of a man-of-war during such a toast.

The potlatcher and his kinsmen would greet the arriving guests and seat them in strict rank. Where each sat, the order in which gifts would be given, by whom, and with what degree of ceremony were all closely reckoned matters of rank, of special inherited privilege. The potlatcher would very often have a special "secretary" to help him sort all this out, and this person or another would announce to the assembled company in awesome detail the sheer outstanding magnificence of the potlatcher in a manner familiar to most of us from observations during the awarding of honorary degrees at colleges and universities. The parallel is uncomfortably close when we realize that many who receive these degrees are being rewarded for having "given away" buildings, endowed chairs, and the like to the college.

The object of virtually all "normal" potlatching was achieved when the title, rank, or crest being validated had been announced and generous gifts were distributed to all of the guests to show by this display of wealth the "worthiness" of the man who claimed the position. Goods were distributed according to rank both in quantity and in quality; and since the other group would naturally have its own ranks to validate, one could expect, as with reciprocity systems, that the bread cast upon the waters would eventually return. Occasionally, however, to make a particularly impressive point of one's wealth, property would be destroyed. This leads us to the curiously familiar phenomenon of "fighting with property."[11]

Our own society has often been cited for its conspicuous consumption, but the rivalry potlatch brings the attempt to overwhelm others with material possessions completely out into the open. These potlatches were not in any way typical, and as noted were probably largely an acculturation phenomenon resulting from the disruptions of white contact. Ruth Benedict, in a widely known book, *Patterns of Culture*, created in many people's minds the notion that this was what the Kwakiutl lived for, but that is obviously not the case.[12]

When villages had been disrupted and the population cut by disease, and when new wealth was pouring in from the white trading activities (not always into the hands of those who had traditional rank), disputes as to who had the best claim to a title might easily arise. The rival claimants would then fight it out by attempting to "out-potlatch" each other. Each would give away or destroy property in the hope of outdoing the other fellow, thereby achieving public validation of his claim. Guests would be laden down with rich gifts, and to further show his wealth, the potlatcher would break or throw into the sea a copper of great value. Carved and painted boxes, even canoes, would be broken or burned, and the highly prized oulachon oil would be poured on the fire around which the potlatch was taking place. Flames would singe the hair of the participants, but for the rival to move away was to lose face, even when, as sometimes occurred, the house itself was in danger of burning down.

Obviously in our own society the aspirant to high social position does not make a bonfire of stereo sets and golf clubs on the lawn of the country club when he seeks admission to its membership, nor does he push several limousines over a cliff to ensure his invitation to society balls. Still, the parallels are there, largely more subtle than in showy contempt for costs, but occasionally emerging blatantly, as in the response of a wealthy yacht owner when asked its price: "If you have to ask the price, you can't afford it." The potlatch was made illegal under white political administration of the area, although yacht salesmen continued to operate openly in the East.

Recalling the definition at the beginning of this chapter, it is somewhat ambiguous as to whether a chief possesses "power," or, simply as a charismatic leader, "authority." It would appear that Northwest Coast chiefs could exercise considerable control over the doings of their own numayn and, if of sufficient importance, over the entire village. This power, however, was not exclusive to the chief since, as noted, there were many fine gradations of rank within and between the lineages and villages. It has been suggested that a useful distinction is made by pointing out that, in the state, some central authority has a monopoly of power, while in the chiefdom the chief simply had more than anyone else but not exclusive control.

It is also worth noting that the economic power, in the sense of

Sketch published in 1758 by Le Page du Pratz, who observed something of the power of the Great Sun of the Natchez, who were among the last of the once-powerful Mississippian peoples. (Courtesy National Anthropological Archives, Smithsonian Institution)

control of a vital resource such as salmon fishing sites, was vested in the kinship groups as corporate entities, just as it occurs in tribal societies. The chief or noblest member of the particular lineage could exercise considerable discretion in the use of these resources and their product, but he did not own them. Even in the potlatch, which is seemingly directed at the glorification of an individual, all the members of the lineage not only benefited by the increase of prestige, but the potlatch could not be carried out without their support. They could be cajoled, shamed, and otherwise pressured, but the chief of whatever degree of nobility could not coerce or guarantee compliance without maintaining consensus among his constituency.

The Northwestern chiefdoms had features that illustrate the thin borderline that distinguishes the chiefdom from the stratified state. Their warfare, while still a matter of raid and counter-raid, as in tribal practice, often had the purpose of controlling important economic resources (fishing grounds) or sometimes the actual destruction of a rival group so as to take over its lands. The war parties were large, forty men in a canoe and several such canoes on a raid, the participants well armed, protected by "slat armor," a distinctly Asian device rather than Mesoamerican. The resources existed to support prolonged warfare, and to some extent so did the motive (the quest for wealth), so that further development might have led these people from the chiefdom to some form of conquest state. The Iroquois, to be examined in another chapter, seem to have been well on their way to some such adaptation through their famous "league."

The power or authority of the chiefs, while largely a matter of prestige, obviously had within it the seeds of "differential access to the basic resources that sustain life," Fried's definition of the stratified society.[13] Had the rank system begun to move toward a less individualistic class system at the time that such economic differentiation occurred, a state would be in formation. The move from chiefdom to some sort of territorial state seems, indeed, so logical a consequence of this level of organization that some have felt that the stable chiefdom is a relatively rare result of special circumstances. The examples offered by these Northwest Coast peoples and the Islanders of Oceania are certainly special in many ways, and both seem to have special defensive and stabilizing mechanisms.

The fascination with rank and the consumption of property through the potlatch may have something of the character of the *carguero* system associated with the stability of closed, corporate peasant villages in the postconquest society of Middle America. Here the people are induced to limit themselves to what have been called the "rewards of shared poverty" and to maintain a stable, equalitarian society by consuming all of their surplus in the "service of the saints." The *carguero* system is an elaborate ceremonial round of fiestas in honor of the saints, which in many places has become the whole point of peasant life and also the means by which stable communities are maintained in the face of a changing world. There will be more of this later in the discussions of future directions for the modern reservation communities since they both represent a type of enclave.

The point here is simply that the consumption of property in the potlatch system and the turning of the focus of life into the pursuit of prestige may have functioned as a stabilizing mechanism similar to the *carguero*. One might speak of the "rewards of shared ostentation" rather than "rewards of shared poverty," but here too property is not accumulated as an end in itself but is quickly disbursed for some higher goal. While the Kwakiutl have been spoken of as "incipient capitalists," the fact is that their interest lay in prestige, not in wealth. In both the peasant communities and with the Kwakiutl, wealth not given away serves no purpose. As with much else, the proving of the point becomes difficult, because the system was swept away before it could be fully recorded or understood.

The few Chichimec groups who do seem to have attained to something resembling the state in historical times are those who appear to have done so under the impact of the Europeans. They are discussed in subsequent chapters.

Some Readings

On states and chiefdoms in general, see the readings previously recommended: Fried (1967), and Service (1964).

Codere, Helen: *Fighting with Property: A Study of Kwakiutl Potlatching and Warfare 1792–1930*, New York: American Ethnological Society, Monograph 18, 1950.

Coe, Michael D.: *America's First Civilization*, New York: American Heritage, 1968. Beautifully illustrated treatment of the Olmec, and informative on the issue of the rise of complex societies in the Americas.

Corkran, David H.: *The Creek Frontier, 1540–1783*, Norman, Okla.: University of Oklahoma Press, 1967. Largely a historical account, with early sections dealing extensively with the nature of Creek social and political organization.

Drucker, Phillip: *Indians of the Northwest Coast*, New York: McGraw-Hill, 1955. Good general coverage of these remarkable cultures.

Prufer, Olaf H.: "The Hopewell Cult," *Scientific American*, **211**:90–102, 1964. A short, readable article. See also appropriate sections of Jennings (1974) and Willey (1968) for this and the Mississippian cultures.

Swanton, John R.: *Indian Tribes of the Lower Mississippi Valley and Adjacent Coast of the Gulf of Mexico*, Bulletin 43, Bureau of American Ethnology, Smithsonian Institution, 1911. Classic work, which includes a survey of colonial sources on contact with the Natchez.

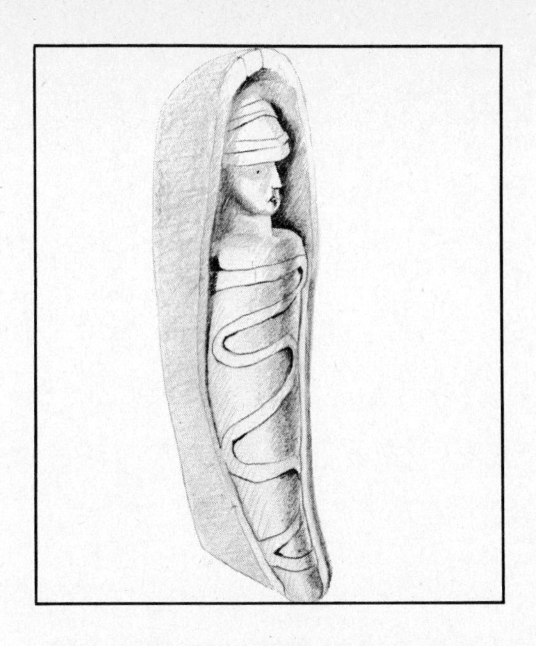

INTERREGNUM: SOME ALTERNATIVE PERSPECTIVES

In this world, things are complicated and are decided by many factors. We should look at problems from different aspects, not from just one.

Mao Tse-tung[1]

Messages from Home and "Elsewhen"

The second part of this book begins with 1492 and the arrival of European influence, which altered forever the independent development of the Chichimec world. In this last chapter on that world's independence, I would like to examine the range and significance of earlier contacts between Old and New World, putting such contacts in the context of a discussion of the relative importance of diffusion and independent invention as concepts of explanation. As the discussion of Mesoamerican influences has indicated, there is no doubt that diffusion has a role to play in our understandings, but there remains the question of when it is appropriate to invoke this explanation to make it something other than an excuse for failing to look further. In considering this question there will inevitably be something to say about the maturation of anthropology that moves it from the "travel and adventure" section of the library to the science section. It will be suggested that much of the formerly, and even some of the currently, popular views of the necessity of outside intervention on Chichimec culture are essentially condescending and racist in their underlying assumptions. Springing from a profound reluctance to admit that any peoples could have devised anything so complex as that represented by the Chichimeca without European help, many theories have "outside influences" responsible for everything more intricate than head scratching. At last count, such influences were postulated to have arrived from Ireland, France, Scandinavia (various Vikings), Phoenicia, Carthage, Egypt, Polynesia, China, Japan, Atlantis, Mu, Lemuria, Israel, and, of course, outer space. In view of what we have already discussed, is this reasonable?

Those Gods-forsaken Chariots!

We can begin by disposing of the more preposterous points of view and in the process establish something of an understanding about the utility of rationality and the scientific method in questions of this kind. There is an element of personal indulgence here since many of the issues addressed are such that professional anthropologists scarcely consider them worth their time. However, as noted at the beginning, this work is directed not at the professional but at the student. Many students take these matters as being very much alive. Perhaps my colleagues will forgive me if I can save them some of the burden of having to explain the business over and over in the same way that we have had to explain that Carlos Castaneda's Don Juan does not really represent your average Yaqui.

Let me make a confession at the start that may make clear some of the vehemence of my treatment of this issue and perhaps save myself from charges of being one of those defensive members of the scientific "establishment" who suppress for some mysterious reason the brilliant insights conveyed to us in crayon on the stationery of asylums. Science, including anthropology, is hard work, and the hardest part of all is having to accept the fact that ideas and insights are valuable only when they can be shown to have some connection with reality. To *say* that something is so simply because it *feels* right isn't going to get us anywhere, however tempting it may be. To insist as we do that ideas, however fascinating, must be supported and demonstrated by orderly reference to the data is necessary, because an insistence that "anything is possible" leads to an abandonment of order and explanation. This is not done out of any fear of asking new questions, because the asking of such questions is the very essence of science. We only insist on asking them in ways that promise some meaningful answers.

"But isn't it possible?" This is the basic question that arises in regard to all of the peculiar suggestions and theories purporting to explain, by reference to spacemen or Lemurians, the development of New World civilizations. A flat "no" makes the student nervous since it seems dogmatic, but the question really is the wrong one. As a lifelong science fiction fan, I am not in a position to deny the possibility of life on other planets or the possibility that if beings exist they could be sufficiently advanced to be spacegoing, as we ourselves are about to become, and therefore the possibility that they *could* have set foot on this earth. Fine! Now the real question is, Is there any reason to believe that this has occurred? Is there anything so otherwise inexplicable as to make it necessary that this should have occurred? Is there sufficient evidence to make this a probable rather than a possible conclusion? Even science fiction, when it is well done, creates an orderly alternative world and not an open-ended randomness. If everything is accepted as equally possible, nothing is knowable!

The appeal of the "outer-space gods" position is really not hard to understand. There was a time not so very long ago when it was perfectly possible, and widely popular, to believe in men who had their heads located in their stomachs or in Amazons who, in order to allow clearance for their bow strings, were mono-breasted. There were lost cities of gold luring on the Spanish conquistadores, and European explorers sought the Christian civilization of Prester John somewhere in Asia. In the Himalayas perhaps Shangri-la did exist eternally young. The problem is that there is no place left to put Prester John's kingdom or the Amazons, and it is somehow depressing to realize that we *know* the sources of the Nile and *know* that the Himalayas are just cold and uninhabited except by mountain climbers and Sherpas who strike for higher pay. A sense of wonder and mystery has been lost, and it is sorely missed and cannot be replaced by dry and unexciting reality. Jacques Cousteau is perhaps the last in the great tradition of "explorers" who can enthrall us with something really new. Even his frontier, the ocean floor, is rapidly becoming unsuitable as a place to hide the wonderful as it becomes mapped in minute detail. The sense of wonder now impels us into ourselves—"inner space," which is still largely unexplored—and into outer space, where still may lurk the kingdom of Prester John. I and most other scientists share this quest, but we must remember that the Spaniards did not look for Prester John in Barcelona, and we, like them, must look to the truly unknown and not distort what we already understand. The past, which also used to be open to any interpretation the observer cared to make, is no more mysterious today than are the Himalayas, and not only are there no Amazons, but there never were, not even in the "lost civilizations" of the non-European New World that are the subject of this book.

Before getting on to serious consideration of the actual relations of the Old and New Worlds, let me make some comments on Erich von Däniken as a symbol of current confusions.[2] There are real issues at stake that will shortly be addressed, but virtually none of them needs to be raised in order to put his and similar writings into perspective. Thousands of archaeologists, historians, and geologists have for generations worked quietly away at unraveling the record of man's unwritten past. Bit by bit, at great cost in thought and energy, indeed sometimes at the cost of their lives, these individuals have begun to put together a coherent body of understanding. Then now and again someone comes along who dredges up bits of these findings, distorts them, insults us all, and makes a pile. If serious scholars seem somewhat testy about the whole business, remember the current levels of compensation for professors—no gold of the gods for them. The truth unfortunately takes a while to tell and isn't half so entertaining as what can be concocted if sales are the only goal. So herewith a few points of general utility in making an evaluation of the flood of "gods" books.

1 The Charlatan Rule—When a man with an idea spends a great deal of time comparing himself to the persecuted great thinkers of the past and insisting that the "scientific establishment" is out to get him—watch out! Anyone who seriously believes that scientists are out to suppress each other's findings, presumably because any deviation from the norm is going to destroy their disciplines and put them in the streets to beg bread, knows nothing of the nature of science. There is an excellent book by Thomas Kuhn (*The Structure of Scientific Revolutions*) in which he points out that science proceeds by devising a set of commonly agreed-upon rules that seem to account for the phenomena to be explained.[3] These rules, then, are continually tested, and as they increasingly fail to do the job of explanation, they are abandoned for a new set that will work better. The point is that they are constantly tested but not abandoned until they fail. We may sometimes be a bit slow to give up, and we certainly are not going to do so for no reason whatsoever. An idea stands or falls on its merits, and complaints about persecution are not characteristic of great thinkers, past or present.

2 Racism rides again—It is noticeable in the von Däniken writings that the mysterious odds and ends that can be explained only by the intervention of gods (because the peoples involved were apparently too stupid to think of anything for themselves) are virtually all of something other than good old white European background. *We* don't need gods to explain the spinning jenny or the flush toilet or even the atomic bomb, but those nonwhites out there couldn't even move rocks around and pile them up without divine guidance. Surely the ethnocentric and racist bias evident in this sort of view is long since out of date. We have had to accept that African cultures reached high levels of sophistication before white contact and that such things as the Benin bronzes did not require European guidance. Must we turn to spacemen to support our propensity for looking down on others?

3 So new?—Somehow the "chariots" hypothesis is touted as something original and new and stimulating. There used to be a school of thought that insisted that all civilizations were derived from Egypt. When the principal advocate was once asked what all the rest of the world was doing while waiting for the Egyptians to get around to spreading the good word, he said, "Nothing." The Greeks, long before the time of Christ, were convinced, as have been a great many other peoples, that all miraculous inventions like agriculture and metallurgy were given by the gods. So what else is new?

4 Context, what context?—The ignoring of context while collecting evidence is the major point of failure in many extreme diffusionist efforts. The basic technique is to scrounge through thousands of years of human history and prehistory, and the hundreds of civilizations that compose it, and here and there, with hardly any bother at all, pick up some peculiar oddment that suits one's argument. The trick is to ignore studiously all aspects of the society that don't suit the point to be made and to totally ignore where the thing you have plucked out fits into that background. Artistic expression can be highly imaginative, and petroglyphs or rock carvings that depict a fantastic range of men, beasts, monsters, gods, and what have you exist in many parts of the world. Now this one here with the elephant nose won't do, but aha!—this one looks sort of like a man wearing a space helmet if you squinch up your eyes a little. Do we really believe in half-man and half-animal creatures just because somebody drew one? Did Salvador Dali ever see a floppy watch? Maya art illustrates a rich and varied pantheon of gods and men in a highly stylized and elaborate form. With ready imagination one looks vaguely like somebody lying down in approximately the same posture assumed by our astronauts in early flights. Which proves what? I won't go on, but selecting your evidence to prove your point is an old practice, and it hasn't become any more praiseworthy or convincing over the years.

5 Impossible?—In a film based on one of the "chariots" efforts we receive an accompaniment of mysterious music and portentous voice tones all suggesting, as the books repeatedly do, that the Maya, the Inca, or the Egyptians performed impossible feats by means that obviously no human being could manage without outside assistance. The "charioteers" approach ignores the magical ingredient that underlies most of these astounding wonders—sweat! Easter Island, a favorite choice of the spurious wonder-makers, has been so thoroughly investigated that every step of the process of making and erecting the huge statues is well understood,from pecking them from base rock with crude stone tools to erecting them on their platforms. The pyramids of Egypt and Mesoamerica, source of much of the fatuous ohs and ahs, are the product of a lot of labor, simple tools, and engineering principles so obvious (earth ramps) that almost anyone could have built one. The Inca of Peru built sometimes with closely fitted, mortarless stone, and this is presented in such a way as to imply the use of atomic molecular slicing machines. It is a well-known technique that requires a lot of labor for the careful beveling and fitting of the stones. This is either an example of lifting a technique out of context on purpose or an incredible illustration of mental laziness, since the briefest inquiry would have shown the true situation. It is hard to say whether it is perversity or ignorance that insists that peoples like the Hopewell of the Chichimec tradition built their enormous animal-shaped effigy mounds for the edification of space travelers since the mounds could only be seen in their entirety from the air. Obviously any massive construction cannot be perceived as a totality from every side and angle, but that doesn't mean, for example, that the Pentagon was designed to be admired solely by aviators.

6 Unknown?—There are, really and truly, some items of ancient civilizations whose purpose is not clearly understood. Unexplained, however, does not mean that they are inexplicable, but just that we haven't figured them out as yet. Archaeologists have some bad habits, including the tendency to call anything they can't figure out a "ceremonial" object, but objects of religious purpose are sometimes otherwise quite meaningless. One thinks of Steinbeck's "Doc" explaining the fact that stinkbugs pause in their wandering and thrust their rears in the air as prayer, based on the theory that whenever human beings do anything that peculiar they are probably praying. *Deux ex machina* is a characteristic of cheap theater and also of cheap thinking when spacemen are rung in to get us out of the bind of having to admit we don't know what something is good for. The number of things we don't understand gets smaller and smaller, and generally the unknown turns out to have some logical connection with the society that produces it. Recall the peculiar "birdstones" that made no sense until the use of the atlatl was demonstrated. Patience, please.

7 I could cry!—While one could be charitable and assume that much of the "charioteers" approach is simple misinterpretation, some of it is so clearly questionable that one is tempted to see it as intentional misrepresentation, or as crashing incompetence. In this regard let us simply mention the implication that the deep wells of the Yucatan peninsula of Mexico are somehow connected with the blast effects of ascending spacecraft. Anyone who took the slightest trouble to really look into the matter would discover that such sinkholes, called cenotes, are a common and easily understood phenomenon in a great sheet of limestone such as this area represents. To act as if there were some mystery here is unforgivable. Compounding this form of deception are more recent "revelations" of evidence, such as golden objects and tablets which no one else has seen and which those who are said to have seen deny. *Playboy*, in its interview with von Däniken, takes note of this and several other instances of demonstrable error which do not appear to trouble von Däniken, who is quoted as saying, "It's true that I accept what I like and reject what I don't like."[4] Indeed, the whole atmosphere of that interview reminds one of those who conduct seances that don't work when scientific observers are present. You must have faith, and to ask questions is to reveal yourself as a nonbeliever who, because of nonbelief, can never understand. Those who question only do so because their minds are narrow. Nonsense!

8 Enough!

"Elsewhen"

There was a time when the world was younger and little was known of past history even in our own lands. It was only in the late 1700s that the view that the world was created in 4004 B.C. fell from popularity when counting biblical generations was abandoned in favor of geological time reckonings. So little was known that virtually any explanation was as reasonable as another and fantasy and science ran parallel. Then it was not impossible to believe in a lost continent such as that first described by Plato in his *Timaeus* under the name Atlantis. There could have been such a land somewhere in the western sea. Remember that Columbus had no knowledge of the existence of North and South America and indeed went to his grave convinced that they were merely large islands such as Atlantis is described as having been. If there were such places, then perhaps migrants from them could have been the founders of the American cultures and indeed the Americans themselves the descendants of survivors of some Atlantean catastrophe. No one knew for certain how old anything was, and the oldest and most unusual peoples most Europeans were familiar with were, of course, the Old Testament peoples, the tribes of Israel and later the Egyptians. It was not then unnatural that comparisons made with these familiar things, and connections postulated if resemblances did exist. What is difficult to understand is the persistence of such sixteenth-century thinking through the seventeenth, eighteenth, and nineteenth centuries, and even in a few notable cases into twentieth-century literature. Too much is known now to allow current proponents of the fantastic any more legitimacy than the flat-earth society.

It is to be hoped that the reader of the last few chapters has perceived the basic argument against all the "interventionist" theories called in to explain the condition of the New World peoples. The Maya and Aztec, with their complex societies on a hitherto unsuspected continent, were rather a shock to the Europe of the sixteenth century, which had no place in its history or cosmology for these peoples. They had to be fitted in somewhere. Today, after much patient and relatively unspectacular investigation, we have pieced together a long and logical sequence of development from primitive beginnings such as illustrated by the Big Game hunters. We can see over the thousands of years a gradual and consistent evolution of the traditions of the New World that led to the complex peoples that so dazzled the Spaniards. This is not to insist that all is known that needs to be known or that some radical reinterpretations will not yet be found essential as our work proceeds, but we have gotten to the point that it all begins to fit together, and the strange lands of Mu and Atlantis or wandering Israelites are not only no longer necessary to fill the gaps but have become a positive embarrassment to fit into the sequence. The subject of the last part of this chapter is some very real indication of transoceanic contact supported by mounting evidence, but this is oriented toward very limited and very late influences. With regret for lost innocence and the wonders once at every hand, let us pay passing tribute to the delightful theoreticians of the past.

Shalom, White Man

The oldest and in many ways the most persistent origin theory is that based on biblical interpretation, which makes the American Indians the descendants of one of the "lost tribes" of Israel. The first suggestions of this view came, very shortly after initial contacts, from the Spanish who saw many puzzling elements in Mesoamerica which seemed to suggest some form of Judeo-Christian influence. The Old Testament indicates that the Assyrians carried away ten of the twelve tribes of Israel in 422 B.C., leaving only the tribes of Judah and Benjamin. Biblical scholars in general seem to believe that these tribes are "lost" in the sense that their members were absorbed and dispersed among the peoples of the Near East, but many have taken the story to mean that the ten tribes actually physically migrated to somewhere outside the biblical area. They have turned up in the most remarkable places, including, of course, the New World, although there were still earlier appearances, as in Britain where the Celtic peoples were once identified as these Semitic wanderers.

Maya carvings with rather prominent noses, beards, and other supposedly Caucasoid features were used early as evidence of the Israelite presence in America. Customs which we now know to be remarkably widespread were in those early days only previously known from the Bible, and so where the levirate (the practice of a man marrying his brother's widow) was encountered it was assumed the tribes had gone. The levirate, sacrifice, myths of a great flood, dietary restrictions, circumcision, and the like were all put forward as incontrovertible evidence.

Supposedly Hebrew words were found in American Indian languages, but unfortunately for the amateur linguist, language is a complex phenomenon and almost any language will yield to the diligent searcher some resemblance to another to which he seeks to show connection. Some such superficial connection has been shown for Indian languages with Celtic, Sanskrit, Greek, and Latin, among others. There are only a limited number of sounds to which human languages assign meanings, and in the thousands of combinations of these that each language uses there will inevitably be the occasional coincidence of roughly the same sound being used for approximately the same meaning. The trick is to show more fundamental resemblances of structure, and in this no Indian language shows connections at any significant level with any Old World tongue.

The failure to find anything demonstrably Semitic about the Indians on close examination, combined with the relative accuracy of dating biblical events, has been significant in the virtual disappearance of this point of view. It has become embarrassingly obvious that the cultures of the New World like the Olmec and the Maya, which were the source of much of the "evidence," had developed their distinctive characteristics much too early to be the product of this particular diaspora. The Olmec were well established by 1000 B.C., with roots going back at least a thousand years earlier in the same area. Simpler traditions, as shown above, go back at least another 8000 years.

A version of this Middle Eastern biblical invasion survives and is very strongly held by the members of the Church of Jesus Christ of Latter-Day Saints, more commonly known as the Mormons. The Book of Mormon, presented by Joseph Smith in 1830, is as open to interpretation as is the Bible itself; but it undeniably populates the New World with Middle Eastern peoples called Jaredites, Nephites, and Lamanites. These peoples purportedly raised great cities and fought stupendous battles throughout the New World long before Columbus, and finally destroyed themselves and lapsed into a barbarous condition after a great battle near the hill Cumorah where Joseph Smith later found the tablets that tell the story. Mormon archaeologists, in their efforts to support this image, have identified the past civilizations of Mesoamerica and South America preceding the modern Indian with one or another of these peoples. One interpretation, that of Thomas Stuart Ferguson in *One Fold and One Shepherd,* has the Jaredites arriving at a very early date, approximately 3000 B.C., with other Israelites entering the picture around 600 B.C.[5] This view, whose dates are somewhat more consistent with the facts, also allows for the existence of other peoples already settled in the Americas and aims only at the explanation of the high cultures. Non-Mormon archaeologists remain unconvinced.

Mysticism and Mu!

There are a number of related schools of thought also of considerable antiquity and also having living adherents today, but most of these make little attempt at scientific demonstration and, indeed, in heated moments, denounce the scientific method in favor of some personal versions of mystical insight. Much they claim to know is simply unknowable. I am, of course, referring to the champions of the lost continents of Atlantis, Lemuria, and Mu, though the latter appears to be only an alternative label for Lemuria. This view was originally presented quite seriously as an explanation of New World origins again by Spaniards immediately after the conquest, and it reached a high point of reasoned presentation in *The Problem of Atlantis* by Lewis Spence in 1925.[6] It has since fallen on hard times, and its principal modern supporters are the Rosicrucians and the Theosophist societies, which are frankly mystical in orientation. It is unlikely that Plato meant to be taken so seriously—any more than Tolkien would have us search for Middle Earth.

Atlantis, as the name obviously implies, is in the Atlantic Ocean, generally placed somewhere around the Azores. Mu-Lemuria is a more recent innovation, placed in the Pacific Ocean and encompassing most of the islands there as its remnants by its principal proponent James Churchward.[7] Although it is not central to our concern, these are purported to be the great mother civilizations for all the world, not just the Americas, and the founders of Indian and Egyptian as well as Mayan thought. This view suggests that savages stay savages unless assisted from the outside, and human cultural development is not the result of an evolution from simple to complex but a history of a degeneration from a higher level attained first by Mu-Atlanteans—much like the Greek notion of a preceding Golden Age. This does not fit the facts.

How can we who endorse the idea of a high and dry land bridge between Asia and the New World deny the possibility of a former continent which is now submerged? The land bridge can be easily documented by geologists and can be accounted for by a known geological process involving the fall of sea levels when great ice sheets lock up much of the world's water. In coastal areas of shallow water, relatively small fluctuations in water levels can expose or submerge large land areas. But Atlantis and Lemuria, to be believable, require a set of circumstances that fly in the face of all that is understood about geology.

As the Atlanteans are fond of pointing out, there are indeed historical instances of sudden change in land form, including such things as the volcano of Paricutin that thrust itself into existence in western Mexico around 1940, or the subsidence of Port Royal in Jamaica into the sea. These and other such fluctuations, dramatic though they may be to the persons involved, are very minor geological alterations and nothing like the cataclysmic changes necessary to account for the subsidence of an entire continent to great depths beneath the ocean far from any shore.

Perhaps the most fundamental problem with the sunken-continent mystics is that their basic idea is so old that it predates an understanding of the age of the earth or the fundamentals of geological process. The death knell of the 4004 B.C. date for the creation of the earth calculated by the Bishop of Ussher from biblical generations was only sounded by Charles Lyell in 1832 with the publication of his *Principles of Geology*. That work was the culmination of a long struggle between the "catastrophists," the believers in continuous divine intervention through such means as the flood, and the "uniformitarians" who argued for much slower natural process to account for the state of the earth. That is the point which scuttles the Atlanteans and the Mu-men, for the necessary level of change that their theories require, equivalent, for example, to the upheaval of the Rocky Mountains, would necessarily date many millions of years in the past and no one remotely human would have been around to see it.

There are many places on the ocean floor where a temple or two located on some small sunken volcanic island could be tucked away unnoticed, even with present levels of mapping of the deeps. There is, however, as noted at the beginning of this section, nowhere left to put whole continents, even granting, as we do not, that such large bodies could have been lost without a trace. Perhaps that should be the final observation of this section: Nothing, absolutely nothing, has ever been produced to indicate the existence of the lost lands, let alone any evidence of their influence on the Americas. The Mu-men cannot even effectively play the usual game of finding Atlantean themes in American archaeological remains because they have no genuine Atlantean examples on which to base their comparison, except those produced by their own imaginations.

Rah, Rah—Ra!

Thor Heyerdahl's voyage in the papyrus raft *Ra* from Egypt to the Americas is the latest step in a long tradition that seeks to show connections between the pyramid builders of the New World and the Old. The fascination with this point of view may in part be due to the obvious resemblance of one pyramid to another, but I suspect it is also fed by the general familiarity of the public with Egyptian archaeology. Because of its early development and the publicity granted by the media, archaeology (in most people's view) involves a pith-helmeted Englishman burrowing through a pyramid, risking the wrath of mummies and their curses. A brief consideration of this perspective can permit a transition from the purely fanciful to the barely possible.

Many of the Atlantean theories already mentioned include Egyptian-American resemblances as part of their proof of common origin, although some have Egypt being derived from America rather than the more popular other way around. The "heliocentric" school, stressing the primacy of the Children of the Sun (Egyptians) in the rise of all civilizations, not just the American, hit its high point around 1924 with the work of G. Elliot Smith and W. J. Perry.[8] This extreme diffusionist school was based on a truly exclusive view of human inventiveness in which virtually all the arts of civilization could only have developed once under ideal circumstances in the valley of the Nile and spread from there. The cultures of the Americas and everywhere else for that matter were barely above that of apes until the Egyptians reached them. Though there are a multitude of obvious objections to this remarkable view, let us simply point out that Egypt is *not* the earliest agricultural civilization—it follows that of Mesopotamia by some considerable time, and this alone discredits it as the mother of them all.

Heyerdahl represents a mixture of this earlier grasping at evidential straws and a modern view that admits to some degree of limited contact and influence.[9] He is not among those who claim that the Indians are actual migrants from Egypt or that everything of any sophistication is necessarily the product of foreign intervention. At this point we encounter a very real problem in archaeology, which is that if one admits transoceanic contact, how much importance does one attach to it in determining the development of New World peoples. Heyerdahl is among those who sees profound influences in art, architecture, and religion far beyond those that most scholars see as reasonable. His view is closer to that of Smith and Perry in assuming that elements of religion such as sun worship and the use of pyramidal mortuary structures are part of an entire complex of Egyptian traits transplanted whole.

Heyerdahl's main claim to fame is not archaeological at all, and most of the evidence he advances is a familiar rehash of earlier Egyptian-influence zealots. What he has done is to cure a number of anthropologists of what one writer has called "thalassophobia" (fear of the sea) with his remarkable voyages.[10] The papyrus *Ra* sailed from Egypt to the Americas, but earlier, Heyerdahl, in support of his theories regarding Peruvian influence in Oceania, voyaged on the raft *Kon-Tiki* from Peru to Polynesia and is currently, I understand, contemplating something similar from Mesopotamia to the New World. While these adventures are dramatic and perhaps do help to open academic minds to the possibility of travel across oceans on relatively primitive craft, it should be borne in mind that they show only that it could be done, not that it was done. In the case of the *Ra* it took two tries, the first raft sinking before arrival; Heyerdahl's difficulties have served to reinforce already existing conviction that while transoceanic contact was possible, it was exceedingly difficult, and probably accidental.

Bodhisattvas and Berserkers

If, in spite of protestations, the impression has been given of harsh dismissal of intriguing ideas, perhaps amends will be made by examining the almost equally remarkable kinds of contact that do receive serious consideration. Very few professionals will now deny that some kind of pre-Columbian contacts occurred, though the validity of any particular piece of evidence for this is often hotly debated. The general tendency is to allow for the possibility of contact but to minimize its importance in determining any significant aspect of the New World cultures.

Much to the chagrin of the fans of Columbus, it now seems almost beyond question that visits were made to North America by Norse sailors almost 500 years before the "discovery" of America. Ample historical documents exist to show that people who had settled Iceland by A.D. 800 also colonized the west coast of Greenland by the late ninth century. For sailors who regularly voyaged from Scandinavia to the remote seas around Iceland and Greenland, as well as to the Mediterranean and even to the courts of Byzantium, it was no great additional feat to have touched on the relatively nearby coasts of North America.

There is indeed considerable historical documentation, references to voyages by Eric the Red, Bjarni Herjulfson, and Thorfinn Karlsefni, to show that some sort of contact was made with western lands variously named Markland, Helluland, and Vinland, all lying to the west of Greenland. These contacts all center around A.D. 1000 and there is little reason to doubt their authenticity. One account indicates a colonization attempt and references are also made to timber from these western lands being used in barren Greenland. As of the time of this writing there is no solid archaeological evidence available to prove beyond question where such visits took place, but that is not so remarkable when we consider that the contacts were apparently infrequent, brief, and involved only a very few persons.

In these Norse references we have an unproven but remarkably strong case for European contact with the people that they called "scraelings"—Chichimeca! Such contact appears, however, to have left no discernible alteration in Indian society of the sort that the transoceanic diffusionists normally postulate so freely from the most unlikely contacts. Taking only the more obvious possibilities, we find no northeastern Indians who copied Viking sailing craft or their weapons, both highly visible and easy to emulate. At the presumed time of contact, the Norsemen had just accepted Christianity, which spread rapidly among them, but we find no indication of its introduction into America. The total lack of anything demonstrably Norse in the face of certain contact is strong reinforcement for our hesitancy to accept the origin of basic American traits as the result of ephemeral visits from abroad. It is a European fantasy that other peoples make gods of the first white men they see.

Contact from Japan or China, while not as clearly historically documented as the Viking excursions, now seems the most likely source of any significant influence. There are occasionally historical oddments seized upon by the enthusiasts who support oriental contact such as the voyage of Hsu Fu in 219 B.C. from China to search the Eastern Seas for medicines. The voyage probably ended in Japan, but since Hsu Fu never returned, it is slim "evidence" for Chinese-American contact. More significantly, there is accumulating evidence for seaworthy craft and at least coastal trade for very early dates in the Orient. Fore and aft sails and flat-bottomed hull shapes are known from documents and archaeology to have existed around the time of Christ or at least by the second century A.D., and some few bits have been found that suggest dates as early as 1000 B.C., though all regard this as speculative.

In modern recorded history there have been numerous incidents of drift voyages to the New World from the Orient. Anyone in the northwestern United States is aware of the frequent appearance of Japanese glass fishing floats on the American coast. In the past, fishing boats with living crews have found themselves similarly blown off course by storms and have ended accidentally drifting to the west coast of America. Currently there are few who would argue that given the existence of sea-going craft at an early date such accidental arrivals could not have occurred with survivors finding themselves living with Chichimec or Mesoamerican peoples. There is at present nothing to suggest in any believable way that there was any regularity of contact through trade routes or actual Asian colonies in the New World. If the pattern of influence is to be based on very infrequent and unplanned culture bearers (shipwrecked sailors!), considerable doubt is cast on the complexity of traits they could have transmitted. While all of us use plastics and steel, few of us if shipwrecked could show anyone how they are made. An exhausted, bedraggled fisherman speaking unintelligible gibberish is not likely to strike anyone as particularly godlike or deserving of being listened to in religious and political matters. Cortes was treated seriously on arrival in Mexico, but he came with an organized expedition of armed men equipped with horses and cannon. Earlier, isolated, individual Spaniards had fallen into Mexican hands, and far from becoming rulers, were enslaved or sacrificed.

Made in Japan

If the possibility of Asian contact is granted, we are still left with a question of the importance of such contacts in influencing the nature of New World cultures. Strangely, since the west coast of America is a logical landing point, most of the evidence for contact appears in the high cultures of Mesoamerica. Since much that is of importance in the Chichimec area is derived from there, we can use some of that specific material to examine the general issue of extent of influence.

In the first place there is nowhere in the New World any trace of any object of Old World origin. I do not mean simply an item with "Made in Japan" stamped on the bottom, though pottery might easily include some such maker's mark—and pottery endures. There is nothing made of bronze or steel or any other material not native to the traditions of the Americas nor any plant or animal remains of other than American origin. If contacts were few and far between, the failure to find such evidence archaeologically is not remarkable, but it is disquieting nonetheless after all of these years of searching not to have located one inscription or tool.

No fundamental life-sustaining items, skills, or techniques can be shown to have Asiatic origin. One can recall from the discussion of agriculture that none of the plants essential to life in the New World—corn, beans, squash, manioc, potatoes—occur anywhere in the Old World before Columbus. Even the *idea* of domestication, occurring as it does at such an early date, predates Southeast Asian agricultural development and the means for transoceanic spread. Once agriculture exists, much complexity follows, as has been seen, through harnessing its potential. Once we admit that this does not have an Asian or other Old World origin, the case for critical influence from abroad is much weakened.

As with agriculture, it seems disquieting that none of the supposed visitors would have been able to introduce something so basic to their own cultures as metallurgy, leaving instead their presumed influence only in matters of art and religion. In Mesoamerica copper was widely used, and work in gold and silver highly developed, but nowhere do we find iron and bronze tools so essential to all of the Old World cultures. The "lost wax" casting technique was employed in Mesoamerica and is frequently offered as evidence of Old World influence because it is admittedly a far from obvious procedure, but nowhere were items of metal (made in this way or in any other) important basic tools or implements. Stone was everywhere preferred over metal for utilitarian purposes right to the time of Cortes. Iron pyrite was ground to make mirrors, and these are compared to the bronze mirrors of China as evidence of influence, without, however, any attempt to explain the difference in materials.

One of the most spectacular items lacking in the New World was the wheel. Until recently it appeared to have been completely absent, but now here and there in Mesoamerica we have found wheeled *toys*. Nowhere have we any evidence that the wheel was put to any practical use. This may be partially explained by the absence of any suitable domesticable draft animals in the New World to pull wheeled vehicles. There are, however, a great many uses for the wheel beyond haulage and the lack of its use is a mystery in many ways.

One very basic aspect of New World technology does seem, in the minds of many, to have a possible Asian origin, and that is pottery. The argument here as in many other cases involves an appraisal of human inventiveness. Is the making of pottery of tempered, fired clay so complex as to preclude its having been invented more than once? Admittedly we do not assume invention of pottery making in the Chichimec area but are convinced that it spread there from Mesoamerica. Did it spread to Mesoamerica from somewhere else? There is rather remarkable evidence from Valdivia in Ecuador of a pottery complex at approximately 3200 B.C., (which would make it the oldest known), that appears to have remarkable similarity to the pottery being made in the Jomon culture of Japan of about the same time. There is considerable debate suggesting that the similarities are only coincidental, but many are persuaded that there is good reason to accept a Japanese intrusion in Ecuador at this time. Among other considerations, the pottery, which is relatively sophisticated, has as yet not been shown to have developed from any more primitive tradition in Ecuador, although that, of course, does not rule out the possibility. Some later Ecuadorian material includes pottery models of houses of Asian type, depictions of the "coolie yoke," and ceramic headrests—all remarkably suggestive of Asian influence.

The Valdivia material represents the only situation where a large number of traits presumed to be Asiatic occur together as a complex in one place and time. For the rest, the case for Asian influence is much diminished by the habit of patching together odd, isolated traits from all over the New World and through 2000 years of time. Around the time of Christ at Teotihuacan, the great classic city of Mexico, we discover cylindrical pottery jars on tripods that resemble bronze jars of the Han in China. Thousands of miles away and a thousand years earlier in time, the feline motif of the Chavin culture of Peru (Jaguar) and the Chou of China (Tiger) had certain similarities that invite comparisons. Both of these and dozens of others similarly selected are usually presented together to make the case for foreign contact—without regard for context or any real attempt to explain why such a haphazard dispersal would occur.

In general, the bulk of the evidence offered for cultural influence falls into areas of artistic or religious expression where great variability exists and where accidental duplication of a particular motif or design among so many is hardly inconceivable. An emphasis on the lotus occurs, as well as the previously mentioned feline motif. Seated figures are shown holding lotus plants and in a posture characteristic of the bodhisattva of Buddhism. The cross is frequently shown, as is the "tree of life" theme; all these and many others have Old World counterparts. The question that remains to be resolved is whether these are so unusual that they must have spread from culture to culture, or whether, as with the pyramidal form of construction, they are so simple as to be frequently and separately invented. The question is ultimately one of contextual analysis, since while the pyramids of the Old and the New Worlds look superficially so much alike, the Mesoamerican version is primarily a temple structure and the Egyptian a mortuary or tomb. While the seated bodhisattvas certainly do look somewhat alike, do they have the same meaning or cultural associations? Only when we have filled in the gaps to answer such problems of association can we give any definite answer to the diffusion problem.

Until we can sort out the matter with hard evidence, positions taken quite often seem simply to be a matter of personal taste. Perhaps we can point out the reason why the overwhelming majority of archaeologists seem skeptical about transoceanic influence as an important factor by mentioning "Occam's razor." William of Occam suggested a kind of logical test for theories, and that is that the simplest theory is best! If a thing fits in reasonably well with all that has gone before it and is none too complex, then assuming that it was invented in place is far simpler than the conjuring up of heroic voyages by persuasive and skillful Asians. If a thing can be invented once, why not twice? If we are not surprised at the choice of the tiger as a Chinese religious symbol, presumably as a consequence of its obvious strength and ferocity, why is it so remarkable that another people should similarly and independently place importance on an equally strong and ferocious beast, the jaguar? If, for whatever obscure religious motive, you want to pile something up as high as it will go, a conical-pyramidal shape can easily result—as can readily be observed by watching a child trying to mound up sand on the beach. If you fiddle with highly plastic clay for hundreds of years and make thousands of shapes and designs, is it inconceivable that you will duplicate someone else's design occasionally, particularly as with some of the Valdivia material if the point of comparison is something so simple as a horizontal zigzag pattern?

No one now claims that everything in the Chichimec traditions is derived from elsewhere, and once it is admitted that clear evidence is lacking for any important influence, the reader, like everyone else, is free to draw his or her own conclusion. No one claims that the Indians are any less inventive than other peoples, or that they fail to produce at the proper times and places the needed incidence of genius. Ample evidence exists to show that ideas and inventions are products of the needs and circumstances of the societies in which they occur. The repeated incidence of simultaneous invention, one example of which is the famous instance of Darwin and Wallace both producing the integrative concept of evolution at the same time, suggests that when the ingredients of an invention are present someone will be on hand to put it together. Innovation is a constant, ongoing human process and the real issue is not whether some idea will occur to anyone but whether it is appropriate to the needs of society and will be accepted. Hero, a Greek, invented the basic principles of the steam engine before the time of Christ, but it was put to no use then, as the wheel was put to no use in the New World. The intricate web of social evolution that has been examined so far in this book demonstrates a level of creativity that no one denies as equal to that of any other region of the world.

On the Eve

There may have been pre-Columbian contacts between the Chichimeca and Asia and Europe, but they seem of so little significance that we must search and argue as to what they were. By 1500, however, with the arrival of the first outriders of European domination, the end was in sight for the independent development of the Indian cultures. In 1512 Ponce de Leon, with his expedition to Florida, was the first to open contact between European and Chichimeca. Coronado pushed northward from the already conquered Mesoamerica in 1540, penetrating deep into the plains of the West. By 1565, St. Augustine in Florida was established, the oldest continuously occupied site in the Chichimec area, and Santa Fe was established in New Mexico by 1610. In less than three hundred years from this time there would be no independent Indian cultures.

To grasp the magnitude of the events that followed European contact, one should consider the situation as of the year 1500, when Columbus was already in the Caribbean, but no one had actually touched the shores of America. The size of the Indian population north of Mexico has been variously estimated from 1 to 15 million people at the time of first European contact. Recent reappraisals seem to suggest that early estimates were much too low and failed to take into account the sweep of European diseases far in advance of the marching frontier, which decimated populations long before whites arrived to observe them. Others have suggested that there may have been a willingness to accept the lowest estimates because cutting a million people down to 500,000 is not so alarming as reducing 15 million to 500,000! Although the figures are still very approximate, it now seems that something closer to 10 million is a more realistic appraisal of the Chichimec numbers before Columbus.

Although all of the explorers were met immediately by the Indian inhabitants on arrival, nothing is more typical of the period than the constant use of terms that stressed the unused and unoccupied character of the "New" world. Virgin forests, untouched and unexplored, lay everywhere, to make the reputation of the explorer who was the first European to set foot on and put a name to these wonders. The problem is that they already had names, and the Indians who stood there and watched the "explorer" move into "unknown" territory had known that territory for thousands of years. As the next chapters suggest, nothing is more revealing than the tendency of the Europeans to treat the Indians as equivalents to the trees which, in the logger's telling phrase, had to be removed to "let a little daylight in the forest." In modern times we have encountered the "vacuum ideology" in Indian education which suggests that the Indians have no cultural experience worth considering in the educational process. In reading historical documents of the period of the explorers, there is the disquieting feeling that, for the recorders of these documents, the Indians didn't exist at all, and certainly there was no awareness of the complexity and diversity represented by these millions of people.

As of 1500, all of the life-styles that have been examined were represented across the face of America as well as a great many more that will be considered as the tide of settlement is explored. Along the lower Mississippi, the sacred, eternal fires burned atop the temple mounds, and kings still ruled complex social orders. The desert bands roamed their wastelands and not yet had the horses that the Spanish lost come into Indian hands, thus transforming their lives. The people who were to become the Sioux were still outside the Plains, and they resembled more closely the settled agricultural tribes surrounding them than the proud horse nomads they were to become. The Okipa ceremony was performed in the earth-lodge clusters of the Mandan, who were not yet diminished by disease or threatened by the horsemen. The pueblos stood all along the Rio Grande, and the mysteries of the sacred universe of Kachinas were observed in the kivas. The Athabascans, who would be called Navaho and Apache, were simple hunters and gatherers, though the Navaho had become more settled than their Apache cousins through association with the Pueblos. The longhouses of the Iroquois stood among fields of corn, and hundreds of the villages of their Algonquin enemies were scattered along the coast, where settlement by Europeans, who would sweep them before all others into oblivion, was to begin. The great towns of the Southeast, Creek and Cherokee, and others of what would be known as the "civilized tribes," flourished as the heirs of the great Mound Building traditions. The wealthy fishermen of the northwestern coastal rain forests practiced their elaborate arts and erect monuments to the glorious lineages of their chiefs. On the coasts, in the mountains, in the valleys—everywhere flourished the bands and tribes of the American Indian, followers of hundreds of distinctive ways and speakers of many languages.

Some Readings

Phillips, Phillip: "The Role of Transpacific Contacts in the Development of New World Pre-Columbian Civilizations," in Robert Wauchope (ed.), *Handbook of Middle American Indians*, vol. 4, Austin: University of Texas, 1966, pp. 296–315. Well-reasoned presentation of the *in situ* position.

Riley, Carroll L., et al. (eds.): *Man Across the Sea: Problems of Pre-Columbian Contacts*, Austin: University of Texas Press, 1971. Collection of articles touching on most of the major issues, with a sampling of a wide range of positions.

Wauchope, Robert: *Lost Tribes and Sunken Continents: Myth and Method in the Study of American Indians*, Chicago: University of Chicago Press, 1962. Delightful and authoritative account of the full range of madness and sense in this area.

Willey, Gordon, and Jeremy A. Sabloff: *A History of American Archaeology*, San Francisco: Freeman and Co., 1974. Places these matters in the context of the development of American archaeology.

PART II

CONTACT, ACCULTURATION, AND ACCOMMODATION

CHRONOLOGICAL OUTLINE FOR PART II

First Settlements and Permanent Contact

1565 Spanish at St. Augustine

1608 French at Quebec

1607 English at Jamestown

1626 Dutch at Manhattan

Colonial Era: 1565–1775

1622 Openchancough's uprising—Virginia

1649 Iroquois League conquest of Hurons

1680 Pueblo Revolt (reconquest by 1692)

1754–1763 French and Indian Wars

1763 Pontiac's uprising—Detroit

1768 Treaty of Ft. Stanwix—Iroquois League cedes rights to "Ohio country"

1637 Pequot War—New England

1675 King Phillip's War—New England

1715 Yamasee War—Carolinas

1763 French defeated and expelled

1763 Royal proclamation to limit settlement east of the Appalachians

1775 Continental Congress assumes authority over Indian affairs

Revolutionary / American Transition: 1775–1803

1778 Treaty with the Delaware (first American treaty)

1784 Treaty of Ft. Stanwix (2d) "gives peace" to the Iroquois and reserves land for their use

1787 Northwest Ordinance accelerates westward expansion of settlement by organizing Western territories

1789 Constitution gives Congress authority over Indian affairs (Article I—Commerce clause)

1779 American forces destroy Seneca villages and break the power of Iroquois League

1786 Secretary of War made responsible for Indian affairs

1789 Henry Knox as Secretary of War repudiates "right of conquest" and guarantees fair treatment in purchase of land

1803 Louisiana Purchase—Jefferson makes proposal to remove Indians west of the Mississippi

Removal and Expansion: 1803–1850

1806 Office of Superintendent of Indian Trade established

1825 Treaty of Indian Springs—Principal Chief McIntosh of the Creeks executed for agreeing to removal

1817–1842 Seminole Wars

1832 Black Hawk's War—Sauk and Fox badly defeated in attempts to reclaim ceded lands

1812 Confederated Western tribes, led by Techumseh, ally themselves with British in War of 1812

1824 Bureau of Indian Affairs created in War Department

1830 Indian Removal Act

1831–1832 *Cherokee Nation v. Georgia* and *Worcester v. Georgia*—Supreme Court defines "dependent domestic nation" doctrine

Removal and Expansion: 1803–1850 (cont.)

1834 Indian Intercourse Act asserts exclusive federal control over Indian affairs

1846 Texas Indians brought under federal jurisdiction upon statehood

1848 Treaty of Guadalupe Hidalgo with Mexico brings all southwestern tribes under federal jurisdiction

1832–1842 Removal of southeastern civilized tribes (the "Trail of Tears")

1846 Oregon Country jurisdiction acquired in settlement with British

1849 Bureau of Indian Affairs becomes part of Department of Interior

Reservations and Resistance: 1850–1890

1850–1854 California statehood and creation of organized Territories (Minnesota, 1849; Oregon, 1848; Utah, 1850; New Mexico, 1850; Kansas, 1854; and Nebraska, 1854) spells an end to removal

1862 Red Cloud's War temporarily secures Black Hills for the Sioux and pushes back frontier

1867–1868 Indian Peace Commission negotiates last treaties including Sioux, Navaho, and Nez Perce

1872 Modoc War (Captain Jack)

1876 Battle of the Little Bighorn

1854–1855 "Stevens" Treaties—wholesale treaty making with all Washington Territory tribes

1862 Minnesota Sioux uprising

1866 Half of "Indian Territory" taken from civilized tribes jurisdiction—13 new reservations created

1869 Grant's "Peace Policy"

1871 Congress unilaterally ends the making of treaties with Indian tribes

1877 Chief Joseph's War

1890 Wounded Knee—last armed resistance to placement on the reservations

Allotment and Assimilation: 1887–1928

1887 Dawes Severality Act (General Allotment Law)

1889 Oklahoma Land Rush I—Oklahoma District opened to white settlement

1898 Curtis Act extends allotment to five civilized tribes; governments dissolved

1902 First oil leases in Indian territory

1906 Burke Act eases trust restrictions and makes possible land transfers

1907 Oklahoma becomes a state

1917 Policy liberalization in BIA accelerates granting of "fee simple" ownership

1924 All remaining Indians granted U.S. citizenship. Voting rights come slowly with Arizona last (1948)

1887 14,000 Indian children enrolled in federal schools (Carlisle founded in 1879)

1893 Oklahoma Land Rush II—Cherokee Outlet opened to white settlement

1901 Oklahoma Indians become citizens

1902 *Lone Wolf v. Hitchcock*—Supreme Court confirms congressional authority and defines Indians as "wards" of the government

1908 Congressional act "frees" many Oklahoma allotted lands for sale

1922 All Pueblo Council formed to resist threat to their lands by Bursum Bill

1928 Meriam Report —"The Problem of Indian Administration"

The "Indian Problem": 1928–?
Reorganization under Collier and the New Deal

1933–1945 John Collier Commissioner of Indian Affairs

1934 Indian Reorganization Act establishes tribal councils and limited self-government

1934 "No interference with Indian religious life will hereafter be tolerated." (Collier's Annual Report)

1933–1941 Day school enrollment triples while boarding schools decline

1944 Foundation of National Congress of American Indians

1933 Civilian Conservation Corps camps provide jobs on reservations and attack ecological problems

1933–1937 Land Allotment is halted, and by 1937 tribal lands have actually increased for the first time

1934 Johnson-O'Malley Act allows for contracts with the states for Indian services (primarily schools)

1941 U.S. entry into World War II creates loss of funds and support for Indian programs

1945 Collier resigns

Termination and Assimilation

1928–1943 Senate Indian Affairs Committee investigation—reports issued tending toward termination

1947 Senate Civil Service Committee asks BIA to indicate tribal degree of readiness for withdrawal of federal supervision

1948 Relocation Service Program—field offices set up in major cities to assist Indians to find employment

1953 H.C.R. 108—Congress declares its termination policy urging tribes "be freed from Federal supervision and control"

1946 Indian Claims Commission to compensate tribes for lost lands, but also aimed at finalizing claims

1948 Hoover Commission recommends "assimilation must be the dominant goal of public policy"

1953 Pub. L. 280 encourages states to assert criminal and civil jurisdiction over reservations *without* requiring Indian consent

1961 Several tribes terminated, including Menominee of Wisconsin and Klamath of Oregon

1946 Tribal attorneys retained on many reservations as result of Claims Commission cases

1956 Industrial Development Program—funds provided to encourage on-reservation industry

1961 Presidential Task Force on Indian Affairs Reports

1962 Manpower Development and Training Act applied to reservations—many federal programs become directly involved on reservations

1966 Rough Rock Community School (Navaho), OEO-supported experimental/demonstration school stressing direct local control

1968 Lyndon B. Johnson Presidential message stresses "self-determination" as goal

1970 Richard M. Nixon Presidential message calls for renunciation of "termination" policy and again stresses self-determination

1971 Zuni and Miccosukee undertake programs of "home rule"/self-administration

1974 Menominee regain status as federally recognized tribe ("untermination")

1954 PHS (U.S. Public Health Service) takes over Indian health services—appropriations vastly increase

1961 Land Consolidation Program—much eased by priority purchasing program

1961 N.I.Y.C.—activist National Indian Youth Council formed

1964 Economic Opportunity Act creates Community Action Program agencies on reservations under direct tribal control

1968 Pub. L. 280 amended to require Indian consent

1968 A.I.M.—radical American Indian Movement founded

1971 N.I.T.C.A.—National Indian Tribal Chairmans Association founded

1971 Navaho Community College Bill guarantees support for Indian-operated community college

1974 *United States v. Washington*—Boldt decision on Indian treaty rights

1975 Pub. L. 93–638 (The Indian Self Determination and Education Assistance Act) provides opportunity for Indian self-administration under grant and contract procedures

VII
CIVILIZATION, SALVATION, AND LAND CLEARANCE

"It's only me from over the sea," said Barnacle Bill the sailor.
Anonymous

Europe and the several nations that composed it in 1500 were, of course, totally unknown to the Chichimeca; and the Chichimeca were equally unknown to the Europeans, barring the few and largely ignored rumors of "scraelings" from the Scandinavians. Before plunging into the subject of Indian-European contact, it would be best to pause here to consider the situation of the Europeans themselves that led up to what is to follow. Around 1500 there began an incredible explosion of European peoples upon the rest of the world, ending in a global dominance, the final outcome of which has yet to be seen. No part of the world remained uninfluenced, and the fate of the Chichimeca is remarkable only in the totality of its capitulation. While Asia and Africa have seemingly begun to reassert their independence, the Americas have become irrevocably part of the West. There is no real hope of adequately explaining this marvel in these few pages, but there is some purpose in reminding ourselves that it was indeed a fantastic event.

Europe? To the Greeks, the men of Northern Europe were simply barbarians who because of their violent and rather unintelligent nature did not even make particularly satisfactory slaves. To the Romans, who conquered them all, they seemed remarkably resistant to the benefits of civilization though they remained under Rome's influence for centuries. The Chinese, heirs to the ancient "Middle Kingdom," knew of such peoples at the end of distant trade routes but regarded them as no more important than other barbarians. Through most of recorded history, Europe, or at least the northern portion outside the Mediterranean world of Greece and Rome, has been a squabbling collection of minor and insignificant "statelets." It seems unlikely that in 1500 anyone could have predicted the events that were to come.

In 1453, Constantinople, the capital and last bastion of the Eastern Roman Empire (founded in A.D. 330), finally fell to the onslaught of the Ottoman Turks. The Ottoman Empire was itself the successor to an Islamic tradition that had in the sixth and seventh centuries driven deep into Europe, occupying most of Spain and not finally expelled until 1492. The Ottomans by 1500 had not only destroyed Byzantium, last remnant of Roman greatness, but also subjugated much of central Europe. As recently as 1236, the eastern borders of the European states had been ravaged by the armies of Genghis Khan, only the latest of many waves of Eastern peoples to disrupt these divided and weak lands. Although slowly successful in driving the forces of Islam from Europe itself, the counterattacks represented by the Crusades were totally without lasting result. Only the Scandinavians (the Vikings), in their intrusions into European Russia, did more than defend what they already had.

Europe was not unified at this time, although there was a degree of commonality in adherence to Christianity, with the authority of the Pope being variable in its importance. Italy, Germany, and France did not yet exist in their modern form, and wars raged periodically between the divided fragments that would eventually unite. Individual trading cities of Italy—Venice, Genoa, and others—were more influential in their control of trade routes than were the developing territorial states. Spain, which was to take the first steps in the Americas, had been engaged since the seventh century in reconquest, slowly pushing back the Moslem forces in the course of which the small kingdoms of the peninsula were forged into a single nation. Ivan the Great, first to take the title of Tsar, assumed the throne of Muscovy in 1462, only then beginning the final elimination of Tartar intrusion into European Russia. All in all, the situation of Europe was not impressive.

Many changes were going on below the surface in the medieval period that may account for the expansion of European power. City life and the merchant class so vividly illustrated in Venice had emerged to challenge the settled order of noble and peasant. Devastated by plagues and famine in the fourteenth century, losing perhaps a quarter of her total population, Europe had begun a process of harnessing energy more efficiently. Wind and water power and more efficient plows, new sources of metals and techniques for their use, more seaworthy ships all began to make themselves felt in this period, though their immediate impact was not dramatic. The great industrial revolution was still in the future and played no part in the early stages of European expansion.

Though Europe had for brief moments seen powerful bursts of political unification, as with the empire of Charlemagne, it was only immediately prior to the events of expansion that there was a stable trend toward centralization of state authority. Kings like Henry VII of England and Louis XI of France at the end of the fifteenth century had begun a process of restraining the power of nobles and asserting the primacy of the central government, which may well have been the most important factor in the ability of European nations to mount their assault on the world. Though by no means as absolute in their authority as the rulers of Asia, the kings of Europe had at this point the ability to act with some certainty of being obeyed, allowing concentrated and coordinated use of the burgeoning resources of Europe.

Whatever the ultimate causality, the apparent focus of the expansion was the questing after trade routes and particularly the routes to the Far East and its exotic riches of spices and silk. Constantinople had thrived as middleman for this trade, but the Italians had become heirs to it, although they were severely limited by the intrusion of the Ottoman empire into the overland route. Frustrated and too weak on land, the Europeans turned to the sea to find ways to tap the rich possibilities of trade. The results were phenomenal.

Portugal was first off the mark under the direction of Prince Henry "The Navigator" who encouraged and financed expeditions along the coasts of Africa. The expressed motives were various but centered around the search for trade with the East and a Christianizing emphasis, directed at the search for a means to take the forces of Islam by flank. They sought to contact and ally themselves with eastern Christian kingdoms like the mythical realm of Prester John. Vasco da Gama had penetrated into the Indian Ocean by 1498. By 1510 the Portuguese had established a permanent trading station at Goa, reached the Moluccas by 1513, and by the 1540s had established trade with China and Japan. The Spanish took off in the opposite direction with the expedition of Columbus to open a route to the Indies. The Dutch were not far behind and came to dominate the Eastern trade for a time with the establishment of the Dutch East India Company in 1602. The English burst out in both directions, setting up their own dominance in the East with the British East India Company in 1612, and in the West with colonies in the New World; Jamestown was founded in Virginia by 1607. The French entered the race and established a fort at Quebec in 1608 while also pushing into the East.

By 1900 the world belonged to Europe. Four continents—North America, South America, Africa, and Australia—were totally controlled by Europeans. Large parts of Asia (India, Burma, Indo-China, the East Indies) and all of the myriad islands of the Pacific including Hawaii and the Philippines were "possessions." China, still independent, was repeatedly humiliated by European power and only Japan asserted a strong position, having become heavily Europeanized herself. In the process, whether as cause or effect, Europe underwent a scientific and industrial revolution and erected a worldwide market economy to sustain it. In 400 years the little states of Europe had transformed the world in their own new image and created an empire greater than Genghis Khan ever dreamed of.

Iron Men and Wooden Ships

Some aspects promoting the success of the Europeans are fairly obvious, others far less tangible. The technological impact of cannon and efficient ocean-going ships on which to mount them cannot be missed, but what of the significance of vastly increased literacy which slowly developed after 1500? The spread of the printed word allowed a degree of mass communication and consequent coordination of thought and action never before possible. Many cultures had developed literate traditions, but these were confined to small elites; the Europeans were the first to move toward general literacy. Gold and spices dazzle the imagination, but the grubby mechanisms of commerce and exchange may be more critical. Banks, bills of exchange, and the limited-liability company had all been devised in Europe by this time to coordinate the free flow of trade. Much of the world was subjugated by corporations—the East India Company, Hudson's Bay Company, and so on. Even the mechanical manifestations of European science reflected something more fundamental in the shift from a traditional acceptance of things as they were to an age of inquiry and experimental, scientific investigation symbolically represented by men like Francis Bacon. The age of discovery and conquest was also the age of the enlightenment, the age of Newton, Descartes, and Luther, as well as Cortes. Even in religion there was a

The paintings of John White, a member of the Roanoke Colony (the first English settlement in the New World), offered the first glimpse of the Native Americans in contact with the English. White's work was reproduced as engravings in 1590 by Theodor de Bry. (The Rare Book Division, The New York Public Library, Astor, Lenox and Tilden Foundations)

revitalization of spirit in the Protestant Reformation and the Counter-Reformation.

Whatever the underlying circumstances, it was, first and foremost, sea power that established the European hegemony. Given the existence of motives—the quest for trade and the zeal for defense of Christianity against Islam—the sea provided the opportunity. Seeking to take Islam by flank, Europe ended by surrounding the world on the seas. Control of the seas provided the mobility to intrude everywhere and the means to coordinate and support the intrusion.

The Mediterranean world had long been dominated by the rowing galley, a type of vessel adapted for ramming and serving as a platform for the clash of hand-to-hand fighting across the decks. As late as 1571 Venice and the Turks fought a decisive naval battle at Lepanto relying on galleys. These light and open vessels were in the long run unseaworthy in open waters and unsuitable as stable gun platforms. The new ships that swept them from the seas combined elements from both the North European and the Mediterranean traditions. These first windjammers, like the Spanish and Portuguese caravels, depended on sails through a square-rigged arrangement balancing forces against a rudder and stern-post. Decked and high-sided and stoutly built, these vessels could keep to the seas in any weather and, powered by the wind rather than rowers, were able to cover vast distances tirelessly, and with large payloads.

Navigation had also reached a critical point at this time. The compass, although still crude, had long been in use. Celestial navigation was well understood, and simple but effective instruments like the astrolabe had been developed. Charts and maps, while also still simple, had begun to be more accurately prepared. Finally, practical seamanship had been brought to high levels through a long naval tradition.

Gunpowder and cannon were widely known, and Europe developed at this time techniques for the casting of iron cannon, heavier than bronze but far cheaper. These, combined with ships on which to mount them, created formidable weapons. Once the system of mounting such cannon in broadside batteries was developed, most efficiently by the British, it remained unchanged and unchallenged for centuries. With these ships and these weapons, the men of Europe could go where they would, eluding opposition and gaining a foothold anywhere that their cannon could reach. For those who would understand the full implications of sea power at its height, I recommend highly the Horatio Hornblower novels of C. S. Forester, which show the British Navy strangling the great land-based power of Napoleon.[1]

Strangely, the first contacts of Chichimeca and Europeans reflect little of Europe's superior technology, except in the ability of the Europeans to reach the New World in the first place. In later stages, as shall be seen, much of what happened in the New World was the outcome of European struggles elsewhere, as in the French and Indian Wars, and this introduced early an element of bewilderment in the Indian view of the white man. What the Europeans did in relation to the Indians often had its roots thousands of miles away—outside the vision and understanding of the Indian peoples. The purposes of the Europeans must often have seemed utterly unpredictable to the Indians who had no knowledge of global intricacies. The Louisiana Purchase and Mexican cession of the entire Southwest are both colossal instances of events with profound consequences for the Indian which in their origins had nothing to do with the Indians. The first instance occurred before Indian awareness of European existence, in 1493, with a series of papal bulls that divided between Spain and Portugal the non-Christian western lands for the purpose of Christianization. This pattern of altering Indian life without consulting the Indians continues to the present day with the machinations of the United States Congress, which, of course, is not subject to the will of the Indian.

First Blood

It was the newly forged Spain of Ferdinand of Aragon and Isabella of Castile that made first contact and first conquests in the Americas, but Spain was ultimately of only peripheral importance to the Chichimeca. An examination of the Spanish policies and motives will, however, allow a contrast with the far more critical ones of the Anglo-Europeans. Spain, discoverer of America and long the dominant power, never managed to make effective her policies in the Chichimec area except among the Pueblos of the Rio Grande and, very late in her imperial career, along the coast of California. Spain's most important contribution to the Chichimeca, after the fact of initial discovery, was the inadvertent introduction of the horse to create the warriors of the Plains. Above all, by the example of her great success, she was an element in luring others to the New World. Because of the stranglehold that Portugal and Spain had on the southern routes to the Indies, those who followed turned to an ultimately futile search for a northern passage and ended by establishing colonies in North America.

The first page in the Spanish saga is among the most tragic. The islands of the Caribbean were the accidental prize of Columbus's attempts to reach the East, and the horrible events there had much to do with subsequent policy. The native peoples of this area simply ceased to exist after a very short period of time. Extermination was not at all the Spanish intention but the result of their early, ill-conceived ventures. Here as elsewhere the principal culprit was the introduction of European disease. Diseases like measles, which were not generally fatal to the Europeans who had developed resistance to them, wiped out whole towns of Indians, who as a result of thousands of years of isolation, had no natural resistance. Warfare and enslavement for the purposes of forced labor also took their toll of the survivors of the epidemics. Food-producing land was converted to the growing of commercial crops like sugar cane, and European animals like cattle and horses came to graze on much of the land and destroy the crops. Disease, war, enslavement, and an unbalancing of the ecology all combined to make necessary the importation of black slaves from Africa to work the new Spanish enterprises, resulting in the final elimination of the Indian people as a viable population.

From their Caribbean base the Spanish fanned out. In 1519 Hernan Cortes with 508 soldiers, 16 horses, and 14 pieces of artillery launched himself against the Aztec empire which controlled all of what is now modern Mexico and supported a civilization of millions. In two years the Aztec capital of Tenochtitlan fell, and with that the Spanish controlled the entire area. Not long after, Francisco Pizzaro, with an even smaller army, attacked and toppled the still larger empire of the Inca of Peru. The incredible tale of these events is outside our area of concern, but in both cases the defeat of empires was as much a result of internal dissension as Spanish military prowess. In Peru, the Spanish stepped into a civil war and in Mexico composed the nuclei around which formed a rebellion against the Aztec. Strength became fatal weakness here, for these peoples were organized into centralized hierarchical states much like the Europeans, and the Spanish succeeded quickly and easily by taking over already existing reins of power. The people, already accustomed to centralized authority, slipped far more readily under the yoke of new masters than did the Chichimeca.

Though disease wreaked havoc in these new domains, the Spanish, confronted with the horrors of the West Indies, had given thought as to their purpose in these new lands. Spanish thought of the time was curiously legalistic, seeking formal justification for acts that were seemingly an exercise in naked power. The most remarkable manifestation of this is the *requerimiento* (the requirement), a legal document that the conquistadores were obligated to read aloud to any Indian group they proposed to attack. The document explained (in Spanish, of course) the rights of the Spanish crown and the mission granted to the crown by the popes and informed the Indian audience of its duty to submit to this authority. If the Indians failed to submit they could be legally attacked and even enslaved. Bernal Diaz del Castillo, the chronicler of the conquest, repeatedly shows this orientation when, in discussing some action, he says, "But it was not done in the presence of a notary."[2] Even Cortes, as his first act, founded the town of Vera Cruz to give himself legal standing as the representative of that community in his otherwise "illegal" conquests.

Diaz del Castillo, chronicler and conquistador, sums up very neatly the stand of one element of the Spanish when he says, "We came to serve God and also get rich."[3] There were originally three groups with variant interests: the Crown, the Church, and the conquistadores. While influential at first, the freebooting conquerors were rapidly subordinated to the purposes of Church and Crown. In Spain, Crown and Church were not so easily separated as elsewhere, for, as noted, Spain was the product of the essentially religious war that had raged for centuries to drive the heathen Moslem from the land. While the Crown's principal interest was the increase of its revenue through the harnessing of new taxpaying subjects (gold, in other words), it was, as Diaz del Castillo says, also interested in serving God. The duty to convert the heathen was in fact the justification of all else, for this alone "legally" entitled the Crown to its new domains. Spain had the "right" to conquer only because it had the "duty" to Christianize, and the conquest, therefore, was "just."

This introduces the contrast with the policies of the Northern Europeans—Dutch, French, and English. The Spanish under the central authority of the Crown implemented a consistent policy throughout their domains of conversion/civilization. They sought gold and land, but they also sought the salvation of souls. There is no doubt the Spanish ruthlessly exploited the Indian, but they regarded them as human beings capable of salvation and citizenship, while the other Europeans could never come to any clear agreement on this issue. As the Crown rigidly controlled the economy of "New Spain," so, too, it controlled the place of the Indian, and while that place was not enviable, it was clearly defined and protected. The Church, above all, with the support of the Crown, stood between the Indian and the European, often corruptly, but helping to guarantee some elements of justice for the Indian.

Although the Spanish sought workers for their mines and peasants for their great ranches and plantations, Cortes himself said, "But I came to get gold, not to till the soil like a peasant."[4] The hidalgos of Spain (*hijo de algo*: son of someone) were the product of the wars of the reconquest when soldiers were paid in booty and nobles in land with men to work it. When the last Moors fell with Granada there was no more land to be gained, and only land could ennoble. The aspiring Spaniard in the New World, in contrast to other Europeans, desperately wanted land *with* Indians to work it, while in general the men of the North sought only unencumbered land. Whatever their other faults, the Spanish never sought to inaugurate a program of land clearance as did their counterparts further north, and while their notions of what the Indians were to become did not include any consultation with the Indians, the Indians were always a part of New Spain. The end result is that modern Mexico is a land of mestizos, both racially and culturally, in which the Indian is a vital part, while in the United States the native peoples are isolated, constituting a persistent "problem."

Though successful in the rich and populous lands of the south, the men of Spain moved north seeking the land of Cibola and the seven cities of gold (which, while legendary, were no more fantastic than what they had already found); they failed miserably. At the end of long and difficult supply lines passing through desolate territories, the Spanish found little that was worth the effort. There were no cities and empires to be seized and no rich mines. There were no prosperous towns with workers to support the Spanish overlord and hear his holy mission, no political structures to be seized and manipulated—only small and widely scattered peoples without possessions worth seizing and not numerous enough to enslave. The Spanish tried, but in their attempts to civilize and preach they encountered the difficulty that you cannot convert someone you cannot catch. Though the Spanish set up programs of "congregation" in order to settle the nomads around forts and missions, with some success in parts of northern Mexico, they made little impact on what is now the southwestern United States. Once the horse had spread, the Spanish found themselves under constant guerrilla harassment from Apache, Navaho, Comanche, and others who finally succeeded not only in resisting Spanish control but in driving it slowly back into Mexico. It took the overwhelming sweep of Anglo-American advance to resolve these problems that the Spanish never solved.

A number of European nations made their initial inroads in the North—the Chichimeca. Blocked from the richer southern lands by Spanish power, the cod of the Grand Banks off Newfoundland was an early impetus for settlement and exploration, as was the hope of discovering a northwest passage to the Indies. Although eventually, with the rise of English sea power, some of the islands of the Caribbean were wrenched from Spanish hands, the sea dogs of Queen Elizabeth, like Sir Francis Drake, were little more than pirates in the early days as they attempted to intercept the treasure fleets of Mexico. The earliest British settlers in Jamestown, in their wrangles over the search for gold, had hopes of emulating the Spanish, but lacking treasures and great civilizations to loot, had to settle for the more mundane cultivation of tobacco.

The Dutch very briefly had an influence through their settlement at New Amsterdam (later, of course, New York), but the English quickly replaced the Dutch. Remarkably, there was an attempt by the Swedes to establish a colony that endured for only seventeen years, destroyed by the Dutch just as an early French settlement in Florida was wiped out by the Spanish, who feared for their convoys through the Florida straits. Only the French and English had long-term impact at the level of political control of colonial policy. The French and their policies will be examined in later considerations of the conflict between English and French, which was so important for the Indians of the Northeast. Although the early French explorers like La Salle, Marquette, and Joliet penetrated far into the North American interior along the great rivers well in advance of the English, who were largely confined to the coast, the French never followed up this head start with extensive settlement. The French government seems never to have consistently encouraged emigration on any large scale, and at various times even actively discouraged dissident religious groups like the Huguenots, whose English equivalents (like the Puritans) figured importantly in swelling European numbers in the New World. The empire of "New France" remained essentially a trade empire with the French thin on the ground, scattered among the Indians whose efforts as fur trappers they sought to control. By the 1660s there were only 2500 French in all North America. Because of this primary interest in establishing a stable fur-trading relationship, French concern for Indian goodwill was far greater than that of the English to whom the Indian trade was never so central. The English were far slower in their conquest but more thorough.

Mr. and Mrs. John Smith

It was the English colonies and the nature of the policies underlying the establishment of these colonies that led to the conversion of North America into a European land with the original inhabitants destroyed or confined to reservations. The next chapter will begin the examination of the march of events sweeping away Chichimec independence, but to make those events seem less incredible, it is necessary to stray a little out of strict chronological sequence to examine broad issues of policy and philosophy.

Although the English, like the others, were initially interested in trade and treasure, a dramatic difference rapidly developed in the sudden increase of emigration to the new colonies. Population figures are necessarily vague for early periods, but there were probably not much more than 100,000 Spaniards in all of Spain's vast American empire by 1570. One author suggests a figure of only 300,000 Spanish migrants to Middle America from the first contacts to the end of the colonial period. By way of contrast, the British colonies, which were established in the 1620s, had reached a population of 275,000 persons by 1700 and incredibly by 1790 numbered almost 4 million. In 1763 at the time of English takeover of New France, the French numbered only 80,000 to 100,000. Figures for the Indian population are still more vague, but it is unlikely that there were more than 300,000 Indians in the whole eastern seaboard area, so that the English came rapidly to outnumber their hosts. Indeed, with the introduction of black slavery, the African population of the colonies, by 1790 approximately one fifth the total European population, was larger than that of the Indian.

This invasion, so much more devastating than that of any other European nation, has many roots. England during the period in question was undergoing a relatively rapid population increase, but perhaps more important, a rapid urban growth. This was the period of the "enclosure" laws when large numbers were driven from the land, and from the stable rural society it represented, into the insecurity of the towns and cities. The poor and rootless grew in numbers in relation to the rest of the population. At the same time that there was a need to cope with this segment of the people, there was frequent religious upheaval, Puritan against Anglican and both against Catholic. Under these conditions the existence of a "land of opportunity" found many takers.

The nature of the English system of colonial exploitation also contributed to the realization of the potential for massive migration. In tidewater Virginia, settlement in the early stages was under the auspices of private corporations who sent out colonists as employees of the corporation to work developing tobacco plantations. Land was freely available through a system of headrights granting fifty acres to every new arrival or sponsor, but the "employees" rapidly set up for themselves and had to be replaced continually. Indians in most of the colonial area were never amenable to wage work or enslavement, and until the introduction of black slavery a constant supply of Europeans was required. Similarly, bond servants who had served their fixed period of indenture (usually four years) could then acquire land, and replacements

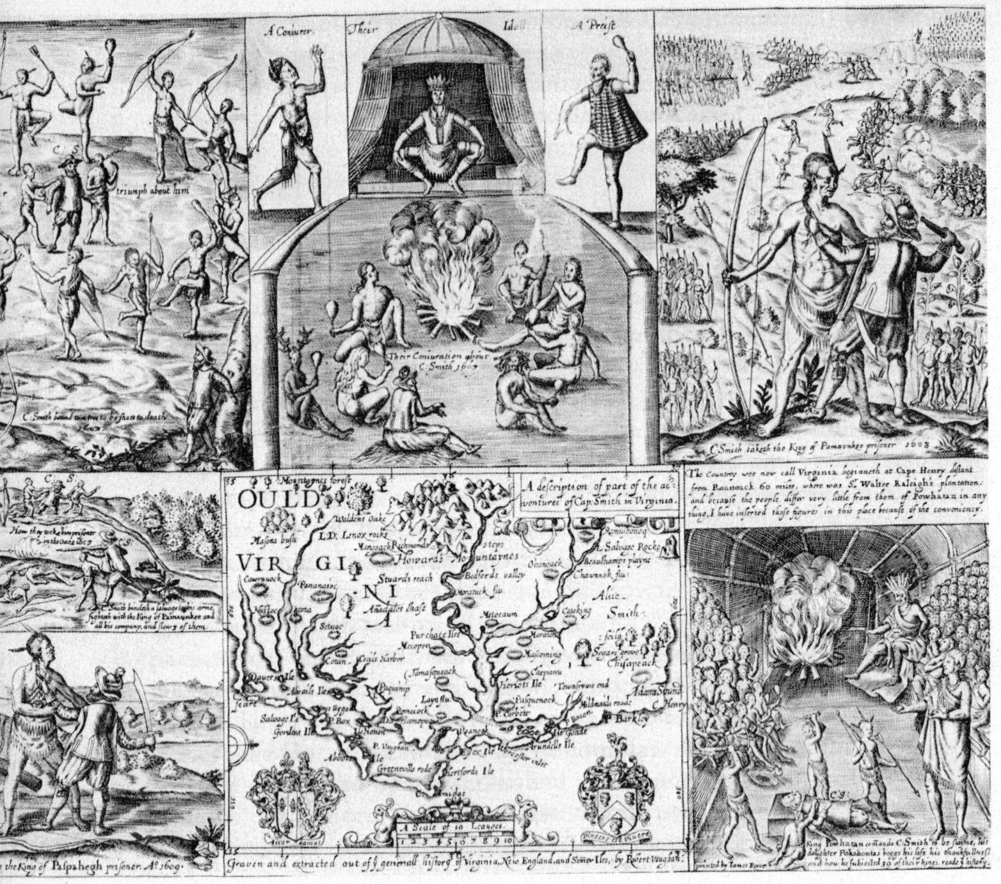

Captain John Smith's map of "Ould Virginia" and illustrations of his "adventures" were included in his Generall Historie of Virginia, *which was published in 1624. Smith freely adapted material from the engravings of de Bry. (The Rare Book Division, The New York Public Library, Astor, Lenox and Tilden Foundations)*

for them would have to be imported. Scarce labor meant high wages as well as ample land. Large numbers, of course, came involuntarily as colonies became an alternative dumping ground for felons sentenced to "transportation," and perhaps as many as half of the total were "bound" voluntarily or otherwise.

From the point of view of the impact upon the Indian, the greatest problem was the combination of these large numbers and their land hunger with the lack of any cohesive program of Indian relations. Although nominally under the direction of the English Crown, the American revolution was clear enough evidence of the weakness of English control. Each colony, separately established for a wide range of reasons, continued to pursue its own course only loosely coordinated by the Crown. The Spanish created a rigidly centralized system able to enforce with some reliability their policies toward the Indian, but every such effort by England was ignored by some segment of the colonials, usually the people on the edge of the frontier. Time and again royal authority set limits to expansion only to find them flouted by the independent Americans.

At the risk of great oversimplification, the essence of the matter was that while the French sought to trade with the Indians, and the Spanish sought to save their souls and put them to work, the British had no use for them at all. The Indians were exploited by traders, enslaved by hacendados, coerced and humiliated by governors and missionaries, but in the French and Spanish scheme of things there was a place for the Indian that was lacking in the Anglo-American's.

The British settlers worried aloud about their justification for taking the land of the Americas, but however much rhetoric was generated by these concerns, it had little or no practical effect. Where the Crown of Spain erected in the "laws of the Indies" a system of control and instruction for relations with the Indians, the Crown of England in its letters of patent generally granted absolute right to lands without mention of Indian rights. Each chartered company or individual, as a matter of practicality or personal philosophy and not according to any formalized state policy, had to make the decision about what relations with the Indians were to be. As late as 1756, Edmond Atkin, a British agent appointed to the southern tribes, could observe, "Some of the Colonies have made no regulations at all in Indian affairs. . . . Seldom if at all (have they) sent proper persons to look into them."[5] Regardless of individual expressions of good or ill feeling which might be quoted by historians to "prove" one thing or another, this lack of coordination and codification amounted to no Indian policy at all.

The Spanish were much concerned with the legality of their land acquisition, resting their actions largely on the exchange of goods, services, and land for the benefit of Christianity. The Virginia Company advertised in 1610 that in their commerce with the Indians they "doe buy of them the pearles of earth and sell to them the pearles of heaven,"[6] but the Virginia colonists, unlike the Spanish, brought with them no cadre of dedicated friars to accomplish their end of the exchange. Both Spanish and French were everywhere engaged in missionary activity as a matter of official policy and with Crown support. Often the proselytizing monks led the advance into new territories and conquests were made on behalf of their mission. The English clergy spoke much of the duty of Christianization, but did little, and not the least of the reasons for this were the lack of state support and the lack of the dedicated religious brotherhoods in the Protestant tradition.

The Massachusetts Bay Company, an avowedly religiously oriented group (Puritans), spoke explicitly of their intentions to fulfill their duty toward the heathen in their original charter. The problem here and with several other of the New England religious groups is that the nature of their creed did not promote evangelical activity. They fled from a corrupt England to seek their own salvation in a purified life which had little room for still more degenerate creatures like the Indians. Salvation is an individual matter in this Protestant approach and not a matter of forms and good works so much as "inner" grace. Eventually there were private organizations like the New England Company, which raised funds for the conversion of the Indian, but the chronicler of that organization notes that for "its first fifty years it was alone in the field."[7] The ministers of all of the English sects concerned themselves primarily with their European flocks, and although there are some instances of mission activity it was, as with all else in Indian policy, not a program but a collection of isolated individual actions. The Christianization of the Indian was never more than a minor and sporadic purpose of English settlement, encouraged but never accomplished.

If the English did not seek the Indians' souls, as the Spanish did, neither did they seek their labor, or, at least, they soon abandoned any hope of harnessing it. The Algonquin and other of the coastal groups, as shall be seen in the next chapter, were small in number and scattered widely throughout the area. Unlike the peasant farmers of Mesoamerica, they were only loosely organized and not accustomed to direction from a central state. The British found them unwilling to work in the fields on any consistent basis even where there were enough of them to make that desirable for the British, and while enslavement was practiced, particularly in the southern colonies, the difficulties were greater than the results.

The Spanish conquest of Mesoamerica was swift and complete, but the piecemeal approach of the British involved them in constantly recurring hostilities. Once the Spanish had usurped the reins of the preexisting state power there was no further significant resistance, but for the British each small tribe or chiefdom presented a separate problem. Their own lack of consistency and ever-growing expansion further prevented stable relations. John Smith said of the Indians: "They are inconstant in everiething, but what feare constraineth them to keepe. Craftie, timerous, quicke of apprehension and very ingenuous."[8] The result in terms of using Indian labor is obvious. Indians were distrusted and feared and even when pacified could not be relied upon. Indian slaves, because of the constant temptation of the possibility of escape or involvement in revolts under these unsettled conditions, were no more useful.

In conflict with the Indians, unable to put them to work, and largely uninterested in their souls, the British had only one continuing involvement with them, and that was in terms of trade. In the South this trade revolved largely around buckskin (tanned deer skins) and in the North around furs of many kinds, particularly beaver for the hat-makers. Certain of the larger and more astute Indian societies managed to forge temporarily successful relations with the Europeans based on this trade, and many became heavily dependent on European manufactured trade goods, particularly firearms. However, as the tide of settlement advanced, the supply of game inevitably declined, and those whites on the frontier who were interested in the trade moved their dealings further and further inland. The decline of game animals, of which the virtual extinction of the buffalo was the most dramatic example, was a minor inconvenience to the whites, only a handful of whom depended on this trade, but a disaster to the Indians whose whole life it was.

The Indian trade was always secondary and readily sacrificed to the primary concerns of the colonists. The French were interested in little else than the fur trade, but the primary orientation of the English was to agriculture, much of it simple subsistence farming but increasingly market cropping. Tobacco in the South was the earliest and single most important export crop, but indigo, rice, and farther north, fish and wheat were all significant. These and the rapidly developing manufacturing and processing industries almost immediately held greater economic importance than the Indian trade, and by the time of independence such trade was of little significance.

Move Over, Brother

The British interest in the Indians was ultimately a negative one. What emerges in an examination of the colonial period is an overwhelming tendency toward acquiring land from the Indians *without* the Indians. The reservation system was only a culmination of a long-standing process of separating the Indians from the land and keeping them apart from the areas of white settlement. Whatever humanitarian motives may be ascribed to the process of continually drawing lines dividing Indian land from European land, as in the frequent insistence that such compartmentalization was for the "protection" of the Indian, the net result was to prevent cultural interchange and cooperation that might have led to some degree of integration. There is in this interest in land without Indians a refusal to accept responsibility for the situation of the dispossessed people that continued up until the time, at the end of the nineteenth century, that there was no more "empty" land to which to move the problem. Until that point the Indians *were* the problem; afterward concern turned to the problems *of* the Indian.

The Virginia colonies started the process after the second of their "wars" with the Powhatan confederacy in 1646 when they drew a line of separation between themselves and these people. On a larger scale, one of the outcomes of the French and Indian War was an attempt by the Crown to define an outer limit to colonial settlement roughly along the lines of the Appalachians. The area west of the line proclaimed in 1763 was to be reserved for the Indians. A glance at the map in Chapter 11 shows the inexorable march of the Indians' "cessions" of land under this system of "treaties." The most dramatic of these and the most unilateral was the Removal Act of 1830, enacted under the auspices of President Andrew Jackson, which cleared virtually all remaining Indians to the west of the Mississippi.

Land was acquired by purchase in many cases, although, as our examination of the treaty system will show, it was unlikely that the seller fully understood the transaction. It was often acquired by "right of conquest" with the aftermath of every conflict between Indian and white usually involving the cessions of some amount of land. More curiously, "the right of conquest" cost the Indians their land when it was not they who were conquered. After the revolution, the new United States asserted their right to vast tracts of land "granted" to them by the defeated British and occupied by Indians who had no active part in the war. Florida, Louisiana Territory, and other areas all "changed hands" according to such a theory, much to the surprise of the Indians when they were informed.

Often the land was simply taken over if it was adjudged to be "unoccupied." It was not long before such obviously unfair acts could be "justified" by the savage and violent reaction of the Indian in his resistance to such encroachment, but other doctrines were also advanced. Like the Spanish, the British settlers, although they did little about it, put forth their Christianizing and civilizing mission as fair exchange. The new United States added a kind of secular crusading aspect with the doctrine of inexorable advance through "manifest destiny." My personal favorite is the argument that the Indians were not using the land anyhow. As wrote John Winthrop, one of the original Puritan settlers:

> As for the Natives in New England, they inclose noe land, neither have any settled habytation, nor any tame Cattle to improve the Land by, and soe have noe other but a Naturall Right to these Countries, soe as if we leave them sufficent for their use, we may lawfully take the rest, there being more than enough for them and us.[9]

I insisted in the first chapter that I did not intend to put forth a "devil" theory of history ascribing the fate of the Indian to the action of "evil" men. That is still the case. A thousand instances can be found where men fought and debated in favor of Indian "rights" to balance every case of naked injustice. From the first to the last, most policies and laws regarding the Indians were, at least in part, intended, however

French Huguenots attempted settlement in Florida, near present St. Augustine, only to be destroyed by the Spanish. This de Bry engraving was made from a painting by Jacques Le Moyne, who arrived in Florida in 1564. The Timucuan Indians shown here "in council" are making use of the ritual "black drink." (Courtesy National Anthropological Archives, Smithsonian Institution)

mistakenly, for the benefit of all, including the Indian. The very language of the treaties was often an exercise in poetic humanity, even if the outcomes were not. However, the unfortunate historical reality of the primacy of land acquisition over goodwill is inescapable. The Cherokee were the most dramatic proof of this, since by 1830 they were generally recognized as "civilized," having organized their own parliamentary government, having adopted European housing, clothing, and farming, having become more literate than their neighbors, and having turned entirely peaceful under their own national police force and judicial system. None of this saved them and all the other "civilized" tribes from being uprooted and moved west of the Mississippi. It is extremely difficult to say what more the Cherokee could have done after having argued and *won* their case before the Supreme Court to prevent this. It seems clear that by this late date it really did not matter what steps the Indians took to come to terms with the whites as long as they occupied land that others wanted.

Ultimately, it does not much matter what the European settlers *said* their intentions were or even what they believed in their hearts. Historically what matters is what was done, and in that context the Indian position does not seem to have been very much different from that of the forests. Both were something to be cleared away so that more important uses could be made of the land on which they stood! The Indian may have been hated by some and loved by others, but the most tragic fact that seems to emerge is that more often the posture toward the Indian was to regard him as a nuisance—like crabgrass. Only when some few Indian groups were effectively able to interfere with European plans was serious attention paid to them in the form of treaties and agreements. Only then were treaties kept. But the number of Indian societies that could compel this attention was very few indeed. The "mighty" Iroquois League at its height could field only 2000 to 3000 warriors, and although any of the individual colonies could easily double these numbers, no other Indian group could approach even the limited power of the Iroquois League.

Contact between two societies is a two-way street, as the succeeding chapters will show. However, I have stressed European motives here at the beginning because whatever it might have been that a particular group of Indians had in mind, it was not they who were in control of the situation. Although the colonists may have proceeded ineptly and often at cross purposes with one another, it was they who exercised whatever choice might exist. If things did not come out the way they had planned, it was not because the Indians chose otherwise. They certainly tried—through flight, and warfare, and messiahs—to influence the course of events, but ultimately it was beyond their power. How and why this came to be will, it is hoped, emerge in the following chapters.

Some Readings

Cipolla, Carlo M.: *Guns, Sails and Empires: Technological Innovation and the Early Phases of European Expansion, 1400–1700,* New York: Pantheon Books, 1966.

Clough, Shepard B., et al.: *European History in a World Perspective,* vol. 1, *Ancient Times to 1715,* 3d ed., Lexington, Mass.: D. C. Heath, 1975. The student should consult this or one of the many other general surveys of European history.

Gibson, Charles: *Spain in America,* New York: Harper and Row, 1966.

Hanke, Lewis: *The Spanish Struggle for Justice in the Conquest of America,* Boston: Little, Brown, 1965. Classical account of the legal struggles and soul searchings of the conquerors.

Nash, Gary B.: *Red, White and Black: The People of Early America,* Englewood Cliffs, N.J.: Prentice-Hall, 1974. Very readable account of the interaction of Indian and White in initial contact.

Peckham, Howard, and Charles Gibson (eds.): *Attitudes of Colonial Powers Toward the American Indian,* Salt Lake City: University of Utah, 1969. Invaluable collection of essays.

Generally useful sources for the historical chapters

Hodge, William: *A Bibliography of Contemporary North American Indians,* New York: Interland Publishing, 1976. Supplements Murdock's larger but less currently focused compilation of sources.

Kappler, Charles J.: *Indian Treaties: 1778–1883,* New York: Interland Publishing, 1972. Reprint of Kappler's collection of Indian treaties originally printed for U.S. Senate use in 1904.

Spicer, Edward H.: *A Short History of the Indians of the United States,* New York: Van Nostrand, 1969. Short, accurate, readable, and insightful.

Washburn, Wilcomb E.: *The American Indian and the United States: A Documentary History,* 4 vol., New York: Random House, 1973. Excellent resource containing basic documents of Indian-White contact, ranging from the reports of Indian commissioners to acts, ordinances, and debates of Congress, including numerous critical legal decisions. Texts of treaties and court cases mentioned will be easily found here or in Kappler.

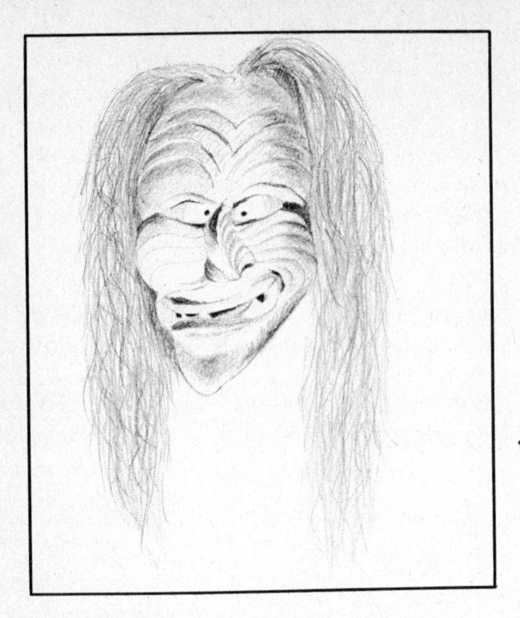

VIII

TREATIES AND TEARS

It is said that God is always on the side of the heaviest battalions.
Voltaire

"Acculturation comprehends those phenomena which result when groups of individuals having different cultures come into continuous first-hand contact, with subsequent changes in the original cultural patterns of either or both groups,"[1] and that is the theme which will be followed for the rest of the book. Much of this will concern itself with planned, purposeful change, such as the setting up of the reservation system and the various attempts to turn nomads into farmers, but there is much more to "contact change" than this. By the definition given above and in actual truth, death, individual or social, can be considered an acculturation phenomenon. As indicated, disease introduced by Europeans decimated and often more than decimated the Indian populations. This factor alone was sufficient to lead to the disintegration of some Indian societies or, as was more common, to weaken them to the point that small pressures would push them over the edge. One result of contact change I am obviously suggesting is the elimination, through one means or another, of one of the societies in contact.

The East Coast was populated by a myriad of Algonkian-speaking tribes including the Mohican, who are remembered primarily because of the book *The Last of the Mohicans* by James Fenimore Cooper. (Confusingly, there were also tribes called Mahicans and Mohegans.[2]) Similar book titles would have been appropriate for a great many other tribes if written within a short time of contact. Ruth Underhill in her book *Red Man's America* listed such tribes under a subtitle, "They Have Gone," and indeed they have.[3] In recent years groups of persons have identified themselves with these vanished peoples, but the reality of their "Indianness" will require examination at another later point. Suffice it to say that the genetic, legal, and cultural connections of these revived ones is much debated. As distinct autonomous societies recognized as such by themselves or others, most Algonkians ceased to exist in their ancestral lands within a very few years of contact. Some survived as peoples by fleeing before the white advance. These included the remarkable Kickapoo (who really do exist outside of *Li'l Abner* comics), who wound up in Coahuila, Mexico, and Oklahoma, after wanderings that put Ulysses to shame.

A great deal of this destruction of peoples and their societies was unintentional, but some was not. The Pequot were very nearly wiped out by warfare with the whites, and the broken remnants were scattered among other peoples, which finally extinguished their existence as a group. The Puritan fathers who accomplished this used methods whose intentions cannot be mistaken, as in the attack on the fortified Pequot settlement at Mystic, Connecticut, where "there were about four hundred soules in this Fort, and not above five of them escaped out of our hands."[4] That is to say they were all killed, about which the same author had this to say: "Scripture declareth women and children must perish with their parents; sometimes the case alters: but we will not dispute it now. We had sufficient light from the word of God for our proceedings."[5] The Pequots, one must add, were not blameless innocents, but history records the fort was surrounded, burned, and all who fled the flames slaughtered.

The options open to the Indian peoples in these early stages were decidedly limited even when they began to recognize that white settlers were destroying their game, occupying the best land, and interfering with their movements and their lives. Resentments led occasionally to outbreaks of war as a class of Indian response, presumably with the hope of throwing the devils into the sea! Powhatan's confederacy in Virginia, under Powhatan's successor, Opechancanough, twice attacked the colonists, and was broken up as a cohesive unit as a result of the second attack. King Phillip, a leader of the Wampanoags, led a similar uprising in New England with a number of allied tribes, which resulted, as did all such attempts, in military defeat and further disruption of the Indian societies. In every case armed resistance did little more than accelerate the decline of the peoples who attempted it. In many cases it is difficult to say, as it often is in warfare, who began the fighting (conflicts with the Susquehanna, Esopus, and others); but the end result was always the same—defeat.

Disease and death in battle are overt and obvious causes of decline. More subtle was the ever-increasing unbalancing of the ecological system on which Indian life, with its mixture of the hunt and cultivation, depended. An excellent illustration is the consequence of tobacco cultivation, which very early became a focus of colonial economic activity in the southern areas. Tobacco could be grown on a given piece of land for three to four years, but the soil would have been exhausted in that time and would optimally have to be left to "rest" for up to twenty years to regain its fertility. Obviously the land would have to be cleared of forest for these purposes and the amount of land cleared would have to be four to five times as much as the amount in cultivation at any given moment to allow for the "resting" period. As a result of tobacco growing in one part of Maryland, timber had become scarce by the 1720s.[6] There are parallels of interest to the archeologist in the limitations imposed on the density of Maya settlement in the Yucatan of Mexico, as a result of a similar rotating pattern of cultivation, and in the small size of the settlements in the tidewater tobacco areas. For the present purpose it should simply be indicated that not only was there a torrent of ever-increasing European settlement, but in areas of this sort the land taken from Indian hands was far greater than that suggested even by the growing population figures.

The clearing of the forest, the preempting of water (settlements clustered along watercourses), and the confiscation of the best, most fertile land not only eliminated or reduced Indian agricultural productivity but effectively wiped out game resources which were very nearly as vital to their subsistence. Destruction of their means of livelihood was in the long run a more devastating blow than the immediate population losses brought about by disease and warfare, because it allowed no possibility of recovery.

The Algonkians also had other troubles—the Iroquois!

Sachems and Saviors

Dekanawidah and Hiawatha were, according to the legendary Iroquois historical accounts, the creators of the Great League of the Iroquois. (The

Hiawatha of Longfellow's poem is largely derived from Ojibwa legend and has nothing to do with the real one.) Dekanawidah, more god than man, enlisted Hiawatha, a Mohawk, as his spokesman to persuade all of the Iroquois tribes to band together in the "great peace." The result was the League, consisting of the Onondaga, Mohawk, Seneca, Oneida, Cayuga; the original "Five Nations" later expanded to six with the addition of the Tuscarora. When this actually occurred is a source of considerable debate, but most agree that it was sometime in the sixteenth century, although whether it was a direct result of white contacts is still disputed. Other groups in the area also formed confederacies of sorts, but none was ever so successful as the League. The League by no means included all of the Iroquoian-speaking peoples. Some, such as the Huron, who were Iroquoian in speech, were deadly enemies of the League, although in general the power of the League was directed against Algonkians.

Whatever its beginnings as some sort of offensive/defensive alliance to assist the member tribes to deal with their hostile neighbors, the League rose to prominence and importance through an attempt to control for its own profit the fur trade. The northeastern tribes very rapidly became dependent on a wide range of European trade goods, another acculturation process involving the creation of new needs. Guns and powder were critical items, but household utensils of metal, steel knives and hatchets, and the calumet (a combination of pipe and hatchet) all replaced aboriginal items and became necessities. Wampum, belts formerly made of shell beads traded with the coastal Algonkians and primarily important as a kind of mnemonic record-keeping and message medium, came to be a kind of medium of exchange and were mass-produced by traders. When their own immediate hunting grounds declined in trapping productivity, the Iroquois expanded into the territory of other tribes and sought to have all trade in furs funneled through their own hands. To some extent because of its organization, but perhaps equally because of its access to a large number of guns early on, the League became the dominant Indian military force in the Northeast, controlling or influencing, from their upper New York State home, peoples from the coast to the Great Lakes and the Ohio country.

The League has been introduced here because it acted as the nether millstone for the atomization of the Algonkian peoples. The competition over the fur trade was ultimately expressed in armed struggle between the French and British colonies, culminating in the French and Indian Wars and the elimination of the French in 1763. All of the various "wars"—King William's War, Queen Anne's War, King George's War, etc.—inevitably involved the alliance of Indian groups. The Hurons were the most powerful of the French allies, but many of the Algonkians were allies as well, while the Iroquois were relatively consistent supporters of the British.

A war of raid and ambuscade, with the burning of crops and homes, raged periodically through the frontier areas, completing the decline of the coastal groups. Some, such as the Delawares, were allowed by the Iroquois to flee into lands under their control at the price of accepting Iroquois dominance and agreeing to being used as a kind of buffer by being settled between the Iroquois and the advancing white tide of settlement. Others, such as the Kickapoo, survived by fleeing beyond the Iroquois lands. The rest underwent atomization, a breaking down of their societies, until each individual confronted white society on his own and found what place he could in that structure. Always at the lowest levels, of course, these remnant peoples became more or less assimilated into colonial society, vanishing as an organized, autonomous culture.

Forest Statesmen

The League of the Iroquois is worth describing in greater detail as one of the few at least temporarily successful adaptations to white contact and also as a vehicle for further discussion of Anglo-American "treaty" policies. Since much of the League's success depended on a delicate balancing act between rival European powers, the end of Iroquois prominence is coincidental with the American Revolution and the emergence of a single government uninterested in placating the Indians for higher European political motives. As shall be seen, the triumph of the colonists in the Revolutionary War was an unmitigated disaster from the Indian point of view.

The League was a curious mixture of kinship principles of a tribal character underlying a political state. The "government" of the League was a central council which met at least once a year at Onondaga and more frequently when circumstances required it. The council was made up of hereditary legislators called sachems, fifty in all, apportioned unevenly among the member tribes. The sachems voted according to a caucus system (each delegation voting as a bloc), and the disproportion of representation did not have any great effect because of the necessity for all significant decisions to be unanimous. The council was responsible only for "foreign affairs," that is, matters affecting the League as a whole, and each tribe maintained its own councils and total control of internal affairs.

The sachem titles (some of which were of higher rank than others) were hereditary in particular matrilineages within each of the tribal groups. In that context, however, they were elective, suitable candidates nominated by the women but ratified and accepted by the men. Such a choice was necessarily ratified by the tribal group as a whole even though the candidates could only come from the particular lineage. In addition there were "Pine Tree chiefs," apparently men of great reputation as warriors who were allowed to speak in the great councils, but who could

Cornplanter, brother of the prophet Handsome Lake, was himself an important Seneca sachem during the last days of the Iroquois League. Painting by F. Bartoli, 1796. (Courtesy of the New York Historical Society, New York City)

not vote. The decision-making process, given the limited mandate of the council, was necessarily a matter of endless oratory to bring about some consensus. Toward the end of the colonial period the limitations of such methods were shown in the inability of the League to present a united front in the British-American conflict, with some segments even within a single tribe, the Seneca, being on opposite sides in the struggle.

There is considerable debate in archaeological circles about the time of the arrival of the Iroquois in the Northeast area. Until recently, the general view was that they were intruders in modern times from the

Southeast, but opinion has begun to shift and allow them much longer residence in the area. There was not a great deal to distinguish them from their Algonkian neighbors except perhaps a more complete reliance on agriculture than some of the northern peoples. The Iroquois were matrilineal in kin organization, and it was the women who owned and worked the fields. The men during the great days of the League wandered far afield in search of peltry, raiding their enemies and conducting complex diplomacy in trade and war. They would frequently absent themselves from their longhouse villages for months, even years at a time, while the women remained in place tending the fields and the household. This is what was meant in an earlier reference to a society of nomadic men and sedentary women.

The system of matriclans was one element of stability since most of the clans had named equivalents in all Five Nations, and the Iroquois sought to regard all members of the League as kinsmen to one degree or another. Like the southeastern peoples, the actual functioning unit for most important matters was the village, and the internal structure of the village was largely a matter of clan relationships. The tribes which possessed their own councils met infrequently as a group and acted together less reliably than the village unit or even the League as a whole, since the League limited itself to broad matters in which its authority was recognized. Much of the warfare engaged in was the usual tribal business of clan vengeance and feud, and the League as an instrument of internal peace functioned to channel that hostility toward external enemies to the benefit of the Iroquois. Theoretically, according to the Dekanawidah legend, the Iroquois had a great mission (much as the Aztec saw themselves as "Soldiers of the Sun") to bring all nations to the "white roots of the Great Tree of Peace"; and their warfare was waged with this ideological justification. Even today some Iroquois are engaged in a sort of pan-Indian movement which seeks to accomplish this task of unification under the banner of the "Great Tree of Peace."

The Utmost Good Faith[7]

The dealings of the Iroquois with the Anglo-Americans can serve as the reference point for a discussion of the development of Indian "policy" and the underlying concepts of the treaty system. For a compilation of pertinent documents, see the invaluable collection by Charles Kappler, *Indian Treaties 1778–1883*.[8]

In the last chapter the general pattern of philosophical justification for the taking of Indian land was introduced. This can be summed up by the principles of the right of "discovery" and the right of "conquest" as more or less legitimate and recognized means of transferring land according to the nonexistent but much discussed "laws of nations." In view of the relatively disorganized character of the Indian societies and the scattered pattern of population, curious variants were added to these broad principles based on the notion that land not used for agricultural purposes was freely available to whoever chose to claim it. In practical terms the general tendency was to treat Indian "chiefs" or "kings" as if they were European sovereigns and to coerce or seduce them into signing "treaties" which acknowledged their acceptance of European political sovereignty. Lands were thus "purchased" or "ceded" through agreement in these treaties. Again in practical terms these treaties were worth only what the parties to them chose to accept and only for so long as it pleased them. Obviously there was no higher authority of "law" to enforce agreements between sovereigns, and at this early stage each Indian group was treated as an independent "nation." European nations recognized each other's "rights"—as the series of wars between the French and English showed—with no more care than those of the savages. If they were more scrupulous in these relations, it was a matter of recognizing the weightier consequences of chicanery against a sovereign that possessed armies and fleets.

Similarly, the Iroquois, because of their relatively greater power, were treated with some deference in treaty matters. In effect, the British, through a series of treaties, sought to buy Iroquois assistance against the French and to enlist Iroquois influence over their dependent and tributary tribes. Tribes which had no such influence received no treaties and no recognition and respect of rights even when those had theoretically been granted. Because of many treaties made with "chiefs" who possessed no real binding authority, wars were provoked—the purchasers sought to take possession of their land from peoples who had no notion that it had been sold. The Iroquois, in the Treaty of Fort Stanwix of 1768, sold off the claims of themselves and all of their allies to lands south of the Ohio River. The principal occupants and users of these lands were the Shawnee who naturally resisted the transaction. An often quoted statement by Chief Joseph of the Nez Perce sums up this sort of procedure:

> Suppose a white man should come to me and say, "Joseph, I like your horses and want to buy them." I say to him, "No, my horses suit me. I wll not sell them." Then he goes to my neighbor and says to him, "Joseph has some good horses. I want to buy them but he refuses to sell." My neighbor answers, "Pay me the money and I will sell you Joseph's horses." The white man returns to me and says, "Joseph, I have bought your horses and you must let me have them." If we sold our lands to the government that is the way they were bought.[9]

As noted in previous discussions, none of the Indian leaders possessed the power to bind and loosen his followers and dispose of land at will. As a general rule land was regarded as property only in the context of belonging to the tribal group as a whole, and while its use might be granted and revoked by the appropriate decision in council, the concept of "fee simple" ownership was utterly alien to the Indian. Chiefs, even the sachems of the League, whose decisions did not suit their followers, could not enforce their will, reliably offering, as noted, plenty of openings for charges of bad faith and treachery. As also noted, while the Crown might seek permanent and stable Indian relations, the "long knives" (frontiersmen) did not, and the Crown could no more control their tumultuous relations with the Indians than the Indians could restrain their peoples from seeking blood vengeance.

This clearly chaotic treaty-making period took on an entirely different character when the colonists won their independence and asserted complete authority over the Indian peoples. From the beginning of the new nation, the Articles of Confederation, the Constitution, and the Northwest Ordinances all pronounced the supremacy of the federal government in the regulation of Indian affairs. It was a long time before the individual states ceased to interfere in this relation; indeed, at the time of this writing, state courts in the state of Washington continue to attempt intervention in the matter of control of Indian fishing. Still, from the beginning the principle existed, however vaguely, of an exclusive right to regulate Indian relations vested in the federal government, although a "Bureau of Indian Affairs" was not created until 1824. The general procedure continued to be the making of treaties until 1871 when Congress unilaterally declared an end to this policy.

The new United States began with a new form of conquest theory. When Britain at the Treaty of Paris (1783) ceded the lands east of the Mississippi and south of the Great Lakes to the new nation, the policy of the new government was that the United States had gained ownership as well as sovereignty over these lands by right of having defeated the British Indian allies as well as the British themselves. The policy was that each Indian nation must therefore come to separate peace terms with the United States, at which point they might be allowed to retain some portions of their lands if the new government saw fit. The fact that a great many Indian tribes either were neutral or had supported the rebels seems to have impressed no one.

The Second Treaty of Fort Stanwix in 1784 with the then Six Nations of the Iroquois was an arrogant expression of this policy which cost the Iroquois the support and respect of their former dependents and tributaries for their abject surrender to the Americans. The Iroquois had indeed supported the British more than they had the rebels, and for this they paid dearly in land and in the effective dissolution of their League and in the loss of their power. Power, however, shifted to a western confederacy of tribes in the Ohio country, who were not so completely in the Americans' grasp as were the New York Iroquois. The turmoil resulting in the border country led Henry Knox as Secretary of War to enunciate a new policy in 1789 which declared that the Indians were the legitimate possessors of the soil and that it could be taken from them only by a process of purchase and negotiation. This repudiation of the conquest theory did not, however, relinquish American sovereignty and was essentially a pragmatic recognition that the previous policy was unrealistic. The growing tide of Indian land cessions between 1784 and 1810 clearly indicates that the expansion did not cease.

In 1803 with the completion of the Louisiana Purchase came the suggestion from President Jefferson that a solution might be reached by removing the Indians to the territory west of the Mississippi, setting limits to American expansion much as the British had attempted to do with their Appalachian limit to settlement. The British for their own imperial purposes had continued to encourage the resistance of western Indian groups to American expansion, and this policy found its final expression in the alliance of many Indian groups with British forces in the War of 1812. By 1806 Tecumseh and his brother, known as the "Prophet," had begun to form a federation of their own Shawnees and other western tribes to resist further white encroachment on their lands. The idea of uniting to deny the whites further land was to recur again and again in Indian movements of reaction. Tecumseh fell in the War of 1812 but had for some years inflamed the whole border to violent resistance, aided by the widespread belief in the mystical powers of his brother. In the Treaty of Ghent signed in 1814, the British in effect abandoned their Indian allies to the complete control of the United States, removing for the last time any alternative to accommodation with that government. The pattern of that accommodation became increasingly apparent as the government pushed westward a line of forts and imposed treaties forcing the Indians into territories across the Mississippi.

The culmination of this phase was the Indian Removal Act of 1830 which called for the removal of *all* Indians from the area east of the Mississippi, rather than the piecemeal approach that had been followed since the War of 1812. The specific impetus for this action was the pressure being brought on the federal government by the state of Georgia to extinguish sovereignty and land title held in her territories by the so-called Civilized Tribes. Georgia had claimed, as did many other states, lands stretching to the Mississippi and only gave these claims up to the federal government on receipt of promises to extinguish remaining Indian land claims within the state's boundaries. President Monroe publicly endorsed in 1825 the policy of removal and took limited action, such as the Treaty of Indian Springs with a Creek minority faction led by the mixed-blood leader William McIntosh, in which lands were ceded and agreement obtained for removal. McIntosh was executed by the Creek for this deed and the treaty was repudiated. Sufficiently blatant fraud was discovered to cause then President John Quincy Adams to negotiate a new treaty in 1827. This gave the Creek better terms but still

In the U.S. Census Extra Bulletin on the Five Civilized Tribes, this house was referred to as "Residence of Charles Journeycake, Chief of the Delaware Indians, Cherokee Nation, 1890." Clearly, the far-wandering Delaware absorbed much of the material culture of the "civilized" whites. (Courtesy National Archives)

contained the agreement for removal. We can best examine the events surrounding the removal by a consideration of the situation of the Cherokee; their resistance provoked many legal maneuvers, including the doctrine of "dependent domestic nations" in the Supreme Court case of *Worcester v. Georgia*—which did not save the Cherokee from removal but did rationalize the treaty system.

Removal and Revitalization

When a human society finds itself disintegrating because none of the normal procedures which characterize it are having the appropriate result, the possibility of a social movement of some sort may arise. The basic requirements for such a movement are a failure of the existing social structures and a conscious awareness on the part of the people that such a failure has occurred. Generally the people have begun to sink into anomie, a condition of purposelessness characterized by high suicide rates, alcoholism, and other indicators of despair. If, in the situation where traditional structures have failed, an appropriate program of remedial action is put forward by a leader or leaders that promises relief, we may find the development of a social movement. The military and political movements like those of Tecumseh represented such a conscious and purposeful attempt to rectify the undesirable conditions that afflicted Indian societies. In this section two other sorts of movement will be examined: the formation by the Cherokee of a political state modeled on European lines (an eminently practical sort of movement) and the religious movement of Handsome Lake, often known as the Longhouse religion, which did much to transform the declining Iroquois after the collapse of the League.

The Cherokee, who at one time were located further east, had at the opening of the nineteenth century gradually yielded land and settled into northern Georgia, Alabama, and adjacent areas of Tennessee. They had involved themselves, as had the Iroquois, in British-American disputes and had suffered as a result, but in the process of contact they had taken on many of the characteristics of the white society. Aboriginally much like the description given of the Creek, the Cherokee were by this time recognized as "civilized" because they dressed in white style, erected log cabins, owned slaves, and in general behaved superficially much like their white neighbors. Unlike the Iroquois, their linguistic relatives, the Cherokee had by and large accepted farming in the white fashion by the *men* as a viable adjustment, as trapping, hunting, and warfare became inappropriate or impossible patterns for male accomplishment. They had refused to join with other tribes in the uprising led by Tecumseh and had indeed acted in concert with the Americans to suppress a faction of Creeks that did rebel. The Cherokee were, however, subject to continual pressure from the expanding white frontier and particularly from the inhabitants and the government of Georgia to cede lands and move further west. Andrew Jackson, on behalf of the War Department, arranged with a handful of chiefs—as early as 1817—the cession of lands, and a few Cherokee were removed at this time.

Under these pressures, however, the Cherokee leaders, notably John Ross and other "mixed bloods" acting in cooperation with the traditional leaders, began what amounted to a planned, purposeful attempt to restructure their political organization in such a way as to retain their unity and allow them to more effectively resist the incessant white pressures. This effort was much aided by the remarkable Sequoia who, as indicated, devised a method of writing the Cherokee language which allowed the publication of a national newspaper, the *Cherokee Phoenix,* and facilitated increased communication and concerted action among the people. Literacy in their own language is reported to have been higher than literacy in English for the surrounding whites.

At their capital of New Echota, Georgia, the loose leadership pattern (much like that of the Creeks) was gradually shifted to an increasingly centralized form partially copied from white procedures and partially traditional in character. A bicameral legislature was established along with a written constitution, but elements of kinship usages were retained in the selection of governmental representatives. A strong national council was established to represent all Cherokees and had the exclusive power to act in land and other legal negotiations with the whites. A system of judiciary districts and a national police force ("Regulating Companies") acted to enforce the power of the government and to restrain the local leaders from selling land piecemeal to the whites. In this the police force was exempted from clan vengeance in the pursuit of its duties, and later all clan feuds were declared to be illegal in order to preserve, as with the Iroquois, the internal unity of the people.

Although never accepting Christianity in large numbers, the Cherokee nation encouraged missionary activity in its lands, but with an insistence that any mission must include schools. The general effect of the drive toward governmental unity and increased education and literacy resulted in an effective revitalization of Cherokee society within a remarkably short time. Left to themselves, the Cherokee seemed to be well on the road to a viable accommodation as a prosperous enclave within the larger society. It was not to be.

Andrew Jackson became president in 1828, and that partisan supporter of the superiority of "states rights" over the Indians brought the conflict to a head. In 1830 Georgia asserted that her laws applied in the Cherokee country with the Catch-22 proviso that no Indian could bring suit against a white in the courts or even be a witness in such cases. Indians, then, had no recourse whatever when whites encroached on their lands. The Cherokee, united as a people, took their case to the Supreme Court in the landmark *Cherokee Nation v. Georgia* in which Chief Justice John Marshall ruled against their attempt to gain an injunction. In the process, however, Marshall set forth the "domestic dependent nation" doctrine; and while ruling that the particular case was improper because the Cherokee could not act as a foreign nation, he openly invited further suit. A missionary apprehended under Georgia law served as the cause for the second landmark suit of *Worcester v. Georgia* in which Marshall ruled against the enforcement of state law to the extent that it interfered with the exclusive power of the federal government to regulate Indian affairs. Even Marshall made plain his belief that the Indian governments ultimately had to yield when he said, "The exercise of the power of self-government by the Indians, within a state is undoubtedly contemplated to be temporary. . . . A sound national policy does require that the Indian tribes within our states should exchange their territories, upon equitable principles, or eventually, consent to become amalgamated in our political communities."[10] Jackson already had authorization for the Indians' removal in the Bill of 1830 and is reputed to have said, "Justice Marshall has made his decision; now let him enforce it!"[11]

Inevitably with federal and state authorities against them, and their own system torn by these events, a minority of chiefs led by one known as The Ridge signed a treaty in 1835, agreeing to removal and ceding all remaining lands for $5,600,000—a matter of pennies per acre. Repudiated again by the legitimate government of the Cherokee, the treaty was nonetheless enforced by the United States in the now infamous "trail of tears," when the Cherokee people, inadequately supplied, were forced from their homes on the long march to Oklahoma. Figures can be debated, but none can doubt that thousands died in that removal, which went on until 1838. Choctaws, Chickasaws, and Creeks were similarly rounded up and marched westward. Under Oceola, the Seminole (actually a composite group of southeastern tribes) in Florida, fought a war that lasted until 1842 before the majority were removed, although small bands were never rooted out of their strongholds in the Everglades. Such fragmentary holdouts form the basis of the only Indian reservations that today survive east of the Mississippi. No major organized tribes were allowed to remain except for the Iroquois. At least 50,000 were swept away in this period, but as shall be shown in the next chapter the Cherokee revitalization was not yet crushed and was to be an important factor in the events in the "Indian territory."

Obviously there is little in the treatment of the eastern Indian tribes that could be described as just. A military officer said of Chief Joseph, "I think that, in his long career, Joseph cannot accuse the Government of the United States of one single act of justice."[12] Something similar could be observed of the removal period. Yet before slipping into a demon theory, some hard facts should be remembered. As noted, something like 50,000 Indians were removed in Jackson's campaign in the Southeast. But immigration to the United States in the 1830s was 500,000, in the 1840s 1,500,000, and in the 1850s 2,600,000. The population of the United States was 5,308,483 in 1800, 17,069,453 in 1840, and 31,443,321 by 1860! Something had to give before this torrent of growth and expansion, and it is unrealistic to suppose that the interests of the Indian would have prevailed regardless of the abstract justice of their position. In the same light, let us also consider that Jackson, in upholding "states rights" over the power of the federal government, was simply in tune with a conflict and a sectional dispute that would find its ultimate expression in the American Civil War. The issue of states rights was at least what the South claimed that war was all about, and had Jackson reneged on the solemn compact with the state of Georgia, that conflict might have been provoked earlier than it was.

"Gaiwiio": The Code of Handsome Lake

The Iroquois by 1800 were reduced to life on small, scattered "reservations" left to them by treaty in the aftermath of the onrush of white settlement and were without the means or land resources to live in their traditional patterns. Anthony Wallace in *The Death and Rebirth of the Seneca* has referred to their settlement at this time as "slums in the wilderness."[13] Some Iroquois who had sided with the British, principally those led by the Mohawk Joseph Brant, were given land in Canada in 1784; and this later became the "Six Nations Reserve" where dissidents set up an entirely separate "league" which still exists today. State and federal governments and private land speculators continued to cajole, threaten, and steadily nibble away at the remaining Iroquois lands. Rival leaders Cornplanter and Redjacket struggled for opposing policies, with Cornplanter's desire for friendship and accommodation with the Americans eventually triumphant, though at the cost of loss of all influence with those western tribes who continued to resist.

For the men particularly there was a great loss of purpose and self-respect. The once-mighty League had been defeated and humiliated at every turn and could only abjectly accept what it was given. Diplomacy and warfare were no longer pursuits allowed to the Iroquois men, and the fur trade had fallen to other hands in territories outside the remaining reservations. On every side was the example of the prosperity of the flourishing white communities in bitter contrast to the poverty and pointless life of the Iroquois, who were urged to emulate a life-style based on single-family agriculture alien to the clan-organized tribes whose women, not men, were responsible for the farming. Small wonder that alcoholism flourished and the tormented people sought scapegoats by accusing one another of witchcraft.

One Seneca, Handsome Lake, was a brother of Cornplanter and himself the holder of a hereditary sachem title. He was one of those who had succumbed to alcohol, but in 1799, at the age of about 50, he began to experience a series of prophetic visions. Handsome Lake had as a young man participated in the great days of the League and was witness to the contrast of that period with their fallen state. Past glories were sufficiently alive, at least in memory, to be the more painful for their mockery of the "slums in the wilderness."

Under such circumstances and usually at the hands of a man who, like Handsome Lake, bridged both worlds, several American Indian groups gave rise to religious movements which aimed in one way or another to restore past glories or create new utopias. These have been called "nativistic" movements, but I prefer the term used by Anthony Wallace, "revitalization," since the movements did not differ significantly from those that arose in Western societies, and the categorization implied by "nativistic" is condescending.[14] Christianity can be called a Jewish nativistic movement, but the term is never used in that way. In a general way, by an examination of the Handsome Lake movement we can gain insight into a class of religious social movements generated by contact disruption which seek to revitalize a dying social matrix. Others will be considered later, but since Wallace is both a theoretician of social movement and the author of a remarkably complete study of this particular religion, it will be examined somewhat more closely.

Cornplanter's people had been in the thick of the events of dissolution, and Handsome Lake would have been witness to it all. The village on the so-called Allegheny reservation was also close by a demonstration model farm of the Quakers which sought to educate the Indians while offering a degree of theological tolerance. Handsome Lake, like most of the prominent Indian prophets, was not only a man of both old and new Iroquois worlds but also a man acquainted with some part of the possibilities of the white world. At a time when his people were consciously aware of the failure of their old ways but not yet totally destroyed by events, as the Algonkians had been, Handsome Lake brought to them a message, a code of life, which offered an alternative to disintegration. It was a new way—Gaiwiio!—part white and part Indian in inspiration but accepted as profoundly Iroquois in final form. He began to formulate his message through dreams in accepted Iroquois fashion in 1799 and preached his doctrines, religious and social, until his death in 1815. In the 1850s a church based on his teachings was founded as an established part of the Iroquois culture. In this period a renaissance took place in Iroquois life.

The Iroquois were very interested in dream fulfillment, having theories about the consequences of their frustrations equivalent to those of the Freudians. A message brought in a dream was assumed to have great significance; and when Handsome Lake was taken through heaven by angels in a series of visions, it was fully in accord with Iroquois procedure. The message that he brought back for the salvation of his people was a mixture of the traditional and the new, but the most important element was the social or practical gospel transmitted through the religious doctrine. The angels showed him the pitfalls of sin and the rewards of virtue. He even spoke with the deceased George Washington, who reinforced the truth of the angels' message.

Theologically the heart of the Handsome Lake religion was that each people had its own way to God and each should have its own ritual which would be conveyed by its own messiah. Jesus was the messiah of the whites and while Indians could follow his road, the true way of the Indian people was the one told to Handsome Lake, who was himself the equivalent of Christ in his capacity as prophet to the Indians. In fact as the message developed, the traditional ceremonial calendar of Seneca observances, the Worship Dance, Great Feather Dance, and the like, became the appropriate means through which Indians should honor the creator. In this as in much else, Handsome Lake preserved the old ways while reinterpreting their significance in the new context. Theologically his principal innovation was the emphasis on Heaven and Hell and the necessity to follow the Gaiwiio as the road to salvation.

Much more important from our point of view than the theological reformation is the use of the revival of spirit to sanction and support a new way of life designed to remedy real problems faced by the Iroquois. Handsome Lake's gospel was intensely practical. He preached temperance to a people much disrupted by alcoholism and succeeded in mobilizing tribal and even federal authority to suppress the sales of liquor in the Iroquois country. Like our own Prohibition, the drying up was never complete, but drinking behavior was at least brought under the control of disapproval. Less usefully, Handsome Lake strongly condemned witchcraft and was unfortunately responsible for a considerable degree of antagonism when he encouraged witch-hunts and even executions of witches. In this area, under the pressure of his brother and others, he eventually modified his message to minimize the insistence of stamping out witchcraft, just as he abandoned attempts to forbid the "secret societies," such as the False Faces, to operate. Pragmatically he simply insisted that they be reinterpreted in the light of his own theology.

Cornplanter had long been an advocate of education and the adoption of white technology, while Handsome Lake only gradually accepted the necessity of some such alteration in traditional ways. However, with the force of supernatural sanction behind him in his role of prophet, Handsome Lake was able to succeed in transforming Seneca life in this direction where his politically powerful brother had failed. Let it also be remembered that much of the transformation was not finally accomplished until the establishment of the Code of Handsome Lake as an organized and formalized religion in the 1850s, long after his death.

In a political sense, Handsome Lake endorsed a policy of unity and an absolute prohibition of further sales of land to the whites, though again pragmatically he allowed some sales so as to consolidate the reservations. He accepted and preached the virtues of the nuclear family as the basic residential and economic unit, in the white fashion, and contributed to the breakup of the longhouse village clusters in favor of family farms dispersed among individually rather than communally worked fields. As the people shifted to this pattern, they also gradually accepted patrilineal naming and inheritance patterns. The old matriclans having been disrupted, a new approach was preached and accepted, modeled on the visibly successful white custom.

The Quakers had a vigorous program of technical acculturation at their model farm and made available instruction and equipment in weaving, carpentry, metallurgy, and all the other essential skills of rural life in the nineteenth century. They did this while visibly maintaining a life of conspicuous virtue and impressively refraining from enriching themselves through their influence over Indian leaders. Though initially conservative, the Code of Handsome Lake came finally to accept this pattern that the Quakers sought to teach and made it the economic base of a new life.

As the Iroquois were moved toward a more successful adaptation based on emulating white rural patterns (as had the Cherokee, although not with religious sanction), there was also an insistence both theological and social on maintaining a boundary between the Indian and the white societies. The doctrine did not condemn white ways but simply labeled them inappropriate for Indians, as for example, whiskey was regarded as useful to whites but not to Indians. There was a remarkably modern air about the effect of some of this on seeking to create a viable enclave as a part of a plural society. As the discussion in the final chapter indicates, some of Handsome Lake's ideas were quite sophisticated in the sense that they resemble the best current conceptions as to how pluralism is to be maintained. A passing example: Though resistant to education at first, the Code finally endorsed a sort of bicultural education system in which Iroquois ways as well as white ways would be taught in the schools. Handsome Lake actually hoped to limit white education to a few who would act as go-betweens with the white society, but the basic notion is very similar to trends that will be discussed later in regard to contemporary educational policy for the reservation.

For a time, the message of Handsome Lake succeeded in transforming the life of his people from a condition of disintegration to one of newness and "revitalization." In the long run, as with the Cherokee, the pressure of white society proved too much for even this new adjustment, as more land was lost and factions grew up again among the people. In modern times, problems remain that require new solutions, but the Longhouse religion continues to be a part of Iroquois life. If in the long run the pressures were too great for complete success, still the vitality of the Longhouse religion carried the Iroquois through the worst of historical times when white rapacity was unbridled. Though they have lost land in recent years, as with the Kinzua Dam project, they have come through intact as a people to a time when their continued existence is supported rather than deplored by the larger society. There are few others in the Eastern states who survived these years as a people.

Staying Out of the Melting Pot

The Cherokee and Iroquois both represent examples of conscious and purposeful movements on the part of Indian peoples to remain independent, autonomous societies. Though they accepted and even actively sought to adopt many white customs, their intention was to adapt to the new circumstances as a people and to remain a people. This, which will be discussed further as "enclavement," is a kind of acculturation phenomenon that can be compared broadly to "assimilation." Assimilation, which overtook most Algonkians who were not destroyed or did not flee, refers to a process focused on individuals who become incorporated into a society not their own. The Algonkians and others became part of the phenomenon that Americans at times have praised and at other times condemned—the melting pot. There are today in the Eastern states a great many persons whose ancestry includes some degree of Indian admixture and who may indeed identify with that ancestry. The society to which they belong and whose customs they observe is, however, American and in no sense Indian. The alternative to this, exemplified by the Iroquois and Cherokee, is the survival of the society as a society even though it adapts to new challenges and incorporates new ways. As seen in the next chapter, the reservation system and the federal policies associated with it have, entirely contrary to their intentions, helped to create a situation where many peoples west of the Mississippi have been given an opportunity for such an adaptive survival, though they have been held in suspended social animation for many decades.

East of the Mississippi the Iroquois stand alone as a people who have come through the challenges from beginning to end and have remained in some sense a viable enclave. Here and there are very small groups which, because of the relative undesirability of their land or its inaccessibility, were for all intents and purposes overlooked. The Seminole in the Everglades are the best example, although there remain Cherokee in the mountains of North Carolina. The far northern territories of Wisconsin are another instance where Indians (the Menomini) remain intact on a reservation, presumably because of their isolation and the lateness of white settlement in the area. In this same area small groups of forgotten Indians remain but without federal reservation lands—the Ojibwa, the Chippewa—always in small pockets.

For those who were removed to the West, the end of the struggle was not at hand. The Cherokee treaty which arranged for their removal also assured them that the new lands granted in the "Indian Territory" would not be incorporated into any state or territory without the consent of the Indians. Unfortunately what had been called the "Great American Desert" beyond the Mississippi River became increasingly attractive to settlers. California became a state in 1850 and Texas still earlier in 1845, while the entire Southwest not already included in the Louisiana Purchase was taken from Mexico in the treaty of Guadalupe Hidalgo in 1848. The westward movement was not over.

The events in the East had had an unpredictable and incomprehensible quality for many Indian groups, since the acts of their white "allies" were not visibly the result of the happenings in America, but connected in ways no Indian could perceive with Bombay and London. Fittingly the events in the East, unbeknownst to the whites, had created alterations in the Indian societies across the Mississippi. As the coastal peoples had been pushed inland and the Iroquois intruded into the Great Lake and Ohio country, a "domino effect" influenced other peoples (who had no direct contact with the events in the East) to move out into the Great Plains. The Sioux, and others whose homeland had been further east,

The second council house constructed by the Chickasaw at Tishomingo in the Indian Territory, with members of the Chickasaw Senate and House seated in front (1890). Despite all efforts, the Chickasaw and other "nations" were dissolved into the state of Oklahoma not long after this photograph was taken. (Courtesy National Archives)

moved west ahead of others and encountered and adopted the horse, which was spreading northward after its introduction by the Spaniards. By the time the advance of white settlement crossed into the West, it was confronted with a new challenge ultimately of the whites' own creation, though they did not know it—the Sioux!

Some Readings

Billington, Ray A.: *Westward Expansion: A History of the American Frontier*, 4th ed., New York: Macmillan, 1974. Widely used text giving useful temporal background. In this, as in many historical texts, the Indians appear only when important in Anglo-American doings. Much of the time one searches in vain for reference to the Indians hidden in the background of the "frontier."

Gearing, Fred: *Priests and Warriors: Social Structure of Cherokee Politics in the 18th Century.* Memoirs of the American Anthropological Association, No. 93, 1962.

Prucha, Francis Paul: *American Indian Policy in the Formative Years: The Indian Trade and Intercourse Acts,* Cambridge, Mass.: Harvard University Press, 1962. Fundamental work in the field.

Sutton, Imre: *Indian Land Tenure: Bibliographical Essays and a Guide to the Literature,* New York: Clearwater Publishing, 1975. Invaluable, and covering far more than the title suggests.

Wallace, Anthony: *The Death and Rebirth of the Seneca,* New York: Knopf, 1970. Excellent study of the Iroquois situation with an emphasis on the Handsome Lake religion.

IX WARRIORS AND WAGONS

The only good Indians I ever saw were dead.
General Philip Sheridan[1]

The "winning of the West" is a tale far too complex to tell here in sufficient detail to do it justice. Any literate American student is aware of the rough outline, and the concentration here must necessarily be on the aspects directly related to the fate of the Indian peoples. Though more spectacular in some of its military aspects and certainly better remembered in both fact and fiction, the collapse of the Indian cultures west of the Mississippi River did not take as long as those of the East. The legacy of their collapse remains today in the reservation system, which was developed as it became impossible to continue to sweep the Indians ahead of the path of American advance. While the French were effectively eliminated after the Louisiana Purchase and the Americans were consistently the leading players in this phase, the situation remained complex, with Spanish/Mexicans in the Southwest and along the coast of California, Russians extending settlements into the Northwest and northern California from their Alaskan base, and the Hudson's Bay Company intruding into the Oregon country from its Canadian domains.

Most cessions of Indian land to the whites took place in the West between 1850 and 1890, with the greatest rush coming after the end of the Civil War in 1865. Explorers like Lewis and Clark had much earlier determined the extent of the western country, but for a long time it was regarded as the "Great American Desert" since much of it was relatively treeless grassland, ill-adapted to the kinds of agriculture typical of the East. New techniques later made this "desert" produce much of the wheat of the nation and of the world, but the initial opening of the West was largely a matter of getting to the coast—California and the rich lands of the Oregon country. Most important, perhaps, in speeding events were the periodic gold rushes to California, Nevada, Colorado, Montana, and the Dakotas. Here whole towns were constructed virtually overnight, some to endure as permanent settlements like Denver, others to become ghost towns. In this same era, the great transcontinental railroads were built and a web of 250,000 miles of rail laid between 1850 and 1900. The consequences of the railroads for the Indian were many, but most profound was the role of the railroad companies in promoting settlement. The entrepreneurs were encouraged by federal grants of vast amounts of public land along the right-of-way, and to recoup their investment sought actively to bring settlers to these barren areas.

Unlike the inexorable wall of settlement that pushed forward from the East to the Mississippi, the western penetration was a matter of narrow corridors along the main routes to the coast and to the gold fields, leaving some Indian areas untouched while others further west were disrupted immediately. The many small California groups like the acorn-gathering Pomo were already facing annihilation while the Sioux continued to hold intact their northern plains. The tide flowed around the so-called Indian Territory, which did not become the organized territory of Oklahoma until 1890, and the lands of the various tribes which had been removed there were not completely opened to settlement until statehood in 1907. The overall picture is difficult to present coherently since the action swayed back and forth across the whole vast West. In one place the Indians won a war and in another made a lasting peace while in a third they were wantonly massacred. Fortunately for simplicity of presentation, if not for the Indian, the end was everywhere the same—the reservation system. Wherever there was land that the onrushing settlers found desirable the Indians were eventually removed from it and placed in some more remote and less useful locale. The end of this process was that with few exceptions land held by the Indian was by definition economically undesirable, else the Indians would not have been given it or allowed to retain it. This clearly created problems for those who, once the Indian had been ensconced in a desolate reservation, sought to promote "development." Develop what?

In an attempt to give some coherence to a treatment of this convoluted process, this chapter will focus on the careers of two Indian groups during this period. These are the Sioux, whose fate illustrates much that is common to all Northern Plains Indians, and the Navaho, who, while unique in the success of their adaptations, do allow a springboard for the discussion of events in the Southwest. For the rest the rough outlines will be discussed of the rise and fall of the Indian Territory of Oklahoma which became a catchall depository for Indians from all over the nation.

Way Down Yonder in the Indian Nation!

A place to start is after the removal of the Southwestern tribes in the 1830s, beginning with the events in the "Nations," as they were often called. The Indian Territory was the archetype of the system of reservations, although lands had frequently been "reserved" for various tribes by treaties prior to the establishment of the Nations. The final form of what we know as the reservation system took shape in a flurry of treaty making by the Indian Peace Commission in 1867, but the essentials were contained in the policies behind the formation of the Indian Territory. Part of the program of isolation was the Indian Trade and Intercourse Act of 1834, which insisted that no one could enter or trade within the reserves except federal officers and their duly licensed agents and traders. This was never completely or successfully enforced, but it reveals government intentions.

At this stage the general thrust behind the reservation system was simply to get the Indians out from underfoot. The Bureau of Indian Affairs was a branch of the War Department until 1849, and joint military-civilian control of the reservations continued long after that. There was often expressed a more positive emphasis, even by men like Jackson, that the removals and creation of the reservations were for the good of the Indian. The notion suggested was that proximity to white settlements was corrupting and disruptive to the Indian way, which could only be preserved in isolation. There was considerable truth to this doctrine since any perusal of American history will show that the central government was never in effective control of the frontiersmen during the westward expansion and, like the English Crown before it, could never really count on enforcing its treaties and policies if the local settlers wanted otherwise. The military, often portrayed as villains, was more often desperately caught in the middle. The majority of the Indian wars were in no sense conscious acts of policy like the Removal but the results of local provocation of Indians to the point of violent reaction, which the army was then called in to suppress. A great many army officers were, unlike Sheridan, highly sympathetic to the Indians' position and appalled at the utter lack of justice in some of the policies they had to carry out. The most frequent cause of stress was the local American population which would ride roughshod over the solemnly guaranteed rights of the Indian; when the Indians rebelled, they were punished for their resistance by a reluctant military.

The territory established for the Indians was of course already occupied, although thinly, by the Osage and Kansa, and treaties had first to be made with these peoples to get them to accept limited reserves and yield the rest of the area. Comanche and other Plains nomads who ranged through the western portions of the territory were not consulted in these early stages, but their hostility toward the newcomers from the East was a major factor in later problems. The largest part of the land, particularly the better watered and timbered eastern portions, was allocated to the civilized tribes—Cherokee, Choctaw, Chickasaw, and Creek. They were also given broad rights over much of the west in the "Cherokee Outlet." Even before the complete resettling of these peoples, small reserves had been established in the northeastern portions of the Nations for others from the East. More peoples came as expansion proceeded and treaties were negotiated. Shawnee from Ohio and Delawares who had once lived in the state that bears their name arrived earliest. Sauk, Fox, Wyandot, Miami, Chippewa, Pawnee, and even a small group of Seneca were persuaded or coerced into the Nations and were followed by still more whole groups or fragments, including some of the much-traveled Kickapoo. The allocated territory at one point included much of eastern Kansas but gradually shrank back to the dimensions of the present state of Oklahoma.

As the frontier moved into the West, there developed a system of putting the Indian groups encountered onto individual pockets of land near their homelands and surrounding them with whites, but for some time an attempt was made to stuff many of these peoples into the Nations. The civilized tribes, who held most of the land, had to give up some of their solemnly guaranteed holdings if these new groups (mostly Plains horsemen) were to be accommodated. This was facilitated after the Civil War when the Nations were accused of having sided with the Confederacy. It is true that Cherokee and Choctaw regiments fought for the South, notably at the crucial Battle of Pea Ridge in Arkansas. However, not all of the civilized tribes supported the South, though many of their more prosperous men were themselves slaveholders, and none of the tribes did so in official and unanimous fashion. On these grounds, nonetheless, the civilized tribes had the western territories removed from their control to make room for the warrior tribes of the West who were being rounded up and herded into these lands.

Close, but No Cigar!

The civilized tribes, in particular the Cherokee, had made in the Southeast an extensive and highly successful adaptation of their own cultures to incorporate much European technology and much of the organization of the whites. They were at this point entirely self-sufficient and as prosperous in general as their white neighbors whom they had come to resemble closely. Then they were uprooted and marched to Oklahoma, wiping out the steps which had brought them so close to a stable enclavement within the larger society.

In the new lands new problems were added to the simple fact of having to start from scratch. The lands allotted to them were not so well watered or timbered as the lands forfeited in the Southeast, so new techniques had to be mastered, and some traditional pursuits such as hunting declined. In their attempts to build new farms and houses and communities, these tribes were further hampered by hostility between themselves and the horse nomads of the western section of the Nations, which sometimes amounted to outright warfare. There were similar altercations between some of the eastern tribes themselves; within each group there had risen a degree of factionalism that was never to completely disappear. Leaders thought responsible for agreeing to the Removal were assassinated and deep divisions grew up between the traditionalists (usually called "full bloods") and the progressives (called "mixed bloods"), although the terms really were political or cultural and had little to do with actual genetic admixture.

Still, in spite of all these confusions, the southeastern tribes reestablished themselves successfully under these new conditions. They individually organized new governments, and the Creeks and Cherokees took the lead in attempts to call together pantribal councils which could have eventually become the nucleus for some form of overall governing body. The Cherokee reestablished their schools and legal system at the same time that they built new farms along the available sources of water. The trend toward acceptance of a new adaptation to white patterns continued, with Christianity becoming firmly established and the Baptist church often taking the place of the old ceremonial community buildings in the center of the settlements. The clan organization had largely declined in favor of a white style of bilateral kinship organization, though these traditional forms and some aspects of ceremonial life (particularly curing rituals) never disappeared and were to be revived in later times of trouble.

To anyone familiar with the problems of modern reservation communities (discussed in the final two chapters), the destruction of the Cherokee organization is an ironic joke. The reservations have perpetuated the Indian in a condition of dependency at a level of poverty while spending vast sums of money to achieve assimilation and autonomy. In the new land as in their old the Cherokee supported themselves and were on a par with their western American counterparts economically and educationally. Their governments, while never perfect and always divided, did as well as most territorial and state authorities on the frontier to provide order, and their educational system successfully promoted a general literacy. By the late 1800s the Cherokee had accomplished on their own and in the face of great difficulty virtually all of the goals that current administrators of Indian affairs hold out only as distant possibilities. Their only aid in this was the payments received of pennies per acre in compensation for lands taken in the Southeast, so that the government—far from investing vast sums in Cherokee development—actually could be said to have made a profit on the Removal.

Almost from the beginning, however, there was pressure to "open" the Indian Nations to white settlement. By the 1870s waves of settlement had swept around both sides of the Indian Territory. Pressures grew around the "anomaly" of the Indians occupying perfectly usable land while white settlers were being forced to trek further and further into the arid and unproductive lands of the Southwest and western plains. The railroads which had been allowed to push their lines across the Nations (although not granted land rights) did much to encourage the opening of these lands to white settlement in order to increase their own traffic and profits. The break in the integrity of the Indian Territory came with the "Oklahoma District"—a 2-million-acre area around present Oklahoma City and squarely in the middle of the Territory, which had been purchased by the United States from the eastern tribes with an apparent eye to making it available to more of the western tribes being gathered up. However, it was technically in the public domain, and pressure mounted for its settlement.

"Boomers," settlers from Kansas, began to move illegally into the disputed area in ever-increasing numbers, and the thinly spread army was hard put to keep throwing them out. In the face of this pressure, Congress gave in and extinguished remaining Indian title to the Oklahoma District, and on April 22, 1889, there occurred one of those events always remembered in American history although never with reference to the Indian. The District was thrown open to settlement and was inundated by 100,000 homesteaders within a few hours of the firing of the gun that allowed them onto the land. Within a year, Oklahoma was recognized as a territory, and in 1893 the great land rush was duplicated when the Cherokee Outlet in the northwestern part of the territory (6 million acres) was similarly thrown open. By 1898, the Dawes and Curtis Acts that led to the piecemeal usurpation of the majority of the land remaining in Indian hands had been passed.

The Dawes and Curtis Acts will be discussed in the next chapter as part of the "assimilationist" doctrine developed during the reservation period, but their impact on the Indian Territory cannot be left unmentioned in this sequence. The Dawes Act, or "General Allotment Act of 1887," was intended to encourage the hunting and nomadic western tribes to settle on individual freeholds and adopt agriculture in the white mode. This was to be accomplished by breaking up the communally held reservations and granting land on an individual basis of 160 acres per householder. The civilized tribes were exempted from this act or at least from the provisions that made the allotment compulsory. It was presumably expected that they would support such action, but one lesson all of the southeastern peoples had learned was never to give up control of the land, and most resisted the allotment program. This resulted ultimately in the Curtis Act of 1898 which extended the allotment program to the civilized tribes and at the same time dissolved their educational and governmental systems. By 1891 arrangements had been made to allow the government to lease Indian lands held "in trust," and in 1902 the first oil leases were made in the Oklahoma Indian lands. By 1907 Oklahoma was a state, and the remaining Indian lands came under intense pressure for further sales.

In fact by 1907 the legal status of all Oklahoma Indians (who were made citizens of the United States in 1901) was not substantially different from their American neighbors, although the federal government continued to exercise some degree of supervision over "trust" relations, particularly in regard to mineral and oil rights. The end of this has been the complete assimilation of many Oklahoma Indians into white society, while curiously, as discussed later, there remains a strong, persistent Indian identity in many communities, and organizations have arisen that continue to give structure to these remaining pockets of "Indianness." The survival of the enclaves aside, the formal reservations and special "national" status of the Indian territories were extinguished by the end of the first decade of this century. For many this destruction of their structured community relations meant poverty and despair and deepened the division between mixed blood and full blood, even resulting in a conservative revitalization movement—the "Red Bird Smith" movement which revived some traditional practices that had already begun to decline.[2] The "stomp ground" or central ceremonial plaza was reinstituted in many traditionalist communities during this period.

Lakota, Nakota, Dakota—Sioux?

In the imagination of the American people the tribes known collectively as the Sioux *are* the Indian. The name itself appears to be a contraction of a French mispronunciation of a Chippewa word for their enemies meaning "little snakes." The various groups of Sioux called themselves in different dialects by one or another of the terms in the section heading above. Since even the modern Sioux generally tend to refer to themselves as Sioux rather than one of the variations of Dakota, we will leave the Dakota label for the states that took it for themselves along with the land of the people who used to own both land and name. While there were speakers of the language stock called Siouan who were settled village agriculturalists—Mandan, Omaha, Kansa—*the* Sioux were the Plains nomadic tribes immortalized in a thousand western novels and movies. This was the real thing: war bonnets, counting coups, scalping, buffalo hunting, teepees, painted faces, and wild mounted charges swooping down on the wagon trains. Amazingly, the period of contact that produced this legendary impact lasted only from 1850 to 1880. The Sioux had only fully developed themselves as Plains buffalo hunters, built around the horse and the gun, by 1800 and didn't come into intensive contact with whites until 1850 when troubles developed along the Oregon Trail which traversed their territory. All were confined to reservations by 1881. The Great Plains held many other tribes—Cheyenne, Comanche, Crow (Siouan speakers), Kiowa, Arapaho—whose names are also well known; but the ferocity, tenacity, and occasional success of Sioux resistance to conquest in their brief but spectacular career is without parallel.

The Iroquois' success can be partly attributed to their early access to a plentiful supply of guns. Other eastern peoples pressured by the Iroquois but better armed than those still further west tended, in a sort of "domino effect," to pass the pressure along. The Chippewa of Minnesota seem to have influenced the gradual drift of some Sioux out onto the Great Plains, though the movements of the Teton Dakota appear to have begun quite early. Once there, the Sioux encountered the northward drifting horse, first made available by the Spanish in Mexico. Although horses were undoubtedly lost from the very beginning, the revolt of the Pueblo Indians, which threw the Spanish out of their settlements along the Rio Grande in 1680, accelerated the passage of horses into Indian hands, as did the continuous raids of Apache, Navaho, and Comanche on Spanish settlements. The horse and the pattern of its use drifted from tribe to tribe, drawing Minnesota agriculturalist and Great Basin nomad alike to the new life made possible by the "great dog."

Horse nomads, with the mobility granted by their domesticated animals, were not nearly so limited in their complexity as the hunting and gathering foot nomads, such as the Shoshone. Additionally in the Great Plains there existed another animal whose pursuit on horseback completed the adaptation—the bison. With the horse (and soon the gun) these great beasts in their countless millions could be so effectively pursued as to produce a stable subsistence. For some horse-rich groups like the southern Kiowa, even a surplus economy was possible, leading to social sophistication based on wealth differences more like that of the

The horsemen of the Plains, like these Nez Perce sketched by Gustavus Sohon at the time of the Treaty of Walla Walla, left an enduring mark on our image of the Indian peoples and on their view of themselves. (Courtesy Washington State Historical Society)

fish-rich Kwakiutl than that of the simpler Shoshone bands. During most of the year the operational social unit for the majority of Plains tribes was a small group, apparently resembling the simple organization of the Shoshone bands, but during periodic gatherings for collective buffalo hunts, pantribal organizations made themselves known. Such hunts often involved fire drives, surrounds, and jump hunts (driving over cliffs) and produced great amounts of food, but this was workable as a reliable base only because techniques of preserving the meat were developed—primarily the drying of meat into "jerky" (from the Spanish *charqui*) or the mixing of meat with fat and berries to form pemmican. Both forms of food could be kept for months stored in skin parfleches and could carry a group through the harsh Plains winters when game was scarce. Wild plants were gathered when available, and sedentary agricultural tribes like the Mandan were raided or traded with, as occasion might dictate, for corn and other products. Only tobacco was grown by the Plains nomads on a regular basis.

In the move to the Plains and with the adoption of horse nomadism, the Sioux and others streamlined and to some extent simplified their material culture. Highly breakable pottery was abandoned in favor of other containers such as skin bags, although, since the Plains adaptation and white trading influences grew up almost simultaneously, there was a rapid switch to utensils of metal. In a general way the technology developed following the same principles used by contemporary manufacturers of good-quality camping and backpacking equipment—to make the articles durable, lightweight, and compact and to design them for easy disassembly (as in the case of the teepee). The Plains Indians added to this prescription a factor of availability and placed heavy reliance on the buffalo, using hide, rawhide, sinew, bone, horn, intestines, and even the euphemistically labelled "chips" which when dried made a passable fire. The people of the Plains truly used every part of the buffalo but the grunt, although perhaps it is necessary to remind the reader once again that on the occasion of really massive kills much was wasted.

Organizationally, most of the year was spent within the bands—largely bilateral kin units generally organized around one or more important charismatic leaders. Thus the famous Sioux "chiefs," such as Red Cloud or Sitting Bull, tended to have large personal, voluntary followings; however, other bands were far smaller. Some Plains tribes preserved clan organizations, but the pattern of small-band wandering for most of the year tended to make these less significant than in the sedentary agricultural settings in which they had originally been developed, though the Sioux maintained a patrilineally oriented tendency in group formation. Higher levels of organization involved voluntary associations and systems of ranking of leaders, revolving in both cases around prowess in warfare.

The life of the Plains tribes involved a considerable interest in raiding neighbors (other horse nomads and the sedentary agricultural peoples like the Mandan and Arikara). The source of this emphasis on male aggressiveness and bravery in warfare is debated, but it springs at least in part from the jostling that went on in the Plains as new tribes attempted to establish a place as buffalo-hunting nomads. Territorial conquest or carving out hunting grounds may have been an initial impetus, but as the new adaptation matured, the warfare remained as a highly ritualized and limited pattern of raid and counter-raid, which some have suggested functioned to maintain tribal solidarity while at the same time insuring stable boundaries. Horse stealing, an honorable undertaking, was surely a motive, particularly for the northern peoples like the Sioux who had to get their horses from more well-endowed southern neighbors (who had Spanish herds to raid). As shall be seen, some of these southern peoples tended to treat the Spanish as a natural resource to be exploited in the same way as the buffalo.

The standing of a man in his group was largely a function of his accumulation of war honors (the feathers in the headdress of some groups represented these) through a rather elaborate system of score-keeping usually referred to as "counting coup." Stealing a horse, being first to contact the enemy, touching a foe with a special "coup stick," and, of course, killing an enemy were all honors of this sort. Touching an enemy with the coup stick ranked higher than killing him. One can imagine a green army recruit from Massachusetts frantically struggling to reload his muzzle loader, ramming in the cartridge, ball and wadding, while a wildly whooping horseman, face hideously painted, galloped straight at him, only to strike lightly with a gaudy stick and ride on. Someone else would probably kill him, however, and although coup could be counted it would be of lesser value on the fallen corpse.

The fascination with these exploits was reflected in many ways, including the decorating of clothing and teepee covers with records of important coups with much the same intent as the Indians of the Northwest Coast displayed crests. The standing of a "chief," a man whose advice would be heeded and who could form and lead raiding parties, depended in large part on his score of bravery. Voluntary associations among the Plains tribes were largely warrior societies, membership and subsequent standing in which were again a function of warlike prowess. These associations served as an element of tribal cohesion, being activated during annual gatherings for the Sun Dance or on the occasion of large hunts. They acted largely as a kind of camp police at these times and could form the nucleus for large-scale war parties.

Spirit "power" was another road to prestige and leadership in the fierce Plains society. Some important "chiefs" were also shamans (Sitting Bull, for example) of great reputation for their supernatural force as well as their wisdom in council. As mentioned, the Indian peoples in general did not make a very clear distinction between sacred and secular domains, at least not in our terms. There were important curing societies as well as warrior societies, and positions in the important events seem to have been based on a mixture of spirit power and war honors. The spiritual emphasis reached its height in the Sun Dance, which was organized by the shaman. The Sun Dance, as previously noted, was a great annual event which served to reinforce the tribal identity through reenactment of mythology, and self-sacrifice through mutilation and ordeal of a few men who thereby gained much power.

The Light Cavalry Finale

No other group challenged the United States expansion on such a large territorial scale and so successfully (if temporarily) as the Sioux. Seminoles had held out in their inaccessible swamps, and the Modoc Captain

Jack and his tiny band were to hold a patch of lava field in California against overwhelming force, but none forced the halt or withdrawal of Manifest Destiny as did the Sioux. Some of the reasons for their success were tragically also part of the reason for their final failure.

The success of the Sioux (and other Plains horsemen) would make sense to any military commander who had fought light cavalry in open steppe or grassland and to the modern American commander who has attempted to cope with elusive guerrilla bands. As nomads, the Sioux, like the modern guerrilla, never had to defend any particular place at any particular time. They sought only to dominate a region, not to hold forts and farms and towns. These they could raid as they chose, leaving their enemies the task of pursuing them. They were a people who could move men, women, children, and old people at a faster speed than green, heavy cavalry and infantry could follow. Heavy cavalry refers here not to armored cuirassiers but to the elaborate equipment and larger horses of the U.S. troopers, who could not survive without elaborate lines of supply in areas where the Indians and their horses were entirely self-sufficient. The people needed only time to hunt and a supply of arms to continue to fight indefinitely. Red Cloud, using these harassing tactics against a line of army forts set up to protect the Bozeman Trail to Oregon, managed to force the withdrawal of the forts and obtained a treaty guaranteeing they would not be reestablished.

In 1862 some Sioux remained in Minnesota, scattered along the Minnesota River, all that remained of their homeland after a series of treaty-induced land cessions. These Indians, usually called Santee Sioux, rose up in the Minnesota Massacre and overran large parts of the state, killing hundreds and driving thousands of whites from their homes, before military units could be mobilized to control those who did not flee to join their western relatives. This was apparently like most Indian military actions, largely spontaneous and uncoordinated, and so devastating only because it was unexpected and widespread. The reprisals were harsh, with 306 Indians condemned to hang, though President Lincoln intervened to insist that those whose only crime was fighting be treated as prisoners of war. Only thirty-eight could be convicted of atrocities, and they were finally hanged on a single massive scaffold. The western Sioux, while they did not participate with their relatives, were disturbed by these events and the military columns that passed through some of their territory in pursuit of the "hostiles."

As the tide of white settlement moved westward, it involved a swirling series of raids and counter-raids between Indian and white. These included some now-famous actions, such as the Chivington Massacre of Black Kettle's band of Cheyenne in the aftermath of furious warfare that had erupted in the Colorado country with the Cheyenne and Arapaho. The Sioux were occasional allies of these tribes. The struggle around the Bozeman Trail ended with a treaty in 1868 establishing the

Great Sioux Reservation west of the Missouri River and including the disputed Powder River and Big Horn country as hunting grounds. Relative peace was maintained until the Black Hills country was overrun with prospectors as the result of rumors of gold in 1875.

The Sioux, who until this time had never had their movements significantly restricted, were suddenly told that the boundaries of the reservation were to be scrupulously observed. The Indians resisted this suggestion. The result was a campaign by the Army in 1876 to round up all of the wandering bands and concentrate them on the remaining assigned lands. The immediate dramatic outcome was "Custer's Last Stand," in which that much-discussed officer led his men to disaster at the hands of the Sioux and their allies. By the latter part of the same year, however, the Army, led by General Terry, had rounded up most of the Sioux, although a few diehards like Sitting Bull eluded them. Sitting Bull held out in Canada until 1881 before accepting a place on the reduced reservation.

The end of the Sioux resistance and that of other Plains tribes might not have come for some time, since white settlement remained scanty in the Sioux hunting grounds. The key to the Plains adaptation was the buffalo, and by the latter part of the 1870s the great southern herds had ceased to exist, to be followed by the virtual extinction of the northern herds in the early 1900s. Without the buffalo, the Indians of the Plains had no choice but to accept the white man's ration of beef and confinement on the reservations. The buffalo, seemingly an inexhaustible resource, was slaughtered so efficiently and indiscriminately by whites as to tip them almost to the edge of extinction. Occasionally hunted for food and often just shot from trains for the "sport," the buffalo perished under a demand for their hides for use as machine-drive belting and other such purposes of the new industrial age. While there were millions of them, millions were slaughtered each year until there were no more. Without them, the Plains horse nomadic adaptation ceased, as had that of the Big Game Hunters of prehistoric times.

To the Sioux goes the honor and the tragedy of the last major armed clash of American and Chichimeca: the battle or massacre of Wounded Knee that has in our own time become an important symbol for Indian activists. This last clash, in 1890, was the outcome of a revitalization movement, the Ghost Dance, and the fears raised by that movement in the minds of white authorities.

The movement originated among the Paiute of Nevada as the result of the teachings of the Prophet Wovoka, the son of a traditional shaman, who in addition to possessing this heritage of spirit power, had traveled extensively and was closely in touch with white religious movements of the area, many of which in this period, including Mormonism, emphasized the imminence of the messiah's return. In 1885 the Prophet had a vision, indeed was said to have died, and in the spirit world saw a preview

Custer's Last Fight *is probably the best-known depiction of this last victorious battle of the Plains peoples. Momentarily united, the tribes soon dispersed and were defeated piecemeal and placed on reservations. (Courtesy Anheuser-Busch Corporation)*

of a new life for the Indian people, and was instructed in the procedures necessary to bring it about. The Paiute were by this time in a bad way, broken into small groups and living on the fringes of the encroaching white towns and ranches. The message from Wovoka spread from the Paiute far and wide, and many tribes, hearing of this prophecy of hope in a time of despair, sent, as did the Sioux, emissaries to be instructed in the necessary ritual.

The message of Wovoka was widely scattered and variously interpreted, since, unlike the Code of Handsome Lake, it never took a final written "official" form. The essence was a promised new world in which the whites would be absent, the dead ancestors resurrected, and most important for the Plains peoples, the virtually extinct buffalo would once again cover the prairie. All would live and prosper harmoniously in this new state of things. The approach necessary, other than a code of personal morality of essentially a Christian character, was the Ghost Dance. A simple circle dance of this kind was common to a great many Chichimec groups and easily adapted to this new purpose. Special songs were sung and the circle dance went on for hours through the night, and some specially favored would succumb to the hypnotic quality of the chanting and dancing and undergo visions of the new world to come. The dancing had to be done to hasten the coming of the new order.

The Sioux, defeated and confined to reservations under military supervision, were hungry since the buffalo had nearly vanished and the government rations were cut off in this critical year. Memories, of course, were still sharp of the days of glory and freedom, and the great leaders such as Sitting Bull and Red Cloud still lived as a potential focus for new directions. Like the life of the Iroquois at the time of the preaching of the message of Handsome Lake, current conditions stood in brutal contrast to a recent glorious past and in even sharper contrast to the power of the whites. The hopeful message of the Ghost Dance religion took rapid root under these circumstances, and many Sioux began to dance.

With their heritage of warlike aggressiveness, the Sioux could scarcely be expected to turn to an utterly accepting and peaceful religion overnight; so their interpretation of the dance reflected their anger and their past. A feature of their version of the dance was the "Ghost Shirt," a garment painted with symbols and worn in the dancing, which made it bullet-proof. Clearly the Sioux wished to help the millennium along rather than leaving it all in the hands of the spirits. The agent on the reservation and the Army became alarmed at the menacing quality of the Ghost Dancers and began to move to suppress the movement.

Indian Police sent to bring in Sitting Bull, who was said to have lent support to the Ghost Dance, became involved in a shooting melee with his followers. At this remove it is difficult to be judgmental with the scanty evidence available, and it will only be noted that many believe that the great leader was deliberately murdered, while others insist that his was a tragic but accidental death. The finale occurred when a band of Sioux led by a man called Big Foot was ordered to be brought into the agency, having wandered outside its prescribed grounds in search of game. The members of the band were apparently wary because of pressures being put on Ghost Dancers, and Big Foot's band was known to contain many enthusiastic dancers. The events that followed the Army's operation to round up Big Foot's band are now almost as symbolically important as Custer's Last Stand, so that truth or falsehood seems to have become of little importance to anyone. The band was contacted by troops, agreed to come in, and was surrounded by soldiers with their weapons strategically placed. Confusion and nervousness on both sides flared when the Army insisted that the Indians surrender their arms. This was in progress when firing broke out. Who fired the first shot has been debated, but there is no question that the troops immediately poured an overwhelming fire into the camp of partially disarmed Indians. The warriors who could retrieved their weapons and began to return the fire while the women and children withdrew under this cover. Massacre or battle? The Indians lost at least 300 dead in men, women, and children and probably more. Only a few of their wounded could be counted because a number of them escaped, some perhaps to die unrecorded. The Army lost twenty-five men, many, it is said, caught in their own cross-fire.

It was an incident not really very dissimilar from many that preceded it. It is remembered more than others perhaps because it was the last. It was also recorded in photographs, which showed the grotesquely frozen bodies of the fallen—perhaps serving as a forerunner of our televised battles in Vietnam in stirring public revulsion.

The Earth Surface People

Like the Sioux, the Navaho represented, at the point they entered the historical record, a culture containing many European elements. The Navaho have as a matter of fact such a long history of successful adaptation to other cultures as to have prompted Evon Vogt to characterize them as the embodiment of a model of "incorporative" acculturation.[3] This model emphasizes the relative lack of disruption that occurs when the borrowing culture has the opportunity to pick and choose and modify the elements it will accept into its own cultural pattern. Such a program of nondirected change figures importantly in this book's consideration of possibilities for new directions for reservation-administered communities. The key to Navaho success, prior to their final loss of autonomy to the Americans, appears to have lain in their control of the conditions of contact with the settled Pueblo peoples and later with the fortunately none-too-numerous Spanish-Mexicans.

The Athabascan-speaking Navaho (Diné) seem to have arrived in the southwestern area they now claim as their homeland no earlier than A.D. 1000, and there is even strong opinion favoring an arrival as late as the 1500s. They and their cultural and linguistic cousins the Apache are in any case recent arrivals as such things go, and their nearest relatives (speakers of the Na-Dene language stock) are far in the north, in subarctic Canada (various hunting tribes—Kutchin, Slave, etc.), and along the coast of the Northwest among the salmon-fishing chiefdoms. Both Apache and Navaho, arriving from the north and the east, seem to have come as relatively simple hunters and gatherers with a material technology that has left few distinctive traces and systems of social organization that have apparently been so heavily influenced by their more complex Pueblo neighbors as to be beyond reconstruction. The Navaho who were concentrated in the Anasazi country of the Four Corners area came under heaviest Pueblo influence, while the Apache scattered more widely through the mountain highlands of Arizona and New Mexico were generally less directly influenced.

The Navaho discussed in Chapter 5 have an elaborate mythology which includes supernatural beings who taught them weaving (Spider Man and Woman) and White Bead Woman who gave them corn, as well as life. As a matter of unromantic fact it was clearly the Pueblo peoples who taught them both weaving and the cultivation of corn. It is indicative of the thoroughness with which the Navaho have integrated these things into their own culture that their myths do not much reflect the borrowing. The Pueblos, as indicated earlier, had settled villages, agriculture, weaving, and pottery by around the time of Christ, and the late-arriving nomadic Athabascans adopted these things along with much else of a less traceable and tangible nature. The Navaho supernaturals, the Yei, who are represented by ritual dancers at ceremonials, bear a considerable resemblance to the Pueblo Katchina, who are similarly impersonated.

The Navaho are not, however, to be regarded as slavish imitators or indiscriminate borrowers. The dancers may resemble Katchina impersonators in costume but the focus of the ceremonial, as we saw in Chapter 5, is curing, and the organization around the "Singer" is in no way characteristic of the Pueblos. The Navaho have remained Navaho, taking those parts of other systems they may have found useful or attractive and modified them to suit their own purposes. (Some modern dancers I have seen whose upper bodies are customarily painted white have reduced the work involved by wearing T-shirts and painting only the exposed parts.) The most obvious key to Navaho cultural adaptation has been a kind of pragmatic opportunism combined with a determined adherence to a sense of common identity.

European contact in the Southwest was much earlier but less devastating than the slow tide moving toward the Sioux from the Atlantic coast. The Spanish who conquered the Aztec by 1521 sent expeditions, such as that of Coronado, deep into the Plains by 1540 and established the settlement of Santa Fe by 1598. In their dealings with the nomadic peoples of this area—Navaho, Apache, or Comanche—the Spanish ultimately created the instrument of their own undoing. The raiding depredations of the newly horsed horse nomads of the southern Plains and the Southwest effectively prevented Spanish expansion into the American West except along the Rio Grande, where a symbiotic relation was developed with the Pueblo peoples who cooperated with the Spanish in resistance to the raiders.

The Spanish program of establishing missions and encomiendas found little success with the Chichimeca except among the Pueblos, who, like the complex peoples of Mesoamerica, were town dwellers. The wandering nomads could neither be preached to nor organized if they could not be caught, and it was not long before the possession of the horse made a nearly hopeless task impossible. Even the Pueblos were not participants in a state level of organization accustomed to hierarchical obedience on a large scale. Only during the Great Pueblo Revolt of 1680 did the Pueblos momentarily act all as a unit in driving out the Spanish, and their reconquest was made simpler for the returning Spaniards because the organization of the revolt quickly vanished to leave each town on its own. Many fled during this period to take refuge with the Navaho. The Hopi Pueblos of the high mesas of northern Arizona remained free from reconquest, located as they were in the midst of the hostile nomads and isolated from the Rio Grande centers of the Spanish.

Spanish impact was further modified and placed at the mercy of the nomads by the peripheral importance of the area in Spanish and later Mexican schemes. The relatively scantily populated and arid north had little worth conquering compared with the fertile south. Except for the mining towns that grew up where precious metals were found, the tide of settlement remained far distant from the isolated Rio Grande communities. The supply lines were long and frequently interrupted, and the Spaniards on the scene were never sufficiently numerous to impose their will or overwhelm the Indians by sheer size of population. Some estimates indicate that by the 1800s, after more than 200 years of residence, there were no more than 18,000 non-Indian Spanish-Mexicans in the entire area of New Mexico.

The Navaho quickly adapted themselves to the Spanish presence in a pattern of raiding, much like that described for the northern Plainsmen except that here the Indians were able to maintain this balance and remain autonomous. From their permanent settlements, the Spanish mounted *entradas*, expeditions to pursue the raiding horsemen, but they could never sustain the campaigns long enough to seriously discommode the elusive nomads. The Spanish took Navaho slaves, but the Navaho captured Spanish in turn. Of necessity in a matrilineal society the offspring of Spanish-Mexican women came to form a clan of their own which continues to exist today, known as the Mexican clan. The Navaho sought horses, as did all others, but, unique among the Chichimeca, adopted the Spanish-Mexican pastoralism and became sheepherders as well as raiders. The hardy Moreno sheep came to seem to the Navaho a part of the definition of life itself, and a man reckoned his worth in sheep as much if not more than in horses. Navaho agricultural activities became a part of a pattern of transhumance, with fields tended at the summer grazing grounds and abandoned as the flocks were moved to higher fields. Young men raided the Spanish and the Pueblos and later the Americanos to increase their flocks of horses and sheep, while the women and children tended the stock and the garden plots.

As they took Hispano stock, they borrowed, adapted, and incorporated into their own Navaho lifeway much else of value. Silverworking, for which the Navaho are today justly famous, was learned from the Spanish, and Spanish designs though much modified still remain. Weaving they already had from the Pueblos, but the possession of wool from sheep led to new techniques. They borrowed loom patterns to make woolen cloth, cloth that is still made today in the famous Navaho rugs and blankets. The dress of the men came to be modeled on the Hispano *charro* (cowboy) costume, and the saddles and bridles were modeled on the Spanish, though as always, modified to suit Navaho tastes. Fruit trees, metal implements, guns, and much else of value they took and made their own but always in their own way.

The Spanish had been miraculously successful in their Christianization efforts in Mesoamerica, but the few missions that were established in Navaho country were destroyed and the friars killed. Only in the Spanish settlements along the Rio Grande was Christianity triumphant, although even the Pueblos maintained their aboriginal cults secretly side-by-side with their new profession of Catholic faith. The only Christian Navaho were servants and slaves held in settlements. The rest continued to build a version of their traditional hogans (log houses) and remained scattered in dispersed "outfits" of matrilineally related families, never submitting to Spanish programs of concentration and congregation into town and village life.

In the face of this system of preying upon the Hispanos like wolves on a caribou herd, it is easy to imagine the consternation and disbelief of the Navaho and Apache when they were informed by American authorities, subsequent to the Treaty of Guadalupe Hidalgo, that they were to cease their raids and that the lands they occupied now formed part of the United States. The Indian point of view, that the Mexicans could scarcely give away what they had never owned, was no more considered in this case than it had been when British and French ceded lands they had never controlled. The admission of Texas as a state in 1845 led to war with Mexico, which cost her not only Texas but other lands nominally under her control that now comprise all or parts of the states of Arizona, New Mexico, Oklahoma, Colorado, Utah, Nevada, California, and Wyoming, as well as, of course, responsibility for the Indians and their lands. Hispano land titles were guaranteed (and in many cases respected) under this treaty, but among the Indians, only the Pueblos, who were regarded as to some extent "civilized" and difficult to distinguish from Mexicans, preserved land rights.

The Navaho (and still more their Apache neighbors) were unimpressed and continued their life-style as before, raiding Mexicans or Anglos as occasion offered. The Army built small forts in the Navaho country and treaties were made with some "chiefs," but those who were not followers of the particular chief ignored the treaties. The land was sparsely settled, and military efforts were never pursued and certainly were never successful in altering the Navaho way. Inevitably, however, the land began to fill up with ranchers and miners, particularly along the Santa Fe Trail to California and the gold fields. During the Civil War when the regular Army was otherwise occupied, the Navaho raids reached an intolerable point, and volunteer troops under the now-famous Kit Carson were ordered into Navaho country in 1863. Carson and his men seldom encountered the elusive Navaho in direct, open battle; but as the accidental destruction of the buffalo had undercut the northern Plainsmen, the Anglo-Americans purposely destroyed Navaho livelihood. The troopers burned crops and either carried off or killed sheep, cattle, and horses wherever they found them, pursuing a ruthless scorched-earth policy.

The result was not a conquest but a capitulation, as word was sent out to the starving and harassed Navaho to gather at Fort Defiance. In 1864, over 2000 gave themselves up to be marched to Fort Sumner (also known as Bosque Redondo) in the first stage of the "long walk" still remembered by the people. Eventually some 8000 were confined in the camp at Fort Sumner along with elements of their enemies, the Mescalero Apache, who had arrived earlier. Many never surrendered and held out as refugee groups in the isolated mesas and mountains until the pressure eased. The Fort Sumner captivity was intolerable to all parties. The site lacked water, the land was virtually worthless for agriculture, and the people were vastly overcrowded. The Army had to feed and administer the Indians and maintain order among the hostile groups in a situation where obviously the only object achieved was preventing Indian raiding, since the camp could never be more than a place of impoundment. The Navaho were fortunate in that their homeland in the Four Corners was sufficiently barren and isolated to be of no particular interest to anyone, and their insistent pleas finally resulted in the granting of a treaty in 1868 that allowed them to return to the lands bounded by the sacred mountains of their mythology.

The return was none too soon, for the first of the intercontinental railroads was completed in the next year. By 1883 the Atlantic and Pacific (owned by the Santa Fe) ran along the lower boundaries of the Navaho country, breaking it into checkerboards of Indian and white land since the government granted alternate sections along the right-of-way to encourage the builders. It is doubtful that the Navaho would have been allowed to retain any of this land had the railroads been pressing through the barren lands of northern Arizona at the time the treaties were made. Navaho "luck" in the lack of exploitable resources and agricultural potential and their isolation from centers of white population or major migration routes allowed them to retain a measure of autonomy on their own original lands that was unique. The luck held, since the treaty reservation of only 3,500,000 acres has consistently expanded over the years (unlike almost every other Indian land base) until it is now over 15,000,000 acres, covering much of northern Arizona and parts of adjacent Utah and New Mexico.

After the defeats and humiliations of the period of captivity, the Navaho, unlike many other groups, did not sink into the apathy and despair so characteristic of the reservations. The reasons for this are many, and will be examined in the following chapter where the reservation system in its early phases is considered. Much of the success was the result of isolation on undesirable land, but the Navaho also rebuilt their mixed pastoral and agricultural economy with the few stock that were returned to them after Fort Sumner. They were promised much in their treaty and received little, but they held to their part of the bargain and raided no more. Their warlike habits only reasserted themselves once, when efforts to force Navaho children into schools led to armed resistance. Navaho troubles began anew later as a result of their own success, when their stock began to produce a problem with overgrazing.

The Last Roundup

All over the West the story was the same, varying only in the details of speed and violence employed in encapsulating the Indians on reserved pockets of land. By 1890 most of the reservations had taken essentially their modern form, although through the actions of the Dawes Act much of this land, technically Indian "trust" land, was still passing into white hands.

In some places the speed and brutality of removals was awesome. California, inundated with Anglo settler-miners in the gold rush of '49, almost completely destroyed the native population before reservations could be established in the middle 1850s. Some of this story is known in sadly detailed form from the Indian point of view because of Ishi, a Yahi Indian, who was the last survivor of his people and who managed to live a free existence until 1911 hiding from white contact. His story was told through Theodora Kroeber, the wife of A. L. Kroeber, one of the founders of anthropology, since Ishi lived and worked at the Berkeley department of anthropology in his last years.[4] Rape, murder, starvation, enslavement, and forcible prostitution were all visited upon the Yahi and others till many vanished completely, the rest to survive in tiny pockets of land, rancherias, mostly located in the relatively undesirable and desolate sections of southern California.

A tiny band of Modocs who had been placed on an Oregon reservation with their rivals, the Klamath, sought to return to their home country along the Lost River in southern Oregon and provoked the Modoc "war" of 1872–1873.[5] Led by "Captain Jack," the band at one point held off over a thousand soldiers with no more than thirty or forty warriors in the desolate lava beds of northern California where they made their stand. Captain Jack was primarily remembered for the embarrassing success of his resistance and for a massacre of negotiators at a parley. He was hanged and his people deported to the Indian Territory.

Ishi, the last of the California Yahi, as he appeared just after his capture in 1911 as the "wild man" of Oroville. Theodora Kroeber's Ishi in Two Worlds *movingly tells the story of the last days of this hunted man while he still tried to live free. (Courtesy Lowie Museum of Anthropology, University of California, Berkeley)*

Similarly Chief Joseph of the Nez Perce refused to abide by treaties signed by other Nez Perce chiefs, which ceded *his* lands in the Wallowa Valley in what is now the state of Oregon, and after some of his band had killed settlers in retaliation for earlier Indian deaths, he began a fighting retreat over a thousand-mile route to escape the thousands of Army troops mobilized to stop him. Probably never more than 200 warriors faced the Army and, with all of their women, children, and old people, consistently outmarched and outfought these troops for four months, again creating national embarrassment. Finally trapped almost at the Canadian border, Joseph and his people surrendered and some of Joseph's words may fittingly symbolize the end of the long struggle:

> Hear me, my chiefs! I am tired; my heart is sick and sad. From where the sun now stands I will fight no more forever.[6]

Some Readings

Andrist, Ralph K.: *The Long Death: The Last Days of the Plains Indians*, New York: Macmillan, 1964. Very readable overview, with considerable Sioux coverage.

Mooney, James: *Ghost-Dance Religion and the Sioux Outbreak of 1890*, Chicago: University of Chicago Press, 1964. Classical study of these dramatic events.

Spicer, Edward H.: *Cycles of Conquest: The Impact of Spain, Mexico and the United States on the Indians of the Southwest, 1533–1960*, Tucson: University of Arizona Press, 1962. Excellent coverage of the Navaho and other peoples of the Southwest.

Tyler, S. Lyman: *A History of Indian Policy*, Bureau of Indian Affairs, 1973. Good treatment of historical development of the reservations and of the Bureau of Indian Affairs.

THE HEADLESS HORSEMEN

"Any Indian . . . who shall resort to any artifice or device to keep the Indians of the reservation from adopting and following civilized habits and pursuits, or shall adopt any means to prevent the attendance of children at school, or shall use any arts of a conjurer to prevent Indians from abandoning their barbarous rites and customs, shall be deemed to be guilty of an offense, and upon conviction thereof, for the first offense shall be imprisoned for not less than ten or more than thirty days."

Rules for Indian Courts, 1892[1]

As we have seen, there were thoughts and occasional gestures toward "civilizing" the Indian from the very beginning, but only with the final establishment of the reservations did the growing federal government come to formulate coherent policy which it could enforce. The problem was no longer where to move the Indians, since there was no place left for them to go, but what to do with them once they had been concentrated and restrained. The problem was particularly acute in regard to the former horse-nomadic buffalo hunters of the Plains and other such wandering folk whose whole means of livelihood had been effectively destroyed by confinement itself. Such peoples were entirely dependent on government "rations," and even those with established agricultural habits were badly disrupted economically.

The basic idea that guided United States Indian policy during this formative period was for the Indians to cease being Indians. The Indians were to learn the ways of Americans and to enter the melting pot, either voluntarily or by force if necessary. This program of assimilation, forced or otherwise, took a number of forms but can be roughly divided into programs directed at deculturation—the direct and purposeful elimination of Indian groups, *as groups,* possessing structures and viable cultural patterns of their own—and assimilation of the resultant decultured and atomized individuals into American society. It was widely agreed that the second, which largely involved various programs of education, could not be successful without the first. The Dawes Act, which will be considered shortly, was praised by Theodore Roosevelt in 1901 in a way that expresses this notion:

> In my judgement the time has arrived when we should definitely make up our minds to recognize the Indian as an individual and not as a member of a tribe. The General Allotment Act is a mighty pulverizing engine to break up the tribal mass.[2]

Roughly speaking, this period of forced assimilation stretches from the passage of the Allotment Act to the time of the Meriam Report in 1928 when its failure was recognized. Assimilation and even allotment had been written into a great many treaties long before the final reservation was formed, but the Allotment Act made this the "final solution" of the Indian problem.

Off with Their Heads

The period in question was referred to and characterized by Edward H. Spicer in his *Short History* as the "superintendency," since Indian Agents, "superintendents," were appointed by the Bureau of Indian Affairs (BIA) to administer the affairs of the reservations when the purely military task of restraining the Indians began to decline and the Army became less directly involved.[3] Indian "police" appointed by the agents replaced the Army as the day-to-day means of enforcing policy, although for a long time the Army remained near at hand and was certainly never gone from memory. While the duty of the military had been simply to control the possibility of Indian depredations, an essentially negative task, the superintendents had the further duty of administering the reservations in such a way as to positively promote federal assimilationist policy.

At this early stage all significant power came to be concentrated in the hands of the agents; later it was dispersed through a bureaucracy. As a matter of policy, traditional leaders were often isolated from their followers and their authority consistently denied and undermined. Traditional "band" organization was intentionally broken in favor of enforced settlements on locations of the agent's choice and usually under his eye. The Indian police (officially authorized in 1878), who enforced the laws, were not chosen from traditional leaders but instead were those whom the agent himself trusted and whose whole position rested on their ability to satisfy the agent in carrying out his orders. All of this was the beginning of the "administered community" where all of the mechanisms of decision making that affected the Indian peoples were removed from their hands and directed by an externally derived "administration." Well-being, indeed life itself, depended not on understanding Indian custom or traditional structures which were now powerless, but on standing in well with the agent who had complete authority to bind and loosen.

Laws were made by the BIA and enforced by the agents who made no provision for Indian "customary law," and who, in fact, strove to stamp out such custom. The Indian courts were administered by Indian "judges," but these were nothing but instruments of the agents who appointed them on the basis of qualifications indicating that "preference shall be given to Indians who read and write English readily, wear citizen's dress, and engage in civilized pursuits, and no person shall be eligible to such appointment who is a polygamist."[4]

The whole purpose of these courts was not, as one might suppose, the regulation of justice but instead the extermination of Indian customary practice. Thus "offenses" that were defined and proscribed in addition to the prohibition cited at the opening of the chapter included engaging in the "sun dance, scalp dance, or war dance or any similar feast. . . ."[5] Similarly punishable were polygamy, immorality, intoxication, failure to perform "road duty," and the general crime of vagrancy for any who had failed to "adopt habits of industry, or to engage in civilized pursuits or employments, but habitually spends his time in idleness and loafing. . . ."[6] Genuinely serious crimes—murder, manslaughter, assault, burglary, larceny—were matters for United States federal courts (as of 1885) and not the Indians at all.

In addition to the immediate backing of the Indian police and the latent threat of the Army, the agent had control of all ration distributions and could withhold these from the uncooperative. For some of the hunting tribes who now had nothing to hunt and were entirely dependent on government "largesse," the possibility of ration withdrawal was an irresistible threat. Obviously the impact of all of this was variable. Groups like the Navaho, wandering across their vast wastelands and following a still viable pastoral pattern, retained much of their aboriginal, loosely knit clan structure because they were less directly in contact with the agencies and because they were less economically dependent once their herds began to multiply. Pure hunters like the Sioux were harder hit in terms of the totality of social disruption above the family level. In all cases, however, the overall direction of the affairs of the reservations, and hence of much of the lives of the Indians, was entirely in the hands of agents without Indian participation in governance. The Indian societies were in essence organizationally beheaded at this point, in the name of civilization and assimilation.

The confusion created by the power of the agents was compounded by the variety of systems employed for their appointment. The Indians not only had no voice in the decision-making process that directed their lives but had considerable difficulty keeping track of who did. The venality, corruption, incompetence, and rapid turnover of Indian Agents was not a malicious plan but the simple result of the political system of the times which allowed the party in power to dispose of these offices along with all others as "spoils" to reward the party faithful. Qualification for the job was more likely to be ability at getting out the vote than sympathy for the Indian or knowledge of reservation problems. Though a shift had begun by 1894, it was not until 1908 that the Indian Service finally became part of the Civil Service system of appointments, protected to some extent from such political musical chairs.

Obviously not all agents were incompetents or scoundrels, but the system did allow a great many whose main interest was their own development to find opportunities to further it. President Grant, as an aspect of his "peace policy," sought to alleviate some of the pitfalls after a congressional commission appointed in 1867 to look into Indian problems recommended, among other things, that all superintendents and agents be removed. Grant quite unconstitutionally turned the choice of agents over to various religious denominations such as the Society of Friends, Presbyterians, Catholics, and the like. For the aficionados of the "lost tribes" school of thought, it is a pity that none of the reservations came under Jewish authority, thus testing the Indians' inherent facility in Hebrew!

Trust Me

This period also saw as part of the deculturation drive a considerable amount of redefinition of the status of the Indians. In 1871, as noted,

The biblical names given these Puget Sound Indians indicate the influence of the Mission of Myron Eells at Skokomish, Washington, on the "civilization" process. During the "peace policy" period, the church boards that appointed the missionary also nominated the reservation agent, in this case Myron's brother, Edwin. (Courtesy Eells Northwest Collection, Whitman College Library)

Congress unilaterally terminated the treaty-making process although continuing to insist that existing treaties would be respected. It was and is the United States government that interpreted what these treaties meant, reserving this right to itself to the exclusion of the states. At the time of this writing, legal horrors have fallen on the state of Maine because a large part of the land of that state was ceded by the Passamaquody in an agreement reached after the Indian Trade and Intercourse Act of 1834 had established this exclusive federal jurisdiction.

If the federal government "protected" the rights of the Indians from local intrusion, who or what regulated the federals? *Quis custodiet ipsos custodes*? (Who will keep the keepers themselves?)

It is the executive branch of the *federal* government which carries out *federal* policy, and the BIA is the specific instrument for Indian matters. It is the executive who interprets what the treaties and legislation regarding Indians mean in any particular instance. If any disagree, disputes are adjudicated in *federal* courts, occasionally requiring some ultimate decisions by the *federal* Supreme Court. In the end the Congress can unilaterally modify or entirely abrogate treaties through legislation if it disagrees with its own earlier decisions; the Supreme Court made this plain in *Lone Wolf v. Hitchcock* (1902). What Congress does, Congress can undo, and the Indians have exactly the same recourse as any other citizen (since 1924, at least) in that they may vote against those representatives who have displeased them. The Constitution protects us all against capriciousness on the part of Congress, but somehow this "protection" did not protect the Indian against such constitutional monstrosities as assigning the governance of the reservations to missionary groups (Grant's peace policy) or the curiosa of arbitrarily imposed morality that was the Indian Offenses Court. In fact the power of Congress in regard to Indian reservations is unrestrained except by the pressure of public opinion and is certainly in no way under the control of the Indian peoples themselves. I do not say that it and the federal government as a whole have not been frequently concerned with and responsive to the views and wishes of the Indian, but, should they not be responsive, the Indians have no recourse, as witness the numerous involuntary programs such as the Curtis Act, or in more modern times the program of termination, both of which were aimed at the dissolution of Indian governments without their true consent. With the loss of their "sovereignty" resulting from their loss of treaty-making power, Indians are at the mercy of federal decisions.

The Dawes Severality Act (General Allotment Act) was the very embodiment of this one-sided power relationship between Indian and federal government. By the time this was imposed the Indians had gone from sovereign nations (recognized in treaties as such) to "dependent domestic nations" (Marshall's doctrine) and were about to become "wards" of the government through the establishment of "trust relationships" that dealt with Indians as legal incompetents. Regardless of the virtues of the act or the noble motives of its supporters, including its framer, Henry L. Dawes, the point here is that the act, as Roosevelt noted, was designed to break up the "tribal mass" and was in no sense a program that consulted Indian wants or opinions at any point. Good was to be done "for" the Indians or "to" them whether they would or no.

The Dawes Act was simplicity itself in conception. Lands held at that time in common by the Indian peoples as part of their reserves would be divided among the individuals making up the tribe. Each head of household was to receive a quarter section of land (160 acres) with supplementary lesser amounts for dependents. This was the same amount of land provided under the Homestead Act of 1862, which allowed any citizen to "homestead" that amount of land in the public domain, and was, at least in areas of reasonably fertile soil, an adequate amount for a viable family farm.

"Surplus" land remaining after the allotments had been made would be sold to provide funds to equip and train the Indians in the necessary skills to operate a successful farm in the same way that the majority of Americans were supposed to aspire to do. Ownership was not to be in "fee simple" but to be held "in trust" for the Indian owner by the government for twenty-five years, or until the government through its superintendent determined that the particular Indian was "competent" and could take title. Acceptance of the allotment also granted citizenship to the Indian allottee, so that many Indians became citizens before that status was conferred upon them all in 1924.

The act was designed to create stout, individualistic, self-reliant yeoman farmers. As Dawes rather poetically said of the Indian, "He is to be led out from the darkness, into the light; he is to be shown how to walk, how to help himself. He is to be taught self reliance, or he will never be a man."[7] That learning to farm would accomplish all of this through pride in property was in accord with the best thought of the time. As to tribal communalism, "there is no enterprise to make your home any better than that of your neighbors. There is no selfishness, which is at the bottom of civilization."[8] Though no one has so clearly recorded the less lofty position, the well-meaning men had the whole-hearted support of others who knew full well that the act would make protected Indian property more openly available to the ambitious. Even at the time (1880) a minority report of the House Indian Affairs Committee stated: "The real aim of this bill is to get at the Indian lands and open them up to settlement."[9]

Of the total original 2.25 billion acres within United States boundaries, land in Indian hands in 1881 was some 155,632,312 acres; the effect of the act was to reduce these holdings to 77,865,373 acres by 1900. Before the program came to a halt, some 90 million acres were removed from Indian hands. Separating the Indians from their "surplus" lands was obviously a successful aspect of the Dawes Act. The positive side of encouraging the formation of family farms was a failure. As early as 1891 white eagerness to utilize Indian land still in trust status and the recognition of the inability of the Indians to make use of it in the ways intended led to legislation allowing such lands to be leased and worked by non-Indians. Much of the transfer of lands involved lands allotted to Indians which were then subsequently sold to whites. Indian agents could arrange to have a particular Indian landholder declared "competent," remove his land from the guardianship of the trust relation, and arrange its sale to non-Indians, with the extent of consultation and explanation offered to the Indian "owner" largely at the agent's discretion. The Burke Act of 1906 formalized this power. Needless to say, lands remaining in Indian hands were those not coveted by non-Indians, being almost by definition unsuitable for development.

The largest amount of land remaining in Indian hands and still held communally was in the Southwest with the larger Navaho and Apache holdings, which were little affected by allotment. Many other reservations, however, were badly "checkerboarded" with white landholdings interspersed among the remaining Indian lands both individually and tribally held. On the lands of the Sioux and the Nez Perce, towns organized, owned, and controlled by whites grew up on the reservations themselves. In modern times, as we shall see, many tribes have been working hard to restore some integrity to their land base by buying back these lands.

Off with Their Hair

At the same time that the superintendency and the allotment program were seeking to break up Indian tribal structures, there was a thrust to "educate" the Indian. A first step toward such education was the suppression of Indian customary practice so as to create a vacuum that could be filled with civilized ways. The missionary societies working in Hawaii and Oceania found it a necessary first step toward civilization to get dresses and trousers on those to be saved. In much the same spirit, the Indian agents promoted civilized dress but were seemingly particularly fixated on the question of hair. Thus the words of an Army lieutenant in 1896: "All energies were bent to compel the adult males to cut their hair. . . . The Indian Office, at my request, issued a pre-emptory order for all to cut their hair and adopt civilized attire; and in six weeks from the start every male Indian had been changed into the semblance of a decent man. . . ."[10]

Such superficial "civilization" was of course meaningless except in furthering the disintegration of the Indian society through humiliation and degradation of those who persisted in its ways. The key to assimilation was soon believed to lie in education for the young, who could be brought to take their place in civilized society, leaving the ways of their hopelessly savage parents behind. The Indian service gave very early signs of believing, as did Nikolai Lenin in the principle, "Give us the child for eight years, and it will be a Bolshevist forever."

Richard H. Pratt was the director of the Carlisle Indian School in Carlisle, Pennsylvania, from its foundation in 1879 until 1904, and his views represent a policy never exclusively pursued but in its outline predominant until the 1930s. Pratt announced it as his aim in educating his pupils to "kill the Indian in him, and save the man."[11] He was drastically opposed to schools located on or anywhere near the reservations, and this emphasis on off-reservation year-round boarding schools has persisted in diminished form into recent years. Pratt went beyond the isolation of Indian students from their parents, coming eventually to oppose any form of "Indian schools" and insisting that the only hope was to destroy the reservations and scatter the Indians among the general population. His own version of this at Carlisle was the "outing system" where Indian students were placed with white families over their vacations or when possible for the entire year. In regard to the allotment program, he insisted that it could only be beneficial if Indian lands were scattered among white neighbors and not allowed to continue in isolation.[12]

Although Pratt was an extreme advocate of "civilization through deculturation," he was more typical than not among educators. Boarding schools on the reservations were begun at about the time of Carlisle's founding, along with day schools, often operated by missionaries. A contract system was inaugurated in which government funds were supplied on a per capita basis to those providing a "Christian" education. This resulted ultimately in court battles which curiously were resolved in 1908 with a decision that support of sectarian schools *was* permissible. Part of this reliance on the missionary as teacher was the fact that, then as now, it was difficult to attract trained and competent personnel to the isolation and difficulties of the reservations; those religiously motivated were likely to be more useful and willing than others. In the same way, the emphasis on boarding schools was not entirely a matter of stressing deculturation. As was found much later when moves toward day schools were pushed, the scattered patterns of population and the poor roads on the larger reserves like the Navaho made attendance at a day school a problem.

In general the schools, day or boarding, secular or mission, were Draconian in their discipline and thoroughly assimilationist in philosophy and approach. The boarding schools in particular featured a pattern of total control reminiscent of boot camp, and many of their personnel, such as Pratt, were indeed of military background. Students were strictly segregated as to sex, wore uniforms, marched in formation everywhere, and were entirely without privacy even in their dormitories. A Sioux once humorously told me of dances he was marched to where the teachers went about the room checking to make certain they could see daylight between the dancers. The savage beatings, many reports of which survive from this period, cannot be viewed out of context. The times were such that any schoolchild, white or Indian, could reasonably expect to have his bottom strapped or his hand swatted with a ruler. The difference seems to lie in the fact that the Indian students had no possibility of parental intervention to restrain the temper of teachers. It is certain that, given the difficulties of crossing cultural and linguistic barriers, the occasions on which whip-worthy offenses were committed must surely have been more frequent in Indian schools than in white.

Offenses in the schools were much like those noted in regard to the Indian courts. It would appear that the greatest of crimes was the speaking of any language other than English, since the schools sought above all else to impart that tongue. At the boarding schools, students from various tribes were deliberately intermixed in the dormitories to prevent any cultural or linguistic communication between members of the same tribe. Osage and Sioux, having only English in common, would presumably be forced to use that as their lingua franca, and any persons caught speaking to their own kinsmen in native languages would be dealt with severely. This de-Indianization was sometimes carried to ludicrous extremes, as in the suggestion by a commissioner to his staff in 1889 that in dealing with pupils "they should carefully avoid any unnecessary reference to the fact that they are Indians."[13]

The filling of these schools was not a voluntary matter, and agents were free to use force if necessary to insure that the schools met their quotas. The Navaho who scrupulously refrained from violence after Fort Sumner came close to revolt shortly after their return. In an incident narrated as "The Trouble at Round Rock," armed resistance was offered to the agent responsible for rounding up school children.[14] It must be remembered that the children sent to boarding schools were as young as 6 years when thrown into this situation—away from kinsmen or anyone who could even speak their language. It is no wonder that there was a consistent problem with runaways, and given the remorseless tone of it all, it is not surprising that truants would be sent back in shackles when "recaptured" by the authorities.

As we shall see, the Meriam Report of 1928 clearly revealed that all of this was not only misguided as to means but unjustified by results. The Indians did not become the enlightened yeoman farmers of the American dream through education and allotment.

The failure of education during the superintendency period seems to have been not only a function of the ignoring of inherent difficulties of cross-cultural education, completely replacing one knowledge and value system with another, but also a paucity of schools, teachers, and funds. A great many Indian children did spend some time in these institutions, but there were never enough schools to serve the total population even had the system existed to insure that they would attend. All figures are debatable, since counting Indians seems an unreliable affair (in 1970 the BIA showed more Indians in its reservation areas of responsibility in Alaska, Arizona, and New Mexico than the census showed Indians for all three states!). One can presumably rely on the figures provided in the Commissioner's annual report in 1906 that 24,762 children were enrolled in federal schools (37 percent in off-reservation boarding schools), but what percentage of the actual Indian school-age population that represented is less certain. The total Indian population was generally put around 250,000 during this period. The Navaho situation is admittedly one where the difficulties of schools have been great, but as late as 1942,

Kluckhohn examined figures indicating that only 28 percent of the school-age children were enrolled in any school, public or private. Kluckhohn's studies also showed that enrollment figures were further deceptive in that few children consistently attended year-round. Like Civil War figures for men on the firing line, as opposed to "aggregate total," the figure for the number of Indians actually sitting in chairs on any given day was much smaller than that for those enrolled.[15]

The schools themselves were ill-equipped and poorly staffed and funded. In 1887, with an enrollment in 227 schools of 14,333 students (federal or contracted), the total funds available were only $1,226,415. Whatever was done, to however many students, it was done on the cheap. The aim was never a "higher" education but, as the name of Carlisle suggests, a practical or "industrial" education, much like that in the early days of the Hampton Institute. The Indian was not to become a doctor or lawyer (certainly not Indian chief) but a mechanic, blacksmith, or farmer—and that in white society, not Indian. Pratt spoke approvingly of a young man who ran away from Carlisle to become a stoker on a ship as a "good serviceable Indian."[16]

The ideal result of these preparations was, of course, the vanishing of the Indian into the crevices of the larger society. Unfortunately the general result seems to have been at best the creation of "marginal men" and the raising of expectations that could not be fulfilled. Again, reliable figures cannot be provided, but it seems apparent that the vast majority of those "educated" to one degree or another returned to their tribal communities rather than becoming dispersed and assimilated. Again Kluckhohn suggests that over 90 percent of the Navaho boarding-school students returned to life on the reservation even though specifically prepared for life in the general society. The cause of this was probably two-fold. The Indian students, not unreasonably, came to value the security of life with their own people (and the sense of community and belonging to be found there) more than the possibility of greater material success off the reservations. The promised material success off the reservations was also more illusion than reality since the climate of the times was not one that would allow even the acceptance of Irishmen ("no Irish need apply") into a condition of equality, let alone barbarous savages. In areas of heavy Indian population, it was not just blacks who were forbidden to use the front door.

Unwelcomed and ill-prepared for participation in the larger society, Indian pupils found after many years' absence (students were not generally encouraged to return to the reservation while in school) that they were no better prepared for the life on the reservation. The skills that they may have learned, while inadequate for the larger society, had little or no relevance to the realities of the reservation. To the extent that children had been successful in the schools, they had succeeded by becoming as un-Indian as possible. As the Navaho said about children

Puget Sound Indian students at the Skokomish Indian School in 1888. (Courtesy Eells Northwest Collection, Whitman College Library)

returning from boarding schools in the 1960s: "They don't know who their relatives are." The behaviors expected among kinsmen in a matrilineal clan system of mutual cooperation and sharing are not only intricate but in many cases run contrary to the strongly individualistic emphasis of the white Protestant ethic. Having learned English, probably ungrammatical and accented, the students also discovered that they spoke bad Navaho after many years of disuse. The marginal man, instead of having achieved assimilation, was not at home in either of the two cultures. In the kingdom of the blind, the one-eyed is in big trouble.

The Unvanishing American

Since governmental policy was so clearly dedicated to assimilation and elimination of the reservation enclave, it is not surprising to find that little effort was dedicated to improving life conditions on the reservations. Who puts new tires on a car if it is about to be traded in? Why paint if you're selling the house? The Indians were not destined to remain on the reservations, so no preparations needed to be taken. Why deal with a situation intended to be no more than a temporary holding action?

By and large each reservation was left with extremely limited funds under the discretion of its agent in matters of economic or other forms of development. Indian health, for example, was not specifically provided for until 1909 with the appointment of a medical supervisor, and the Indian Health Service was not created until 1911. The program had funds of $40,000 in 1911 for a population of over 250,000 persons. In spite of deplorable conditions and lack of care, the Indian population from its low of 250,000 began to climb after 1900, reaching 336,000 by 1920 and beginning a startling growth to its present level of over 1 million.

Some agents managed to introduce stock raising by providing the necessary animals. This met with noticeable success with the Navaho, who already favored such a life, and even with the Sioux, who proved amenable to cattle raising. The Sioux and others were, however, undermined in their nascent adaptation by the leasing of their grazing lands by the agents to non-Indians and by the checkerboarding brought about by allotment. Here and there, as with the Pima, agricultural tools were supplied and instruction in smithery and other farming skills was provided. Agricultural development was noticeably retarded, particularly in the Southwest, by the preemption of water rights by non-Indians. The government was forced in 1907 to fight the issue to the Supreme Court, which inaugurated the Winters Doctrine, allowing the government to reserve water for Indian use in spite of the Western states' adherence to prior-use rights.

"Industry" began to be systematically approached in the 1920s at a few locations, but in the early years the only industries were those associated with the administration of the Indians. Small towns grew up around the agencies composed of the employees and dependents of the "educated" Indians and non-Indians who maintained the police, schools, and administration of the reservation. Whatever development occurred in terms of road building, sanitation, and the like was concentrated in these agency towns with little effect on the rest of the reserve. To the extent that Indian resources, such as timber or mineral deposits, were exploited at all during these years, it was by non-Indians through arrangements like those used for land leasing, with the funds received held "in trust" and administered by the government.

As already noted, the only Indians who had been making great strides toward adopting a white mode of life as a group were the civilized tribes in Oklahoma. Here the assimilationist distaste for Indian self-determination and group survival in any form resulted in the wiping out of developed governments and a fully functioning school system and, by special act in 1908, a rapid removal of land through allotment. Everywhere, whatever else might be happening, land continued to leave Indian hands. Teddy Roosevelt attempted to remove 2,500,000 acres of forested Indian land and include it in the national park system. His unilateral action, two days before the end of his term in office, was finally declared invalid, but it stands as an early example of a struggle between conservationists and Indian development. Between 1917 and 1920 there was a drive toward "competency" declarations turning over Indian land to individual owners in fee simple. Commissions granted title to 10,956 parcels of land, most of which, as with the newly allotted lands in Oklahoma (which were found to have mineral resources), rapidly found their way into non-Indian hands. The Indian might not be vanishing, but his land continued to do so.

The results of the action of Roosevelt's "mighty pulverizing engine" were many and varied, as the next chapter will show, but the one result that it did not produce was the result it most ardently and ruthlessly sought—the vanishing through assimilation of the Indian peoples. Their life-style, their economy, their land base—all were "pulverized"; but somehow the Indians continued to prefer to think of themselves as Indians and remain in communities, however disrupted and poverty stricken, with others who also thought of themselves as Indians. Some left, but most remained, and whether this persistence of Indian identity through these times of trouble was a matter of federal incompetence or Indian strength is something many have debated.

Some peoples, like the ever-adaptable Navaho, managed to retain their aboriginal ceremonial system more or less intact through all of these deculturative efforts. In the Navaho case it was largely a function of their being widely dispersed, which made supervision nearly impossible. The Pueblo peoples developed during the Spanish period a dual system that Dozier has referred to as "compartmentalization."[17] They became, as required, nominal, visible Catholics attending church under the direction and coercion of non-Indian priests. At the same time, however, they maintained the traditional ceremonials and the structures that supported them, simply keeping these from the Spanish eye. With the coming of the Americans, pressures upon the "pagan" aspect of the Pueblos was again intensified. The result was simply to increase the secrecy and the defensive social controls that enforced it; so the Pueblos continued to keep a public Christian face while preserving their Katchinas and other such symbols of belief underground (literally, in the case of the kivas).

For most peoples the social and communal aspects of their belief systems were effectively suppressed, although cultural transmission at the personal and family level was preserved. While sun dances could not be held, there was nothing to prevent old men from passing on the myths of the days of glory or to restrain an eagle doctor from instructing an apprentice. Still, by the end of the superintendency, most Indians were counted as nominal members of some Christian sect, and many of them had actually become participants in these churches.

One curious and unlooked-for development (by the government at least) in this period was the rise of a new religion generally known as the Native American Church (or Peyote Church). Weston La Barre, author of *The Peyote Cult,* suggests rather ironically that the spread of the church among so many different groups may in large part have been facilitated by the intertribal contact at the boarding schools and the use of English as a lingua franca.[18] It has eventually become one element in a general pattern of pantribalism that may have indeed had its beginnings in the forced mixing bowl of the boarding schools, where while Indians did not come to think of themselves as whites, they did apparently begin to identify with Indian peoples other than their own tribal units.

The story of the Peyote Church is too long and complex to tell here in any detail, but its rough outline may serve to illustrate the fact that the Indian peoples were not as passive in the face of the events of the superintendency as the historical record might seem to suggest. Clearly much was going on among the powerless peoples to redefine their lives, and most of that necessarily took place outside the vision of history as represented by the agents who would have interfered had they known of it. To the extent that the agents *did* encounter the church or evidence of the use of peyote in ritual, they sought to suppress it along with all other paganism.

As noted earlier, the use of hallucinogenic drugs was part of an overall pattern of consciousness altering as a religious principle in the Chichimeca. The Native American Church utilizes peyote (*Lophophora williamsii*) sacramentally in the context of lengthy and complex ritual. Because a "drug" is used, Peyote Church members have continued to suffer persecutions into modern times long after programs for the stamping out of "paganism" were generally abandoned. Though such arguments have no real place in this book and the case is presented in proper detail in references provided, I will remind the reader that this consciousness altering is a religious act, not recreation. Peyotists do not seek to "get it on" any more than one could logically accuse the congregation at communion of "boozing it up" on the sacramental wine.

Peyote was used in pre-Columbian times primarily in Mexico, particularly northern Mexico, and most authorities agree that it diffused from there in comparatively recent times into the Southwest and southern plains. Whether the basic ritual associated with peyote was also derived in this way or created on the foundations already existing in the Chichimeca (a Red Bean cult, for example) is much debated. Whatever the details of origin, some form of the peyote ritual was becoming widely spread among Indian groups by the early 1900s.

David Aberle, who studied Navaho peyotism, characterizes the movement as "redemptive," that is to say, focused on the salvation of the individual rather than a transformation of society itself.[19] Following the "peyote road" allows individuals to obtain the spiritual power they require to cope with their own problems in an imperfect world. Navaho peyotists consider that the ritual has some curative powers, and it is widely believed that the power of the peyote allows a person to resist the temptations of alcohol. Such a movement was obviously very appropriate in the times when no realistic possibility existed of altering the world around the Indian peoples but when strength could be sought in order to endure.

Peyotism as a religion is syncretic, or fusional. It is fundamentally "Indian" in its ritual forms and notions of spiritual power but has mixed with it (in many of the variations) a number of Christian elements. In some ways it is reminiscent of the Handsome Lake religion in its emphasis on a separate "Indian way" to worship the one God of the Christians, although not all peyotists see it in that light. The all-night ritual of singing and drumming while ceremonial corn-husk cigarettes are smoked and peyote eaten is relatively uniform in broad outline from tribe to tribe. The uniformity may partly be due to the traveling "road chiefs" who organize rituals and teach the proper techniques but who cannot be thought of as priests, since they claim no special powers beyond knowledge of the peyote way. Like other aspects of pan-Indianism, the rituals, feather fans, corn-husk cigarettes, crescent-shaped ash altars, thunderbird symbols, and the like cannot clearly be associated with any one pre-Columbian tribal belief system but appear to be as syncretic in their combinations of a variety of Indian belief and symbols as they are in incorporating Christian elements.

The Peyote cult is probably only a single indicator of a general pattern of common experience producing a sense of common identity. The Indian peoples, whatever their aboriginal differences—bands, tribes, chiefdoms, states—were being dealt with as if they were all simply "Indians"; and the reservation system, while failing to completely eradicate "Indianness," did begin to produce a sort of cultural uniformity. Modern intertribal gatherings, often called the "powwow circuit," feature displays of costume and war-dancing contests which seem largely Plains in their origins but which have been accepted by all Indians as at least symbolic of their common identity. In describing the process of adaptation, it makes sense to speak of "U.S. reservation cultures" rather than treat each people separately, even though each tribal group retains its own distinct core.

Beet Farmers?

In a stout defense of a scheme to develop Indian character and self-reliance by inaugurating the cultivation and processing of sugar beets, Commissioner of Indian Affairs Francis Leupp in his report of 1906 said, "The Indian takes to beet farming as naturally as the Italian takes to art

Peyote persons? Although the photograph was simply titled "Three Musicians" when taken in 1894, the three men (Comanche, Kiowa-Apache, and Kiowa) hold what appears to be the paraphernalia of the peyote ritual. (Courtesy National Anthropological Archives, Smithsonian Institution)

or the German to science."[20] In view of this level of sophistication, one could be permitted to disagree with or at least doubt the observation contained in this same report by the superintendent of the Asylum for Insane Indians in South Dakota, who rather defensively said, "It is clearly established in our experience at this asylum that what some people term 'enforced education and civilization' of the Indians has nothing whatever to do with causing insanity among them."[21]

The reservation communities (if that word applies at this point) were riven with factionalism between "mixed blood" and "full blood": those who sought to assimilate or at least cooperate with the agents (mixed bloods), and those who clung to or reverted to traditional ways or resisted in some form the efforts of the agents (full bloods). Utter dependency, both economic and social, had been promoted by putting all of the mechanism of governance in the hands of the agents. The reliance on compulsion and decision making without consultation had produced a climate of distrust, suspicion, apathy, and despair. Edward H. Spicer used a label for those in the somewhat similar Japanese relocation camps of World War II which would apply here—"Impounded Peoples."[22] The impounding process in both cases led to a self-defeating mechanism—the administered community—which we will contend by its very nature cannot achieve any end but its own perpetuation.

This superintendency period took away without replacing. It eliminated or rendered ineffective the traditional structures in the name of assimilation, without achieving assimilation. Having failed to assimilate, it also failed to provide any structures through which life could be lived successfully on the reservations or by which Indian peoples could begin to move toward some form of self-help and self-determination. Seeking assimilation, the superintendency saw beginning to emerge a permanent client population.

Some Readings

Leacock, Eleanor Burke, and Nancy Oestreich Lurie (eds.): *North American Indians in Historical Perspective,* New York: Random House, 1971. Wide-ranging series of essays, many useful but the quality is mixed.

Prucha, Francis Paul: *Americanizing the American Indians: Writings by the "Friends of the Indian," 1880–1900,* Cambridge, Mass.: Harvard University Press, 1973. Revealing collection of statements by historically important figures.

Prucha, Francis Paul: *American Indian Policy in Crisis: Christian Reformers and the Indian, 1865–1900,* Norman, Okla.: University of Oklahoma Press, 1976. Definitive but heavy going.

Spicer, Edward H. (ed.): *Perspectives in American Indian Culture Change,* Chicago: University of Chicago Press, 1961. Capsule analysis of the pattern of acculturation of six Indian groups with an integrative chapter by the editor. Best work of its kind.

Washburn, Wilcomb E.: *The Assault on Indian Tribalism: The General Allotment Law (Dawes Act) of 1887,* Philadelphia: Lippincott, 1975. Short and well done.

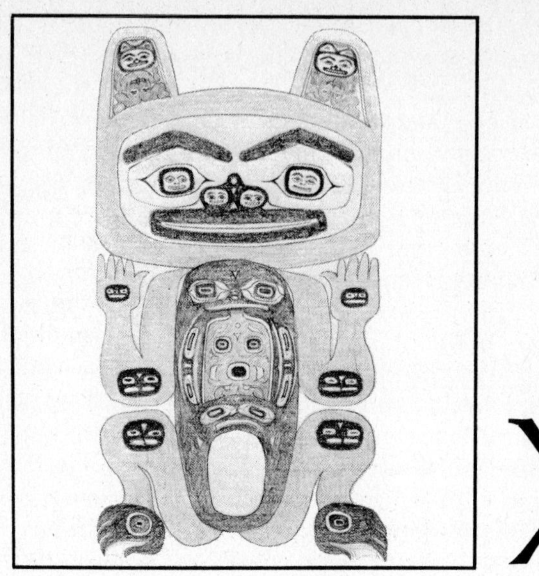

XI SECOND THOUGHTS

To the egress!
P. T. Barnum[1]

No realistically definite date can be given for the turning point in Indian policy that shifted it away from the assimilation-at-any-price positon. Frequently, however, 1922 is cited, since a series of legal and political battles that raged around the Pueblos seems to have focused and organized the "friends of the Indian" and brought conditions to public attention. By 1933 John Collier, who had been most active in these battles, especially in the American Indian Defense Association, became Indian Commissioner and a "new deal" was definitely a conscious feature of his term under President Franklin D. Roosevelt. The reorientation of policy and attitudes lies somewhere in this decade of furor and rethinking and as with much else probably owes its success to factors that had nothing directly to do with the Indian. The new deal for the Indians was ultimately only possible because of the more general New Deal administration of FDR which sprang out of concern for the "one third of a nation, ill-housed and ill-fed" produced by the general American economic depression. Since *all* the Indians were demonstrably in this condition, it became impossible to ignore them in a national climate of reconstruction and recovery.

In our times when a Secretary of Agriculture has been disgraced because of reports of privately told racial jokes, it is difficult to imagine the atmosphere that would allow a Commissioner of Indian Affairs to publicly denounce the assembled elders of the Taos Pueblo as "half animals" and throw the lot into jail for practicing religious rites which had been previously branded as "obscene and pornographic." The public vilification included charges that the Pueblos were "agents of Moscow," which is a rather early occurrence of the red-baiting that later became so popular in the McCarthy era that the Indians themselves engaged in it.[2] Specifically, a spokesman for the American Indian Federation, a group opposed to the Indian Reorganization Act, denounced it as "communistic, subversive and dangerous to our nation."[3]

The Pueblos had survived the Spanish through their dual Christian/Pueblo religious structures only to find their religion and themselves under attack once more as a sort of pagan theocracy. The real point, of course, was, as always, land. After the war with Mexico, the Anglos found the Pueblos, who were orderly, well-governed, town-dwelling agriculturalists, many of whom spoke Spanish, hard to tell apart from the Mexicans. All in all, they seemed "civilized" and so were not brought under the "wardship" of the government during the early creation of the reservations as were their "savage" neighbors, though agents and schools were provided for them. By 1913, encroachments of the settlers had prompted the government to act to bring the Pueblos under its full jurisdiction and protection.

Albert Fall, Secretary of the Interior, is primarily remembered in American history for the Teapot Dome scandal involving misuses of public oil lands. Fall did not confine himself to this one memorable deed but attempted in a similar fashion to usurp Indian rights. He sought at one point to declare lands that had been granted to the Navaho (not by treaty but by "executive order") under federal control for the purposes of oil exploitation. The legal differences between "treaty" reservations and "executive order" reservations remain a much debated issue. He sponsored an Indian Omnibus Bill whose apparent purpose was to finally distribute all remaining Indian properties on a per capita basis and dissolve the tribes. The Pueblo struggle, which brought Indian problems into the light of day, was the result of the Bursum Bill sponsored by Fall, which would have had the effect of granting white "squatters" clear title to Pueblo lands.

The stripping away of a bit more Indian land was in itself scarcely remarkable, but the proposed bill brought on a furor without parallel. Fall was ideally cast as the villainous antagonist; around the Pueblos rallied a remarkable collection of "friends," from Collier to the poetical Oliver La Farge and the populist hero Robert La Follette. The Pueblos organized themselves into an "All Pueblo Council" to meet this threat, the first time they had been so united since the Pueblo Revolt of 1680. The Pueblos eventually defeated the Bursum Bill, but a crusading spirit and sense of further wrongs to be righted carried the "friends" on to more general protests. Hubert Work, who replaced the disgraced Fall in the midst of it all, responded to the mounting tide of protest to appoint the Committee of One Hundred to investigate the Indian situation. This gesture was unsatisfactory to many and eventually a nongovernmental agency was chosen, the Institute for Government Research (Brookings Institute), whose findings (generally known as the Meriam Report) were published in 1928 as "The Problem of Indian Administration."[4]

The "Indian Problem"

The Meriam investigators surveyed the Indian conditions and found them deplorable and said so in a document that is by and large dry and understated. They suggest calmly that part of the problem lay in the low levels of funding and understaffing for Indian facilities. Conditions reported at the Hiawatha Hospital for Insane Indians (the same mentioned in the last chapter in the 1906 report) indicated some of the stern reality of this mild observation when they noted that a trained nurse had been appointed for the *first time* in 1927, that there were no records available for their study, and that the director, the only professional, was on leave at the time of their visit. Boarding-school children were noted to have been fed for 11 cents a day and to have worked at least half days to support their own education under the guise of "industrial training." In spite of its dry quality, the report and its impact are high drama.

The very first sentence of the report stated that "an overwhelming majority of the Indians are poor, even extremely poor, and they are not adjusted to the economic and social system of the dominant white civilization."[5] This "adjustment" was of course the long standing assimilationist goal, and the authors of the Meriam Report had not abandoned hope, as witness the first of their major recommendations that the Indian

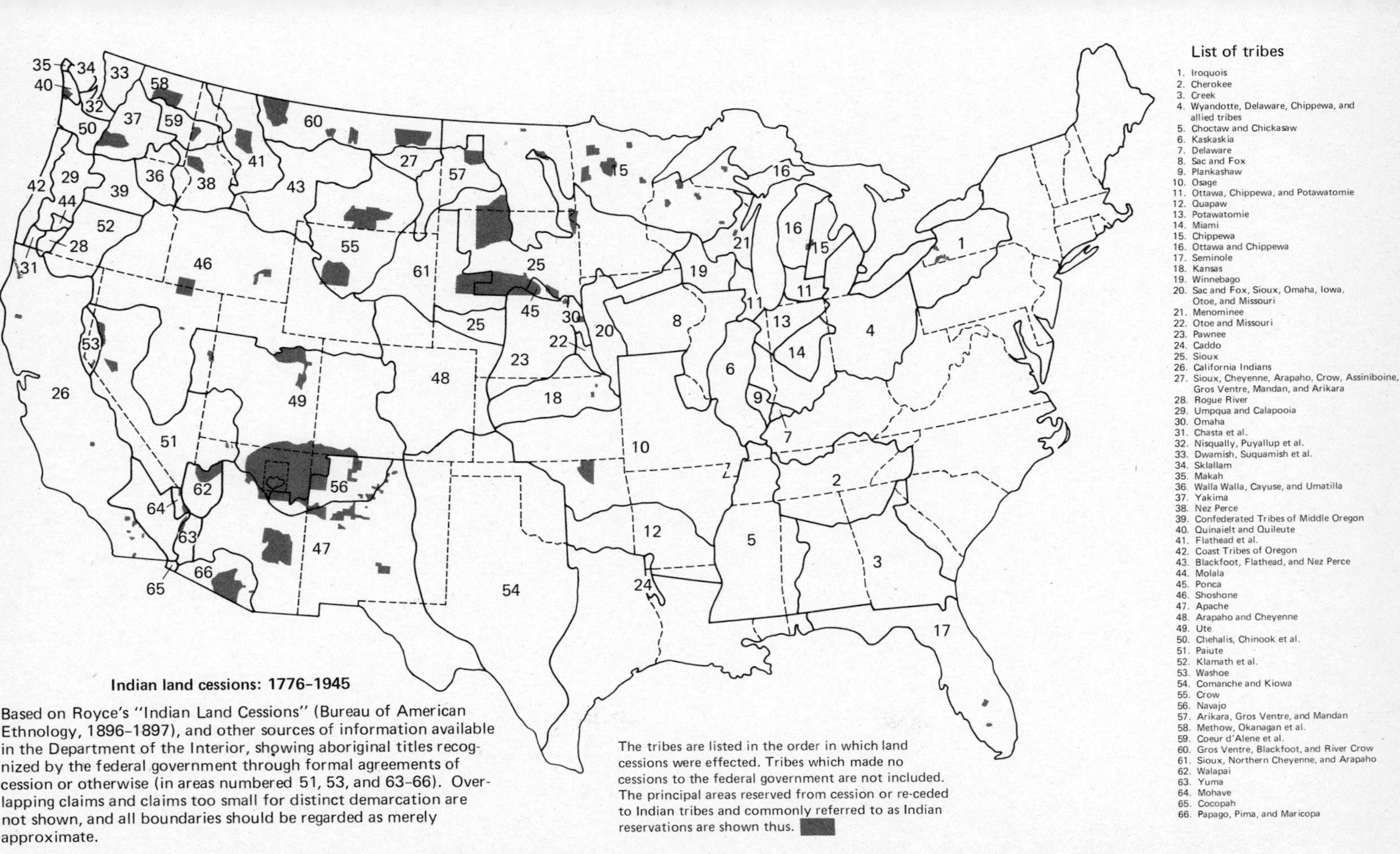

The inexorable march of Indian land cessions is shown in this map prepared for Felix Cohen's Handbook of Indian Law. *(Courtesy Bureau of Indian Affairs)*

Service become an "educational agency" for the Indians "so that they may be absorbed into the prevailing civilization. . . ." But in that same sentence they sound a new concern and alternative theme, *"or be fitted to live in the presence of that civilization* at least in accordance with a minimum standard of health and decency" [italics added].[6] This was a new recognition—that the problem might take some time, effort, and resources and that while waiting for the glorious future to arrive, it might be necessary to do something about the miserable present. It was also a confession of the failure of previous policy.

There was even in their statement of "A General Policy for Indian Affairs" recognition that some Indians "wish to remain Indians . . ." and a recommendation against attempts "to force individual Indians or groups of Indians to be what they do not want to be, to break their pride in themselves and their Indian race, or to deprive them of their Indian culture. Such efforts may break down the good in the old without replacing it with compensating good from the new."[7] In general, the expectation remained that the Indians would seek to achieve prosperity by merging with the larger society, but the small gesture toward accepting those who didn't choose that path was a turning point. "He who wants to remain an Indian and live according to his old culture should be aided in doing so."[8] The effort was justified, they went on to point out, by health considerations, if nothing else, since the Indians lived in proximity to white communities.

Remarkably astute in part, the report is also sometimes naive and occasionally reverts to the condescending rhetoric of earlier times, as when it speaks of the Indians having a "pauper point of view" brought about by the ration system, or that "the typical Indian is not industrious, nor is he an effective worker when he does work."[9] Even at worst, however, there are nuggets of insight as in the suggestion regarding dependency: "Anything else done for them in a way that neglects educating to do for themselves will work in the same direction."[10] Put as a moral statement deploring sloth, this is distastefully preachy, but the position that will be examined and supported in this book's final discussions is that a client population prevented from making its own decisions or controlling its own destinies is self-defeating. John Collier picked up and amplified this theme when he suggested as one of his own basic guiding principles, "The experience of responsible democracy is, of all experiences, the most therapeutic. . . ."[11] The report itself paid service to restoring viable organization but repeatedly deplored remaining vestiges of structure or those newly emerging, like the peyote movement, wherever they appeared to interfere with assimilation. The peyotists or any other ceremonial curers were seen as interfering with health education rather than as a vehicle for revitalization.

Just how bad things really were on the reservations the investigators admitted was unknowable because of the paucity of available information and records. Still, a picture emerges from the report of a people on the bottom of the scale in every reasonable index of human misery. For those who sought comfort in the unreliability of the figures, the researchers noted that in those few cases where they had reason to believe that the data had been most reliable the picture that emerged was worse, not better. The Indians were clearly, in a phrase later used by the Office of Economic Opportunity, the "poorest of the poor."

Health figures revealed tuberculosis as the most serious problem, with rates for that disease ranging up to seven times that of the general population. Infant mortality rates were in some cases two to three times that of the general population. Many others were more difficult to calculate, but there was a general belief that venereal disease rates were very high in spite of the lack of testing. One contract physician is reported to have declared 85 percent of those on his reservation to be suffering from syphilis with no tests or documentary evidence at all. As the report stated in regard to education, a "fundamental need" was a "change in point of view";[12] this was a problem in medicine as well. In regard to medical as well as all other services directed at Indian well-being, there was a constant theme of inadequate funding and staffing combined with minimally trained and grossly biased personnel. In 1927 there were sixteen active Public Health Service nurses in the field. Doctors were concentrated in the hospitals and schools, and there were only 104 filled permanent positions with an additional sixty-one "contract" physicians offering some part-time help. This was for a population scattered over many states and numbering in the neighborhood of 300,000.

Health obviously is not simply a function of lack of medical attention but one of environmental circumstances that promote susceptibility to disease. Sanitation was reported as virtually nonexistent, with even privies being a rarity. Housing was declared to be primitive and overcrowded even in such government facilities as the boarding schools. Sanitary water supplies were nonexistent; reliance was everywhere on hand-hauled water from open sources. Diet was inadequate wherever measurable, even when supplied by the government, including that for boarding schools. The lack of roads and vehicles, combined with concentration of facilities in agency towns or entirely off the reservations, aggravated a situation of isolation that prevented any effective use of what little medical attention was available.

These environmental conditions were in turn partly a product of economic conditions which limited Indian abilities to alleviate their problems. Sadly, the Meriam reporters felt called upon to dispel the myth of the oil-rich Indians which lives on in modern comic strips. They pointed out that a crude calculation on a per capita basis of the value of all Indian property, tribal or personal, land and possessions, every stick and stone, showed three quarters of the people owned or could lay claim to no more than $3000 even if all tribal property and assets were divided on a per capita basis. Actual income levels were still more remarkable with 97.8 percent having an annual income level of under $500 dollars, and these crude figures *included* agriculture products grown for home consumption; 71.4 percent were shown to have incomes less than $300. Some individual reservations showed figures that were either absurd miscalculations or incredible tragedy. The estimate for the Navaho was $17.00 annual per capita income! A good deal of these princely incomes were unearned, that is, the result of land sales, lease payments, or annuities. Earned income figures show 96.4 percent of those surveyed having less than $200 annual income. It is noteworthy that many BIA services provided in this period were in fact "reimbursed" out of these pitiful levels of tribal income.

There were, in fact, rich Indians in the form of some 2826 Osage who had a per capita income in 1927 of $19,119! This oil windfall did not last, and it is in any case no more "typical" of the Indian than the Kennedy family was of the Irish.

Education, which was to have been the great panacea, had on the face of this evidence alone clearly failed in moving the Indian into the mainstream. The schools were examined, and while they appeared to be successful in getting Indian children into the schools in large numbers, no one was certain, as elsewhere noted, how many there were to be gotten. Regardless of numbers, the quality of the education offered was suspect, as is suggested by the fact that only 1043 out of 16,257 surveyed were found to be at their proper grade level, all others being at least one year retarded, and the majority considerably more (in relation to the general population). Literacy rates, presumably an end product of adequate education, revealed further failure. Arizona, with its large Indian population, had a rate of 67.8 percent illiteracy. North Dakota was in far better shape with a rate of 29.6 percent. The schools, like the medical facilities, were reported as inadequate in every way, from overcrowding to lack of towels.

The blame for it all was placed directly on the policies of the federal government, particularly the actions taken under the allotment program, which the reporters said had done much to induce the poverty of Indian life. For the rest, the great cry of the Meriam Report was for more and better: more money, more equipment, more personnel, more planning, better training, better pay, better standards, better personnel. Although the report touched on the fundamental problem of the place of the Indian as Indian in American society, its solutions, like most social reform then and now, were palliative and aimed more at the symptoms than at the causes. Like all of the prior assimilationist doctrine, the focus ultimately was on the individual Indian who was to be helped *as an individual* rather than a member of a viable alternative culture. The notion of dealing with the community *as a community* emerges occasionally, but in the long run

The "Hiawatha" Hospital for Insane Indians, Canton, South Dakota, at approximately the time of the Meriam Report. (Courtesy South Dakota Historical Society)

the approach is essentially like that of contemporary programs of drug rehabilitation where the addict is treated but the social situation which promoted the addiction is ignored. Ghettos and reservations *as wholes* are usually ignored in such therapeutic enterprises, and the Meriam Report was no exception.

Curiously, the report talked of problems of community organization under the heading "Women and Family and Community Life." In general, when problems of community were discussed, the word was more or less synonymous with family or local group and did not refer to the Indian cultures as wholes. Although the report did stress at one point in this section the necessity for community reorganization and the involvement of Indians in administration and decision making, it was primarily couched in terms of assisting the superintendents in their tasks. At best it was presented as a problem on the same level as improving Indian housekeeping skills and not as the essential key to pluralism.

Collier and the I.R.A.

The Indian condition had been discovered and deplored before the Meriam investigation, although never on so large and dramatic a scale. One presumes that in the normal political order of things, some highly visible gestures would have been made to placate aroused public indignation and all would have returned after a bit to the status quo. President Hoover appointed as Commissioner of Indian Affairs Charles Rhoads, who, while clearly a man of good will, accomplished little in a practical or fundamental way, though many beginnings and gestures were made in accord with the Meriam Report's recommendations. In fact, a radical redefinition was required of federal Indian policy, and the FDR administration and the Great Depression provided the opportunity. There was a climate of radical innovation which found our collapsed laissez-faire economy being revived by any and all means—federal bank holidays, price and wage fixing, Supreme Court packing, and an alphabetical flurry of work-relief projects—WPA, CCC. In the midst of this the restructuring of the BIA was scarcely politically noticeable.

John Collier, appointed in 1933 as Indian Commissioner, began with the active cooperation of Secretary of the Interior Harold Ickes and President Roosevelt himself. He launched a vigorous attack on Indian problems, the most lasting expression of which was the Indian Reorganization Act of 1934. Eventually Collier was to run afoul of the Congress and spend much of his twelve years as commissioner in explaining himself and protecting his programs, but for the first four years, problems of Indian reservation life were assaulted in the same spirit as the Depression itself. As the Depression made possible early changes, World War II reduced the funds available and diminished the interest previously focused on Indian and other internal affairs. This decline was symbolically highlighted by the removal of the Bureau of Indian Affairs headquarters from Washington to Chicago for the war years.

The Wheeler-Howard Act, or Indian Reorganization Act (I.R.A.), had as its primary focus the creation of some degree of Indian self-government and self-administration. Tribes were invited to draw up constitutions and form governments to which the Bureau would gradually relinquish power as competency was developed. Most reservations, with some notable exceptions such as the Navaho, voted to accept "reorganization," although many had felt that the electoral process was not fully understood by the Indians nor truly representative of their will. Certainly the constitutions promulgated under the act were not drawn up by the Indians themselves and were in virtually all instances faithful copies of Anglo-American conceptions of representative democracy, copied from "models" provided by the BIA. The customary organizations of Indians and their procedures and law received little more attention here than they had gotten under the superintendents. The I.R.A. constitutions also granted powers of control and approval to the

BIA and the Secretary of the Interior which the tribes are currently fighting to revoke. Still, the Collier administration did create a mechanism which, however un-Indian, allowed the possibility if not the immediate reality of self-government. For the first time since the reservations were created, the Indians had some hope of a workable mechanism for controlling their own destinies. An accompanying piece of legislation, the Johnson-O'Malley Act, provided for further regularization of Indian communities as communities in the fabric of the United States by allowing the federal government to contract with or otherwise arrange for state and other local authorities to provide services to the reservations. The principal outcome of this was the payment of per capita funds to public school districts to defray the cost of educating Indian children whose parents paid no local property taxes.

Collier put a stop to the old allotment program and pressed unsuccessfully for a return to tribal status of already allotted lands. He did succeed in beginning a process of consolidating checkerboarded lands, and during his administration the amount of land in Indian hands began to grow rather than decline. In these years of the Oklahoma dust-bowl disasters he worked hard for conservation measures to improve and restore Indian lands, and in the process, through the programs of the Civilian Conservation Corps (CCC), provided much wage work for Indians. In some ways the Depression was a boom time for Indians since the great public work projects created to help the mass of unemployed brought more work and higher wages to the reservations than had ever existed when the general economy was healthy.

Collier was also responsible for or representative of a turnabout in philosophy that was in stark contrast to previous assimilationist doctrines. His administration officially was insistent that the Indians could and should remain Indian! Reread the opening part of Chapter 10 and compare it with this statement made by Collier in 1934:

> No interference with Indian religious life or expression will hereafter be tolerated. The cultural history of Indians is in all respects to be considered equal to that of any non-Indian group. . . . The Indian arts are to be prized, nourished and honored.[13]

The extent to which BIA personnel observed this admonition was, of course, variable and still is. A highly practical administrator, Collier was also something of a romantic, particularly in his public writing. Thus he says, "The deep cause of our world agony is that we have lost that passion and reverence for human personality and for the web of life and the earth which the American Indians have tended as a central, sacred fire since before the Stone Age."[14] Aside from the purple prose, one wonders what period is "before the Stone Age" and how Collier knew about it!

The overall shift in emphasis toward creating viable Indian communities on the reservations also took tangible form in the shape of the day schools. At a time when the rest of the nation was moving from the one-room country school to the consolidated school district served by a bus system, Collier began a program of decentralizing which in effect went in exactly the opposite direction. At the isolated Navaho community of Rough Rock, an example of this kind of school still stands, in proximity to a new consolidated boarding school. The building is small and simple, built of native materials, and, in contrast to the new school, blends in with its surroundings. These schools were meant to serve as community centers with the teacher or teachers serving a broad adult-education and community-resource role beyond simple classroom instruction. The acceptance of the continued existence of Indian communities required an emphasis on life on the reservation, and, in theory at least, instruction was to provide skills useful for life either on or off, as the individual might choose.

The BIA accepted a relatively low level of technical excellence in teacher training, equipment, and other pedagogical matters in order to accomplish wider if more limited instruction, in much the same way the modern Mexican government has attempted to provide *everyone* with four years of schooling before pushing on to more sophisticated levels. Later programs of the Office of Economic Opportunity in housing had a similar emphasis on getting people out of situations of living in abandoned car bodies into *improved* housing, even if standards were not those of surrounding white communities. In both cases well-meaning persons opposed the programs because they felt Indians were being given second-class education and housing, which was true. What was not understood was that, since it was impossible to leap directly from no education and car-body housing to university graduation and split-levels, an insistence on such high standards would mean no improvement at all. Second class is an improvement over fifth class.

The wage work brought by the CCC was of course ephemeral, but during the Collier years, as part of making the reservations viable, a wide range of economic development schemes were at least begun. At this time (and to the present day) the fact that Indian lands were by definition isolated and without development potential led constantly to frustration. The sins of the land-grabbing fathers were visited in the form of frustration on the redemption-minded sons, as they tried to make economically viable lands whose common characteristic was that no one had thought them worth stealing. Still, loan funds were arranged and both industrial and subsistence efforts were encouraged at the same time that measures to promote off-reservation wage work continued. Steps were taken to provide the underlying economic infrastructure necessary for development: roads, electrification, skilled workers, and the like.

With the discovery of the misery of the Indian people, Collier, and indeed all succeeding administrations, have attempted to provide the "more" called for by the Meriam Report. More roads, more schools, more hospitals, more doctors, more teachers, and, inevitably, more administrators. With occasional interruptions, as in the crisis of the war years, the BIA budget to provide services for Indian peoples has grown ever larger. The Meriam Report showed a total budget in 1928 of just under $15 million, including tribal funds. In 1955 the budget for the BIA alone, without consideration of tribal and other funds, was just over $94 million, and by 1968 the BIA figures suggested a total of federal expenditures of $425 million, although by this point the Department of Health, Education, and Welfare (HEW) and the Office of Economic Opportunity (OEO), as well as others, were spending very nearly as much as the BIA. Things did get better under all these efforts, but by the sixties, when the OEO began to encourage the tribes to operate Community Action Programs, the figures produced still showed the Indians, as has been said, as "the poorest of the poor." The 1977 budget of the BIA, which was originally committed to "working itself out of a job" and withering away like the Marxist state, was over $1 billion, and the latest studies show little has changed for all this expenditure of "more."

A Little Bit Pregnant!

Unfortunately, just as there is no such thing as being a little bit pregnant, there is no salvation in being a little self-determining. Even Collier, whose sincerity could not be doubted in efforts to develop Indian governments, fell victim to the temptation to use power when it is available. For the expert who watches someone doing a bad job in his area of expertise, there is a virtually irresistible temptation to take a hand and set matters straight. However, to let others make decisions only when you agree with them produces a sensation of futility and boredom much like playing poker, as they say, "for fun" (no money). In his attempts to explain the brouhaha attendant upon the Navaho stock reduction program, Collier asked aloud whether it would have been better "in this one case of stock reduction and range management to have used authority, frankly and absolutely (the authority existed). . . ."[15] That was and is the problem. The authority existed and, whether occasional or constant, it was and is used to direct Indian affairs without Indian consent and, as in this case, sometimes in direct opposition to expressed Indian desires. Collier's experiences with the Navaho illustrate the point.

By 1933 the Navaho had developed an almost complete reliance on a mixed gardening and pastoral pattern of subsistence with sheep raising being the principal focus. In the process Navaho population had grown and with it the flocks of sheep, goats, and horses. The result was soil erosion due to overgrazing and an ever-increasing, spiraling decline in the carrying capacity (number of animals that could live on a given unit of land). All of this was quite apparent to the experts of the Soil Erosion Service and acceptable as an analysis to the officials of the BIA. The solution was equally obvious and acceptable and included, in addition to other land management procedures, the unavoidable need to reduce at least temporarily the number of animals being grazed in order to allow the land time to recover. Once reduced, the numbers would have to be maintained at a proper level through a system of grazing permits controlled through a structure of grazing districts on the reservation. The end result would be (and was) a halt in soil erosion, an overall increase (through selection and culling) in the quality and quantity of meat and wool per animal, and over the long run an increase in the productive capacity of the land. All perfectly reasonable and correct but regarded as utter, murderous madness by most Navaho!

Although the experts were probably *right* (as they usually are), most Navaho simply never could come to accept that the way to have more sheep was to destroy sheep. Analogies understandable to primarily urban Americans are difficult to conjure up, but the situation is not too far removed from one in which you are asked to cull the number of dollar bills in your wallet on the promise that those that remain will be fatter. Actually that is indeed what the government in its battles against inflation attempts when it asks labor unions to restrain their wage demands in the face of increasing costs so as to interrupt the inflationary spiral. The unions in general do not do it, but the Navaho, as it turned out even under Collier's program of self-government, had no such choice. They had only the freedom to make the right decision, not the wrong one.

The Indian Reorganization Act carried a rider that those who adopted tribal constitutions must also accept and endorse conservation measures. Given the circumstances surrounding the reduction program, the Navaho voted against it. They did not adopt the I.R.A. pattern of government but continued on under their own system of tribal council, which had been in operation since the early 1920s. In his book, *The Peyote Religion among the Navahos*, David Aberle associates the rise of that movement for the Navaho with the disruptions of the stock reduction program and in the process gives an authoritative account of events. From our point of view, the important thing is the blow dealt to the process of self-government, and this is expressed in the letter of a Navaho spokesman quoted by Aberle: "We Indians don't think it is right for Collier to tell us we should govern ourselves, and then tell us how to do it. Why does he want to fool us that way and make us believe we are running our country, when he makes us do what he wants."[16]

The Navaho tribal government did indeed vote in favor of the grazing measures eventually, but only under enormous pressures from the BIA, including Collier. Until the I.R.A. could be implemented, the provisions for loan funds and other economic programs were withheld. The Navaho were reminded, as Collier noted, above, that the authority did exist to proceed without their consent. They were not offered alternatives other than disaster. One million sheep were reduced to about 500,000 through purchase and destruction, done in some cases before the seller's eyes in violation of all sense of reality. Sheep and horses were life itself to most Navaho, and their well-being was tied in with Navaho conceptions of the harmonious balance of the world. Shooting sheep and burying them in pits with lime did not accord well with these beliefs.

The Navaho, as always, eventually recovered, but most observers agree that for many years the primary result of the reduction program

The reduction of Navaho flocks, such as these photographed by Edward Curtis, led to Navaho rejection of the Indian Reorganization Act. The limited carrying capacity of the arid Navaho canyonlands is obvious in this photograph. (Edward Curtis)

was hostility and distrust of the many government programs and anyone connected with them. The Navaho tribal government itself long labored under the stigma and all BIA programs were viewed with suspicion, and cooperation and participation were withheld.

Collier did many things right and began the turn away from the assimilationist program of destruction, but in the last analysis, he ran hard aground on the problem of the structural relationship between the Indian peoples and the BIA. That problem, as we shall see, remains the one insoluble issue throughout all phases of Indian-Anglo relations up to the present day. The Indian Self-Determination Act of 1975, which will be examined, was a long step toward achieving what its title implies, but even it continued to contain such phrases as "with the consent of the Secretary of the Interior." The Collier administration vividly illustrates the problem of clinging to ultimate authority while promoting self-determination.

Ready or Not

Inevitably the Collier administration generated opposition, particularly in the area of "re-Indianizing the Indian," and for attempting to develop viable reservation communities, it was accused of retarding Indian assimilation. Assimilation as an end had not died, of course, and began to revive as a dominant policy around 1946 to 1948. In 1946 an Indian Claims Commission was created to hear and settle outstanding disputes of the tribes with the federal government over treaty and other rights. It carried with it a strong implication of a final tidying up of Indian affairs prior to concluding them, although the monies it eventually awarded were important resources for the development of many reservations. In 1948, the Hoover Commission, looking into Indian affairs, proclaimed once again, "assimilation must be the dominant goal of public policy."[17] The end result of these and other happenings was the move toward "termination," a word which still has a special and worrisome sound to Indian peoples.

The ultimate expression of this new revival of the desire to be done with the Indian was House Concurrent Resolution 108 passed by the Eighty-third Congress in 1953. H.C.R. 108 said among other things that it sought "to make the Indians within the territorial limits of the United States subject to the same laws and entitled to the same privileges and responsibilities as are applicable to other citizens of the United States, to end their status as wards of the United States, and to grant them all of the rights and prerogatives pertaining to American citizenship. . . ." It named specific tribes which "should be freed from Federal supervision and control and from all disabilities and limitations specially applicable to Indians. . . ."[18] Nowhere in its lofty language did it express the fact that the Indians gained freedom but lost rights and protections guaranteed by solemn treaty and ultimately ceased to exist as self-governing peoples under the stipulations of the Indian Reorganization Act. The allotment act (Dawes Act) had similarly misleading tones.

In the modern United States "freedom" and "equality" are still remarkably powerful words, and it is hard to argue with anyone who is in favor of these things. In Washington State, where I currently live and work, the furor over the judicial decisions about Indian rights to 50 percent of the fish catch has tended often to take this tone: "The Indians should be free and equal. They should have the same opportunities as everyone else—no more and no less. In our democratic nation there should be no special privileges or specially privileged classes." It all sounds good. Except when we remember, as I hope the reader of this book will do, how the Indians got to where they are.

In this special case in Washington State, the federal courts have taken the position that the Indians are exercising no special privilege but simply doing what was guaranteed and reserved to them by solemn treaties which are the supreme law of the land. In these treaties the Indians in effect gave away all right to the land area of the state of Washington and in return were allowed to retain a little land to live on, their lives (the treaties were largely written under duress), a few annuities for leaders, some meaningless promises, and the right to fish and hunt in "usual and accustomed places." "Equality" in this case means to strip from the tribes what is left to them after all else is taken. The analogy comes to mind of a mugger who reads in the papers the day after the mugging that when shaking down his victim he overlooked a valuable ring and, as a result, protests vociferously that his victim must share this with him equally. In this case actually the situation is more like that of a small child who, having bullied those smaller than him for years, suddenly comes out on the side of brotherhood and pacificism when confronted with a larger opponent. For the fiscally minded, the comparison has been suggested of "freeing" the holder of tax-exempt government bonds to pay taxes like everyone else. Freedom or a failure to honor obligations?

Whatever the philosophical implications, H.C.R. 108 was the culmination of a process whereby Congress insisted that the BIA draw up lists of those tribes who were ready to have their special federal status "terminated." The tribes named in the resolution were those that had been determined to be immediately ready to begin the change in status. The choices had been made on the basis of the Bureau's appraisal of the degree of "acculturation" (assimilation, in our terms), adequacy of economic resources, willingness of the states concerned to take over some degree of transitional responsibility, and finally the expressed desire of the Indians involved to make this move. The Klamath of Oregon and the Menominee of Wisconsin are the two major groups who in fact went through the process of termination, although there were several smaller groups, like some California Indian "rancherias," pocket-size reservations with a handful of members, who were also terminated. The Menominee not only went through it into the status of "Menominee County" and "freedom" by 1961 but had fought their way *back* into reservation status by 1974. The Klamath stayed terminated, though at the time of this writing there are reasons to believe these and other nonreservation groups may attempt to recover federally guaranteed tribal status.

Both the Menominee and Klamath tribes had a certain level of apparent prosperity for the same reasons—timber lands which through curious historical accident had neither been clear-cut nor removed from tribal hands. The Menominee had since 1908 been operating a successful sawmill and a "sustained yield" cutting operation largely as the results of Robert La Follette's efforts in arranging legislation to protect and promote their lands. By comparison with other Indian tribal groups, there were relatively high educational and income levels, and the tribe seemed to want the change. The state was willing to assume a good deal of responsibility in easing the transition for the new "county." There was also provision for the infusion of federal funds to the state and county to similarly ease the period of transition. It was done.

Looking back on the events that followed termination, it is difficult to see why the outcomes were not anticipated. Economically the most obvious and utterly predictable event was an enormous increase in the tax burden that the Menominees as individuals and as a corporate entity (Menominee Enterprises Inc.) had to pay. Lands held in federal trust and funds earned from these were exempt from taxation. When the corporation took over management of the tribal sawmill and supervision of the lands, it all became subject to taxation, as did the holdings of individual Menominees. What had been a profit-making enterprise affording employment for many Menominee rapidly began to degenerate toward bankruptcy under the new arrangements. Efforts to broaden the tax base and to provide further income led to the Legend Lake Project, a land development scheme which if completed would have taken something over 5000 acres of land out of Menominee hands. The Menominee who had successfully resisted allotment and retained their land base were in danger of losing it under the new system of "freedom." There was the possibility that ownership of tribal resources would go into non-Menominee hands; a substantial percentage of the bonds given each Menominee had already been transferred and the stock which conferred voting control was scheduled to become publicly available. The management had in any case been largely in non-Menominee hands throughout. An opposition group, DRUMS, began to focus resistance and resentment, which began to turn into outrage when the loss of land involved in the Legend Lake Project became known and understood.

Let us note that prior to termination the Menominee were indeed better off than most reservations, where termination could lead to self-sufficiency only through the economic principle of "taking in each other's laundry"—providing services to themselves. As I noted in a 1974 article, figures supplied for 1960 income on the Navaho reservation showed over half from wages connected with services of one sort or another supplied to the Navaho which they would have to pay for themselves under total economic autonomy.[19] The Menominee before termination were able to pay for many of these services but only under protection of special federal status. Whereas the Menominee were reduced to a poverty level by termination, most Indian reservations would have been completely destroyed by the withdrawal of federal services and payroll. A later report shows many tribes without sufficient income to even pay their tribal officers. Costs increased in general while services declined. Income fell as obligations mounted.

The Menominee in fact were not in control of their affairs during most of the period in question because most of the "stock" voted in Menominee Enterprises Inc. was that held in trust (for minors) by the First Wisconsin National Bank. In elections before 1970 few Menominee voted their shares, so the bank's bloc vote was decisive. Only in 1970 under the impetus of the DRUMS organization did the Menominee themselves vote in sufficient numbers to reduce the impact of the bank, though it remained substantial. Further loss of control was evident in the school system, which was merged with the surrounding communities for economic reasons, as were other functions, such as the courts. Money was saved, but the Menominee voice in Menominee affairs was diminished. It is now apparent that the move to terminate the Menominee (if it was intended that they remain in existence as a group) was premature and ill-conceived despite the obvious good will of local and state authorities. The Menominee pulled back from the edge and regained tribal status as a reservation, leaving unanswered the question of how the transition to tribal autonomy is to be achieved except to suggest that termination is no more of a solution than the allotment program.

The Klamath were less lucky since they (78 percent at least) did not decide to retain their tribal resources intact as a group as the Menominee had done through Menominee Enterprises Inc. Instead they liquidated (by a vote which many have disputed) their lands and distributed the monies on a per capita basis. These were substantial sums ($40,000 to $50,000), and the temptation to opt for the dissolution of resources must have been overwhelming. Many tribes which have received settlement money from sources like the Indian Claims Commission have run into similar difficulties. The Umatilla Reservation in Oregon is an example where the majority of enrolled tribal members live off the reservation itself. Such reservations have often found irresistible the temptation to divide up award money (from the settlements of the Indian Claims

Commission) individually rather than investing it en bloc in the reservation. If the state of Washington were awarded a sum of money and the electorate asked whether they wanted their share directly or invest it in the future, how many of us would vote for the future? The off-reservation members of one such tribe actually mounted an attempt to terminate their home reservation and distribute the assets.

The inevitable appears to have occurred. The assets distributed have apparently largely been dissipated, since welfare and dependency costs for the state in the former reservation area have risen rather than declined. Whatever the individual disposition of their funds, the Klamath had traded their continued existence as a tribe for those funds. Wisely or foolishly spent, there will be no further share in the tribal resources and no assistance from the federal government because the Klamath no longer remain a recognized tribe. Some 22 percent who chose not to distribute income were placed under the aegis of a private bank in a sort of collective trust arrangement not unlike that formerly exercised over them by the federal government, but this new relationship was made revokable by vote at fixed dates. The tribal roles were closed and with withdrawal of federal support and recognition the Klamath technically have ceased to exist.

The one sure and certain effect the efforts at termination had was to create a fear and resistance among reservation leaders that they might be next. Programs designed to increase Indian involvement or to develop economic resources have, since the program of termination, been treated with cautious suspicion. The question is always being asked: Is this a move toward termination? If we accept this responsibility, will it be used to prove that we should be terminated? Willingness to trust the government, obviously never very high considering Indian history, fell to new lows after H.C.R. 108.

At roughly the same time as these termination activities were taking place, further assimilationalist pressure was evident in the increase in the effort devoted to "relocation." Relocation was a program actually begun in the 1930s and meant just what it said. The object was to find Indians jobs off the reservations and assist them in relocating themselves. Obviously in the 1930s the national job market made nonsense of this program, but with the drive toward termination such efforts were much increased in the 1950s. Relocation offices were set up in major cities, including Chicago, Washington, D.C., Dallas, and Los Angeles. In the climate of the times, many Indians came to see the program as a kind of personalized termination, and to avoid the stigmata of this association, it has come to be called "Employment Assistance."

As with most such programs the relocation efforts are benign in intent, but have been tarred with the termination brush. There in fact has been an increase in the number of Indians living in urban areas (25,000 in Los Angeles, for example); and for those who seek to find a place in these strange and often hostile environments, the BIA program offers them help in training for a job, finding the job, and then eases the transition with assistance in finding a home and other such simple but critical details. The success rate is debated. Critics say most eventually return to the reservations. The Bureau says most stay once relocated. It is undeniable that the shift to off-reservation life has increased, but whether that is attributable to the relocation program is open to question. In its disguise of "Employment Assistance," it is certainly an aid to those who do wish to try the city, but in philosophy it is not very different from the aims of Richard H. Pratt in the early days of the Carlisle Institute when he sought to isolate his pupils from the contaminations of the reservation community and then disperse them to the winds.

In the same year as it enacted H.C.R. 108, Congress also passed Public Law 280, a further reflection of a desire to be done with the Indian. Pub. L. 280 allowed the individual states to assert their criminal and civil jurisdiction over reservations within their boundaries. There was no provision in this for any degree of Indian consent. The object was to remove the Indians from the peculiar special situation where crimes on federal trust land (the reservations) were heard in federal courts, or, for minor crimes, in the tribal courts. Who could be tried, where, and for what was admittedly confusing, but Pub. L. 280 met considerable opposition from the tribes when they realized the implications for their loss of special autonomous status. Washington State is again an example where judicial battles had been fought and in 1977 were still being fought as to the applicability of state law to reservations. The law was amended in 1968 to require tribal consent, but those states like Washington which had already asserted jurisdiction did not feel compelled to give it up.

The jurisdiction problem is particularly acute when it comes to matters of state and local taxes. Trust lands and the income from them cannot be taxed even in the Pub. L. 280 states, but complex legal wrangles revolve around virtually all other areas. Particularly vexatious are the business dealings involving non-Indians on reservation lands or non-Indians who have transactions with reservation businesses. Who issues fishing licenses? One group of Chippewa has won the right to issue their own automobile license plates! Do non-Indians pay state taxes on cigarettes and liquors bought on the reservation? They do in the state of Washington according to recent decisions.

What Now, White Man?

Fortunately for the Indians, at least in terms of their survival as a group, the wave of termination came at a moment when the current of political tolerance and encouragement for ethnic groups and their continued existence was moving in the opposite direction. Civil rights legislation, black power, brown power, women's rights—all began to assert themselves as the nation moved into the 1960s and 1970s; the Indians were once again saved as a people by events in the larger society over which they had no control. The Kennedy administration, the War on Poverty, the Office of Economic Opportunity—all begun for reasons that originally had nothing to do directly with the Indian—began to sweep away the neoassimilationist stance and strengthen the moves toward self-determination begun by John Collier.

In these decades, for the first time since the abortive establishment of the civilized tribes in Indian Territory, the views of Indians themselves have been solicited in a serious way and their right to some voice in their own affairs once again asserted. As we shall see, the Indian peoples have not been passive in the face of all the political maneuverings, but only recently has the extent to which they might regain control of their own affairs been recognized, and only recently have Indian spokesmen and organizations begun to tentatively move to seize the opportunity.

The Kennedy administration appointed a Task Force on Indian Affairs which discovered once again the misery of the Indians, but its recommendations retained some degree of the termination taint. Lyndon Johnson in 1968 delivered a presidential message, "The Forgotten American," which for the first time gave sign that the powerful force of the presidential office was going to be focused to renounce the doctrine of termination. He spoke of "freedom of choice: an opportunity to remain in their homelands if they choose, without surrendering their dignity . . ." and of a "policy of maximum choice for the American Indian: a policy expressed in programs of self-help, self-development, self-determination."[20] Richard Nixon in 1970 sent a special message to Congress in which he specifically urged the renunciation of the termination doctrine, but no legislation directly resulted. Gerald Ford expressed himself in favor of self-determination and against termination, as has Jimmy Carter, but only in speeches, and there has been no binding legislation.

Pub. L. 93-638 (1975), the "Indian Self-Determination and Education Assistance Act" in Section 110 specifically says that "nothing in this Act shall be construed as . . . authorizing or requiring the termination of any existing trust responsibility of the United States with respect to the Indian people."[21] But the findings of the latest investigation of the Indian condition suggest that this statement is not believed, and while some groups have seized the opportunities this act offers, many have not, partially for this fear. In fact Congress has yet to state flatly and as irrevocably as possible that termination will never be revived as a policy, and until this is done the legacy of suspicion will continue to distort the Indian situation.

So where are we now?

Some Readings

See the previously recommended Tyler (1973) for a general outline and Washburn (1973) for texts of documents.

Collier, John: *Indians of the Americas,* New York: Mentor, 1947. Collection of Collier's essays which shed much light on his programs and philosophy.

Hood, S.: "Termination of the Klamath Tribe of Oregon," *Ethnohistory,* **19**:379–392, 1972.

Lurie, Nancy O.: "Menominee Termination: From Reservation to Colony," *Human Organization,* **31**:257–270, 1972. Fuller information is available on the Menominee Restoration in the record of hearings of the House Subcommittee on Indian Affairs (Pub. L. 93-197) for the first session of the Ninety-third Congress, 1973.

Meriam, Lewis, et al.: *The Problem of Indian Administration,* Baltimore: Johns Hopkins, 1928. Essential reading for any serious student of Indian policy.

Spicer, Edward H.: "Sheepmen and Technicians," in Edward H. Spicer (ed.), *Human Problems in Technological Change,* New York: John Wiley, 1952. An analysis of the Navaho stock-reduction program, covered more fully in David F. Aberle, *The Peyote Religion among the Navaho,* Chicago: Aldine, 1966. Spicer also includes other case studies of problems in directed change on the reservations.

Spicer, Edward H.: "Indigenismo in the United States, 1870–1960," in Deward E. Walker (ed.), *The Emergent Native Americans: A Reader in Culture Contact,* Boston: Little, Brown, 1972. Examination of the nature of movements of support for the Indian peoples in a broader pan-American context.

Walker, Deward E. (ed.): *The Emergent Native Americans: A Reader in Culture Contact,* Boston: Little, Brown, 1972. Wide-ranging and well-organized collection.

XII WHAT IS TO BE DONE?[1]

Our mission here on earth is to change our environment not adjust ourselves to it. If we become maladjusted in the process, so much the worse for the environment.

Robert Maynard Hutchins[2]

The United States census of 1970 reports that there are now 827,108 Indians on and off the reservations. More correctly, there are 827,108 persons who think of themselves in this way or admit to it, since the current census practice is to rely on "self-classification" in such thorny racial matters. That same year there remained 39,642,413 acres of land in tribal hands and under federal trust, another 10,697,622 acres individually allotted but also in trust, and 237,483 acres of state reservation land. Canada has something over 260,000 "registered" Indians on and off Crown lands or "reserves," and in some areas, such as British Columbia, it is estimated that there may be as many non-status Indians as there are officially recognized Indians. There are unquestionably over a million of the Chichimeca who still think of themselves as Indians, and more than half of these still live on land of special status: state or federal reservations in the United States and reserve bands in Canada. If the Chichimeca of northern Mexico, who are properly part of the culture area under consideration, are counted, the numbers are still larger. The current Indian birth rate is almost double that of the general population, and in 1972 the BIA estimated that in areas under its jurisdiction nearly half the population was under sixteen years of age, a proportion typical of a rapidly expanding population, not a vanishing race.

The Indians remain, as does some of their land, and unfortunately their status, as the poorest of the poor. The "more" proposed in the Meriam Report has over the years produced "better," but compared with the criteria which define levels of poverty for the nation as a whole, the Indians remain on the bottom in health, education, earnings, and general life conditions. The hopeful difference today is not that things are getting better in these areas (which has happened) but that it would seem that those charged with this responsibility have begun to strike at the root causes of the problems rather than apply social Band-Aids. Given the levels of funds expended, the paucity of results has caused many to reappraise approaches to Indian self-sufficiency and prosperity. After many decades of staring fixedly at the trees, those in charge have apparently sighted the forest.

By *reductio ad absurdum* let us remind ourselves before going further that in the solution of the "Indian problem" as it exists today there is a decision to be made. It is the same decision that has faced the American people (European-derived) before. Are the Indians to continue as Indians? This choice is as always in the hands of the majority population. I do not ask whether Indians are to survive as Indians in the genetic sense, since preventing that would involve genocide. I ask whether Indians are to continue as separate societies with separate cultural systems on their own land and under their own direction. If not, the answer is simple. Pull the plug. Sociocide!

Tomorrow morning or any morning Congress could call a halt to the trust relationship, distribute the fair (or unfair, for that matter) value of tribal properties to the individual Indians, close down all federal offices, and walk away. The Indians, so few in number (relatively), would slide into the poverty statistics of the various states without much real impact. After all, let us realize that as of 1970 there were very nearly as many persons living in the United States who had been born in Cuba (born

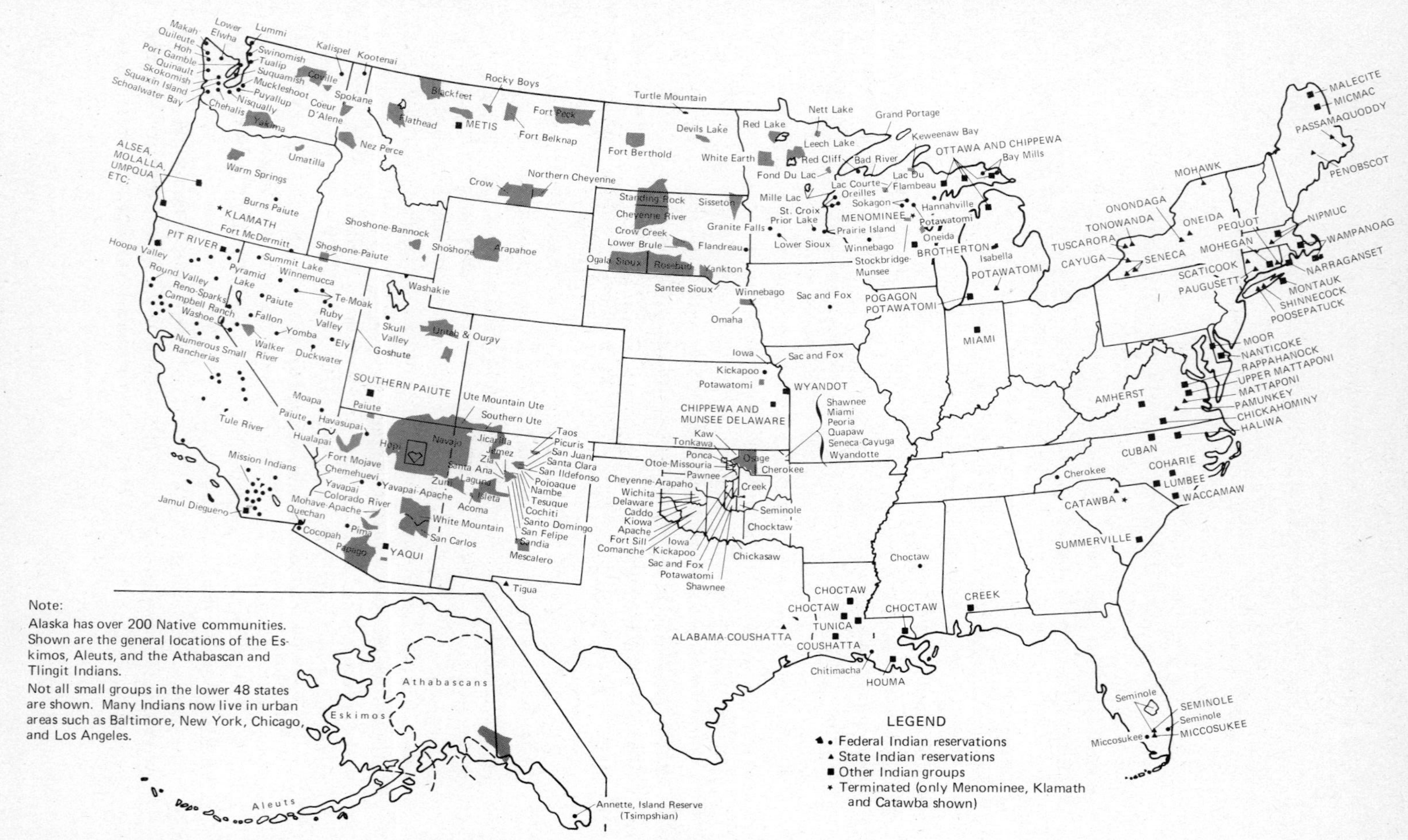

Present-day Indian lands and communities. (Courtesy Bureau of Indian Affairs)

there, not simply of Cuban descent) as there were Indians living on federal reservations—400,000-plus in both cases. The total Indian population on these reservations is less than one-half of 1 percent of the population of the United States. After a disastrous generation of adjustment, possibly two, there would be nothing left but tiny pocket ghettos, rural and urban, easily coped with by local authorities.

Why not?

I have my own answers, but only you, assuming you are one of the 200 million-plus who make up the "majority" population, can truly decide. This has been true since the Indians passed up their chance to push the Pilgrims off Plymouth Rock. Assuming you do want something other than this final solution and will stay your collective hand, we can go on to ask, how can the Indian people be brought to a stable and prosperous condition of pluralism? I have tried to avoid advocacy and subjective polemic all along, and while I have strong emotionally based views I have tried not to intrude them. In this chapter some of my own views may slip through.

The final presentation is an essentially linear and compartmentalized sampling of the problems and emergent solutions of the reservation cultures. A point should be emphasized: that in social matters one cannot proceed a bit at a time. If you want to improve reading skills with employability in mind, then arrangements must be made for electrification. If you want to control epidemic disease, you must renounce termination. What have these to do with one another? The first is fairly obvious except that no reading teacher would conceive it as part of her task. A Navaho child living in a traditional hogan (one room and dirt floored) with illiterate parents, devoid of reading material, may still seek to read, only to be prevented by lack of electricity. Gas for the Coleman is expensive, and the parents have little cash income. Do we start our reading program with rural electrification or upgrading parental income levels? Obviously the total problem, not just one fragment, must be attacked. Doctors, however medically efficient, will fail to control disease if their patients do not seek attention and refuse to put sufficient faith in the physician so as to follow directions. The problem is complex but is, at least in part, a function of a general distrust of any government official or program. A people live in their past as well as in the present, and for a reservation resident to put faith in the United States government is a dubious, indeed illogical, proposition in view of that past. Why believe the doctor any more than any other official? Recent public furor about involuntary sterilization of Indians may be based in truth, but what is sadly more important is that the Indian people readily believe such a rumor whether it is true or not.

The latest (at the time of this writing) discovery of the "Indian problem" is represented by the series of reports prepared by the American Indian Policy Review Commission (A.I.P.R.C.), a congressionally organized body headed by Senator James Abourezk of South Dakota. The commission sent out a series of "task forces" whose reports ranged from questions of fiscal management to alcohol and drug abuse. Predictably, of course, the reports once again discover Indian poverty and the failure of past programs. More significant, they focus again and again on the issue of the need for some fundamental redefinition of the Indian in relationship to the federal government. New structural arrangements are called for in almost every area as a response to the discovered conditions. While governmental rather than private, as was the Meriam Report, these commission reports are only recommendations and require legislation to be put into effect. Whether Congress agrees with these recommendations (most task forces were made up largely of Indians, not members of Congress) remains to be seen. The reports, like the earlier Meriam effort, are uneven in quality and objectivity. Much of the material is undigested and presented without analysis or comment. The rather remarkable inclusion of a "statement" by Marlon Brando in the report on "Trust Responsibilities and the Federal Indian Relationship" is an example.[3]

Whatever the merits or flaws, the reports indicate that the problems remain essentially as they were before. I will discuss them only briefly, touching on economic conditions, educational levels, the state of poverty, and life conditions. More important, I hope to indicate that the dilemma of this matter of the structural relation between Indian people and the larger society, legal and administrative, underlies and complicates all effort in any direction. That structural relation is in the process of being redefined by the federal government, and at the same time the Indian peoples have begun to respond to new opportunities with greater competency and confidence. Some possible consequences are the major concern of this chapter.

Been Down So Long

The most persistently irritating problem, from the point of view of non-Indian administrators and legislators, is the economic status of the Indians. They remain a client population, consuming goods and services at a level greater than they produce. The reservations are not economically self-sufficient, and poor as the life conditions are, they are beyond the ability of the reservation economies to support on their own. The A.I.P.R.C.'s *Report on Tribal Government* notes a 1972 study of financial dependency on the White Mt. Apache Reservation which showed that federal funds accounted for 81 percent "of all reservation expenditures." They also examined a random sample of tribal governments in terms of their costs against their tribal incomes and found that 37.5 percent "were unable to pay their normal government operating expenses."[4]

Realistically there will never be peace and security in the relation between the Indians and the government until this dependency is eliminated. The Indians will remain forever at the mercy of federal purse strings and the general electorate will complain of the costs. Few will ever stop to consider the history of this nation in relationship to the price Indians have involuntarily paid to arrive at their present condition. The Indians, I am sure, would be glad to refund all monies paid, cancel the deal, and reclaim North America. We, as a nation, seem ready to condemn the South Africans for retaining possession of lands acquired at about the same time and in the same way as we acquired ours, but none seems ready to "give it back to the Indians." The truth is that, now, at this moment, Indians cost money and that problem must be solved, regardless of historical justice or the lack thereof.

Rather than reviewing again, as many have done, the dreary statistics of poverty, let me simply quote from President Nixon's message to Congress (July 1970):

> Economic deprivation is among the most serious of Indian problems. Unemployment among Indians is ten times the national average; the unemployment rate runs as high as 80 percent on some of the poorest reservations. Eighty percent of reservation Indians have an income which falls below the poverty line; the average income for such families is only $1500.[5]

Unemployment, underemployment, and poverty-level family income remain the characteristics of reservations today, as they were at the time of the Meriam Report. These, however, are only individual symptoms of the general lack of development of the reservation economies and need to be considered in this broader light. The A.I.P.R.C. reports provide much information but in complex form. A. T. Anderson, a special assistant for the commission, has written a short, popularized summary of the commission materials and findings, *Nations Within a Nation*, which the student will find useful for an up-to-date overview of poverty conditions.[6]

An economist friend once commented that development on the reservations was very nearly an insoluble problem because if there had been anything to develop, it would already have been done. Perhaps there is more hope than that, because the A.I.P.R.C. reports and the Meriam Report before them paint a picture of managerial miscalculation which, while depressing, does leave the hope that something might be done if purposeful planning were finally brought to bear. The BIA clearly emerges in these most recent studies as an organization dedicated to the maintenance of the reservations, not their development. It possesses neither the inclination nor the ability to effect development, and the managerial experts of A.I.P.R.C. cite many examples to back up a picture of an organization which, far from assisting development, quite often stands in its path, while simultaneously urging the tribes forward.[7]

The problems of the various reservations are not all the same, but there are certain general problems that apply to virtually all attempts at solutions of the development dilemma. A sampling is in order, but neither a comprehensive picture nor effective schemes of solution can be offered in this simple introduction.

The lack of resource base has already been indicated, and there is little to be done about that. Tribes have been authorized from time to time to acquire additional lands and have them brought under "trust" status, but by and large the capital has been lacking to actually accomplish much in the way of such expansion. Capital for investment in development of any kind is a principal problem for the reservation economies. Internal capital is very nearly nonexistent except in the form of monies received from the Indian Claims judgments, or accumulated income in the federally controlled trust accounts. These controlled funds are invested by the government and the capital or its earnings can be used by the tribes only with federal consent. Federal investment policy has typically been very conservative, stressing minimal risk rather than maximum gain. For some tribes these are considerable funds, but for others the amounts are negligible if considered as the base for significant economic advance.

The principal source of investment capital for an underdeveloped economy, Indian or otherwise, is external capital—in this case principally federal development program funds. In addition to the BIA itself, there are a great many programs of the Economic Development Administration, the Department of Housing and Urban Development (HUD), and other such agencies which provide some amount of development capital. There are, in fact, a great many sources of funds available to the tribes which are either not being used at all or are being used only by the larger, better organized tribes who have the staff to locate funds, apply for them, and make maximal use of them when received. For the majority of tribes, the tribal government, which is most often unpaid and part-time, cannot cope with the intricacies of the pursuit of the federal dollar.

Some available funds are primarily concerned with long-range development of economic self-sufficiency and infrastructural investment (funds primarily concerned with the economic base of roads, power, water, and so on). More funds, however, are budgeted for maintenance investment (primarily devoted to operating administrative facilities at present levels) or for therapeutic investment (treating symptoms rather than causes). The BIA administrative budget is an example of the first, and welfare assistance is an example of the second. The majority of funds expended by the government fall into the maintenance category, and while these expenditures are certainly necessary for sheer survival, they are *maintenance* costs and have little or nothing to do with change.

Infrastructural development has not been great in the past, and currently the major funding focus appears to be improved housing, which tends to fall into the therapeutic rather than the developmental category. "Developmental" in this simplistic scheme means any productive activity which creates tribal income and provides employment for the reservation population on a self-sustaining basis. Income derived from any source is obviously welcomed, but if dependency is to be eliminated, the income must be earned from productive activity rather than "taking in each other's laundry." As explained before, the major source of income is monies paid to Indians for supplying services to themselves—an economic dead end. In fact, a great deal of the money expended on the reservations in administration or on such projects as road building does not place jobs and income in Indian hands even on a temporary basis since non-Indians are often employed to do these tasks.

Most economic problems tend to have a chicken-egg quality to them, as in the lack of Indian on-reservation enterprises to provide a "multiplier" effect for Indian income. Money paid to Indians is immediately spent off the reservations or in enterprises on the reservations owned by non-Indians. There are very few Indian entrepreneurs operating businesses on the reservations. The multiplier is the effect produced when the money, rather than immediately draining out of the reservation economy, bounces around from Indian worker to Indian business to Indian government. The more such internal transactions the greater the multiplication of the impact of each dollar entering the reservation economy. Indian private enterprise and tribal enterprise are both limited by a lack of capital, although loan funds, such as those supplied through the Indian Financing Act, have helped (there is now a Kentucky Fried Chicken stand at Chinle on the Navaho reservation as a result of this act), but the amounts available are inadequate. Private lenders are reluctant to risk money in these situations where so much depends on the caprice of federal policy. "Redlining" is obviously not confined to urban ghettos alone. The end result is that money continues to leak off the reservation rather than forming the base for the reinvestment that is so necessary to prevent the leakage—a circular dilemma.

The lack of development capital is not the only economic barrier. There are equally great confusions in the manpower area, including skill levels and work patterns. As we have seen, educational levels are low for reservation populations, and work experiences tend to have been concentrated in unskilled occupations. There is some economic advantage in this since Indian wage expectations are low, and cheap labor is an attraction for any labor-intensive enterprise. Currently most of the operations which have located on the reservations, such as fishing fly-tying or electronic subassembly, have tended to be labor-intensive.

The lack of general education will gradually solve itself as the school systems become more effective under tribal control, but for the moment low levels of facility in basic areas, such as literacy, remain a serious problem. Specialized work skills—for example, welding, carpentry, and the like—have been promoted through a variety of programs of manpower training, which is in fact a major area of federal development investment. The problem is that efforts concentrated here are useless if there are no jobs which require the skills developed, and, as we have seen, few effective efforts have been made to develop enterprises to employ the trained. One frustrating result is that some Indian people have come to regard training programs as a kind of seasonal job, and neither they nor anyone else seems to mind that the ultimate end of achieving stable employment is never reached. Of course the trained men could leave the reservation and go to where the jobs are, but that is the least likely result of all as experience should surely have taught by now.

Having for so long been in a marginal economic position, the Indian workers have naturally enough adapted their expectations and habits to that situation. Whether it is to be regarded as an inherently Indian custom or the result of a rural variant of the "culture of poverty," many of the work patterns of Indian populations create difficulties for development. Clearly important traditional cultural differences are very often either unknown to developers or ignored as insignificant. Navaho ceremonial life requires workers to be absent from their jobs for short periods to meet their obligations to kinsmen. While the fact that these occasions are less predictable than the arrival of Christmas and Easter complicates planning, there is no reason that statistical models could not predict absentee levels, since the times of the year when ceremonials occur do tend to cluster. If automobile manufacturers can anticipate and accommodate high absentee rates during hunting season in Michigan, it seems that similar procedures could be made to function on reservations, if careful account were taken of the realities of cross-cultural differences. Clearly Indian administration of Indian enterprises would solve at least part of this dilemma.

Work attitudes and habits may be a more thorny issue. In the absence of regular employment, many reservation populations have become accustomed to a mix of subsistence activities (gardening, stock raising, and so on) and seasonal temporary unskilled wage work. A job becomes a sometime thing that one takes to fill a cash need and then quits when sufficient money is earned to meet the need (if, of course, the job has not already run out, as temporary jobs do). Jobs are very frequently not thought of as ends in themselves, and the work ethic of the Anglo world may not always override other considerations. A man may prefer less well paying work which allows him free time to devote to traditional pursuits; while not economically as rewarding as wage work, these pursuits are more highly valued. A recent study of Shonto (a Navaho community) shows such a pattern and also a decided preference for work of any kind which allows the worker to remain near his home.[8] Railroad work, which is high paying but requires travel, has declined in favor of less well paying local work sponsored by the tribe. While this failure to seek maximal gain at all costs is decidedly non-Anglo, it does have a hopeful side in that it suggests that if jobs are created on the reservations, local desires will guarantee they be filled.

It should be stressed again that despite all that has occurred, the culture of the Navaho (as an example) remains Navaho in its basic assumptions. What seems logical and inevitable to the Navaho may seem bizarre to the Anglo and vice versa. An example that has been noted is the emphasis on sharing with and assisting one's relatives. If a man has a steady job, he is likely to be subject to a high level of demand for help from his less fortunate kin, and to refuse is to be "stingy" and ultimately to show that one is not truly Navaho. A man *must* share, and this violates the work-thrift ethic, because accumulation is not possible, or is severely limited, unless all members of the kin network prosper. To some extent, capital accumulation is a contradiction of basic Navaho values unless it is done on a collective basis. Again tribal administration of tribal enterprises can probably alleviate some of these conflicts.

OPEC and the Chichimeca

The economic position and problems of the Indian are, in broader perspective, remarkably similar to those of the less developed nations of the Third World in their struggle to cope with the economic dominance of the First (Western) World. The rules of development for them are not the same as they were for the Europeans when they were making their own transition from subsistence economies to industrial structures. The difference for both Chichimeca and these others is that the Europeans are already established and holding the economic high ground. The position of the Indians is aggravated because they are certainly "dependent domestic nations" in the economic area if no other. The nature of their economic predicament is much more closely constrained than that of the Third World and is defined by their relations with the United States. The key question for the Third World is what can they produce or process that is competitive in world markets with the First World, which with high technology, skilled work force, and elaborate economic infrastructure can generally produce anything faster, better, and cheaper. In the past the role of the Third World has been as a market, a source of raw materials, and a provider of cheap labor for the growth or extraction of raw materials. Those lucky enough to control resources critical to the survival of the First World (oil and coffee, for example) have in recent years begun to manipulate their control, as in the case of Iran, so as to buy into the developed condition. The Chichimeca unfortunately control no such resources (with rare, accidental exceptions) and given their political dependency could not use the bludgeoning tactic of, for example, the Organization of Petroleum Exporting Countries (OPEC) in any case.

Economically if not culturally, the urban Indians must eventually fit into the productive structure of the cities in which they have chosen to live as individuals. The solutions to their problems are ultimately the same as for virtually any other underemployed, undereducated minority. It is the reservations that are a special problem and a special hope. Other minority populations have spoken of establishing their own autonomous homelands within the fabric of the United States. The Black Muslims, for example, have made some progress toward acquiring land in the South. The Indians still have a land base, however little of it may remain, on which to build their own community, if only it can be made viable. The existence of this base will ultimately have consequences for the urban-based Indian, as the existence of Israel has had for Jews everywhere.

The land in Indian hands is, by and large, as has been repeatedly pointed out, relatively valueless. By virtue of the Winters Doctrine, Indian land does theoretically have superior claim to water rights, but these rights have often been ignored. For purposes of agriculture and stock raising, productivity could be much improved by irrigation (assuming Winters Doctrine rights) and more sophisticated management, but in the long run such pursuits can never support more than a fraction of the reservation populations on other than a subsistence level. The same situation faces the Third World, where wars of liberation have been fought only to reveal that inevitably, in an era of high technology and agribusiness, the small landholder is an anachronism and socialists as well as capitalists must support efficiency over nostalgia. Fewer people are needed on the land, not more. The tribes will surely seek productivity increases, and, as the Israelis have shown, dedication and sophisticated technology can make even the most unlikely land yield.

The land in some cases does have valuable resources, as, for example, in the case of the coal of Black Mesa on the Navaho reservation in Arizona currently being exploited to fuel great power plants. Here there is another ironic problem common to Indians and the Third World. The peoples of the developed world, the United States in this case, have become seriously concerned about the consequences of their technology on the quality of life and the condition of the earth. The power plants pollute and the strip-mining of Black Mesa ravages the landscape. Ecologists (in the political and philosophical sense) object. The response of the Indians seems similar to that of the Third World in general, which is, "First we must, as you did, drag ourselves from the horrors of poverty—by whatever means will serve. Then we will worry, when we can afford it, about these niceties." The far-off risk of DDT poisoning is not very impressive to someone who faces the more immediate threat of starvation if his crops cannot be saved from pests which the DDT will surely kill. Indian leadership has tended to decide in favor of jobs and development at the risk of some degree of damage to the environment.

An example that illustrates the difficulties of conflicts of interest in having the BIA in the Department of the Interior is the situation of the Havasupai. These people, who live in the Grand Canyon, traditionally maintained control of lands along the rim of the canyon. In recent years, apparently fearing that the Havasupai would commercialize the rim lands, or simply disfigure them by their presence, the National Park Service have forbidden Havasupai use of these lands. Long political battles raged prior to 1975, at which time the Indians were granted rights (under trust supervision) to large parts of the remote south rim but with severe limitations on the use of the land. Some of this tastes of the ethnographic zoo approach, since Indians are welcome to dance in the National Park Service tourist centers presumably because that is part of the "natural" environment, but Indians operating their own tourist business are apparently unnatural and not to be countenanced.

Indian lands which have limited exploitable resources in general are sometimes spectacular in their natural beauty: Monument Valley and its eerie stone pinnacles in the Navaho country, for example, or the mountainous forests of the Apache reservations. An obvious line of development is to exploit these scenic resources through the promotion of tourism. The Mexican government earns the major part of its foreign currency through tourism, and that has been a valuable source of capital for the development of the Mexican economy in other areas. The Indian lands are in fact visited by large numbers of tourists, but the money acquired does not end up in Indian hands. The tribes have erected few money traps where tourist dollars can be collected, having left the souvenir, motel, and recreation facilities to be developed and administered by non-Indians. Indeed, the problem of non-Indians benefiting more than the Indians from the exploitation of Indian resources is widespread, as in the BIA tendency to lease the better lands to outsiders rather than develop them for Indian use.

Some few tribes—for example, those in the Warm Springs Reservation in Oregon—have erected their own tourist complexes and so provided jobs for their people and income for the tribe as a whole. This pattern of harvesting the tourist crop will probably increase as other tribes whose lands are appropriate make the necessary investments. The A.I.P.R.C. reports, however, indicate many planning problems and little current success.

The Indians may have something special to sell to our curious consumer society and that is an image. Genuine Indians, performing genuine Indian dances or making genuine Indian crafts! This special image of the Indian has long been exploited by others who name their products Cheyenne or Comanche (off-road vehicles) or market "Indian"

Kah-Nee-Ta Resort Lodge owned by the Confederated Tribes of Warm Springs, Oregon, represents one of the more successful and better-planned attempts to build a tribal economy through tourism. (Courtesy Confederated Tribes of Warm Springs, Rockey/Marsh Public Relations)

patterns in cloth or rugs. There is probably not a college student in the country who doesn't own at least one piece of "Indian" jewelry, most likely made in Hong Kong. If the Indians could simply put their tongues properly in their cheeks, they too could cash in on these fanciful dreams. Much of our economy is built on illusion (after-shave lotions that make you irresistible), and what the Indians have to sell that is unique is that they are Indians. They have very little else.

An area that occurs immediately to everyone for development on the reservations is arts and crafts, but these have no hope of becoming an important source of employment. How many of us are competent artists? Artistic skill and talent are no more common among Indians than they are among others, so only a few will ever be able to produce items of sufficient quality to earn them a living. The study of Shonto points out that while eighty-nine women did some weaving of the famous Navaho rugs, only two produced rugs of high quality and price. Despite the fact that the prices were artificially inflated because of Navaho tribal subsidy programs, the income was only $128.25 per weaver for the year, which, while seemingly low, is in fact a 420 percent increase since the original study in 1955.[9] Craft products are a useful income supplement and can serve to support the "image" for tourism, but by themselves they are not viable. The situation can surely be improved, for those few who seek to pursue crafts, by putting the marketing of the crafts more directly into tribal hands. For Navaho weavers it is often the case that what little profit is currently being made is being made by middlemen at the trading posts who accept weaving in payment for grocery bills, but at wholesale prices written off against inflated retail prices for the groceries. The fine blanket which eventually fetches a price of over $1000 in some Tucson tourist shop may have earned the weaver considerably less than the minimum wage. Some like the Navaho have taken steps to set up their own "guilds" and marketing organizations to insure fair practices—another illustration, if more were needed, of the virtues of self-administration.

The matter of "image" has some demonstrable reality. The Mohawk, as everyone knows, are skilled "high steel" construction workers whose services are sought wherever a building or bridge that is being built goes beyond a few hundred feet in height. They are said to have a natural affinity for this work, and it has become an essentially "hereditary" trade among them, producing for many of them good stable incomes. The fact is that the Mohawk are no more likely to have any actual genetic propensity for high-altitude balance than they are to have the natural rhythm or the taste for mercantile dealing that have been said by racists to characterize other peoples. A far more likely explanation has been advanced which associates their early entry into this field (when a steel bridge was being raised near their reservation) with aspects of their cultural attitudes. The "warrior" mentality which insists that courage be displayed through bravado and that fear be disguised probably underlies the seeming ease with which these first Mohawk workers danced on the girders in the sky. It was not a genetic trait but a cultural norm in favor of *cojones* much the same as that which has established the Navaho and Apache as reliable forest-fire fighters.

Once such an image or belief becomes established, however, it is as real as any other social fact. The Mohawk *are* skilled steel workers and apparently as a group better at it than any one else. A large part of this is presumably because they themselves believe in their skill and such self-confidence is an obvious necessity in that precarious line of work. The rest is the organized, nearly hereditary character of Mohawk steel workers who form a kind of guild which makes easier the entry of a new Mohawk worker into this trade and helps him through the training and familiarization necessary. Whatever the reality, it is clear that at least part of the highly successful adaptation of the Mohawks to white society is a matter of selling an image and can serve as proof of the possibility of such an approach.

In the final analysis it will have to be the Indian tribes themselves who develop their economies, but that can only be done with federal assistance, both financial and technical. The reservations are isolated from markets and resources, lacking in skilled workers, short of capital, lacking infrastructure, and plagued with cross-cultural confusions. Regardless of federal incentives (unless these become massive), private developers will not risk themselves in such an economic-disaster zone. The Israelis have developed ways of getting food out of the Negev desert not because it was a profitable and attractive business enterprise but because they had no choice. It is the same for the reservations. If the Indians wish to remain on their lands, as they obviously do, then they alone have the motivation and dedication necessary to make an economic desert bloom, but for this they need leadership and organization of their own.

Who Speaks for the People?

As noted much earlier, the Indian people have not remained unchanging and unresponsive to the events that have impinged upon them, however little they may have been able to control them. The Native American Church has already been cited as an example of a syncretic, pan-Indian cultural pattern which belongs to no specific tribe and yet is still not Anglo. Many different tribes think of peyotism as theirs and as somehow "Indian," as opposed to "white." Similar phenomena of common identification of the various tribes and the existence of structures through which this unity is expressed are by no means indicative of a total absorption of the tribes into some central common structure, but they do reflect an emerging uniform response to a universal problem. The Navaho may not traditionally have much resemblance to the Sioux, but both respond to the federal government in much the same way, very largely because the structure of federal Indian administration has always treated the tribes as if they were all alike. It is yet another self-fulfilling prophecy.

The cooperation and common identity of pantribalism—"We are Indian"—has complex roots but is, like the culture-area concept, basically a reflection of response to environmental challenge, the environment being the reservation system. Ironically many aspects of pan-Indianism incorporate white-derived stereotypes of "the Indian" as a sort of common denominator, just as English is the lingua franca of these linguistically diverse peoples. Beaded buckskins and feather headdresses similar to those of the Plains horsemen are nearly universally adopted by the Indians themselves as being symbolically authentic expressions of solidarity. Southwestern silver and turquoise are equally universally accepted as generalized Indian.

Powwows (intertribal gatherings) form one structural manifestation of this Indian unity. Many tribesmen travel the powwow "circuit" in much the same way that cowboys follow the rodeo circuit. In fact, many powwows and tribal "fairs" feature such rodeos where cowboy skills are the central entertainment. Powwow activities (regardless of location or tribe) tend to feature "Indian" dancing (particularly "war dancers") and drumming and singing in much the same competitive atmosphere as the rodeo, with prizes offered for the finest dancers and musicians. "Indian" arts and crafts are displayed and judged for prizes along with "Indian" costumes, and very frequently there are beauty contests in which costume is stressed. These costumes and dances are very nearly always of the Plains pattern now accepted as generalized Indian, ignoring the wide variety of patterns of dress and dance associated with the individual pre-Columbian cultural patterns.

Formal organizations also exist which "represent" in one way or another a degree of Indian unity. Some, like the Indian Rights Association, have existed for a very long time but have largely been dominated by Indian "friends" and as such are not strictly to be regarded as Indian. The National Congress of American Indians (N.C.A.I.) founded in 1944 is probably the oldest and still one of the most effective of the organizations which are Indian-conceived and -dominated. The National Indian Youth Council (N.I.Y.C.) was founded in 1961 partially in reaction to feelings on the part of younger leaders that the N.C.A.I. was too conservative and was principally a lobbying organization for the "establishment" of the reservations. Tribal chairmen, who are certainly the most influential and powerful of current Indian leaders, banded together in 1971 to coordinate their actions in national policy matters, through the National Indian Tribal Chairmen's Association (N.I.T.C.A.). Throughout the late sixties and into the seventies a great many small special-purpose organizations arose, often seeming to be "protest-oriented" in the confrontation style of the sixties. The American Indian Movement (A.I.M.), founded in 1968, was the best known of these through its part in the spectacular events of the "Trail of Broken Treaties" when a protest march on the BIA headquarters in 1972 ended in the "trashing" of that building. Still more attention was focused on A.I.M. after the armed clashes at Wounded Knee in 1973 and the subsequent trials of such leaders as Russell Means. The newsletter *Akwesasne Notes* gives a sampling of issues currently debated.[10]

Who speaks for the people? This is by no means so simple an issue as the media have made it seem by their concentration on A.I.M. and similar flamboyant movements or actions such as the occupation of

Alcatraz Island. In fact a great deal of this level of "representation" springs from young and essentially urban Indians rather than reservation-oriented Indians. For a time one might have supposed that certain Oscar-winning movie stars were important Indian spokesmen if the extent of media coverage were to be the criteria for representativeness. It is difficult enough to say who is an Indian at all and the profusion of "spokesmen," usually self-appointed, for "my people" can be truly alarming. Since a great many persons subscribe to the "it takes one to know one" theory in ethnic matters, any who claim to be of "the people" are likely to be listened to as if they were truly representative through some mystical, racial, collective consciousness. Often the only thing "Indian" about some such Indians are the beads and turquoise they so ostentatiously wear and some small quantum of "blood." The limitation of a genetically derived level of awareness of the problems of the Indian people is indicated by the words I once heard from a "spokesman" for a northwest coastal tribe in which these totally nonagricultural people were credited with a great reverence for "our mother corn." As there were once "professional" Irish, there are now professional Indians who seemingly make a business out of being "spokesmen." The influence of such "leaders" with the Indian peoples themselves is extremely limited, but unfortunately strong, out of all proportion, in the wider society.

No one group or person speaks for the people since, in spite of an increasing degree of pantribal unity, the people are not one. The Navaho are still the Navaho and, while not Anglo, are not Sioux either. The problems of the tiny rancherias of California are not the problems of the state-size Navaho reservation. The urban activist for "civil rights" has little in common with the Comanche eagle doctor. The one real commonality is the need to come to some sort of terms with Anglo society so as to survive as peoples.

The constitutions springing from the Indian Reorganization Act gave rise to a kind of Indian leader—the tribal chairman—whose central position has made him probably the most effective and most representative of the many who claim to speak for the people. Very often in the past the chairmen have been simple tools for the administrative convenience of the BIA, and these and other excessively cooperative "Uncle Tomahawks" are the target of the young activists' protests and derision. In some cases, however, the chairmen have become spectacularly successful representatives of their tribes and have gained policy influence in national as well as tribal circles. Peter McDonald and his predecessor as chairman of the Navaho, Raymond Nakai, have both had wide impact on policy although they have inevitably been controversial figures in tribal politics. Many others could be named whose efforts have gained the tribal chairman's role a degree of importance beyond that of almost any other office.

Theoretically, the chairmen are the chief executives and administrative officers of their tribes, functioning as the agents of elected tribal councils. In fact, because of the administrative dominance of the BIA, which has in the past retained virtually all real day-to-day as well as long-range governmental functions in its own hands, this executive role of the chairmen has largely been an illusion. Some of the larger tribes do in fact have considerable governmental structure of their own, performing planning, policy, and administrative functions that are not directly in the hands of BIA officials, but in most, the tribal government is a part-time and very frequently unpaid shadow organization.[11]

It is the federal government from whom all blessings flow, primarily the BIA, but other agencies and programs such as the Department of Health, Education, and Welfare (HEW), and the Public Health Service (PHS) are increasingly important funding sources. This being the case, the most important asset of the tribal chairman in the absence of true administrative functions has been his ability, on behalf of his people, to manipulate and cope with these federal agencies. One can think of the chairman as an official tribal hunter stalking the "Fed-beast" through the bureaucratic forest. To flog the image into the ground, he must go out and bring back the federal bacon while holding the termination wolf from the door. In a phrase used by Robert Bee, an anthropologist and a student of Indian government, their primary responsibility is "to get something for the people" and a failure to perform this function is frequently the criterion for removal from office.[12]

While many chairmen have been spectacularly successful at this hunter's task, most of the smaller tribes do not have the staff or money to allow them to discover more than a small fraction of the programs for which they are eligible, let alone complete the paperwork to get them. Even for the successful, it should be noted that the job is simply to get the programs—not to administer them. This form of government resembles a kind of lobbying expertise and is in no way to be regarded as an automatic preparation for actual self-administration.

Much of this intricate business of dealing with the government has fallen into the hands of the "tribal attorneys" who first became commonly retained to deal with the cases of the Indian Claims Commission in the late forties. Rarely Indian, some of these attorneys have been no better than they should be, while others have been accused of taking advantage of their clients' legal ignorance for their own advantage. But as Henry Dobyns pointed out in a study some years ago, the attorneys have taught the tribes an important lesson about the virtues of self-administration.[13] The attorneys work directly for the tribe itself and represent the tribe directly, not the tribe and the federal government simultaneously. Bureaucratic reality being what it is, BIA officials will have at best mixed loyalties and will not press for the interests of the tribe when they conflict with the federal government which is, of course, where most of the conflict does lie. The Spanish word for lawyer—*abogado* (advocate)—expresses the essential function of the lawyers, and this the BIA cannot be relied upon to perform. It is the tribe itself which pays the attorney (often on a contingency basis: no success, no pay), but the bureaucrat knows that his pay as well as his job security depends not on the tribe but on standing in well with his higher-level chiefs whose heads rest securely on their own shoulders only so long as Congress is pleased. Like the expectation that the BIA will work itself out of a job, the notion that federal employees will pay more attention to the wishes of the Indians than their real bosses is structurally absurd.

In dealing with lower level bureaucrats, all of us have been confronted with the arrogance of helplessness and incompetency: "I am sorry but there is nothing I can do." "Mr. Ferndock is the only one who can change that and he's gone for the day." The effective Indian leaders have long since perfected the "congressional end run" as a tactical response. They are as aware, as are those of us who call for the manager, what it is besides water that flows downhill. The entire tribal council of the largest tribe in the United States has no real power over the most lowly BIA clerk because there is no real structural articulation between tribe and BIA except a general admonition to "consult." The expert tribal hunters zip straight to Washington, preferably to Congress, and present their grievances there. The most casual congressional inquiry sends ripples down the bureaucratic structure that become an imperative tidal wave when they reach the omnipotent/impotent clerk. Obviously this is another structural absurdity serving to obstruct development and maintain the condition of administrative dependency.

"With the Consent of the Secretary . . ."

Included in the I.R.A. constitutions and even in the current Indian Self Determination and Education Assistance Act (Pub. L. 93-638), the phrase "with the consent of the Secretary" mocks the authority of the tribes and is a constant reminder to all of the location of the ultimate source of power on the reservation. John Collier and the failures contingent upon his invocation of this ever-threatening authority illustrated some time ago the need to give *real* irrevocable responsibility to tribal governments if the cycle of dependency were to be broken. All local governments are restrained to some extent in the range of their decision making by the authority of the federal government. Only the Indians find every aspect of their lives so persistently crosscut by this authority that any reliability in local choice and decision making is unlikely. After so many generations of outside control, the reservations lack the structure to implement self-administration and the people of the reservations lack any expectation that there is reality to promises of self-determination. As noted earlier, the reservations have long since had all traditional structures for ordering life disrupted, and by preempting decision making, the BIA has effectively beheaded the communities.

I have occasionally referred to the reservation as the "administered community." I have written elsewhere of this phenomenon, as have others, as a self-perpetuating system which is inherently incapable of producing viable and independent enclaves.[14] Administration can lead only to continued administration. In reference to the World War II Japanese relocation camps, Edward H. Spicer said, "Public policy involving the future of human communities must be made by those communities, or the destruction of some of the most important human qualities is certain to take place, resulting in frustration, apathy, and dependency."[15] These are certainly characteristics of the reservations, and the reservations are unique only in that they represent a situation where the administered condition is sustained over generations rather than a few years.

As we have seen, the peoples of the reservations have (from their point of view) been subjected unpredictably and uncontrollably to capricious and often apparently senseless events. Stock-raising programs are inaugurated, and then the animals are sold off. Irrigation projects are developed, and then the lands are leased to outsiders. Schools forbid children to speak anything but English and then become bilingual. Day schools are built and then closed. Children are rounded up and taken to boarding schools. Ceremonials are forbidden and then encouraged. Whether or not on any given day the life of a particular Indian family is affected by these administrative bolts from the blue is perhaps not so important as the knowledge that nothing can be undertaken with the certainty that the uncontrollable and unpredictable outsiders will not intervene in it or forbid it.

At this individual level the results are often a sort of permanently maintained apathy—why bother? An artifically sustained state of anomie or normlessness, usually associated with the disintegrating society, is, under the system of administration, maintained just above the point of collapse but with all the consequences in misery and despair associated with social disruption. Alcoholism, suicide, and other indicators of despair remain extraordinarily high on the reservations. The administrators spend much of their time attempting to alleviate such symptoms, which their administration itself may be largely responsible for producing. Perhaps it was with something like this in mind that Vine Deloria spoke of a "leave us alone law."[16]

An administered community is a type of enclave within a larger society in which essential and vital functions necessary to the continued existence of the group are performed by structures which are controlled from outside the community itself. Schools are such social structures, which in the normal society prepare the child to become a functioning member of his or her own society. Until recently, however, schools on the reservation were instruments of assimilation controlled by outsiders and designed (however unsuccessfully) to make the Indian child a functioning member of a society other than his own. Whatever the Indian peoples might want taught to their children, the structure which performs the enculturative function of formal education is lock, stock, and videotape in the hands of others who are in no way responsible to the Indians for the content or manner in which the function might be performed.

In a situation such as this, it is not simply a case of the Indian community lacking structure of its own to perform vital functions, but there is in fact a destructive stress built in. The Indian peoples *do*, through the structure of the family, ceremonials, storytellers, peer groups, and other nonformal structures of enculturation, pass on some large part of their own idea of what the child should know, so much so that educators whose aim has been assimilation have felt themselves locked in a battle with "grandmother" for the mind of the child. At the same time, using Murray Wax's felicitous phrase, a "vacuum ideology" has prevailed in Indian education (as it did in the national project Head Start) which suggests that the Indian people have no culture and that the educator's task is to fill a vacuum, not support a viable tradition.[17] Much the same notion lay behind the transportation of ghetto children to see a cow so as to remedy "cultural deprivation" in the Head Start program.

"No tickee, no laundry—no structure, no function" was a popular phrase among my graduate school buddies which expresses rather irreverently the essential point. Talk of self-sufficiency, autonomy, independence, or any other label denoting the elusive goal of Indian community self-determination must remain only talk as long as the model of administration is retained. How can Indian communities take responsibility for their own affairs when they are denied access to the mechanisms which regulate those affairs? They can gain no "therapeutic experience" (Collier's phrase) or any other kind of experience as long as the mechanisms are designed and run by outsiders. Bitter though it may be for "experts" to accept, as it was ultimately impossible for Collier to accept, the only path to Indian self-sufficiency is to turn over the structures of administration and stand back, leaving the Indian peoples to make mistakes as well as succeed. When the newly installed BIA Director of Indian Education, William G. Demmert, was asked in 1976 how to go about changing the structure of Indian education, he said:

> In my judgement there's only one way. You give the money and the control over the money directly to the community. You give the school board sign off authority over the budgets.[18]

A seemingly simple statement, but the implications for the acceptance of a nonadministered model along the lines of the "sustained enclave" are profound. As we have already seen, the reservations are not yet self-supporting economically and will not be for some time, under the best of circumstances. Now and for some time to come it will be necessary to "sustain" the enclaves through a continuing infusion of federal funds. The difference will be that while the funds continue to come from outside, they will be managed and administered by the tribes themselves, a process which can, it is hoped, lead to the recapitation of the beheaded communities. Demmert's statement is particularly significant for its recognition and encouragement of Indian structures of self-administration; the school boards referred to (commonplace mechanisms everywhere in America) did not exist on reservations before 1966, at least not composed of Indians or with any actual authority.

Since the first of the locally Indian-controlled (technically at least) boarding schools went into operation at Rough Rock near the center of the Navaho reservation in 1966–1967, many steps have been taken which seem to indicate something of the way to de-administer the reservation communities without termination of special federal status and support. Administration is self-defeating. Termination has been seen to be tantamount to sociocide. Is there a third way that leads to the sustained enclave?

Let My People Go?

The Rough Rock demonstration school, which has spawned several imitations (although most Indian schools are still not Indian-administered) and whose founders went on to establish a community college for the Navaho reservation, was itself a product of a more general phenomenon—the Office of Economic Opportunity (OEO) and, in particular, its Title II, "Urban and Rural Community Action Program," which had among its other mottos, "The maximum feasible participation of the poor." Rough Rock school was as a matter of fact an offspring, a special project, of the Research and Demonstration Office. The "ordinary" Community Action Program (CAP) agencies set up on the reservations were an eye-opening experience for all concerned as to the potential in a "contract" procedure of federal support without direct administration.[19]

There is no room here to tell the story of the rise and fall of the OEO, from its first glory days when young bureaucratic gunslingers thrust money and power into the hands of those who had never had it before, to the final emasculation of what embarrassingly enough turned out (briefly) to be a government-sponsored revolution in power relationships. Before the poverty warriors were driven back to the hills and the charity/welfare establishment returned to its proper role of supervising the poor, much had changed and that included the Indian leaders' conception of what could be done. The Indians found themselves directly tapped into a fast-moving and powerful (briefly) federal agency which was sometimes alarmingly eager to use its considerable clout on their behalf in confrontations with practically everyone. More important, the tribes learned that they could plan and operate complex programs on their own if technical assistance and financial support were provided. As with a sheep-killing dog, a taste of blood ruins a pet forever.

Although no one seems to admit an official connection, the Self Determination Act (Pub. L. 93-638) is obviously a direct lineal descendant of the Economic Opportunity Act of 1964, particularly Title II mentioned above. The CAP agencies were local organizations composed of "representatives" of the target populations, not branches of some central bureaucracy. Obviously fiscal control was maintained, but the essential mechanism was a granting procedure with no direct administration by OEO itself after initial grant approval and subsequent refunding reviews. Pub. L. 93-638 proposes to do precisely the same thing for virtually the entire range of services currently being operated on the reservations by the BIA or other federal agencies. There is a particular emphasis on schools, presumably because that has already been shown to be workable. There is little doubt that the tribal chairmen made very favorable contrasts between the innovative and locally directed CAP agencies and the traditional BIA administration of Indian affairs, and this has provided much of the impetus for the new direction.

The path of contractual enclavement has not yet been embraced with wholehearted enthusiasm by either the BIA or the tribes although as mentioned earlier, the Zuni and Micosukee have undertaken a wide range of former Bureau functions through such procedures. One pitfall is the fact that while the act says that it shall not be construed as "authorizing or requiring the termination of any existing trust responsibility" (Sec. 110),[20] it does not specifically forswear the government's intention to move toward the goal. It contains a few ominous phrases, stressing, for example, "an orderly transition from Federal domination of programs for and services to Indians to effective and meaningful participation by the Indian people . . . etc." (Sec. 3),[21] which *could* be misinterpreted to imply some sort of termination goal in the absence of specific irrevocable renunciation of that specter. This same section declares "commitment to the maintenance of the Federal government's unique and continuing relationship with and responsibility to the Indian people" without, however, spelling out what that responsibility *is*.

There are, to my mind, other flaws in the bill, as, for example, the emphasis in the education statement on the intention to make it possible for the Indian children "to compete and excel in the life areas of their choice" (Sec. 3),[22] which is focused on the individual and says nothing about the Indian *community* and its survival. There seems some echo of education as the road to assimilation remaining here. The major flaw of this bill, however, is the phrases which make it plain that the Secretaries of the Interior and of the Department of Health, Education, and Welfare can accept or decline the contracts, regulate them according to rules of their own devising, revoke them, or continue them at discretion. There is an injunction to "consult" with some nebulous group of "national and regional Indian organizations" but only "to the extent practicable." Power remains with the Secretaries and their delegates (presumably the Bureau). The purse-strings are very short since the contracts are normally to run only for one year and for a maximum of three.

Having said enough to point out that the bill does not accomplish all that could, and eventually must, be done if true self-determination is to exist, I hasten to point out that it is a good and substantial first step in that direction which, however flawed and incomplete, gives hope of eventual success. The bill does not guarantee a transfer of authority from the Bureau to the tribal governments, but it makes it *possible* to move in that direction. The tribes may fail to pursue their opportunities or the bureaucrats may make use of the obstructive possibilities written into the bill to throttle true local decision making, but the chance is there! The limitations and loopholes are in fact not so great as those written into the Economic Opportunity Act, and that bill, at least for a time, was administered in such a way as to create structure where no structure had existed before; and that, it is suggested, is precisely what is needed on the reservations. Contracting properly done can provide the experience and support necessary to recapitate the headless horsemen in a way that continued direct administration can never do.

Title 25 and Catch 22

The Self Determination Act speaks of Indian tribes repeatedly, as does all such legislation, but the final issue I want to address is the desperate need for some clear-cut definition as to what a tribe is and what its legal relationship to the local, state, and federal governments might be. Title 25 of the United States code theoretically expresses the current state of Indian law, but the A.I.P.R.C. task force on "Law Consolidation, Revision and Codification" said of this that it was "packed with statutory provisions which are either superseded by subsequent legislation, obsolete by virtue of the passage of time, redundant to prior legislation, or in total conflict with present policies relating to the administration of Indian affairs."[23] The Bureau of Indian Affairs operates on the basis of a "manual" of regulations which is equally obscure, contradictory, and incomprehensible. What is an Indian tribe?

Over the years there have been a number of court cases which seem to affirm some basic characteristics of the tribal status. There has also been an increasing legislative recognition of the likelihood of continued tribal existence. There seems to be gradually emerging an assertion of the special nature of the relationship of Indian tribe and the federal government in which Congress exercises plenary power over all Indian affairs. The states are excluded from this relationship and may not intervene or interpose since the tribes possess some degree of inherent sovereignty equivalent in many ways to that of the states themselves. The rights which tribes possess, such as fishing rights, are not special privileges granted to them by the states or federal government but residual rights retained because they have never been specifically relinquished to the federal government by treaty or statutes. The controversial decision of Federal Judge Boldt in *United States v. Washington* is the most recent and most dramatic affirmation of this general view. It grants Indians rights to fishing which cannot be restricted by the state of Washington.[24]

The fact that court decisions are still necessary indicates that there is no clear recognition on the part of states that the tribes do in fact possess the characteristics of sovereigns, of a dependent domestic nature. As we have seen, the policies of the United States government over the years since first contact with Indians have changed repeatedly, so the truth is that the current status of tribes, a contradictory amalgam of earlier purposes and decisions, needs to be clarified and restated in modern terms. There can be no doubt that as original possessors of the land, the Indian tribes as *tribes* have a special character in relation to the United States government to whom they relinquished their lands. As *persons* Indians are simply citizens like anyone else.

Much as the Indian leadership deplores the paternalism of the "feds" and bemoans their lack of freedom, the fact is that the only thing standing between the tribes and social extinction is the federal government. The states have invariably shown an inevitable tendency to favor the interests of the majority of their voting citizenry over the minority of Indians, who seldom vote. Whatever goodwill the states possess toward "their" Indians cannot be relied upon to override local concerns, as countless cases of dispute over land, water rights, taxes, hunting and fishing, and the like have indicated. Sympathy for the "quaint" Indians vanishes when someone's economic ox is gored, as in the recent outrages over land claims in Maine or fishing rights in Washington. The Indian tribe or reservation and its rights and obligations must be clearly defined and not forced to rely on the ephemeral goodwill of public opinion.

The tyranny of the majority over the minority is one of the dangers of the democratic system of government that the Founding Fathers sought to control and protection against such tyranny has found much expression in recent years in civil rights legislation. The special quality of the Indian position, however, makes such protections a problem. The so-called Indian Civil Rights Act of 1968 guaranteed *individual* Indians federal court protection against the actions of their own tribal govern-

Yakima Tribal Council in session. The extent and structure of tribal self-government and self-determination remain the principal problems for the Indian peoples. (Courtesy Yakima Nation Media Services)

ment and courts if civil rights were violated. A laudable notion—except that it constitutes in this case another interposition of the standards and structures of the larger society on the Indian and his own mechanisms of social control. I do not say that the tribes should violate basic human rights, but I do say that it is necessarily up to them to define what these might be if we do not once again wish to introduce destructive stress that will prevent effective self-administration.

Obviously the "Indian problem" is still with us, and once again we are at a turning point in our approach to the solution. Many recommendations are being advanced from many sources, and it seems certain that by the time this book appears some amount of new legislation will have been introduced into Congress as a result of the latest investigations. It seems extremely likely that the BIA will be shifted entirely out of the Interior Department or made into a relatively autonomous branch in the Department in order to remove the unending conflicts of interest between Interior's primary concern (land and resources) and the Bureau's concern (people). In this context, assuming success of the contracting procedure, one can expect the BIA to be redefined as a technical-assistance agency rather than a governing and administrative entity. The BIA may begin to take on the role most helpful for the relatively cloutless Indian peoples, which is that of advocate and wielder of federal clout on their behalf.

It also seems very likely that the matter of legal definition of tribes vis-à-vis the states and the national government will not be immediately resolved. There are precedents that might be applicable, as, for example, the special status of the District of Columbia, which is outside state jurisdiction and has become increasingly self-governing while remaining in a special relationship with the federal government. Perhaps the solutions to the questions of self-government for the District of Columbia and the creation of a series of Indian "Districts" could follow similar patterns. Could all the Indian governmental entities be lumped together as a single fifty-first state, ignoring the lack of geographical continuity in favor of cultural continuity? Granting the Navaho some sort of status equivalent to a state has a certain logic because of their size and numbers, but if tribes are to be dealt with individually, then what of the California rancheria of twenty people? For the smaller groups, perhaps the model of the All Pueblo Council can apply to situations where confederacies of tribes must operate together if a unit of sufficient size is to be created.

At about this point in my classes I am forced to confess to my students that I don't know the answer to the "Indian problem." I confess it to you if you have not already guessed. I am sure that it will inevitably involve a redefinition of the Indian status so as to allow self-administration, but precisely how that can be legally, economically, and politically accomplished remains unclear. The administered community must go, and something less self-defeating must take its place; that something must be hammered out with the participation of the Indian people. A hopeful beginning has been made with recent legislation, but beginnings of great promise have been made in the past to end in nothing. Still, I am satisfied that there will be no end to the Indian peoples, as peoples, so in that spirit there is no end to this book. The last word is the same as the first word . . . Chichimeca.

Some Readings

Anderson, A. T.: *Nations Within a Nation: The American Indians and the Government of the United States*, U.S. Government Printing Office, 1976. Readable capsule summary of the A.I.P.R.C. reports. The reports themselves are extremely useful as a whole, but large parts are confusing in organization and presentation.

Castile, George P.: "Federal Indian Policy and the Sustained Enclave: An Anthropological Perspective," *Human Organization*, **33**:219–228, 1974. Short summary of the sustained enclave versus the administered community.

Castile, George P.: "An Unethical Ethic: Self Determination and the Anthropological Conscience," *Human Organization*, **34**:35–40. The author wrestling publicly with his conscience and the nature of applied anthropology.

Hertzberg, Hazel W.: *The Search for an American Indian Identity: Modern*

Pan-Indian Movements, Syracuse, N.Y.: Syracuse University Press, 1971. Survey of the development of Indian political consciousness.

Szasz, Margaret: *Education and the American Indian: The Road to Self Determination, 1928–1973.* Albuquerque: University of New Mexico Press, 1974. Illustrates the moves toward self-determination in administration through a consideration of the schools. Like most who have dealt with Rough Rock and other initial experimental steps, too much success is assumed too soon, on the basis of hope rather than evidence.

NOTES AND ACKNOWLEDGMENTS

The sketches at the beginning of each chapter are by Jeanne Bowden Winer. The introductory chapter sketch represents the "God of the Morning Star" from the Mexican Codex Borgia; Chapter 1 shows a cradleboard-flattened skull and archaeologist's trowel; Chapter 2, Papago basketry; Chapter 3, Navaho "Corn People"; Chapter 4, a stylized butterfly (representing "butterfly sickness"); Chapter 5, Turquois Whipping Boy, Hopi Katcina; Chapter 6, a Haida crowned doll; Interregnum, a Clallam doll; Chapter 7, a ship detail (redrawn from de Bry plate); Chapter 8, an Iroquois falseface mask; Chapter 9, an armed cigar store Indian; Chapter 10, a missionary/agent; Chapter 11,

"Bear Coming out of His Hole" (Tlingit); and Chapter 12, the backside of the "Spirit of Death" (Haida). Those drawings not entirely original are largely redrawn from items either in the author's personal collection or in the Eells Northwest Collection of the Whitman College Museum. The cigar store Indian is a very much modified impression based on a piece in the New York Historical Society, New York City. The Haida "death" is redrawn from a doll in the Provincial Museum, Victoria, British Columbia.

The photographs are individually credited, but the majority were taken from an original edition, in the Washington State Historical Society collection, of the 20-volume pictorial work by Edward S. Curtis entitled *The North American Indian* (vols. 1–5, Cambridge, Mass: The University Press; vols. 6–20, Norwood, Mass: The Plimpton Press; 1907–1930). Reproduction was by Gregory J. Hyde and Larry Paynter. The bookplate on page 5 is from an early edition of J. Fenimore Cooper's *The Wept of Wish-Ton-Wish, A Tale* (D. Appleton & Co., New York, 1883). The photograph on page 6 is from Major Lee Moorhouse's *Souvenir Album of Noted Indian Photographs* (East Oregonian Print, Pendleton, Oregon, 1905).

Permission for extensive quotations in the text was granted by the following: the Smithsonian Institution Press, for the quotation at the beginning of Chapter 1 (taken from Aileen O'Bryan, "The Diné: Origin Myths of the Navaho Indians," Bulletin 163, Bureau of American Ethnology, 1956); the University of Washington Press, for the quotation from Smohalla on page 64 and for the quotation from Chief Joseph on page 189 (both taken from Merrill D. Beal, *I Will Fight No More Forever*, Seattle: University of Washington Press, 1963); the University of Oklahoma Press, for the quotation from James Edward Oglethorpe on page 125 (taken from David H. Corkran, *The Creek Frontier, 1540–1783*, Norman, Okla.: University of Oklahoma Press, 1967); and Prentice-Hall, Inc., for the quotation from an Army lieutenant on page 233 (taken from Jack D. Forbes [ed.], *The Indian in America's Past*, Englewood Cliffs, N.J.: Prentice-Hall, 1964).

Chichimeca Introduction and Perspective

1 A gag line, as is "forward into the past," from *Temporarily Humboldt Country*, an entertaining and regrettably accurate short history of Indian-white contact presented by the comedy group "The Firesign Theater." Columbia Records Cs-9518.
2 Charles Di Peso, *Casas Grandes: A Fallen Trading Center of the Gran Chichimeca*, Dragoon, Arizona: Amerind Foundation, vol. 1, 1974. Di Peso has long used the term to refer to the southwest United States and northwest Mexico. He discusses the usage on pages 48–56 of the cited work. I have simply expanded the term to include all of the rest of native North America.
3 Leslie White, *The Science of Culture*, New York: Grove Press, 1949.

4 A. R. Radcliffe-Brown, *A Natural Science of Society,* New York: Free Press, 1948.
5 Lewis Binford, "Archaeology as Anthropology," *American Antiquity,* **28**:217–225, 1962.
6 Anthony Wallace, "Revitalization Movements: Some Theoretical Considerations for Their Comparative Study," *American Anthropologist,* **58**:264–281, 1956.

Chapter 1 First Man

1 Aileen O'Bryan, "The Diné: Origin Myths of the Navaho Indians," Bulletin 163, Bureau of American Ethnology, Smithsonian Institution, 1956, pp. 166–167.
2 For this and a general background to the question, see Gordon R. Willey and Jeremy A. Sabloff, *A History of American Archaeology,* San Francisco: W. H. Freeman and Co., 1974.

Chapter 2 Worlds to Conquer

1 Joseph R. Caldwell, "The New American Archaeology," in Joseph R. Caldwell (ed.), *New Roads to Yesterday,* New York: Basic Books, 1966.
2 Julian H. Steward, *Basin-Plateau Sociopolitical Groups,* Bulletin 120, Bureau of American Ethnology, Smithsonian Institution, 1938.
3 George Dalton (ed.), *Primitive, Archaic and Modern Economies: Essays of Karl Polanyi,* New York: Doubleday, 1968.
4 Walter Kelly, "Robin the Red Breasted Hood," in *The Pogo Stepmother Goose,* New York: Simon and Schuster, 1954.
5 Richard S. MacNeish, "Ancient Mesoamerican Civilization," *Science,* **143**:531–537, 1964.
6 Morton Fried, *The Evolution of Political Society,* New York: Random House, 1967.
7 Edward H. Spicer, "The Yaquis: A Persistent Identity System," paper read at American Anthropological Association Annual Meeting, Washington, D.C., 1976.

Chapter 3 Corn Mother

1 Aileen O'Bryan, "The Diné: Origin Myths of the Navaho Indians," Bulletin 163, Bureau of American Ethnology, Smithsonian Institution, 1956, p. 30.
2 Merrill D. Beal, *I Will Fight No More Forever,* Seattle: University of Washington Press, 1963, p. 32.
3 Richard S. MacNeish, "The Origins of New World Civilization," in *New World Archaeology: Readings from Scientific American,* San Francisco: W. H. Freeman and Co., 1974.

Chapter 4 Left-handed Mexican Clansman

1 Elman R. Service, *Primitive Social Organization: An Evolutionary Perspective,* New York: Random House, 1964.
2 Julian H. Steward, *Theory of Culture Change,* Chicago: University of Chicago Press, 1963.

3 Lewis R. Binford, "Post Pleistocene Adaptations," in S. R. Binford and L. R. Binford (eds.), *New Perspectives in Archaeology*, Chicago: Aldine, 1968.
4 Bronislav Malinowski, *Sex and Repression in Savage Society*, London: Routledge, 1927.
5 Service, op. cit.

Chapter 5 The Great Spirits

1 Aileen O'Bryan, "The Diné: Origin Myths of the Navaho Indians," Bulletin 163, Bureau of American Ethnology, Smithsonian Institution, 1956, p. 156.
2 Ralph Linton, "Nativistic Movements," *American Anthropologist*, **45**:230–240, 1943.
3 Charles Kappler, Jr., "Treaty with the Yakima, 1855," in *Indian Treaties: 1778–1883*, New York: Interland Publishing, 1943, p. 698.
4 Clyde Kluckhohn, *Navaho Witchcraft*, Boston: Beacon Press, 1944, p. 5.
5 Weston La Barre, *The Peyote Cult*, New York: Shocken Books, 1969, p. xiv.
6 Ibid.
7 Carlos Castaneda, *Tales of Power*, New York: Simon and Schuster, 1974.
8 Although this title was invented independently, it resembles the title of an excellent treatment of "emics" and "etics" by Gerald D. Berreman: "Anemic and Emetic Analyses in Social Anthropology," *American Anthropologist*, **68**(1):346–354, 1966.
9 Anthony Wallace, *The Death and Rebirth of the Seneca*, New York: Knopf, 1970.
10 David E. Jones, *Sanapia: Comanche Medicine Woman*, New York: Holt, 1972.
11 Clyde Kluckhohn and Dorothea Leighton, *The Navaho*, Cambridge, Harvard University Press, 1946, p. 163.
12 Leslie A. White, *The Pueblo of Sia, New Mexico*, Bulletin 184, Bureau of American Ethnology, Smithsonian Institution, 1962.

Chapter 6 Lords of the Chichimeca

1 Jacques Soustelle, *Daily Life of the Aztec on the Eve of the Spanish Conquest*, Penguin, 1968, p. 242.
2 Morton Fried, *The Evolution of Political Society*, New York: Random House, 1967.
3 Ibid., p. 13.
4 Ibid., p. 109.
5 Ibid., p. 186.
6 Charles Di Peso, *Casas Grandes: A Fallen Trading Center of the Gran Chichimeca*, Dragoon, Arizona: The Amerind Foundation, 8 vol., 1974.
7 John R. Swanton, *Indian Tribes of the Lower Mississippi Valley and Adjacent Coast of the Gulf of Mexico*, Bulletin 43, Bureau of American Ethnology, Smithsonian Institution, 1911.

8 David H. Corkran, *The Creek Frontier, 1540–1783,* Norman, Okla.: University of Oklahoma Press, 1967, pp. 12–13.
9 Franz Boas, *Ethnology of the Kwakiutl, Thirty-fifth Annual Report,* Washington, D.C.: Bureau of American Ethnology, 1921.
10 George Dalton (ed.), *Primitive, Archaic and Modern Economies: Essays of Karl Polanyi,* New York: Doubleday, 1968, p. 186.
11 Helen Codere, *Fighting with Property: A Study of Kwakiutl Potlatching and Warfare: 1792–1930,* New York: American Ethnological Society, Monograph 18, 1950.
12 Ruth R. Benedict, *Patterns of Culture,* New York: Mentor, 1953.
13 Fried, op. cit., p. 186.

Interregnum: Some Alternative Perspectives

1 Stuart Schram (ed.), *Quotations From Chairman Mao Tse-Tung,* New York: Bantam, 1967, p. 122.
2 Erich von Däniken, *Chariots of the Gods,* London: Corgi Books, 1972.
3 Thomas S. Kuhn, *The Structure of Scientific Revolutions,* 2d ed., Chicago: University of Chicago Press, 1970.
4 Erich von Däniken, interview in *Playboy,* **21**(8):57, 1974.
5 Thomas Stuart Ferguson, *One Fold and One Shepherd,* San Francisco: Books of California, 1958.
6 Lewis Spence, *The Problem of Atlantis,* New York: Brentanos, 1925.
7 James Churchward, *The Lost Continent of Mu,* New York: Ives Washburn, 1932.
8 Grafton Elliot Smith, *In the Beginning: The Origin of Civilization,* New York: Morrow, 1928.
9 Thor Heyerdahl, *The Ra Expeditions,* Garden City, N.Y.: Doubleday, 1972.
10 Edwin Doran, "The Sailing Raft as a Great Tradition," in Carroll L. Riley et al. (eds.), *Man Across the Sea,* Austin: University of Texas Press, 1971.

Chapter 7 Civilization, Salvation, and Land Clearance

1 C. S. Forester, *Captain Horatio Hornblower,* Boston: Little, Brown, 1939.
2 Lewis Hanke, *The Spanish Struggle for Justice in the Conquest of America,* Boston: Little, Brown, 1965, p. 6. Quotes Castillo on this point in the context of a discussion of Spanish legalism.
3 Ibid., p. 7.
4 Ibid., p. 71.
5 D'arcy McNickle, *The Indian Tribes of the United States,* London: Institute of Race Relations, 1962, p. 20.
6 Gary B. Nash, *Red, White and Black,* Englewood Cliffs, N.J.: Prentice-Hall, 1974, p. 41.
7 William Kellaway, *The New England Company, 1649–1776,* New York: Barnes & Noble, 1961, p. 1.
8 Warren M. Billings, *The Old Dominion in the Seventeenth Century: A*

Documentary History of Virginia, 1606–1689, Chapel Hill, N.C.: University of North Carolina Press, 1975, p. 214. Other materials of interest are to be found in Chapter 8, "Indians and Whites: The Conflict of Cultures."

9 Nash, op. cit., p. 80.

Chapter 8 Treaties and Tears

1 Robert Redfield et al., "Memorandum for the Study of Acculturation," in Paul Bohannan and Fred Plog (eds.), *Beyond the Frontier,* Garden City, N.Y.: Natural History Press, 1967.

2 James Fenimore Cooper, *The Last of the Mohicans,* Boston: Houghton Mifflin, 1958.

3 Ruth Underhill, *Red Man's America,* Chicago: University of Chicago Press, 1953.

4 John Underhills (1638), quoted in David R. Wrone and Russell S. Nelson (eds.), *Who's the Savage? A Documentary History of the Mistreatment of the Native North Americans,* Greenwich, Conn.: Fawcett, 1973, p. 60.

5 Ibid., p. 61.

6 Carville V. Earle, "The Evolution of a Tidewater Settlement System: All Hallows Parish, Maryland, 1650–1783," Research Paper 170, Department of Geography, Chicago: University of Chicago, 1975.

7 "The utmost good faith shall always be observed towards the Indians." A provision of the Northwest Ordinance of 1789, quoted in Vine Deloria (ed.), *Of Utmost Good Faith,* New York: Bantam, 1971.

8 Charles Kappler, Jr., "Treaty with the Yakima, 1855," in *Indian Treaties: 1778–1883,* New York: Interland Publishing, 1943, p. 698.

9 Merrill D. Beal, *I Will Fight No More Forever,* Seattle: University of Washington Press, 1963, p. 33.

10 Wicomb E. Washburn, *The American Indian and the United States,* New York: Random House, 1973, p. 2646. See also for texts of other major treaties and court decisions.

11 Marquis James, *The Life of Andrew Jackson,* New York: Bobbs-Merrill, 1938, p. 603.

12 Ralph K. Andrist, *The Long Death,* New York: Macmillan, 1964, p. 317.

13 Anthony Wallace, *The Death and Rebirth of the Seneca,* New York: Knopf, 1970.

14 Anthony Wallace, "Revitalization Movements: Some Theoretical Considerations for Their Comparative Study," *American Anthropologist,* **58**:264–281, 1956. See also Ralph Linton, "Nativistic Movements," *American Anthropologist,* **45**:230–240, 1943.

Chapter 9 Warriors and Wagons

1 Dee Brown, *Bury My Heart at Wounded Knee,* New York: Holt, 1971, p. 166.

2 Robert K. Thomas, "The Redbird Smith Movement," in William N. Fenton and John Gulick (eds.), *Symposium of Cherokee and Iroquois Culture,* Bulletin 180, Bureau of American Ethnology, Smithsonian Institution, 1961.

3 Evon Z. Vogt, "Navaho," in Edward H. Spicer (ed.), *Perspectives in American Indian Culture Changes,* Chicago: University of Chicago Press.
4 Theodora Kroeber, *Ishi in Two Worlds: A Biography of the Last Wild Indian in North America,* Berkeley: University of California Press, 1964.
5 Keith A. Murray, *The Modocs and Their War,* Norman, Okla.: University of Oklahoma Press, 1959.
6 Alvin M. Josephy, *The Nez Perce Indians and the Opening of the Northwest,* New Haven, Conn.: Yale University Press, 1965, p. 630.

Chapter 10 The Headless Horsemen

1 Francis Paul Prucha (ed.), *Americanizing the American Indians: Writings by the "Friends of the Indian," 1880–1900,* Cambridge, Mass.: Harvard University Press, 1973, p. 302.
2 Theodore W. Taylor, *The States and Their Indian Citizens,* Washington, Bureau of Indian Affairs, 1971.
3 Edward Spicer, *A Short History of the Indians of the United States,* New York: Van Nostrand, 1969.
4 Prucha, op. cit., p. 301.
5 Ibid., p. 302.
6 Ibid., p. 304.
7 Ibid., p. 102.
8 Wilcomb E. Washburn, *The Assault on Indian Tribalism: The General Allotment Law (Dawes Act) of 1887,* Philadelphia: Lippincott, 1975, p. 17.
9 D. S. Otis, *The Dawes Act and the Allotment of Indian Lands,* Norman, Okla.: University of Oklahoma Press, 1973, p. 19.
10 Jack D. Forbes (ed.), *The Indian in America's Past,* Englewood Cliffs, N.J.: Prentice-Hall, 1964, p. 114.
11 Prucha, op. cit., p. 261.
12 Richard Henry Pratt, *Battlefield and Classroom: Four Decades with the American Indian, 1867–1904,* New Haven, Conn.: Yale University Press, 1964.
13 Prucha, op. cit., p. 261.
14 Left-handed Mexican Clansman, *The Trouble at Round Rock,* Navaho Historical Series, Washington: United States Indian Service, 1952.
15 Clyde Kluckhohn and Dorothea Leighton, *The Navaho,* Cambridge, Mass.: Harvard University Press, 1960.
16 Pratt, op. cit., p. 310.
17 Edward P. Dozier, "Rio Grande Pueblos," in Edward H. Spicer (ed.), *Perspectives in American Indian Culture Change,* Chicago: University of Chicago Press, 1961.
18 Weston La Barre, *The Peyote Cult,* New York: Shocken Books, 1969, p. xiv.
19 David F. Aberle, *The Peyote Religion among the Navaho,* Chicago: Aldine, 1966.
20 *Annual Report of the Commissioner of Indian Affairs,* Washington: Government Printing Office, 1907, p. 4.
21 Ibid., p. 341.
22 Edward H. Spicer et al., *Impounded Peoples: Japanese-Americans in the Relocation Centers,* Tucson: University of Arizona Press, 1969.

Chapter 11 Second Thoughts

1 Sign supposedly hung over the exit at his American Museum by P. T. Barnum. Irving Wallace, *The Fabulous Showman: The Life and Times of P. T. Barnum,* New York: Knopf, 1959, p. 103.
2 John Collier, *Indians of the Americas,* New York: Mentor, 1947, pp. 150–151.
3 S. Lyman Tyler, *A History of Indian Policy,* Bureau of Indian Affairs, 1973, p. 142.
4 Lewis Meriam et al., *The Problem of Indian Administration,* Baltimore: Johns Hopkins, 1928.
5 Ibid., p. 3.
6 Ibid., p. 21.
7 Ibid., p. 87.
8 Ibid., p. 88.
9 Ibid., p. 4.
10 Ibid., p. 89.
11 Collier, op. cit., p. 155.
12 Meriam, op. cit., p. 346.
13 Tyler, op. cit., p. 128.
14 Collier, op. cit., p. 8.
15 Ibid., p. 166.
16 David F. Aberle, *The Peyote Religion among the Navaho,* Chicago: Aldine, 1966, p. 64.
17 Tyler, op. cit., p. 166.
18 Edward H. Spicer, *A Short History of the Indians of the United States,* New York: Van Nostrand, 1969, p. 218.
19 George P. Castile, "Federal Indian Policy and the Sustained Enclave: An Anthropological Perspective," *Human Organization,* **33**:219–228, 1974.
20 Tyler, op. cit., p. 200.
21 U.S. Congress Public Law 93-638, Indian Self Determination and Education Assistance Act, S. 1017, Ninety-third Congress, January 4, 1975.

Chapter 12 What Is To Be Done

1 "What Is To Be Done?: Burning Questions of Our Movement." Title of a pamphlet of Nikolai Lenin, quoted in Robert Tucker, *The Lenin Anthology,* New York: W. W. Norton, 1975.
2 Robert M. Hutchins, *Freedom, Education and the Fund: Essays and Addresses, 1946–1956,* New York: Meridian Books, 1956, p. 76.
3 Hank Adams et al., *Report on Trust Responsibilities and the Federal-Indian Relationship, Including Treaty Review. Final Report to the American Indian Policy Review Commission,* U.S. Government Printing Office, 1976, pp. 287–297.
4 Alan Parker et al., *Report on Tribal Government: Final Report to the American Indian Policy Review Commission,* U.S. Government Printing Office, 1976, p. 42.
5 Richard M. Nixon, "The American Indians—Message from the President of

the United States," House Document No. 91-363, *Congressional Record* V116, Part 17.

6 A. T. Anderson, *Nations Within a Nation: The American Indian and the Government of the United States,* U.S. Government Printing Office, 1976.

7 Peter MacDonald et al., *Report on Reservation and Resource Development and Protection: Final Report to the American Indian Policy Review Commission,* U.S. Government Printing Office, 1976. See also Warren King and Associates, Inc., *Bureau of Indian Affairs Management Study: Report on BIA Management Practices to the American Indian Policy Review Commission,* U.S. Government Printing Office, 1976.

8 William Y. Adams and Lorraine T. Ruffing, "Shonto Revisited: Measures of Social and Economic Change in a Navaho Community, 1955–1971," *American Anthropologist,* **79**:58–83, 1977.

9 Ibid.

10 *Akwesasne Notes,* Mohawk Nation, Roosevelt, New York.

11 Thomas Weaver et al., *Summary of the Tribal Management Procedures Study,* Tucson: University of Arizona, Bureau of Ethnic Research, 1974. Summary of a series of studies all available separately.

12 Personal communication, June 1977.

13 Henry F. Dobyns, "Therapeutic Experience of Responsible Democracy," in Stuart Levine and Nancy O. Lurie (eds.), *The American Indian Today,* Baltimore: Penguin, 1968.

14 George P. Castile, "Federal Indian Policy and the Sustained Enclave: An Anthropological Perspective," *Human Organization,* **33**:219–228, 1974.

15 Spicer et al., *Japanese-Americans in the Relocation Centers,* Tucson: University of Arizona Press, 1969, p. 20.

16 Vine Deloria, *Custer Died for Your Sins,* New York: Avon, 1969, p. 33.

17 Murray L. Wax et al., "Formal Education in an American Indian Community," in Deward E. Walker (ed.), *The Emergent Native Americans: A Reader in Culture Contact,* Boston: Little, Brown, 1972.

18 William G. Demmert, *Indian Record,* Bureau of Indian Affairs Publication, July–August 1976, p. 3.

19 George P. Castile, "The Community School at Rough Rock," Master's thesis, Tucson: University of Arizona, 1968.

20 U.S. Congress, Public Law 93–638, Indian Self Determination and Education Assistance Act, S. 1017, Ninety-third Congress, January 4, 1975.

21 Ibid.

22 Ibid.

23 Peter Taylor et al., *Law Consolidation, Revision and Codification: Final Report to the American Indian Policy Review Commission,* U.S. Government Printing Office, 1976, p. iv.

24 There is a good general discussion in Taylor of the current state of the law.

INDEX

INDEX

Aberle, David, 240, 256
Abourezk, James, 270
Acculturation, defined, 182–183
Acorns as subsistence base, 45, 48
Adena-Hopewell traditions:
  preagricultural base, 67
  tradition described, 117, 118
Administered communities:
  modern reservation as, 285
  origins, 228
  self-defeating nature of, 285, 286
Agency towns, 238
Agriculture:
  expansability of, 73
  slash and burn technique, 70
Akwesasne notes, 281
Algonkians, rapid decline of, 183
Allotment, 231–233
  under Collier administration, 253
  (*See also* Dawes Act)
Amazons, 139
Ambilineality, 128
American Indian Federation, 245
American Indian movement, 281
American Indian Policy Review Commission, 269, 270, 289
Anasazi tradition, origins of, 74
Anderson, A. T., 271
Animism, 96
Anomie, 285
Anthropology:
  defined, 9–10

Anthropology:
history of, 8–9
physical, defined, 10
Archaeology, defined, 11
Archaic tradition, 41-57
defined, 41
as "efficiencies," 42
as "living in" process, 42
Aridity, 44
Arikara, 212
Artifact, defined, 32
Asian influences, 151–154
Assimilation, defined, 199
Assimilation policy:
failure of, 243
in Meriam report, 250
resurgence after Collier, 258
Astaentsic (Huron), 99
Atkin, Edmond, 175
Atlantis, 143, 146
Atlatl, 45
Atomization, 185, 186
Australopithecus, 23
Authority, 115
Avunculocality, 129
Aztec, 2, 69, 92, 114, 120, 170, 188
Aztlan, 2

Ball court, 120
Bands:
familistic organization, 49–50
leadership in, 50
(*See also* Desert tradition; Shoshone)
"Banner stones," 57
Basketry, 46
Bat cave site, 65
Battle of Pea Ridge, 206
Bee, Robert, 283
Beloved men, 125
Benedict, Ruth, 133
Bentwood boxes, 128
Bering Strait, 25
Big Foot, 217
Bilateral descent, defined, 81
Binford, Lewis, 11, 82
Birthrate, Indian, 267
Black drink, 125, 179
Black Elk, 10
Black Hills, 215
Black Kettle, 90, 214
Black Mesa, 276
Blackwater Draw site, 35
Blankets, Navaho, 279
Blood types, 29
Boaz, Franz, 8, 127, 128
Bodhisattva, 153
Boomers, 308
Bosque Redondo, 222
Bozeman Trail, 214
Brant, Joseph, 196
Buffalo, extinction of, 215
Bullboats, 24, 25
Bulls, papal, 168
Bureau of Indian Affairs, 190, 205, 227, 231, 254, 263
agents, 228, 232, 233
under Collier administration, 252–258
growth of budget, 255
limited responsiveness, 284
reorganization, 291
as resource base, 283
spoils system, 229
structural limitations, 271
Burial mounds, 118
Bursum Bill, 246
"Butterfly sickness," 86, 104

Cahokia site, 117, 122
Caldwell, Joseph, 42
Calico site, 34
Canadian Indians, 267
Cannon in conquest, 168
Capital, lack of, 272
Captain Jack, 214, 223
Carguero system, 135
Carlisle Institute, 233
Carrying capacity, 42, 48
Carson, Kit, 222
Carter, Jimmy, 264
Casteneda, Carlos, 103, 138
Castile, Isabella of, 169
Castillo, Diaz del, 170
Catlin, George, 83
Cayuga, 185
Checkerboarding, 233, 238, 253
Cherokee, 90, 123, 124, 179, 207

Cherokee:
  adoption of "civilized" habits, 193–194
  beloved men, 90
  black drink and, 101
  removal of, 192–195
  revitalization in Oklahoma, 208
Cherokee nation as revitalization movement, 193–194
Cherokee Nation v. Georgia, 194
Cherokee outlet, 206, 208
Cherokee Phoenix, 193
Chichimeca, concept defined, 1–3
Chickasaw, 201
Chief Joseph, 90, 189, 224, 225
Chilkat blankets, 131
China and Indian origins, 150
Chinook jargon, 95
Chippewa, 210
Chivington Massacre, 214
Choctaw, 123, 195
Churchward, James, 146
Cibola, 171
Citizenship:
  of all Indians, 231
  in Indian territory, 209
Civilian Conservation Corps, 253
Civilized tribes, 206
  in civil war, 206
  and pantribalism, 207
  reorganization in Indian territory, 207
  (*See also* Cherokee; Chickasaw; Choctaw; Creek; Seminole)
Clan, defined, 82–83
Class society, 117
Cloth, rabbit fur, 46
Clovis tradition, 32, 40
Cochiti Pueblo, 99
Collier, John, 9, 245, 246, 253, 258
Collier administration, 252–258
  development programs under, 254
  Indian self-determination during, 255
Colonization, pressures favoring, 173
Columbus, Christopher, 2
Comanche, 100
Community Action Program, 287
Compartmentalization, 110, 239
Connubium, symmetrical, 86
Conquest, right of, 178
Consciousness alteration, 101
Constitutions, 252
Contact change, 182
Contractual administration, 288
Cooper, Fenimore, 5, 183
"Copper" (Kwakiutl), 130, 132
Corn:
  diffusion of, 67–68
  origins of, 64–68
Cornplanter, 187, 196, 198
Corporate kin units, defined, 81
Corporations in conquest, 166
Cortes, Hernan, 169
Cotton, domesticated, 69
Coup, 213
Cousteau, Jacques, 139
Coyote, 96
Crafts, 277
Creek, 123–126, 191, 193
  confederacy, 124
  policy of neutrality, 126
  town organization, 124
"Crest" (Kwakiutl), 128
Cross cousins, 85
Cultural relativism, 13
Culture, concept defined, 9–10
Culture areas, 12, 59
  map, 3
Curing, 103–106
Curtis Act, 209, 231
Custer's Last Stand, 215

Dakota (*see* Sioux)
Dali, Salvador, 141
Dating:
  absolute and relative defined, 30–31
  carbon, 14–31
  stratigraphy, 31
Dawes, Henry L., 231
Dawes Act, 208, 227, 231, 232, 259
"Death cult," 119
de Bry, Theodor, 167, 179
Deculturation, 227
Dekanawidah, 184, 185, 188
Delaware, 186, 192, 206
Deloria, Vine, 285
Demmert, William G., 28
Dependent domestic nations doctrine, 194

Depression and Indian affairs, 252
Desert tradition, 35, 43–56
Development and crafts, 277
  cultural factors in, 274
  ecological consideration, 276
  fund sources, 272
  holistic nature, 269
  resemblance to Third World, 275
  and tourism, 277
Diffusion:
  defined, 12
  stimulus, 12
Di Peso, Charles, 120
Dobyns, Henry, 283
Domesticates, New World: plants, 68–69
  resemblance to Old World, 151
Domestication, origins of, 66–67
Dog, domesticated, 69
Draft animals, 152
Drake, Sir Francis, 172
Drugs, 101–103, 240
DRUMS, 260
Dutch, early explorations of, 166, 172

"Eagle Doctor," 109
Easter Island, 117
Ecological analysis, defined, 40
Ecological disruptions in colonial period, 184
Economic conditions, modern, 270
Education:
  as assimilation, 233
  continuing assimilationist policy, 286
  Indian controlled, 287
  and marginal men, 236
  through missionaries, 234
  Rough Rock Demonstration School, 287
  school age population, 235
  at time of Meriam report, 250
  and vacuum ideology, 286
Eells, Edwin, 230
Eells, Myron, 230
Effigy mounds, 118–119
Egypt and Indian origins, 148
Emic, 106, 131
Employment assistance, 262
Enclave, sustained, 286
Enclavement, 199
English, early explorations of, 166
English colonial policy, 172–180
Environment:
  and hunters, 41–42
  limitations for nomads, 46
  of Northwest tradition, 127
Eolith, 32
Eric the Red, 149
Eskimo kin terminology, 84
Ethnocentrism, 13
Ethnography, defined, 10
Etic, 106, 131
Europe, condition of, in 1500, 165–168
Evolution, cultural, 11–12
Executive order lands, 245
Exogamy, 49
Extended family, 49

Fall, Albert, 245
False face society, 109
Ferdinand of Aragon, 169
Feud, 89–90, 124
Fishing rights, 259, 290
Fluted points, 32
Folsom tradition, 27, 32, 40
Ford, Gerald, 264
Forester, C. S., 168
Fort Sumner, 222
French, early explorations of, 172
French colonial policy, 172
French and Indian wars, 185
Fried, Morton, 54, 115, 117, 135
Full bloods, 207, 242

Gaiwiio, code of Handsome Lake, 197–198
Ghost Dance, 12, 100, 103, 107, 214–218
Ghost Shirt, 217
Ghosts, 99–100, 104
"Give aways," 131
Glottochronology, 30
Grant, Ulysses S., 229
  (*See also* Peace policy)
Great American Desert, 200, 204
Great death, 39–40

Great Sioux reservation, 215
Great Spirit, 95
Great Sun, 112, 122–123
Great Tree of Peace, 188

Haida, 126, 295
Hallucinogens, 101–103, 240
Hamatsa, 102
Handsome Lake, 100, 196–199
  religion in, 241
    origins of, 196–199
Havasupai, 47, 277
Head Start, 286
Health Conditions:
  modern, 267
  at time of Meriam report, 249
Henini (Creek), 125
Heyerdahl, Thor, 147
Hiawatha, 184, 185
Hiawatha Hospital for Insane Indians, 242, 246, 251
Hogan, 221
Hohokan tradition, 67, 72, 120
Hoover Commission, 258
Hopewell tradition, 117–119, 142
Hopi Pueblo, 91, 220
Hornblower, Horatio, 168
Horse, Spanish introduction to, 5
Horse nomadism, 210
Horticulture, primacy of women in, 71
House Concurrent Resolution 108, 258
Hrdlicka, Ales, 27
Hsu Fu, 150
Huguenots, 179
Hupa, 58
Huron, 99, 185
Hutchins, Robert Maynard, 266

Ickes, Harold, 252
Incest as cause of illness, 104
Incest prohibitions, 86
Income levels:
  modern, 271
  at time of Meriam report, 250
Indian Civil Rights Act, 290
Indian Claims Commission, 258, 283
Indian Courts, rules for, 226
Indian Defense Association, 245
Indian Financing Act, 273
Indian "offenses," 228
Indian police, 217, 227
Indian Reorganization Act, 252, 256
Indian Rights Association, 281
Indian Self-Determination and Educational Assistance Act, 258, 264, 284, 288
Indian Territory, 205–209
Indian Trade and Intercourse Act, 205, 230
Infantacide, 48
Interior, Secretary of, 253, 289
Iroquois, 87, 123, 180, 195, 200
  dreams and, 107
  False Face Society, 106
  religion of, 100
  trade dominence, 185
Iroquois kin terminology, 85
Iroquois League, 135
  destruction of 196
  founding of, 184–185
  system of organization, 186
Irrigation in Southwest, 70
Isabella of Castile, 169
Ishi, 223, 224

Jackson, Andrew, 194
Japan and Indian origins, 150
Jefferson, Thomas, 8
Jerky, 211
Job training programs, 274
Johnson, Lyndon, 264
Johnson-O'Malley Act, 253
Jomon and pottery origins, 152
Jones, David, 109

Kah-Nee-Ta Resort Lodge, 278
Kansa, 206, 210
Kappler, Charles, 188
Katchina, 109, 110
Kickapoo, 183, 186, 206
"Kill" sites, 35
King Phillip, 184
Kinship nomenclature, 84–85
Kinzua Dam, 199
Kiowa, 210
Kiva, 73, 112

Klamath, termination of, 261–262
Kluckhohn, Clyde, 100, 107, 236
Knox, Henry, 190
Komugi (Kwakiutl), 97
Kon-Tiki, 148
Kroeber, A. L., 223
Kroeber, Theodora, 223
Kuhn, Thomas, 140
Kwakiutl, 10, 78, 116, 127–135
  bilateral kin groups, 128–129
  chiefs and power, 133
  potlatching, 131
  rank and, 129
  religion of, 99
  surplus economy, 127–128
  warfare, 130

La Barre, Weston, 103, 240
La Farge, Oliver, 246
La Follette, Robert, 260
Land:
  losses under allotment program, 232, 238
  map: of cessions, 247
    of modern, 268
  remaining in Indian hands today, 267
Land bridge (to Asia), 22, 24–27
Languages, number and variety of, 30–31
La Venta, 114
Laws of the Indies, 175
Leadership, national, 281–283
Leakey, L. S. B., 34
Leighton, Dorothea, 107
Lemuria, 146
Leupp, Francis, 241
Lévi-Strauss, Claude, 60
Lindenmeir site, 35
Linton, Ralph, 95
Lone Wolf v. Hitchcock, 231
Long house (Kwakiutl), 129
Longhouse religion (*see* Handsome Lake)
"Lost tribes" of Israel, 144–146, 229
Lost wax casting, 151
Louisiana Purchase, 191
Luther, Martin, 1
Lyell, Charles, 147
McDonald, Peter, 282
McIntosh, William, 191
MacNeish, Scotty, 52, 67
Macro-bands, 52, 53
Maize (*see* Corn)
Malinowski, Bronislav, 87
Mana, 97
"Manda," 110
Mandan, 111, 210, 212
  earth lodge of, 87
  population of, 83
  religion of, 101
  rites of passage, 107
Manifest destiny, 178
Manito, 96
Mano and metate, 45, 72
Mao Tse-tung, 137
Marginal men, 236
Marmes man, 31
Marriage, 81
  as alliance, 53, 85
Marshall, John, 194
Massachusetts Bay Company, 175
Matriarchy, 86
Matrilineality, 81, 123
Matrilocality, 49
  relation to matrilineality, 81
Medicine bundle, 111
Mega fauna, extinction of, 39–40
Melting pot, 200
Menominee, termination of, 260
Menominee Enterprises Inc., 260
Meriam Report, 227, 235, 246–251
Meso America, influences on North, 59, 66, 67, 114, 120, 127
Metallurgy, 57, 151
Mico, 123
Micosukee, 288
Migration:
  from Asia, 22
  of horse, 26
Minnesota Massacre, 214
Mississippian tradition, 119–123
  Mesoamerican influence on, 120
  origins of corn in, 67
Mixed bloods, 207, 242
Modoc, 213, 223
Mogollon tradition, 72
  Mesoamerican influence on, 67
  and origins of pottery, 76

Mohawk, 185, 196
as steel workers, 279
Moiety, 83, 112, 124
Mongoloids, Indians as, 28–29
Monks Mound, 117
Monotheism, 96
Monument Valley, 277
Monumental architecture, 117
Moorhouse, Major, 6
Morgan, Lewis Henry, 8
Mormons and Indian origins, 145
Mother's-brother, 86
Mound builders (*see* Adena-Hopewell traditions; Hopewell tradition; Mississippian tradition; Natchez)
Mu, 146
Mummification, 44
Muskogean language group, 123

Naco site, 35
Nakai, Raymond, 282
Natchez, 112, 119, 122, 123
as class society, 122
matrilineal nobility, 122
National Congress of American Indians, 281
National Indian Youth Council, 281
National Park Service, 277
Native American Church, 102, 240, 280
Nativistic movements (*see* Revitalization movements)
Navaho, 7, 10, 12, 60, 61, 64, 90, 218–223, 229, 275
ceremonials of, 99
education and, 236–237
ghost sickness, 104
ghosts and witches, 99–100
hand trembler, 104
incest and butterfly sickness, 104
and incorporative acculturation, 219
kinship among, 88
long walk, 222
origin myth, 21–22
and pastoralism, 220
Peyotism, 240–241
religion of, 98, 106, 109
reservation size, 222
self-determination and, 256
Navaho:
Spanish period, 219–220
stock reduction, 255–258
weaving, 70
New Deal programs, 245
New England Company, 176
Nez Perce, 189, 211, 224, 233
Nixon, Richard, 264
Nomadism, 46–48
Norse sailors, discovery voyages by, 149
Northwest Coast tradition (*see* Haida; Kwakiutl; Tlingit)
Nuclear family, 49
Numayn (Kwakiutl), 128

Occam's razor, 153
Oceola, 195
Oedipus complex, 87
Office, concept defined, 88–89
Office of Economic Opportunity, 254–255, 287
Oglethorpe, James Edward, 125
Oil leasing, 209
Okipa (Mandan), 101
Oklahoma District, 208
Oklahoma land rushes, 208
Oklahoma statehood, 209
Old copper culture, 57
Olmec, 114–115
Omaha, 210
Oneida, 185
Onondaga, 185
Opechancanough, 184
Osage, 206
Ownership, fee simple, 190

Paiute, 216
Pantribal sodality, 80
Pantribalism, 241, 280
Parallel cousins, 85
Passamaquody, 230
Patrilineage, defined, 80
Patrilocality, 81
Peace policy, 229, 231
Pemmican, 211
Pequot, 4, 183
Persistent systems, 60–61

Peyote, 102–103
Peyote cult, 103, 240, 242, 280
Phratry, 83
Pima, 78
Pine tree chiefs, 186
Piñon nuts as subsistence base, 45, 48, 52–54
Pit houses, 73
Plant collecting as preadaptation for agriculture, 72
Pleistocene, 40
  and land bridge, 25–26
Plow, absence of, 70
Pocahontas, 4, 6
Pogo, 51
Polanyi, Karl, 51, 131
Polygyny, sororal, 86
Pomo, 45, 204
Population:
  during colonial period, 173
  estimates, pre-Columbian, 154
  increase in Anglo: by 1860, 195
    after 1900, 238
  of Indians today, 266
  at time of removal, 195
Portugal, early explorations in, 165
Pot-hunters, 11
Potlatch, 127, 131–135
  rivalry, 133
Pottery, 46
  Asian influences, 152–153
  origins of, 76
  revitalization of traditions, 77
  utility in archaeology, 76
Power:
  political, 115–117
  spiritual, 97–98, 213
Powhatan confederacy, 177, 183
Pow wow, 241, 281
Pratt, Richard L., 233, 234, 236, 263
Preprojectile point tradition, 33
Prester John, 139, 165
Priests, 108
Primates, New World, 23
Property rights, 54
Public Law 280, 263
Pueblo Bonito site, 72
Pueblo revolt, 219
Pueblos, 70, 73, 239
  "All Pueblo Council," 246
Pueblos:
  and Athabascans, 74
  and John Collier, 245
  Great Pueblo Fall, 74
  religion of, 109–110
Puritans, 4
Pyramids, 142, 147, 153

Quakers, influence on Handsome Lake, 198

Ra, 148
Rabbit boss, 53
Rabbit hunting, 52–53
Racial characteristics of Indians, 29
Racism, 13, 140
Radcliffe-Brown, A. R., 9
Railroads:
  Atlantic and Pacific, 222
  growth between 1850 and 1900, 204
  in Indian Territory, 208
Rank, 115–117, 129–130
Rations, 215, 227, 228
Reciprocity, 51
Red Bean cult, 240
Red Bird Smith, 209
Red Cloud, 14, 89, 212, 214
Redistribution, 131
Redjacket, 196
Religious movements, fusional nature of, 241
Relocation, 262
Relocation camps, Japanese, 243
Removal Act, 178, 191, 194
Requerimiento, 170
Reservation system origins, 205
  state jurisdiction, 263
Resource base, lack of, 272
Revitalization movements, 196
    (*See also* Cherokee nation as revitalization movement; Ghost Dance; Handsome Lake; Pan-tribalism; Peyote cult; Red Bird Smith)
Rhoads, Charles, 252
Right of conquest, 190
Right of discovery, 188
Rite of passage, 107

Roanoke Colony, 167
Roosevelt, Franklin D., 245
Roosevelt, Theodore, 227
Ross, John, 193
Rough Rock, 254, 287

Sachem, 186
Sanapia, 109
San Creek, 90
Sand paintings, 106, 109
Santee Sioux, 214
Scandanavia and Indian origins, 149
Schools:
  boarding, 234, 236, 246
  under Collier administration, 254
Science, nature of, 140
Scraelings, 149, 163
Sea power in conquest, 167
Sedentism:
  consequences of, 75–78
  origins of, 73–75
Self-determination:
  and administered community, 285
  and economic development, 274
  under I.R.A., 255
  and Navaho stock reduction, 256
  resurgence of, as policy, 264
Seminole, 195, 213
Seneca, 185, 187, 206
Sequoyah, 12, 193
Service, Elman, 80, 88, 116
Sexism, 13
Shalako (Zuni), 99
Shaman, 108
  antelope, 53
  Shawnee, 189, 191, 206
Sheridan, Phillip, 203
Shonto, 274
Shoshone, 45, 48–49, 52, 108, 210
Sia Pueblo, 110, 112
Singer (Navaho), 109
Sioux, 10, 209–218, 229, 233, 238
  and Ghost Dance, 214–218
  as horse nomads, 210
  origin of name, 209
  social organization, 212
Sitting Bull, 212, 217
Six Nations Reserve, 196
Skokomish, 230, 237
Slavery (Kwakiutl), 130
Slavery of Indians, 176
Smith, John, 4, 176
Smohalla, 63
Snaketown site, 120
Social movements, 193
  (*See also* Revitalization movements)
Sociocide, 267
Sodalities, 83
Sohon, Gustavus, 211
Southern cult, 122
Spain, early conquests of, 169
Spanish colonial policies, 169–171
Specialization, 131
Spicer, Edward H., 59, 227, 243, 285
State, 115–116
  and sanctions, 90
Stereotypes of Indians, 4–7
Stevens treaties, 95
Steward, Julian, 49, 81
Stimulus diffusion, 120
Stinkards, 122
Stock raising, 238
"Stomp ground," 209
Stone boiling, 46
Stratification, 115–117
Structure, social, defined, 13
Sun Dance, 101, 213
Superintendency, 227
Surplus:
  consequences of, 75
  origins of, 75
  redistribution of, 131

Talwa, 124
Taos, 245
Tecumseh, 191, 193
Tehuacan Valley, 52, 65–67
Temple mounds, 112, 117, 120
Tenochtitlan, 169
Teotihuacan, 120, 152
Termination:
  decline of, as policy, 264
  and impact on development, 262
  of Menominee, 260–261
  origins of policy, 258
Territoriality, 53-54
Thalassophobia, 148
Timucuan, 179

Tlingit, 126, 295
Tobacco, 102
  cultivation and ecological disruption of, 184
  origins of, 68–69
Totem poles, 128
Tourism, 277
Trade, importance of, in conquest, 177
Traditions, defined, 58–61
"Trail of tears," 195
Transoceanic influences, 148
  on migrations, 24
Treaties:
  federal supremacy over states in, 230
  origins of, 188–192
  process ended, 230
Treaty:
  of Fort Stanwix, 189
    second, 190
  of Ghent, 191
  of Guadalupe Hidalgo, 221
  of Indian Springs, 191
  of Paris (1783), 190
  of Walla Walla, 211
Treaty rights, modern debates over, 290
Tribal attorneys, 283
Tribal chairmen, 282–283
Tribe, 79–80
  corporate ownership in, 92
  leadership patterns in, 88–89
  legal status in, 289–290
  religious organization of, 108
  and territoriality, 89
  warfare, 89
Trust relation, 232
Turkey, domesticated, 69
Tuscarora, 185

Umatilla, 261
Underhill, Ruth, 183
Unilineages and nomenclature, 84–86
Unilineality, defined, 80
United States v. Washington, 290
Urban Indians, 262, 276

Vacant towns, 118
Valdivia and pottery origins, 152
Vancouver Island, 127
Vespucci, Amerigo, 2
Virginia Company, 175
Vision quest, 101
Vogt, Evon, 218
Voluntary association, defined, 83
Von Däniken, Erich, 140

Wakan, 96
Wallace, Anthony, 107, 196
Wampaoag, 184
Wampum, 185
War of 1812, 191
Wardship, 231
Warfare:
  in bands, 54
  and horse nomads, 212–214
  Northwest Coast, 134
Warm Springs Reservation, 278
Washo, 54
Water rights, 238
Wax, Murray, 286
Weaving, origins of, 69–70
Wheel, absence of, 152
Wheeler-Howard Act, 252
  (*See also* Indian Reorganization Act)
White, John, 167
White, Leslie, 9
White Bead Woman, 21, 64, 98
White Mountain Apache, 270
Winters Doctrine, 276
Winthrop, John, 178
Witchcraft, 100, 105
  accusations of, 100–101
Woodlands tradition, 120
Worcester v. Georgia, 192, 194
Work, Hubert, 246
Wounded Knee, 215–218
Wovoka, 216

Yahi, 223, 224
Yakima, 291
Yaqui, 59

Zuni, 87, 110, 288